Oracle Press™

OCA Oracle Application Server 10g Administrator Exam Guide

(Exam 1Z0-311)

ABOUT THE AUTHOR

Sam R. Alapati is an Oracle Database 10g Administrator Certified Professional (OCP) who manages Oracle databases for the Boy Scouts of America at their National Office in Irving, Texas. Prior to this, Sam worked at Sabre, Lehman Brothers, AT&T, and the NBC Corporation. He also worked for the Oracle Corporation in New York City as a Senior Principal Consultant. Sam has published three other books: *Expert Oracle9i Database Administration*, *OCP Oracle Database 10g: New Features for Administrators Exam Guide*, and *Expert Oracle Database 10g Administration*.

Oracle Press™

OCA Oracle Application Server 10g Administrator Exam Guide

(Exam 1Z0-311)

Sam R. Alapati

McGraw-Hill

New York   Chicago   San Francisco
Lisbon   London   Madrid   Mexico City   Milan
New Delhi   San Juan   Seoul   Singapore   Sydney   Toronto

The McGraw·Hill Companies

The McGraw-Hill Companies
160 Spear Street, Suite 700
San Francisco, California 94105
U.S.A.

To arrange bulk purchase discounts for sales promotions, premiums, or fund-raisers, please contact McGraw-Hill at the above address.

OCA Oracle Application Server 10g Administrator Exam Guide (Exam 1Z0-311)

1234567890 CUS CUS 019876

Book p/n 0-07-226272-9 and CD p/n 0-07-226273-7
parts of
ISBN 0-07-226271-0

Acquisitions Editor Tim Green	**Technical Editor** John Watson	**Composition** G&S Book Services
Production Coordinator Katherine Bishop	**Copy Editor** Harlan James	**Illustration** G&S Book Services
Project Manager Jody McKenzie	**Proofreader** Lori Newhouse	**Series Design** Roberta Steel and Peter Hancik
Acquisitions Coordinator Jennifer Housh	**Indexer** Randi Dubnick	**Cover Series Design** Damore Johann Design, Inc.

This book was composed with Adobe® InDesign®.

To my wife, Valerie

CONTENTS AT A GLANCE

CONTENTS

ACKNOWLEDGMENTS

First and foremost, my appreciation goes to Tim Green, Acquisitions Editor at McGraw-Hill/Osborne, who suggested that I write this book and charted its course over the last year or so. Tim performed a lot of valuable work, including working with the Oracle Certification folks and getting me the necessary materials to work on the book. I'm fortunate to have had Tim's guidance and encouragement in writing this book. I'm immensely grateful to Jennifer Housh, who toiled hard in her capacity as the Acquisitions Coordinator for this book. Jennifer did a marvelous job of coordinating the several drafts and helped provide all the assistance I needed to complete the book on time.

No amount of praise would be too high to describe the contribution of the Technical Editor, John Watson. This book has benefited considerably from John's perspicuous observations, comments, and suggestions. John has helped me avoid several key errors as well as consistently steered me toward the key areas emphasized in the Oracle certification exam. I appreciate the kindness as well as the remarkable efficiency of Katherine Bishop, the Production Coordinator at G&S Book Services. Harlan James's diligent copyediting enhanced my writing and I'm thankful for that. I thank the Project Manager, Jody McKenzie, for managing the long publication process extremely smoothly. My thanks to the Proof Reader Lori Newhouse for a conscientious job that improved the quality of the book and to Indexer Randi Dubnick, who did a tremendous job as well.

I wish to acknowledge the help and support of my colleagues and superiors. Nate Langston, the Director of our Information Services Division, encourages our efforts to be at the cutting edge always. Dave Campbell's considerateness, encouragement, and support have meant a lot over the years, as well as David Jeffress's kindness and helpful nature. I am grateful for the help and support provided by Nate, Dave, and David. Mark Potts as usual helped me during the course of the book and I'm thankful to him.

I'll always be indebted to my father, Dr. Alapati Appa Rao, whose illustrious career is my main source of inspiration while writing books. My mother, Swarna Kumari, has always been supportive of all my endeavors and has always had confidence in me. I thank both of my brothers, Hari Hara Prasad and Siva Sankara Prasad, for their affection and support over the years.

I'm extremely grateful to my wife, Valerie, who has encouraged me to write and supported my writing efforts despite the inconvenience and burden the book-writing task imposed on her. Finally, I wish to thank my children—Nina, Nicholas, and Shannon—for being graceful about my long absences while I was working on the book as well as for supporting my book-writing efforts at home with their kind understanding and patience.

INTRODUCTION

T his book is designed to help candidates taking the Oracle Application Server Certification Associate (OCA) exam. Oracle provides two certification levels for the Oracle Application Server Administration track. The first level of certification is the Oracle Certified Associate (OCA) exam and the second, the Oracle Certified Professional (OCP) exam.

This book is intended as a comprehensive preparation guide for the Oracle Application Server 10g Administrator Certified Associate (OCA) exam (*Exam 1Z0-311 Oracle Application Server 10g: Administration I*). After you earn the Oracle Application Server 10g OCA credential, you'll be eligible for the next rung of certification, which is the Oracle Application Server 10g Administrator Certified Professional (OCP) certification.

If your goal is to become certified as an OCA, you can do so by diligently working through this book, completing all the practice tests at the end of each chapter, and rounding it all off with the two full-length tests, one on the enclosed CD-ROM and the other on the Web. However, your goal should ideally reach beyond merely passing the OCA exam. To benefit from the powerful set of features offered by the latest Oracle Application Server release, you must be able to clearly understand the various features. To this end, I've designed the book somewhat more comprehensibly than a straightforward exam guide. I consistently introduce each OracleAS component carefully and explain how it is used, before going on to the administrative aspects that are more relevant for the exam.

I urge the reader to delve deep into the OracleAS platform by installing and testing all the components according to the procedures I explain in this book. While one can theoretically pass a certification exam by merely reading the relevant books and manuals, I think a true appreciation of each OracleAS component will only come about from actually experiencing it. In general, most folks take the Oracle certification tests on a voluntary basis, in the sense that in the majority of cases certification isn't a rigorous prerequisite for a job involving working with Oracle products. However, the real value, I believe, of becoming certified lies in the mastery of a wide range of skills as a result of the study and practice you put into the exam preparation process. So, as a first step, go to Chapter 2 of the book and follow the instructions for installing the Oracle Application Server on your server, if you don't have an installation on your machine already. There is no substitute for actually logging into the OracleAS Portal or the OracleAS Web Cache or any of the other Oracle Application Server components and performing complex tasks with ease!

The Oracle Application Server is part of the Oracle Platform, which is a comprehensive set of tools to facilitate e-business and is designed primarily to deploy and manage Internet applications. The Oracle Platform has two other major components besides OracleAS 10g. These are the Oracle Database 10g (which stores the data) and the Oracle Developer 10g components (to develop the applications).

exam

watch *You can prepare for the exam by taking the Oracle course Oracle Application Server 10g: Administration I, which is based on the OracleAS 10.2 release of the software at the time of this writing (February 2006). The predecessor to this class was also named Oracle Application Server 10g: Administration I, but was based on the OracleAS 10.1 release. The Oracle Application Server OCA test is validated against both of these courses. Therefore, if you've taken either of the two classes, you're ready to take the exam.*

Oracle provides specific objectives for the exam, which I list at the end of the Introduction. Each of the nine chapters in this book will address the test objectives comprehensively. Since the book is designed primarily as a certification guide, my main focus is covering the exam objectives thoroughly. For a comprehensive look at the OAS 10g product, you may want to refer to some of these other books:

- *Oracle Application Server 10g Administration Handbook* by John Garmany and Donald K. Burleson, published by Oracle Press in 2004.
- *Oracle Application Server 10g Web Development* by Chris Ostrowski and Bradley Brown, published by Oracle Press in 2005.
- *Oracle Application Server Essentials* by Rick Greenwald, Robert Stackowiak, and Donald Bales, published by O'Reilly in 2004.
- *Oracle Application Server 10g J2EE Deployment and Administration* by Michael Wessler et al., published by Apress in 2004.

Of course, the Oracle Corporation has several manuals for the Oracle Application Server, available at http://www.oracle.com/technology/documentation or http://

tahiti.oracle.com. The following Oracle Application Server manuals are of particular importance for an Oracle Application Server administrator. Yes—you do need to be familiar with all of these manuals if you want to be a competent OracleAS 10g administrator!

- Administrator's Guide
- Distributed Configuration Management Administrator's Guide
- Certificate Authority Administrator's Guide
- Containers for J2EE Services Guide
- Containers for J2EE User's Guide
- HTTP Server Administrator's Guide
- Portal Configuration Guide
- Identity Management User Reference
- Single Sign-On Administrator's Guide
- Web Cache Administrator's Guide
- Identity Management Guide to Delegated Administration

In This Book

This book is organized in such a way as to serve as an in-depth review for the OCA Oracle Application Server 10g Exam for Oracle Application Server administrators. Each chapter covers a major aspect of the exam, with an emphasis on the certification objectives specified by Oracle Corporation.

On the CD

The CD-ROM contains the entire contents of the book in electronic form, as well as one practice test that simulates the real OCA Oracle Application Server 10g Exam. For more information on the CD-ROM, please see the Appendix.

On the Web

In addition to the full-length exam on the CD-ROM, you can also access another full-length exam on the Web site, which you can find by following the link provided on the CD-ROM. Together, the two practice tests should put you in the driver's seat as far as exam readiness is concerned.

Exam Readiness Checklist

At the end of the Introduction, you will find an Exam Readiness Checklist. I constructed this table to allow you to cross-reference the official exam objectives with the certification objectives as I present and cover them in this book. The checklist also allows you to gauge your level of expertise on each objective at the outset of your studies. This should allow you to check your progress and make sure you spend the time you need on more difficult or unfamiliar sections. The Exam Readiness Checklist contains the exam objectives exactly as provided by the Oracle Corporation and the Certification objectives in this book that address the official Oracle exam objectives, along with a chapter and page reference.

In Every Chapter

This book includes a set of chapter components that call your attention to important items, reinforce important points, and provide helpful exam-taking hints. Take a look at what you'll find in each chapter:

- **On the Job** notes describe issues that come up often in real-world settings. The notes point out common "gotchas" and address job-related administration issues.

- **Exam Watch** notes call attention to information about, and potential pitfalls in, the exam.

- The **Two-Minute Drill** at the end of every chapter is a checklist of the main points of the chapter. You can use it for a quick last-minute review before the test.

Q&A

- The **Self Test** offers questions similar to those found on the certification exam. The answers to these questions, as well as explanations of the answers, can be found at the end of each chapter. By taking the Self Test after completing each chapter, you'll reinforce what you've learned from that chapter while becoming familiar with the structure of the exam questions.

Some Pointers

Once you've finished reading this book, set aside some time to do a thorough review. You might want to return to the book several times and make use of all the methods it offers for reviewing the material:

1. *Re-read all the Two-Minute Drills*, or have someone quiz you. You also can use the drills as a way of doing a quick cram before the exam. You might want to

make some flash cards out of 3 × 5 index cards that have the Two-Minute Drill material on them.

2. *Re-read all the Exam Watch notes.* These notes will help you focus on the important topics that are likely to appear on the certification exam.

3. *Re-take the Self Tests.* Taking the tests right after you've read the chapter is a good idea, because the questions help reinforce what you've just learned. However, it's an even better idea to go back later and do all the questions in the book in one sitting. Pretend that you're taking the live exam. (When you go through the questions the first time, you should mark your answers on a separate piece of paper. That way, you can run through the questions as many times as you need to until you feel comfortable with the material.) I personally wouldn't take the actual test until I'm able to answer upwards of 95% of the self test questions correctly.

4. *Take the Practice Tests.* As I mentioned earlier, there are two full-length practice tests: one on the CD-ROM and the second on the Web. Make sure you time these tests, so you get used to the pace you must work at on the actual day of the test. Repeat these two tests until you're scoring in the nineties.

Test Structure

You usually will have about 60 or so multiple-choice questions on the exam, and you need to get at least **68%** of the answers correct in order to pass the test. You will be given about 105 minutes to complete the exam. If you work your way through all nine chapters of this book, diligently taking the Self Tests and reviewing your answers and paying close attention to the Exam Watches, you shouldn't have any problem passing the exam with flying colors.

A word of caution regarding questions for which there are several correct choices. If you pick only part of the correct answers, you won't get credit for the answer, even if your pick is among the correct alternatives. Please be very careful that you picked all the possible choices when there are multiple correct choices.

How to Prepare for the Exam

You should read each of the nine chapters, preferably from the beginning to the end, and answer the end-of-chapter review questions correctly. However, most chapters can be read out of order. So, if you are interested in OC4J, for example, you may start with Chapter 7. The point is to cover all nine chapters in any order you wish, since that'll ensure you're covering all the OCA official objectives.

I've covered every OCA certification objective carefully in this book. However, the fact remains that this is a test guide, and thus by necessity, I'm limited as to the length of discussion of any particular topic. I strongly recommend that you refer to the pertinent Oracle Application Server topics in Oracle Corporation's voluminous manuals for in-depth discussion of all the new topics.

OCA tests are rigorous, and you can't expect to become certified by merely "brushing up" on the new features. You must really understand the new concepts from both a theoretical standpoint and a practical one. OCA exam questions typically are divided into questions that test your knowledge of syntax and new commands, on the one hand, and those that test in depth your understanding of how a particular new feature works in practice, on the other. Your basic strategy for questions that test your knowledge of Oracle syntax is simply to learn and remember the new commands and syntax. However, when it comes to preparing for the significant number of questions (often called scenario-based questions) that test your understanding of "how" things work, there is no substitute for actually installing the various OracleAS components and testing various concepts and commands, using material from this book as well as the relevant Oracle manuals.

Use the Exam Readiness Checklist to guide your preparation for the exam. Check off each exam topic after you're fully convinced that you really understand how the command or feature works. You're ready to take the exam when you have checked off all the objectives on the checklist!

Good luck and have fun!

Exam Readiness Checklist (Exam 1Z0-311)

OCA Official Objective	Certification Objective	Ch #	Pg #
Oracle Application Server Key Components and Features		1	
Describe the solution areas addressed by Oracle Application Server	Overview of the Oracle Application Server	1	4
Describe the key components of Oracle Application Server	Oracle Application Server 10g Components	2	44
Analyzing Oracle Application Server Architecture		2	
Explain the different installation options for Oracle Application Server	Installing OracleAS 10g	2	47

Exam Readiness Checklist (Exam 1Z0-311)

OCA Official Objective	Certification Objective	Ch #	Pg #
Explain the installation dependencies of Oracle Application Server components	Installing OracleAS 10g	2	47
Installing OracleAS Infrastructure		2	
Define the installation requirements for OracleAS Infrastructure	Installing the OracleAS Infrastructure	2	68
Describe OracleAS Infrastructure installation types	Installing the OracleAS Infrastructure	2	68
Install OracleAS Infrastructure	Installing the OracleAS Infrastructure	2	68
Start and stop OracleAS Infrastructure	Installing the OracleAS Infrastructure	2	68
Installing OracleAS Middle Tier		2	
Describe the Oracle Application Server 10g Middle Tier installation types and their requirements	Installing the OracleAS Middle Tier	2	85
Perform preinstallation tasks	Installing the OracleAS Middle Tier	2	85
Install the middle tier with Portal and Wireless installation type	Installing the OracleAS Middle Tier	2	85
Verify completion of the installation	Installing the OracleAS Middle Tier	2	85
Access the installed OracleAS middle-tier components	Installing the OracleAS Middle Tier	2	85
Using Oracle Application Server Management Tools		3	
Start and stop Application Server Control	The Application Server Control Interface	3	111
Access OracleAS Component pages of the Application Server Control	The Application Server Control Interface	3	111
Start and stop an OracleAS instance or a component using Application Server Control and Oracle Process Monitoring and Notification interface (opmnctl)	The Application Server Control Interface / Oracle Process Management and Notification Server	3	111 / 102
Use dcmctl utility to obtain configuration information	The Application Server Control Interface	3	111
Managing the Oracle Internet Directory		4	
Explain Directory and LDAP concepts	Directories and the LDAP	4	142
Describe Oracle Internet Directory (OID)	Oracle Internet Directory	4	149
Explain Oracle Internet Directory architecture	Oracle Internet Directory	4	149

Exam Readiness Checklist (Exam 1Z0-311)

OCA Official Objective	Certification Objective	Ch #	Pg #
Start and stop Oracle Internet Directory processes	Oracle Internet Directory	4	149
Identify various OID command-line tools	Oracle Internet Directory	4	149
Connect to and disconnect from the Directory by using Oracle Directory Manager	Oracle Internet Directory	4	149
Managing and Configuring Oracle HTTP Server		5	
Explain the Oracle HTTP Server processing model	Introduction to the Oracle HTTP Server	5	212
Describe the Oracle HTTP Server modules	Introduction to the Oracle HTTP Server	5	212
Specify the server and file locations for Oracle HTTP Server (OHS)	Introduction to the Oracle HTTP Server	5	212
Control the number of processes and connections, manage network connection for OHS	Managing the Oracle HTTP Server	5	230
Configure and use OHS log files	Managing the Oracle HTTP Server	5	230
Configuring Directives and Virtual Hosts		5	
Describe the configuration directories and their scope	OHS Configuration Directives	5	238
Describe the process of merging containers and contents	OHS Configuration Directives	5	238
Configure directories and enable directory indexes	OHS Configuration Directives	5	238
Describe the process of setting up virtual hosts	OHS Configuration Directives	5	238
Use configuration directives such as Option, Alias, and Script Alias	OHS Configuration Directives	5	238
Managing and Configuring OracleAS Web Cache		9	
Start, stop, and restart OracleAS Web Cache	OracleAS Web Cache Management	9	448
Change passwords for administrative users and listener ports	OracleAS Web Cache Administration Tasks	9	455
Specify site-to-server mappings	OracleAS Web Cache Administration Tasks	9	455
Create and configure caching rules	Creating and Configuring Caching Rules	9	465
Set up basic invalidation mechanism	Sending Invalidation Requests	9	476
Set up expiration rules	Expiration Policies	9	473

Exam Readiness Checklist (Exam 1Z0-311)

OCA Official Objective	Certification Objective	Ch #	Pg #
Configure access and event logs	OracleAS Web Cache Administration Tasks	9	455
Obtain basic performance statistics	OracleAS Web Cache Management	9	448
Managing and Configuring OC4J		8	
Create OC4J instances	Creating an OC4J Instance	8	374
Start and stop OC4J instances	Managing the OC4J Instance	8	379
Enable or disable application startup	Deploying J2EE Applications	8	406
Configure OC4J Instance Properties	Configuring OC4J	8	387
Configure web site and JSP properties	The OC4J Configuration Files	8	389
Edit OC4J configuration files	The OC4J Configuration Files	8	389
Managing the OracleAS Portal		7	
Describe OracleAS Portal Administrative Services	Managing the OracleAS Portal	7	333
Describe tools to monitor the OracleAS Portal instance	Managing the OracleAS Portal	7	333
Manage OracleAS Portal users, groups, and schemas	OracleAS Portal Schema, User, and Group Management	7	339
Administer the portlet repository	Administering the Portlet Repository	7	344
Perform export and import of portal content	Exporting and Importing Portal Content	7	348
Configuring OracleAS Portal		7	
Describe OracleAS Portal configuration tasks	OracleAS Portal Configuration Tasks	7	352
Configure the Self-Registration feature to enable users to create their own portal accounts	OracleAS Portal Configuration Tasks	7	352
Configure OracleAS Portal for WebDAV	OracleAS Portal Configuration Tasks	7	352
List the configuration modes of the Oracle Portal Configuration Assistance (OPCA)	OracleAS Portal Configuration Tasks	7	352
Configure Language support	OracleAS Portal Configuration Tasks	7	352
Configure the OracleAS Portal instance dependencies by using the Portal Dependency Setting file	OracleAS Portal Configuration Tasks	7	352

Exam Readiness Checklist (Exam 1Z0-311)

OCA Official Objective	Certification Objective	Ch #	Pg #
Deploying J2EE Applications		8	
Deploy Web applications to Oracle Application Server	Deploying J2EE Applications	8	406
Configure data sources to be used with OC4J	The OC4J Server Configuration Files	8	389
Provide necessary mappings for an Oracle database	Deploying J2EE Applications	8	406
Deploy J2EE applications	Deploying J2EE Applications	8	406
Deploy and register web providers	Deploying J2EE Applications	8	406
Configuring Oracle Application Server Components in OID		4	
Describe identity management	Identity Management and the OID	4	174
Describe the OracleAS Administration Model	Oracle Identity Management	4	175
Explain application-specific access control	Oracle Identity Management	4	175
Manage users and groups	Oracle Identity Management	4	175
Describe relationship between OracleAS Portal and Oracle Internet Directory	OracleAS Portal and the Oracle Internet Directory	4	200
Identify OracleAS Portal entries in the directory	OracleAS Portal and the Oracle Internet Directory	4	200
Managing Access Using Delegated Administration Service		4	
Explain the DAS Architecture	Delegated Administrative Service	4	191
Describe how DAS works	Delegated Administrative Service	4	191
Start and stop DAS	Delegated Administrative Service	4	191
Access DAS home page	Delegated Administrative Service	4	191
Use OID Self Service Console	Delegated Administrative Service	4	191
Manage user entries using DAS	Delegated Administrative Service	4	191
Manage group entries using DAS	Delegated Administrative Service	4	191
Create Identity Management Realm	Oracle Identity Management	4	175
Access DAS from OracleAS Portal	OracleAS Portal and the Oracle Internet Directory	4	200

Exam Readiness Checklist (Exam 1Z0-311)

OCA Official Objective	Certification Objective	Ch #	Pg #
Administering the OracleAS Single Sign-On Server		6	
Describe OracleAS Single Sign-On server components	OracleAS Single Sign-On	6	272
Explain OracleAS Sign-On server authentication flow	OracleAS Single Sign-On	6	272
Manage and configure OracleAS Single Sign-On server	Configuring and Managing the SSO Server	6	277
Administer partner and external applications	Configuring and Managing the SSO Server	6	277
Monitor OracleAS Single Sign-On Server	Configuring and Managing the SSO Server	6	277
Access OracleAS Single Sign-On server from OracleAS Portal	Configuring and Managing the SSO Server	6	277
Securing OracleAS Components Using SSL		6	
Explain Oracle wallet manager functionality	Oracle Wallet Manager	6	291
Manage wallets	Oracle Wallet Manager	6	291
Upload and download wallets	Oracle Wallet Manager	6	291
Manage user certificates	Managing Certificates	6	295
Manage trusted certificates	Managing Certificates	6	295
Enable Oracle HTTP Server, SSO, Web Cache, and Portal to Use SSL	Enabling OracleAS Components to Use SSL	6	296
Managing and Configuring OracleAS Certificate Authority		6	
Explain Public Key Infrastructure	OracleAS Certificate Authority	6	299
Describe Oracle Public Key Infrastructure Management Tools	OracleAS Certificate Authority	6	299
Describe OracleAS Certificate Authority	OracleAS Certificate Authority	6	299
Explain OracleAS Certificate Authority Architecture	OracleAS Certificate Authority	6	299
Access OCA Administration Pages	OracleAS Certificate Authority	6	299
Access OCA User Pages	OracleAS Certificate Authority	6	299

Part I

Architecture, Installation, and Management

Overview and Architecture

CERTIFICATION OBJECTIVES

Oracle Application Server 10g (OracleAS 10g) is a tool whose range spans several important solution areas. OracleAS 10g consists of a dazzling array of components designed to work seamlessly to address a wide-ranging set of application needs. This book deals with the latest Oracle Application Server 10g Release 2 (10.1.2.0.0) version being shipped by Oracle currently. Oracle plans to release versions 10.1.2.0.1, 10.1.2.0.2, and 10.1.3 later on.

In this chapter, we briefly review the following aspects of the Oracle Application Server 10g, Release 2 (10.1.2):

- Key solution areas
- Key components
- J2EE, Web Services, and Internet applications
- Key terminologies

CERTIFICATION OBJECTIVE 1.01

An Overview of the Oracle Application Server

OracleAS 10g is actually part of a much larger Oracle e-business platform that consists of three major components:

- Oracle Application Server to help deploy Internet applications
- Oracle Database Server to store enterprise business data
- Oracle Developer Suite to develop Internet applications

Oracle Application Server, which is described by Oracle as its Integrated Software Infrastructure for Enterprise Applications, is built on an integrated platform designed to take advantage of Grid computing and to help you develop and manage Web-based enterprise applications. OracleAS consists of several components designed to help you run all types of Web-based applications. OracleAS provides the capability not only to deploy Internet applications but also to create and manage enterprise portals and mobile devices, to automate business processes, and to provide real-time business intelligence.

OracleAS 10*g* is a standards-based application server that provides support for running J2EE applications and Web Services. OracleAS Portal, which is an important component of the Oracle Application Server, provides easy information access to customers through a browser or through wireless devices.

OracleAS 10*g* contains an Application Server along with development tools that enable you to create and deploy business applications on a service-oriented architecture (SOA). OracleAS 10*g* presents a common platform for the Web applications you can develop with various Oracle tools such as Oracle Developer, Oracle Discoverer, and JDeveloper. All these applications can be deployed by OracleAS 10*g* and accessed by users. OracleAS 10*g* also follows Oracle's Grid computing vision by designing the product's components so they can be deployed on a large number of low-cost servers, thus providing affordable performance and reliability.

Figure 1-1 shows the OracleAS Welcome page.

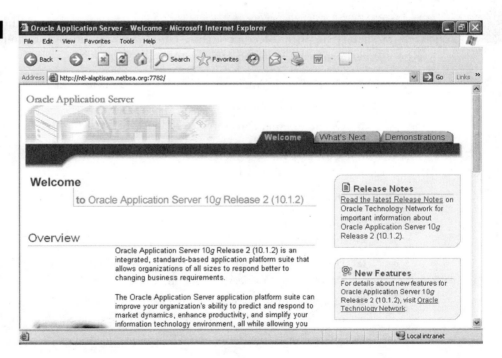

FIGURE 1-1

The Oracle
Application Server
Welcome Page

Key Solution Areas

OracleAS 10g is designed to address several solution areas with the help of its numerous components. You can broadly divide the solution areas into the following subareas:

- Using J2EE, Web Services, and Internet Applications
- Creating personalized portals
- Developing wireless-enabled applications
- Accelerating performance with caching
- Providing business intelligence
- Integrating Web Applications and Services
- Managing and securing the Web infrastructure

Key Components

It's quite confusing for newcomers to find way their way through the huge set of OracleAS application components. The three most important components, which form the guts of OracleAS 10g, are the following:

- OC4J (Oracle Application Server Containers for J2EE)
- Oracle HTTP Server
- Oracle Internet Directory

In addition to the foregoing three essential components, you have the following OracleAS 10g components:

- OracleAS Web Cache
- OracleAS Portal
- OracleAS Wireless
- Business Intelligence (OracleAS Discoverer, Oracle AS Forms, Oracle AS Reports, and OracleAS Personalization)
- Oracle Identity Management (in addition to the Oracle Internet Directory, it includes the Oracle Single Sign-On and the Oracle Certificate Authority)
- Integration, Management, and Security Components

■ Management and Security Components: Oracle Application Server Control, Oracle Internet Directory (OID), OracleAS Secure Developer Tools

I'll now explain each of the key solution areas in detail, with a brief summary of the particular OracleAS 10g component that's designed to address that solution area.

CERTIFICATION OBJECTIVE 1.02

J2EE Applications and Web Services

OracleAS provides complete support for J2EE Internet applications and Web Services. Let's look at each of these in detail in the following sections, starting with J2EE application support.

J2EE Applications

J2EE-based applications are important because they use a standard application platform and component specifications to develop Web-based applications. J2EE applications are written in Java using J2EE APIs. Each J2EE application consists of a set of components, with each component in charge of an area such as database access, presentation logic, and business logic, among others.

J2EE Application Components

You can use the following types of components in J2EE applications:

■ *Servlets*   Servlets are Java application components that work on the Web and enable dynamic Web page creation. A servlet is essentially a small Java program that runs on a Web server. An applet, on the other hand, is a small Java program that runs in a client browser. Servlets take the client browser's HTTP requests, generate dynamic content, and return the HTTP response to the browser.

■ *Java Server Pages*   Java Server Pages (JSPs) can contain static data in a text-based format (HTML, XML) as well as dynamic content constructed with the help of JSP elements.

■ *Enterprise JavaBeans*   Enterprise JavaBeans (EJBs) are based on the server and provide the business logic component.

Java Server Pages are precompiled into servlets when you invoke them, thus converting JSPs into servlets. The JSPs/servlets perform all the user interface work, and the EJBs perform application processing and database access. The first two components taken together can be called the Web component, and the third component can be called the enterprise bean component. All J2EE applications consist of one or more enterprise beans and Web or application client component modules.

Multi-Tiered J2EE Application Model

The various J2EE components can be distributed among several tiers according to their function. Here's a distributed application model based on three machines:

- The Client machine contains the application client, which is usually a Web browser, in charge of nothing more than local window management.
- The Application Server machine sits in the middle and contains the J2EE components along with other middleware. The Application Server machine can serve two tiers. The first, the Web tier, can host presentation services with the help of JSP pages and servlets. The second tier, the business logic tier, can contain the necessary business logic, encapsulated in EJBs.
- The Database Server machine hosts the enterprise database server.

J2EE Containers

Containers are components that contain other components such as servlets; they help manage servlets and provide the runtime support for them. A J2EE application component (e.g., a servlet) doesn't interact directly with other servlets or other types of J2EE components. The container provides the protocols and methods for interaction between various components and the J2EE services. Security checks, state management, and other deployment services are managed by the containers. A container provides the servlets a federated view of the underlying J2EE APIs.

When a client browser makes a request for a servlet, the Web server passes along that request to the container that contains the servlet. The container then converts the HTTP request into a Java method before sending the request along to the servlet.

Any enterprise bean component or Web-based component must be first assembled into a J2EE application and then deployed into a J2EE container. You can specify container settings that include security services, the naming and directory lookup, and the remote connectivity model. Based on the type of component it contains, you can create two kinds of J2EE containers:

■ EJB Containers, which contain all the Enterprise JavaBeans (EJBs) and run on the J2EE server

■ Web Containers, which contain the two Web components—JSP pages and servlets

Note that the JSPs are in effect extensions of the servlet functionality that provides a simple programmatic interface to Web pages. JSPs are HTML pages containing embedded Java code that's executed on the Web server. JSPs are used to provide dynamic functionality to Web-based applications. The Web server will compile JSPs into servlets when they are first requested.

OracleAS 10g Components to Support J2EE Applications

OracleAS 10*g* has two main components, which are designed to support J2EE applications:

■ Oracle HTTP Server

■ Oracle Application Server Containers for J2EE (OC4J)

Let's briefly review these two important OracleAS 10*g* components.

Oracle HTTP Server

Oracle HTTP Server (OHS) is based on the popular Apache Web server and hosts static and dynamic Web pages and Web applications. The HTTP server receives browser HTTP requests and converts the requested URLs into filenames that it sends back to the requestor. OHS serves as the deployment platform for OracleAS 10*g* by providing Web listener services for J2EE (OC4J) and by hosting the Web pages and Web applications for it. The Apache Web server uses modules to extend its basic functionality. Similarly, OHS uses several proprietary Oracle related add-ons or *mods* (short for modules) that extend the basic functionality of the underlying Apache server. The Oracle HTTP Server also provides several load-balancing features. The following subsections describe the main components of the Oracle HTTP Server.

HTTP Listener The OHS uses an Apache HTTP listener, which is in charge of receiving incoming requests and serving those requests by sending them to the appropriate processing utility.

Modules (mods) The Oracle HTTP Server is based on the Apache Web Server, and Oracle provides several modules to enhance the Apache server. Here's a brief explanation of some of the standard as well as Oracle-provided HTTP server modules.

As mentioned previously, the Apache Web server uses modules to implement, as well as extend, its basic functionality. In addition to the standard Apache modules, OHS contains several add-on modules that are specific to the various components of the Oracle Application Server. The following list names the main OHS add-on modules:

- **mod_php** Supports PHP (recursive acronym for PHP Hypertext Preprocessor), the open-source scripting language.
- **mod_security** Protects the Web server from external attacks by providing intrusion detection and protection services.
- **mod_fastcgi** Helps runs CGI programs at a higher performance level.
- **mod_perl** Routes requests to the PERL Interpreter.
- **mod_plsql** Routes requests to the PL/SQL engine.
- **mod_oc4j** Communicates with the OC4J instance.
- **mod_oradav** Supports distributed authoring and versioning.
- **mod_ossl** Supports the Secure Sockets Layer.
- **mod_osso** Routes requests to the optional OracleAS Single Sign-On server.

As you can surmise, each of the add-on modules serves as a communicator or facilitator between the HTTP server and other entities such as the database. For example, the *mod_plsql* module lets the Oracle HTTP Server use the Oracle PL/SQL language in the Oracle database.

Perl Interpreter The *mod_perl* module embeds the persistent Perl runtime environment in the Oracle HTTP Server. The Perl Interpreter runs as a thread within the Oracle HTTP Server, instead of using the Perl Interpreter that may have been installed as part of your operating system.

Oracle HTTP Server Architecture The Oracle HTTP Server employs a modular approach by using modules (explained in the previous section), to enhance its basic capabilities. During an HTTP request life cycle, the various modules are invoked as necessary.

There is a slight difference in the way the HTTP server processes requests on a UNIX system from the way it processes requests on a Windows system. In a UNIX system, a parent or control process spawns several child processes that are identical copies of the parent process, whose job it is to listen to and respond to users' requests. The *httpd.pid* file, located in the $ORACLE_HOME/Apache/Apache/logs directory, contains the process ID of the main parent process. When a request comes into the HTTP server, the child process takes charge of the request for the duration of the request's life cycle.

Note that the parent *httpd* process runs under the root user's account, but the child process it spawns runs as a less privileged user, usually the user "nobody." You must use the User and Group directives to set the privileges for the child processes. You must ensure that the child processes have read privileges to read all the files that they have to handle as part of the client request processing.

A request sent to a Common Gateway Interface (CGI) invokes an additional process besides the child process to handle the CGI program. To reduce the additional overhead caused by CGI programs, the Oracle HTTP Server offers the following two features:

- *FastCGI*   FastCGI eliminates the need for an additional process to run the CGI program.
- *Perl Interpreter*   The Perl Interpreter runs the CGI applications within the Web server processes, without any need for adding to overhead by starting new processes.

In a Windows system, the Oracle HTTP Server runs as a single control process and a single child process. Multiple threads spawned by the child process will serve the client requests.

Oracle Application Server Containers for J2EE (OC4J)

J2EE applications are Java applications that are deployed on a J2EE-compatible server and consist of various types of modules, such as a Web presentation module, a business logic module, and a data access module. If you wish, you can install the various application components of a J2EE application on different machines.

OracleAS 10*g* is built on a J2EE foundation, and it enables the development and deployment of dynamic Web sites using popular programming languages and technologies. OC4J is the core J2EE runtime component of the Oracle Application Server. You can also call the OC4J component the J2EE server component. A

J2EE server component is the runtime component of any J2EE product, and it provides the EJB and Web containers. OC4J is a fast, lightweight, and scalable implementation that's J2EE 1.3 certified; it runs on standard J2SE distributions. OC4J supports the following standard APIs:

- Java Servlets
- Enterprise JavaBeans (EJB)
- Java Transaction API (JTA)
- Java Message Service (JMS)
- JavaMail
- JavaBeans Activation Framework
- Java API for XML(JAXP)
- J2EE Connector Architecture
- Java Authentication and Authorization Service (JAAS)

ℯχαм
ⓦatch   *Java 2 Platform, Standard Edition (J2SE), enables you to develop, deploy, and manage Java applications on a desktop client platform such as a personal computer.*

Although OC4J provides a complete Java 2 enterprise edition (J2EE) environment, you can run OC4J on the standard JDK that comes with your operating system.

The following subsections describe the important features of OC4J.

Oracle Application Server Containers for J2EE Containers   Containers provide runtime support for the various J2EE application components. Each of the components is bundled in the form of a module and added to the J2EE application. Thus, a typical J2EE application will consist of one or more Enterprise JavaBeans, along with Web or application client component modules. The J2EE application modules are modularized to enable the reuse of application components such as user interfaces (e.g., JSP or DHTM) and business logic, which is usually taken care of by using EJB components.

Enterprise JavaBeans (EJB) is the component-based application model for Java and provides system-level services such as multi-threading to facilitate application programming. EJB relies on various standardized services, such as JNDI, JTS, and JDBC, to facilitate application programming and help EJB objects to be interoperable across different EJB servers. An EJB application is a framework for deploying CORBA (Common Object Request Broker Architecture) objects adhering to the EJB specification. A *CORBA object* is nothing but a generic term for programs that conform to the OMG's CORBA specification. CORBA objects can be written in any language and deployed on any machine. An EJB container coordinates the components in an EJB application and thus is one of the primary EJB runtime components.

OC4J provides the following three types of J2EE containers.

J2EE Servlet Containers (Servlet 2.3 specification): A servlet is a small Java program that runs on a Web server. Servlets accept HTTP requests from client browsers and send the HTTP responses back to them. Servlets may also query databases to serve dynamic content to the clients. A servlet *container*, which is a part of the OC4J Web container, controls the runtime behavior of the servlets and provides it the necessary services it needs while it's executing. The servlet container executes and manages the servlets and provides it access to Java APIs such as JDBC so that the servlet can connect to a database. A servlet container also provides the runtime environment for Java servlets.

e x a m

ⓦ a t c h *Both the OC4J Web containers and the OC4J EJB use the Java 2 Platform, Standard Edition (J2SE) infrastructure.*

Java Server Page (JSP) containers (Sun JSP 1.2 specification): Java Server Pages enable the generation of dynamic Web content. JSPs are translated into Java servlets before they are run.

J2EE Enterprise JavaBeans Containers (EJB 2.0 specification): The OC4J EJB Container executes the enterprise beans for J2EE applications and uses the J2SE virtual machine to do so. As explained earlier, enterprise beans implement Enterprise JavaBeans technology and run in the EJB container. Enterprise beans are server-side components that contain the application business logic. There are three types of enterprise beans:

- *Session Beans* These are nonpersistent and generally nonshareable objects. Session beans are used to distribute processing tasks, with each session bean performing a certain task for its client—for example, querying and updating data for a client.

- *Entity Beans* These are persistent shareable objects that continue to exist even after a program has been stopped. Entity beans are used to model complex business entities or a set of actions inside a business process. For example, you can use entity beans to perform computations on a purchase order's items. You typically use entity beans when dealing with business actions that involve data and computations with data. Entity beans have a primary key to help identify them.

> ■ *Message-Driven Beans*   These objects facilitate receiving of
> asynchronous messages, using Java Messaging Services (JMS), which
> is an enterprise-messaging API.

J2EE Services

The various J2EE Java containers described in the previous section manage access to
certain important J2EE services. The following are the important J2EE services:

- Java Database Connectivity (JDBC) is used to incorporate SQL statements inside
  Java programs.
- Java Message Service (JMS) lets J2EE application components create, send, and
  receive messages.
- Java Transaction API (JTA) helps applications handle transactions distributed
  over multiple databases as well as access transaction services from other
  components. Multiple databases correctly know when a transaction ends by a
  committing or rolling back of the transaction's effects.
- Java Naming and Directory Interface (JNDI) provides a standard interface for
  naming and directory services.
- JavaMail Technology enables the use of e-mail notifications.
- Java API for XML (JAXP) supports standard SAX and DOM APIs for parsing
  XML documents, in addition to supporting XSLT transform engines.
- J2EE Connector Architecture enables database access to J2EE applications.
- Java Authentication and Authorization Service (JAAS) serves as a user
  authentication service for J2EE applications.

Web Services

Web Services enable applications to directly interact with other applications using
XML and other Web-based standards. Web Services are business processes that
provide the following features:

- Using the Web Services Description Language (WSDL) to expose and describe
  their attributes and functionality to other services
- Enabling other services to locate a service on the Web (for example, a weather
  service), using the Universal Description, Discovery, and Integration (UDDI)
  registries

■ Enabling remote services to invoke services using Internet protocols

■ Responding to requesting applications over an identical protocol

on the Job *OracleAS Web Services run as servlets in the OC4J servlet container.*

Oracle Components to Support Web Services

OracleAS Web Services is the OracleAS component that provides sophisticated runtime features and solid support for Web Services; they're run as servlets in the OC4J Servlet Container. This enables the OracleAS Web Services to gain the scalability and load-balancing benefits of all J2EE applications. OracleAS Web Services enables the following two types of exchange:

■ Remote procedure call (RPC) style

■ Message-oriented or document style

Here are some key features of OracleAS Web Services:

■ Implementing Web Services using J2EE components as well as Java classes or PL/SQL stored procedures

■ Generating automatic Web Services Description Language (WSDL)

■ Developing Web Services using the same programming concepts and tools as regular J2EE applications

■ Transparently accessing existing J2EE business logic

■ Using common runtime services environment with the J2EE applications

OracleAS 10*g* provides several tools to package, assemble, deploy, register, monitor, and manage Web Services.

CERTIFICATION OBJECTIVE 1.03

Creating and Managing Business Portals

Business portals provide a way to access information from different data sources through a single entry point called a *portal page*. This entry point or page can be customized for an individual user, thus presenting users with relevant information to suit their business needs. Portals are being increasingly deployed by organizations to provide a single source for company-wide information as well as the central point from which to conduct a company's day-to-day business. Business portals offer the following benefits:

- Providing easy access to company-wide information from a single point of access
- Providing access to personalized information based on the job level and type
- Providing nontechnical users an easy way to transmit information across the enterprise
- Enabling multiple applications and user accounts to be accessed through the single sign-on feature

OracleAS Components to Support Portals

Oracle Application Server Portal (OracleAS Portal) is the OracleAS component that addresses the portal solution. OracleAS Portal is a Web-based tool that can integrate data from multiple sources, thus making enterprise-wide data accessible from a single location. Using OracleAS Portal, you can build and deploy sophisticated Web applications and Web sites. Through a user friendly HTML-based interface, you can create database objects as well as build HTML-based interfaces.

You can build OracleAS Portal pages with the help of *portlets*, which are reusable components that provide access to or summarize an information source or applications. A portal client usually accesses the OracleAS Portal application through portlets. You can either use existing portlets that come with the OracleAS Portal, or create your own custom portlets, using the following languages and technologies:

- Java-based applications
- Oracle PL/SQL packages
- Web pages built with technology such as Active Server Pages (ASPs) or Perl
- Web Services

Portlets communicate with the OracleAS Portal through a *provider*. The provider exposes the business application or information source through the portlets. Each portlet can have a single provider, whereas a provider can have multiple portlets. You can divide OracleAS Portal providers into the following two broad categories:

- Partner portlets, created by independent software vendors.
- OracleAS components used as portlet providers. For example, you can use the Oracle Business Intelligence Discoverer tools as a portlet provider.

CERTIFICATION OBJECTIVE 1.04

Wireless Applications

Increasingly, mobile devices are being used as a means of communication. These mobile devices use wireless-enabled applications to communicate in a connectionless mode. On demand, any time, anywhere—information, over a broad variety of devices is the order of the day. The essence of wireless applications is to enable users to access information such as e-mail and calendars as well as key enterprise-wide information, using a mobile device as a wireless client.

OracleAS Wireless

Oracle Application Server Wireless (OracleAS Wireless) is the OracleAS component that provides comprehensive support for wireless and voice applications. OracleAS Wireless enables the building and deploying of Web and database applications, including e-mail, news, and other services, to mobile device users through a common application framework and environment.

Here is how OracleAS Wireless works, in a nutshell: A wireless service will provide a URL request to OracleAS Wireless through a Gateway. OracleAS Wireless will send this request to the intended target after normalizing it. OracleAS Wireless will then transform the response to the markup language used by the requesting mobile device and send it along to the device, using the gateway again. The mobile device might use a variety of markup languages, including target markup languages, such as HTML, WML, HDML, VoiceXML, SMS, and XMPP. The essential point is that the content rendered by OracleAS Wireless is device independent.

OracleAS 10g uses the Wireless Access Protocol (WAP) to make the XML data translation from a device-dependent format to a standard XML message. This enables OracleAS 10g to treat these requests as device independent requests that can be accessed from anywhere.

You can also use OracleAS Wireless to enable connections to OracleAS Portal through mobile devices, in addition to the standard Web browser-based access.

Requests coming from mobile devices to access the OracleAS Portal use WAP, with OracleAS acting as the intermediary between the mobile device and the OracleAS Portal. OracleAS Wireless converts the mobile XML to the mobile device language (e.g., WML or HDML) and sends the requested portal information back to the client through the WAP gateway.

Content from non-HTTP sources such as PL/SQL and SQL queries is also accessible to mobile devices, as long as they use the necessary protocol adapters. OracleAS Wireless provides the API to plug in these adapters.

OracleAS Wireless consists of these four broad component groups:

- The *Multi-Channel Advisor* functions to detect the various types of wireless devices and transform content and application for those devices.
- The *Sensor Edge Server*'s job is to integrate command and response indication equipment such as sensors with various applications.
- A *Mobile Portal* is a wireless portal component employed by end users to access applications and content.
- *Foundation Services* include Java APIs, Web Services, and the like, which help developers create their applications.

OracleAS Wireless uses open platform standards to make development easier and to help integration with applications. Besides the previously mentioned wireless components, various development tools are available to help you develop and test wireless- and voice-based applications. Here's a brief list:

- Service Designer
- Content Development Tool
- Help Desk
- System Monitor

With the help of OracleAS Wireless, you can do the following:

- Develop location-based, voice-enabled, or personalized applications that can be deployed to all types of devices.
- Use advanced messaging techniques such as Short Messaging Service (SMS).

Providing Business Intelligence for the Web

Business intelligence solutions generally include the ability to perform easy analyses of business data to glean valuable information. Business intelligence tools generally possess the ability to perform ad hoc queries, what-if analyses, and reporting and Web-publishing tasks. Businesses often make use of disparate types of information such as OLTP databases, data warehouses, and small data marts. A good business intelligence solution enables nontechnical users to easily access and retrieve necessary information from all these business sources.

OracleAS Business Intelligence Components

OracleAS 10*g* provides several components to aid business intelligence-related tasks. Note that the business intelligence components aren't a part of our OracleAS 10*g* installation—they're an optional component that you can install later on if you wish. These business intelligence tools are summarized in the following subsections.

OracleAS Discoverer

OracleAS Discoverer is OracleAS 10*g*'s main business intelligence component. OracleAS Discover can perform the following types of business intelligence tasks:

- Ad hoc queries and what if analyses
- Complex analysis using Oracle analytic functions
- Customized summary views of data
- Drilling down to detailed views of data
- Web publishing

The OracleAS Discoverer works with Oracle OLTP databases as well as data warehouses and Oracle Applications, thus covering all of Oracle's data sources. The OracleAS Discoverer tool can be accessed in two ways:

- Using an *applet-based client* called Discoverer Plus to perform quick queries and develop short reports. These reports can be viewed with either Discoverer Plus or the Discoverer Viewer.
- Using a *browser-based client* called Discoverer Viewer, which is optimized for performance to view prebuilt reports and detailed drill-down reports. You can also

use the Discoverer Viewer to publish reports to a Portal. The reports can be easily customized to fit a Web site's presentation format.

OracleAS Reports Services

OracleAS Reports Services is a powerful feature for developing and deploying sophisticated reports in any data format from virtually any source. The following are the key features of OracleAS Reports Services:

- Building and deploying reports based on data from just about any source
- Unlimited data formatting capabilities
- Making reports accessible from any browser
- Production of high volumes of reports, using the OracleAS 10g middle-tier load-balancing and caching features
- Ability to generate ad hoc as well as scheduled reports
- Ability to generate reports in HTML, PDF, or XML
- Ability to link to published reports in the OracleAS Portal

OracleAS Forms Services

OracleAS Forms Services provide a middle-tier application framework with the following three major components:

- *Client* This is typically a thin Java client with a Java (or Jinitiator) plug-in.
- *Forms Listener Servlet* The Forms Listener Servlet resides on the middle tier and acts as a broker between the Java client processes and the Forms runtime processes.
- *Forms Runtime Processes* The runtime processes are connected to the Oracle database and manage application logic and processing. It manages requests from the Java clients and communicates with the database server to retrieve the data requested by the clients. Web forms are user processes like any others, and they separate the presentation layer from the application logic layer by presenting the user interface within a browser and the application logic in the runtime process.

OracleAS Personalization

OracleAS Personalization is a product that enables personalized recommendations to users, based on their Web site activity. Personalization includes the recording and analyzing of a user's Web behavior, so that up-to-date personalized recommendations can be made when the user logs in the next time.

Accelerating Performance with Caching

Caching involves storing frequently accessed information so that it can be retrieved faster. Caching in the context of Web applications involves the storing of either partial or complete static and dynamic Web pages on a middleware server. For example, frequently requested Web pages can be stored in a cache and accessed directly from there, thus reducing the need to access the database each time you need to view a particular page. Efficient caching can reduce Web site bottlenecks and enable Web sites to carry much higher user loads.

Caching Web applications can provide the following benefits:

- Serving fresh dynamic content faster
- Providing higher throughput at a very low cost
- Decreasing response time
- Increasing the concurrent user load capability

You can cache data at various levels, including at the client or the server level. Caching solutions that target the browser use browser-caching techniques. Here, our main concern is more about a specified type of Web caching, called server acceleration. A *server accelerator* is a caching engine that substitutes for the actual Web server and caches or stores a copy of the Web server's objects. When the user next makes a request to the Web server for any content that's already in the server accelerator's cache, the content is served directly from there instead of from the Web server. The server accelerator intercepts all requests to the Web servers to determine whether it can serve the request itself, thus decreasing the Web server's load. Because server accelerators can be implemented with inexpensive machines, they are an excellent cost-effective method of scaling up a Web application. A server accelerator cache is also called a *reverse proxy* cache.

OracleAS Web Cache

OracleAS Web Cache is the OracleAS 10*g* component that provides support for the Web-caching solution. The OracleAS Web Cache is a server accelerator type of Web caching solution and provides both server content acceleration and load-balancing services by caching and thus accelerating the delivery of both static and dynamic Web content. The OracleAS Web Cache acts as a content-aware reverse proxy that can be clustered to provide enhanced availability and scalability of an organization's Web servers.

In a simple deployment, the OracleAS Web Cache sits in front of a Web server and caches its content. When a client wants to talk to the Web server, it sends an HTTP request to the OracleAS Web Cache, which serves as a virtual server for the Web server. If the content being requested is already cached, it's served straight from the Web cache. If it isn't in the cache, the Web cache retrieves it from the application server's Web server first. OracleAS Web Cache can run on the same server as the application server, or it can run on a dedicated server. Because the Web cache runs well on cheap commodity servers, a dedicated server can help in avoiding resource contention among various applications.

OracleAS Web Cache supports Edge Side Includes (ESI), which enable the assembly of pages at the network edge. ESI enables partial-page caching and dynamic page assembly using both cacheable and noncacheable page fragments.

Benefits of OracleAS Caching

The OracleAS Caching feature provides the following benefits:

- Speeding up the delivery of both static and dynamic pages
- Reducing administrative and hardware costs
- Providing load balancing among the HTTP servers

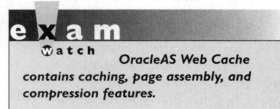

OracleAS Web Cache contains caching, page assembly, and compression features.

OracleAS Web Cache Features

A high-volume Web site can deploy multiple Web caches on commodity servers, thus providing a low-cost server acceleration solution. The OracleAS Web Cache contains several features that enhance the quality of any Web site. The OracleAS Web Cache features can be grouped into the categories outlined in the following subsections.

Content Compression The OracleAS Web Cache can compress documents, including noncacheable Web pages. Because compressed pages are compact, this means that Web browsers get their results back much faster.

Full-Page Static and Dynamic Content Caching OracleAS Web Cache uses separate rules for caching static and dynamic pages that employ technologies such as Java Server Pages. You can also use separate caching rules for Web pages that assemble dynamic Edge Side Includes (ESI) fragments.

Partial-Page Caching and Personalized Page Assembly   The OracleAS Web Cache can dynamically assemble Web pages with cacheable as well as noncacheable fragments. The partial-paging technology enables the Web cache to cache, assemble, and deliver more HTML content.

High Availability and Scalability   You can configure multiple instances of the OracleAS Web Cache to run as a single cluster (called the OracleAS Cluster Web Cache) to increase both the availability and the scalability of your Web applications.

Workload Management   You can also configure the OracleAS Web Cache as a load balancer. You can use an architecture with several application servers to increase scalability and availability. The OracleAS Web Cache can then send requests to the least busy server by using its load-balancing capabilities. Furthermore, when an application server goes down, OracleAS Web Cache can automatically perform a failover to the other functioning servers until the failed server comes back online.

In addition, you can configure the OracleAS Web Cache exclusively as a load balancer by replacing the hardware load balancer with one or multiple caches that don't cache any Web content.

Cache Invalidation and Expiration   OracleAS Web Cache provides a sophisticated means to invalidate and expire outdated Web content, thus ensuring the delivery of fresh content to Web browsers.

End-User Experience Management   OracleAS Web Cache also includes performance-monitoring functionality that provides valuable insight into end-user service levels. You can measure end-user response times for a particular URL or for the entire Web application.

CERTIFICATION OBJECTIVE 1.07

Identity Management

Identity management refers to the deployment of enterprise identities and the control of their access to enterprise applications. You create enterprise entities, create enterprise groups, provision those identities in enterprise services, and manage policies associated with the enterprise identities.

OracleAS 10g Identity Management Components

Oracle Identity Management is a key component of the OracleAS 10g Infrastructure and serves as the backbone of the Oracle Application Server deployment. Oracle Identity Management comprises several components, including the Oracle Internet Directory and the Single Sign-On feature, and provides directory, user management, and security support. Key identity management components are described in the following subsections.

Oracle Internet Directory

Oracle implements the Lightweight Directory Access Protocol (LDAP) version 3, through the Oracle Internet Directory (OID). OID is used to store enterprise-wide security and management information. OID helps to create and manage users across the enterprise by providing authentication mechanisms and a centralized user-provisioning model. All OracleAS 10g instances including the OracleAS Infrastructure instance, the various middle-tier components such as Oracle Single Sign-On and OracleAS Portal, and all applications deployed on the Oracle Application Server use OID as a single store for all types of user information.

OID enables all Oracle components to maintain a single identity for users, thus enabling administration of the user information from a single point. In addition, OID stores configuration information for various OracleAS 10g components and applications, based on which granting of administrative privileges to different users can be managed.

Oracle Delegated Administration Service

Oracle Delegated Administrative Service (DAS) consists of a set of predefined Web based services known as Delegated Administrative Service units. DAS units perform operations such as maintaining user and group entries in the OID. DAS units help users perform directory operations on the OID directory without the need to depend on the application administrator. Application administrators can delegate various user management tasks to the users themselves, using DAS. A user or an application administrator can be granted privileges to modify authorized data and use DAS to deploy and manage OID-enabled applications.

DAS provides a browser-based application called the OID Self Service Console, in which users can access the directory data of their applications that are stored in the OID. Using the Self Service Console, authorized users can perform tasks such as granting access to directory entries or attributes to application users.

Oracle Directory Integration and Provisioning

Directory Integration and Provisioning performs two major functions. *Directory Integration* refers to the synchronization of the OID with other directories and user repositories. *Directory Provisioning* refers to the OracleAS 10*g* features that enable the creation and management of users' accounts and privileges for various Oracle components and applications. Note that Directory Integration and Provisioning also includes third-party applications, which are accessed through standard interfaces.

OracleAS Single Sign-On

Users access various applications through OracleAS Single Sign-On (SSO). SSO enables a user to log in once to the Oracle Application Server using a username/ password combination, and to subsequently log in to all applications that it hosts without having to log in to each of them separately. User information is stored not in the various applications but in the centralized store, the OID. The OracleAS SSO Server stores the user information in the OID and retrieves it from there when users need to be authenticated. Therefore, it's the OID that enables the Single Sign-On capability of the Oracle Application Server. The SSO Server provides transparent logon to all SSO-enabled applications on all application servers in an OracleAS farm.

on the job

You can protect Web sites by using the Secure Sockets Layer (SSL) encryption.

OracleAS Certificate Authority

The OracleAS Certificate Authority manages the use of public-key certificates, which enable the secure and reliable authentication of enterprise users. A trusted entity can issue a certificate to a user after verifying the user's authentication credentials. These certificates are virtually impossible to alter or duplicate, thus providing solid security on both open and closed networks. To prevent the copying of the certificates, you can store them in an Oracle Wallet, which is a secure store for certificates.

CERTIFICATION OBJECTIVE 1.08

Oracle Application Server Architecture

The very first thing you must be aware of regarding the Oracle10g architecture is that it consists of the following *two main components:*

- The OracleAS Infrastructure
- The OracleAS Middle Tier

OracleAS Infrastructure's main job is to support the functioning of the OracleAS middle-tier components. OracleAS Infrastructure enables you to deploy components such as the OID and OracleAS Single Sign-On and OracleAS clusters through using the infrastructure's Metadata Repository. A Metadata Repository is an Oracle database with prebuilt schemas to support Oracle Application Server components and services. Note that if you use just the file system instead of the Metadata Repository, you can't use the OID or the SSO capability.

on the
job

High availability options that are available when using the Oracle Application Server include OracleAS Cold Failover Cluster, OracleAS Cluster (Identity Management), and OracleAS Disaster Recovery.

The middle tier is where the action is—you deploy and run all your applications from there. The middle tier consists of the actual OracleAS components that address each of the solution areas I discussed earlier in this chapter (e.g., the OracleAS Portal and OracleAS Wireless). The OracleAS infrastructure supports the middle tier by providing necessary services such as identity management.

Here are some important points regarding the relationship between the middle tier and the infrastructure components:

- When you install OracleAS 10g, you must install the infrastructure separately from the middle tier, which in essence means that you must perform the installation using the Oracle Universal Installer twice—once for the infrastructure and once for the middle tier. The infrastructure should be installed first, because it must be running in order to install several middle-tier components.
- Several middle tiers can share one infrastructure installation.

■ You can run some middle-tier components without the infrastructure. The infrastructure is optional for the J2EE and Web cache middle-tier types.

■ You can run both the infrastructure and the middle tier components on the same server, if you wish, or on multiple servers. For superior performance, you must install the infrastructure and the middle tier on different servers, but the choice also depends on how powerful your servers are. A very powerful server can accommodate all components without any problems.

on the
ö o b
You can use the same OracleAS Infrastructure to support more than one OracleAS Middle-Tier installation.

The OracleAS Infrastructure

The OracleAS Infrastructure consists of the OracleAS Metadata Repository component and the Identity Management Components. When you use the Oracle Universal Installer to install OracleAS 10g, you must first install the OracleAS Infrastructure components, before you can install the middle-tier components. When installing the OracleAS Infrastructure, you can install:

■ The OracleAS Metadata Repository by itself

■ The Identity Management component by itself

■ The Identity Management component and the OracleAS Metadata Repository together

The OracleAS Infrastructure consists of two components — the Identity Management Components and the OracleAS Metadata repository. Together, these two components provide all the necessary support for the functioning of the various middle-tier components. When you install one or both components of the OracleAS infrastructure, the Oracle HTTP Server, Oracle Application Server Containers for J2EE (OC4J), and the Application Server Control (GUI management tool) are automatically installed by default.

The two components of the OracleAS 10g infrastructure are discussed in more detail in the following subsections.

Oracle Identity Management

OracleAS Identity Management provides security, directory, and user-management services and includes the following components:

- Oracle Internet Directory (including the Delegated Administration Service)
- OracleAS Single Sign-On
- OracleAS Certificate Authority
- Oracle Directory Integration and Provisioning

OracleAS Metadata Repository

The OracleAS Metadata Repository is a collection of schemas necessary for the functioning of the various OracleAS components. The repository itself is part of an Oracle database. Various OracleAS middle-tier components use the Metadata Repository to store data pertaining to those components. The various schemas stored in the Metadata Repository can be grouped into the following categories:

- *Product metadata*   Metadata used by middle-tier components such as the OracleAS Portal and OracleAS Wireless.
- *Identity Management metadata*   Security and identity management-related meta data used by security- and identity-related middle-tier components such as the Oracle Internet Directory (OID), OracleAS Single Sign-On, and the OracleAS Certificate Authority.
- *Configuration Management metadata*   OracleAS instance configuration schema used by components such as the DCM.

OracleAS 10*g* lets you install the OracleAS Metadata Repository into an existing Oracle database; otherwise, it creates a new Oracle Database 10*g* database for this purpose.

Multiple Repositories   You can choose to configure more than one Metadata Repository. This way, you can improve performance by letting different middle-tier components use their own specific repository. Multiple repositories require the creation of multiple Oracle databases, with each database serving as a separate Metadata repository. In most cases, you first register a repository with the OID. You then select the repository you want to assign to a particular middle tier (e.g., the Portal or the Wireless) during the installation of the middle tier.

Installing the Infrastructure on Multiple Servers   You can take advantage of the division of the infrastructure into the OracleAS Metadata Repository and the Identity Management components by installing them on separate servers. Installing the infrastructure components on multiple computers provides the benefits of security, scalability, and availability.

If you choose to install the two components on different servers, you must first install the OracleAS Metadata Repository before installing the Identity Management components. You can also install the various components of the Identity Management on several servers if you wish.

The OracleAS Middle Tier

The OracleAS middle tier contains all the components you need to deploy and manage applications, such as the following:

- Oracle HTTP Server
- Oracle containers for J2EE (OC4J)
- OracleAS Portal
- OracleAS Web Cache

You must install the OracleAS Infrastructure and the OracleAS middle-tier components separately. During the OracleAS 10g installation, you choose the installation option "OracleAS Middle Tier" to install the middle-tier components.

CERTIFICATION OBJECTIVE 1.09

Managing the Oracle Application Server

You manage the Oracle Application Server with several tools. The most important of these is the Oracle Application Server Control tool, which is a GUI tool similar to the Database Control used by Oracle DBAs for database management, and the Grid Control, which is used to manage your entire enterprise, including the application servers, hosts, and databases. The other key tools are Distributed Configuration Management (DCM) and the Oracle Process Management and Notification Server (OPMN). Let's now look at these three tools briefly.

Application Server Control

When you install an instance of OracleAS, the Application Server Control is automatically installed as well and there's no need to configure anything. All you need to do is to make sure that the application control service is running, which must be done before you can access the tool through your Web browser. Using the Application Server Control, you can manage the following:

- A single OracleAS instance
- An OracleAS farm
- An OracleAS cluster

An OracleAS farm is a set of application server instances that are grouped together into one unit and managed together. An OracleAS cluster is a collection of OracleAS instances with identical configuration as well as application deployment.

Figure 1-2 shows the Application Server Control home page.

FIGURE 1-2

The Application Server Control Home Page

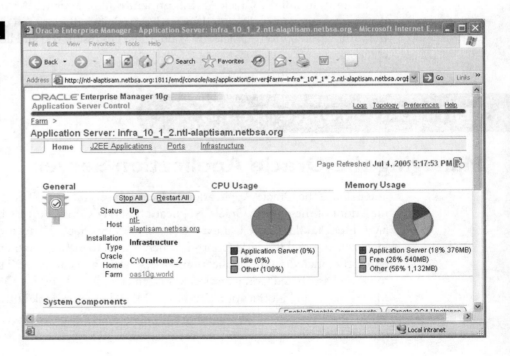

Distributed Configuration Management

DCM is used mainly for configuration purposes and the *dcmtl* utility is used to perform DCM-related tasks.

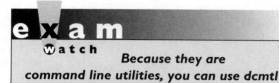

e x a m

ⓦ**a t c h**　*Because they are command line utilities, you can use dcmtl and opmnctl in operating system scripts.*

Oracle Process Management and Notification Server

You can use OPMN instead of the Application Server Control for many tasks, such as the starting and stopping of the OracleAS instance. You use the command line tool *opmnctl* as the interface to OPMN.

CERTIFICATION OBJECTIVE 1.10

Important OracleAS 10g Terminology

Before you install OracleAS 10g, it's a good idea to familiarize yourself with the key OracleAS terms. Some of these terms are relevant to the installation process, but most of them are relevant throughout this book while administering the OracleAS Infrastructure and Middle Tier.

OracleAS Installation

The OracleAS installation refers to the OracleAS software programs and configuration files that are installed in an Oracle Home during OracleAS installation. The OracleAS Infrastructure and the Oracle Middle Tier each has its own separate installation, in a separate Oracle Home.

OracleAS Infrastructure

The OracleAS Infrastructure provides centralized support to the middle-tier components. These services are grouped into three main categories—product metadata, identity management, and configuration management.

Metadata Repository

The Metadata Repository is an Oracle Database 10g database that stores the metadata for the OracleAS instance. The metadata is mandatory only if you're installing certain OracleAS components.

Middle-Tier Components

The Middle-Tier OracleAS components help you develop, deploy, and manage Web-based applications. The various middle-tier components address each of the OracleAS solution areas listed previously in this chapter. The middle-tier components include the OHS, OC4J, OracleAS Web Cache, OracleAS Portal, and OracleAS Wireless.

Directory Server

A directory provides a convenient way to store and retrieve a company's information regarding employees and other resources. Oracle Internet Directory Server is the OracleAS directory server.

Oracle Application Server Instance

An Oracle Application Server instance is the set of processes that operate the various OracleAS components you configure during the installation. After you install either the infrastructure or the middle tier, you must create an OracleAS instance to make the installation functional. You have a separate instance for the infrastructure and for the middle tier. For example, you can name your infrastructure instance infra10_1_2 and the middle tier J2EE_10_1_2. Instance names help OracleAS identify instances, given that you can install multiple instances on the same computer. Once you name an instance, you can't ever change it. The *complete name* of the OracleAS instance will be the product of appending the fully qualified host name to the instance name, as shown here:

```
infra10.myhost.mydomain.com
portwire.myhost.mydomain.com
```

The ias_admin User

During the installation process, you supply a password for a default OracleAS user named *ias_admin*. The user *ias_admin* is the administrative user for OracleAS instances. For example, you log in as *ias_admin* to manage OracleAS through the Application Server Control tool. The username *ias_admin* is the same for all OracleAS instances. Of course, you can use different passwords for each instance.

OracleAS Farm

An OracleAS Farm is a set of OracleAS instances (one or more) that share a single OracleAS Metadata Repository. An OracleAS Farm is a set of application server instances that are grouped together into one unit and managed together. You create the OracleAS Farm by adding OracleAS instances to a common Farm. The Metadata Repository could be a repository created in a new database as part of the OracleAS Infrastructure installation, a repository created in an existing database using the OracleAS Repository Creation Assistant, or even a File-based repository, which doesn't need a database.

on the
❶ o b
You can use the File-based Repository only for the J2EE and Web cache instances. This repository doesn't contain the schemas for the other types of OracleAS installation types (e.g., the Portal and Wireless installation type).

Oracle Application Server Cluster

An OracleAS Cluster is a collection of OracleAS instances with identical configuration as well as application deployment. A cluster of OracleAS instances will appear as a single instance, and function as such. When you make a change to one component belonging to an instance, it will be applied to all similar components across the cluster. For example, if you make changes to one HTTP server, then all HTTP servers in the cluster are affected similarly. If you deploy or change an OC4J application on one instance in a cluster, OracleAS automatically deploys or changes OC4J components across the cluster.

When you create the first instance of a J2EE and Web cache OracleAS instance, you can create a cluster and then add your OracleAS instance to the new cluster. When you subsequently create other instances, you can add them to the

FIGURE I-3

The Application
Server Farm Page

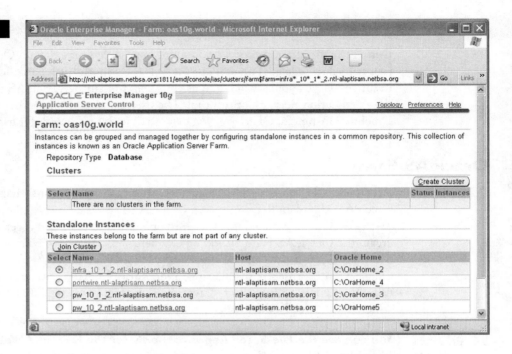

cluster. OracleAS will automatically change the J2EE and Web cache component configuration of the new instance to match the component configuration of the instances in the cluster. When you deploy an application from an OC4J instance, for example, OracleAS will deploy that application across all OC4J instances in the cluster. Figure 1-3 shows an OracleAS standalone instance, farms, and clusters on the Application Server Farm page.

on the
Üo b

In order for you to create a cluster and add members to it, the OracleAS instance must be first a part of an OracleAS Farm.

TWO-MINUTE DRILL

An Overview of the Oracle Application Server

❑ OracleAS 10g is part of the Oracle e-business platform that also includes the Oracle Database Server and the Oracle Developer Suite.

❑ The three most important components of OracleAS 10g are OC4J, the Oracle HTTP Server, and the Oracle Internet Directory.

❑ OracleAS 10g is a standards-based application server that provides support for running J2EE applications.

J2EE Applications and Web Services

❑ OracleAS 10g provides support for running J2EE applications and Web Services.

❑ Servlets are Java classes that work on the Web and enable dynamic Web page creation.

❑ Java Server Pages contain both static and dynamic content.

❑ Enterprise JavaBeans provide the business logic component to J2EE applications.

❑ J2EE containers manage servlets and provide runtime support for them.

❑ There are two kinds of J2EE containers: EJB containers and Web containers. Web containers can be servlet containers or JSP containers.

❑ Enterprise Beans run in the EJB container and contain the business logic.

❑ OC4J and the Oracle HTTP Server support J2EE applications and Web Services.

❑ Oracle provides several add-on modules to the Apache server (e.g., mod_plsql) that are special to the Oracle HTTP Server.

❑ Web Services enable applications to directly interact with other applications using XML and other Web-based products.

❑ OracleAS Web Services enable RPC style and Document style exchange.

Creating and Managing Business Portals

❑ A business portal lets you access information from different data sources through a single entry point, called a portal page.

❏ OracleAS Portal pages are built with the help of portlets, which are reusable components.
❏ Portal clients communicate with the portal through portlets.
❏ Portlets communicate with the OracleAS Portal through a provider.
❏ There are two types of OracleAS portlets: Partner portlets and OracleAS components as portlet providers.

Wireless Applications
❏ Wireless applications enable users to access key enterprise information using mobile devices.
❏ OracleAS Wireless provides support for wireless and voice applications.
❏ OracleAS uses the Wireless Access Protocol to make data translation.
❏ OracleAS Wireless consists of multi-channel advisor functions, the Sensor Edge Server, Mobile Portal, and Foundation Services.

Providing Business Intelligence for the Web
❏ OracleAS Discoverer is OracleAS's main business intelligence component.
❏ You can use OracleAS Discoverer to analyze OLTP, data warehouse, or Oracle Applications data.
❏ Discover Plus is an applet-based client that helps perform quick queries and develop short reports.
❏ Discoverer Viewer is a browser-based optimized tool that's used to view prebuilt reports and drill-down reports.
❏ OracleAS Reports Services helps develop and deploy reports in any data format.
❏ OracleAS Forms Services provides a middle-tier application framework.

Accelerating Performance with Caching
❏ Web caching can help provide higher throughput, reduce bottlenecks, and increase scalability.
❏ A server accelerator substitutes for the original Web server and caches the Web server's content.
❏ A server accelerator cache is also known as a reverse proxy cache.

- ❏ OracleAS Web Cache provides content acceleration and load-balancing services.
- ❏ OracleAS Web Cache supports Edge Side Includes (ESI).
- ❏ ESI enables partial page caching and dynamic page caching.
- ❏ OracleAS Web Cache provides content compression, full page static and dynamic content caching, and partial page caching.
- ❏ You can create multiple instances of the OracleAS Web Cache and run them as a single logical Cluster Web cache.
- ❏ You can configure the OracleAS Web Cache as a load balancer.
- ❏ The OracleAS Web Cache provides a sophisticated invalidation and expiration mechanism.

Identity Management

- ❏ OID is used to implement the Lightweight Directory Access Protocol (LDAP), version 3.
- ❏ All OracleAS instances use the OID as a single store for user data.
- ❏ Delegated Administration Service helps users perform user- and group-related administrative tasks.
- ❏ The OID Self Service console is a browser-based application through which you can perform DAS tasks.
- ❏ OracleAS Single Sign-On enables users to log in only once to OracleAS and subsequently access all applications without having to be authenticated by them again.
- ❏ The OracleAS Certificate Authority manages the use of public-key certificates.

Oracle Application Server Architecture

- ❏ An OracleAS installation consists of two main components, the OracleAS Infrastructure and the OracleAS Middle Tier.
- ❏ The main purpose of the infrastructure is to support the middle-tier components.
- ❏ The middle tier consists of components such as the Web Cache, the Portal, and the Wireless components.

❏ Several middle-tier installations can share a single infrastructure.

❏ You can run certain middle-tier components without the help of the infrastructure.

❏ The OracleAS Infrastructure consists of the Metadata Repository and the Identity Management components.

❏ You can install the Identity Management and the Metadata Repository components by themselves.

❏ The Oracle HTTP Server, OC4J, and the Application Server control are always automatically installed.

❏ You can choose to create more than one Metadata Repository.

❏ You can choose to install the infrastructure components on multiple computers.

Managing the Oracle Application Server

❏ You use the Application Server Control for browser-based management of the Oracle Application Server.

❏ The Application Server Control is automatically installed when you install an OracleAS instance.

❏ You use OPMN (opmnctl tool) for starting and stopping the instance.

❏ You use DCM (dcmtl) mainly for configuration purposes.

Important OracleAS 10g Terminology

❏ An OracleAS installation consists of installing the software programs and configuration files during the installation process.

❏ A directory server stores and retrieves employee and other related enterprise information.

❏ An OracleAS instance is the set of processes that operate the OracleAS components you configure during installation.

❏ The administrative user or the OracleAS instance is named ias_admin.

❏ An OracleAS Farm is a set of instances that are grouped and managed together.

❏ An OracleAS Cluster is a collection of OracleAS instances with identical configuration and application deployment.

SELF TEST

1. Which installation type would you choose, if you were primarily interested in enhancing the speed of your Internet-based Web applications?

    A. Portal and Wireless

    B. J2EE and Web Cache

    C. OracleAS Infrastructure

    D. Oracle Internet Directory (OID)

2. Which Oracle 10g feature supports transparent application failover and automatic session rerouting?

    A. Oracle Internet Directory

    B. OracleAS Clustering

    C. OracleAS Single Sign-On

    D. OracleAS Web Cache

3. OracleAS Web Cache enables you to perform which of the following? (choose three)

    A. Accelerate static and dynamic content delivery.

    B. Implement Oracle Internet Directory.

    C. Reduce administrative and hardware costs.

    D. Potentially perform as a load balancer.

4. Which of the following is (are) not considered an installation type of Oracle Application Server?

    A. Portal and Wireless

    B. Data warehousing

    C. Business Intelligence and data marts

    D. J2EE and Web Cache

5. Which of the following shows the correct OracleAS Infrastructure components?

    A. OracleAS Metadata Repository, Single Sign-On (SSO) server, and the Oracle Internet Directory Server

    B. OracleAS Metadata Repository and Oracle Forms Server

    C. Oracle AS Metadata Repository and OracleAS Portal

    D. OracleAS Metadata Repository and OracleAS Web Cache

6. Which component do you have to install and configure before installing the Portal and Wireless option?

   A. OracleAS Web Cache

   B. OracleAS Infrastructure

   C. Single Sign-On (SSO) server

   D. Business Intelligence and Forms

7. What is the correct order for installing the Identity Management and Metadata Repository on different computers?

   A. The order of installation doesn't matter.

   B. Install Identity Management first.

   C. Install the Metadata Repository first.

   D. You have to install the Identity Management and Metadata Repository components on the same computer.

8. What are the three main OracleAS management tools?

   A. opadmin, ias_admin, and opmnctl

   B. opmnctl, Oracle Application Server Control, and dcmtl

   C. opadmin, dcmtl, lsnrctl

   D. Oracle Application Server, opmnctl, and dcmctl

9. Which of the following is true, when you have to consider both the infrastructure and the middle-tier instances?

   A. All OracleAS instances are part of a cluster.

   B. All OracleAS instances are part of a farm.

   C. An OracleAS instance must first be part of a cluster in order for it to become part of a farm.

   D. An OracleAS instance must first be part of a farm in order for it to become part of a cluster.

10. Which of the following components can run without the OracleAS Infrastructure?

    A. Portal and Wireless

    B. Business Intelligence and Forms

    C. J2EE and Web Cache

    D. Portal and Web Cache

SELF TEST ANSWERS

1. ☑ **A** and **B** are correct because both of them come with the OracleAS Web Cache component, which lets you speed up Web applications by caching content.
   ☒ **C** and **D** are incorrect because neither contains the OracleAS Web Cache component.

2. ☑ **B** is correct because clustering the application server provides transparent application failover and automatic session rerouting.
   ☒ **A**, **C**, and **D** are wrong because those components don't have anything to do with application failover and session rerouting.

3. ☑ **A**, **C**, and **D** all refer to valid OracleAS Web Cache functions.
   ☒ **B** is wrong because the Oracle Internet Directory is a directory service which has nothing to do with the OracleAS Web Cache.

4. ☑ **A** and **D** are valid installation types in OracleAS 10.2.
   ☒ **B** and **C** are incorrect since they aren't valid installation types.

5. ☑ **A** is correct. All three of the components are part of the OracleAS Infrastructure.
   ☒ **B**, **C**, and **D** are wrong because they contain a middle-tier component.

6. ☑ **B** is correct because you must install the infrastructure before installing the Portal and Wireless option.
   ☒ **A**, **C**, and **D** are incorrect because neither of them is a prerequisite for the Portal and Wireless installation option.

7. ☑ **C** is correct because you must install the Metadata Repository before you can install the Identity Management component, which needs the Repository to store its data.
   ☒ **A**, **B**, and **D** are wrong because you have to follow the foregoing order to successfully install the two infrastructure components.

8. ☑ **D** is correct because the three main management tools are opmnctl, Application Server Control, and dcmtl.
   ☒ **A**, **B**, and **C** are wrong since they either don't include the correct tools or include nonexistent tools.

9. ☑ **B** is correct because all OracleAS instances are automatically part of a farm. **D** is also correct because an OracleAS instance must first be part of a farm for it to become part of a cluster.

    ☒   **A** is wrong because all OracleAS instances need not be a part of a cluster. **C** is wrong because an instance must first be part of a farm in order for it to become part of a cluster.

10.   ☑   **C** is correct because the J2EE and Web Cache installation type doesn't require that you install the OracleAS Infrastructure.

    ☒   **A**, **B**, and **D** are wrong because they all contain components that require the OracleAS Infrastructure.

2
OracleAS 10g
Installation

CERTIFICATION OBJECTIVE 2.01

Oracle Application Server 10g Components

In this chapter, you'll learn how to install the two main OracleAS 10g components—the Infrastructure and the middle tier. You must install the two key components separately, as two different OracleAS instances. Whether you use the downloaded installation files or the Oracle CD/DVDs to install OracleAS 10g, you have a choice of three distinct Oracle Application Server product sets, as shown in Figure 2-1.

In OracleAS Release 1 (10.1.0), you had the following installation type options:

- *J2EE and Web Cache* This includes the Oracle HTTP server, which can implement Java 2 platform J2EE applications as well as the OracleAS Web Cache.

- *Portal and Wireless* This installation type includes all the components of the J2EE and Web cache installation type. In addition, it includes the OracleAS Portal and the OracleAS Wireless installation type to enable the deployment of enterprise portals and wireless applications.

FIGURE 2-1

The Oracle Application Server Product Set

- *Business Intelligence and Forms*   This includes all the components of the Portal and Wireless installation type, in addition to the OracleAS Discoverer, OracleAS Forms, and OracleAS Reports.

In OracleAS Release 2 (10.2.0), you have only two options:

- J2EE and Web cache
- Portal and Wireless

No matter which of the two middle-tier installation types you choose, you can always add on the Business Intelligence and Forms component later on, if you wish.

Oracle Application Server Middle Tier

The OracleAS Middle Tier is the OracleAS platform that consists of various components such as the Oracle HTTP Server, OC4J, OracleAS Portal, and OracleAS Wireless. As explained previously, in OracleAS 10g, Release 2, two *middle-tier* installation types are available:

- J2EE and Web Cache
- Portal and Wireless

If you choose the Portal and Wireless option, you'll automatically have the J2EE and Web Cache components as well. Here are the main OracleAS middle-tier components:

- Oracle HTTP Server
- OracleAS Web Cache
- OracleAS Containers for J2EE (OC4J)
- OracleAS Portal
- OracleAS Wireless

OracleAS Infrastructure

The OracleAS Infrastructure supports the deployment of the Oracle Application Server, and includes the following two types of components:

■ Identity Management components, which include the three main identity management-related components: Oracle Internet Directory, Oracle Single Sign-On, and the Oracle Certificate Authority.

■ OracleAS Metadata Repository components, which include an Oracle Database 10g version database containing the OracleAS Metadata Repository.

ⓦatch *Before installing OracleAS Portal and OracleAS Wireless, or the business intelligence components, you must install the OracleAS Infrastructure.*

During the OracleAS Infrastructure installation, you can choose to install the different infrastructure components on different servers or databases. If you wish, you can even install the identity management components on several servers.

OracleAS Developer Kits

Developer Kits include the OracleAS Portal Developer's kit and the OracleAS Wireless Developer's kit, which allow users to create portlets and wireless applications.

CERTIFICATION OBJECTIVE 2.02

Oracle Application Server Topology

The OracleAS Infrastructure and the OracleAS Middle Tier can share the same host computer, or they can be installed on different servers. For performance reasons, it's advisable to install them on different servers. Here are some points regarding the Oracle Application Server topology:

■ You can install the OracleAS Infrastructure and a single instance of the OracleAS Middle Tier with the Portal and Wireless components on the same machine.

■ You can install the OracleAS Infrastructure on one machine and the Portal and Wireless components on another machine.

■ You can install the Oracle AS Infrastructure on one machine and multiple instances of the OracleAS Middle Tier Application Server instances on a second machine. These multiple instances of the Middle Tier Application Server instances could belong to the same or different installation options (e.g., OC4J and Web Cache, Portal and Wireless).

■ You can install the two components of the OracleAS Infrastructure — OracleAS Metadata Repository (Oracle 10g database) and the Identity Management components — on the same or on different host machines.

You can install the OracleAS Metadata Repository in an existing database or in a new Oracle database. By default, the Oracle Universal Installer tool (which performs the OracleAS installation), creates the repository in a new database. You must use the Oracle Application Server Metadata Repository Creation Assistant, if you want to install the OracleAS Metadata Repository in an existing Oracle database.

CERTIFICATION OBJECTIVE 2.03

Installing OracleAS 10g

As I mentioned in Chapter 1, you must perform two *separate installations* to install the two main components of OracleAS 10g, the *infrastructure* and the *middle tier*. In this chapter, I explain the installation process for both the infrastructure and the middle-tier components. In this chapter, I explain the OracleAS 10g installation on a Red Hat Enterprise Linux ES/3.1 server; therefore, the installation procedures I use are mostly Linux (and UNIX) specific.

The installation process is more cumbersome on a Linux/UNIX system as compared to an installation of OracleAS on a Windows platform because you have to ensure that several directories and the necessary users are created before you start the installation. You must also make sure the pertinent environmental variables are set correctly. In Windows, the installation is straightforward. You basically click the setup icon and the Oracle Universal Installer will take care of the installation. Of course, as in the UNIX/Linux systems, you must respond to the installer prompts and make various choices along the way to configure the various OracleAS components. You use the Oracle-provided GUI tool, Oracle Universal Installer, to install OracleAS 10g. Let's start with the steps you must take to prepare for the use of the Oracle Universal Installer.

on the
job

Only the way you invoke the Oracle Universal Installer is different in the Linux/UNIX and Windows systems. Once the installer comes up, the various screens and options are identical under both versions.

The installation process for OracleAS 10g is simple and shouldn't consume more than an hour or so, at the most. However, you must spend considerably more time preparing for the installation.

To successfully install the OracleAS Infrastructure and the OracleAS Middle Tier, you must follow these preliminary steps:

watch
The following three components are always installed during an Oracle Infrastructure installation: Oracle HTTP Server, Oracle Application Server Containers for J2EE (OC4J), and Oracle Enterprise Manager.

- Get the necessary software.
- Check the Requirements.
- Set up the Installation environment.
- Set up the Installation Users and Directories.

In the following sections, each of these prerequisites is explained in detail.

Getting the Necessary Software

You can either download the software or use an Oracle-supplied CD-ROM or DVD-ROM to install the OracleAS 10g software. If you plan on downloading the software from the Oracle Web site, here are the steps you must follow: Log into http://technet.oracle.com and click Oracle Application Server from the list on the left-hand side. Click Downloads. You'll see a list of choices for various types of 10g software downloads. Choose the following:

```
Oracle Application Server—Portal_and Wireless
```

The Portal and Wireless option is the most comprehensive distribution you can choose in OracleAS 10.2. In OracleAS 10.1, it was the Business Intelligence and Forms type installation that was the most comprehensive OracleAS software distribution available to you. The Portal and Wireless distribution has the following three files:

```
as_linux_x86_portal_wireless_101200_disk1.cpio (about 640MB)
as_linux_x86_portal_wireless_101200_disk2.cpio (about 450MB)
as_linux_x86_portal_wireless_101200_disk3.cpio (about 390MB)
```

Unpack the contents of the three files as shown here:

```
$ cpio -idmv < as_linux_x86_portal_wireless_101200_disk1.cpio
$ cpio -idmv < as_linux_x86_portal_wireless_101200_disk2.cpio
$ cpio -idmv < as_linux_x86_portal_wireless_101200_disk3.cpio
```

You'll have three directories, Disk1, Disk2, and Disk3, which contain all the installation files for OracleAS 10g, Release 2. The Oracle Universal Installer will be in the Disk1 directory. I will show you how to invoke the installer later in this chapter.

General Installation Requirements

In the following discussion, I limit most of the installation requirements to the Linux Red Hat Advanced Server (Version 3) operating system, because that's where I'll install the OracleAS 10g software. Your own operating system may diverge from these guidelines in some areas. Please check the installation manual pertaining to your specific operating system for exact details. The following hardware requirements combine the requirements for both the infrastructure and the middleware installations. Make sure you have what you need for the installation before starting the installation. There are two simple ways to perform these hardware checks: You can manually check the requirements, or you can run the *runInstaller* command from the Disk1 directory, which will invoke the Oracle Universal Installer, with the following option:

```
$ runInstaller -executeSysPrereqs
```

When you invoke the installer with the *executeSysPrereqs* option, the installer will automatically check and let you know if you meet the necessary installation requirements. In the following subsections, I summarize the OracleAS 10g installation requirements. Note that these requirements apply to both the infrastructure and the middle-tier installations. In general, the server requirements (e.g., space) are larger for the infrastructure component than those for the middle-tier installation.

Server Hardware

In order to install the OracleAS software, your server must meet some basic requirements regarding processor type, processor speed, and monitor capabilities, which I summarize here:

- Processor Type: Pentium (32-bit)
- Processor Speed: at least 450 MHZ

The monitor should be capable of a 256-color display, which you can check with the following command:

```
# /usr/X11R6/bin/xdpyinfo
```

Network

Following are the network requirements you must meet:

- *Network*   You need either a standalone server or a network-enabled server. You can install on a standalone server first and network-enable it later on, if you wish.
- *IP*   Use either a static IP or a DHCP allocated dynamic IP address.

Memory

You'll need at least 1GB of physical memory for installing and running the Oracle Application Server with just the infrastructure installation or the middle-tier installation. If you plan on running both the infrastructure and the middle tier (Portal and Wireless type) on the same computer, you must have at least 1.5GB in physical memory available. Log in as root and run the following command to check the amount of RAM available:

```
# grep MemTotal /proc/meminfo
MemTotal:        1203934 kB
#
```

Swap/Page

You'll need at least 1.5GB of swap space. You can check the available swap space with this command:

```
# grep SwapTotal /proc/meminfo
SwapTotal:       2040244 kB
#
```

Disk Space

For the OracleAS Infrastructure, you need about 3.3GB. For the Portal and Wireless middle-tier option, you need an additional 700MB of disk space. You use the *df -k* (in kilobytes) command to check the available free space in the directory in which you're planning to install the OracleAS 10g software.

To check the available disk space, run the following command:

```
# df -k
Filesystem      Size Used Avail Use% Mounted on
/dev/sda3       11G  8.7G 1.7G  85%  /
/dev/sda1       99M   15M  79M  16%  /boot
none            588M    0 588M   0%  /dev/shm
#
```

Temporary Directory Space

You'll need about 512MB free space in the /tmp directory. If you don't have this, you can specify a different directory as your temporary directory, by using the TMP and TMPDIR environment variables. You can check current free space in the /tmp directory with this command:

```
# df -k /tmp
```

Software Requirements

In addition to following the operating system and space requirements, you must also ensure that you're using the correct operating system software, including the necessary patches. Of course, software requirements are going to vary, depending on your operating system. In this section, the software requirements for the Red Hat Enterprise Linux AS/ES 3.0 systems are given. Remember that Oracle doesn't support any customized kernels or modules not supported by Red Hat Linux for the Red Hat Linux operating system.

Operating System

You must use either Red Hat Enterprise Linux AS/ES 2.1 or the AS/ES 3.0 system if you're using the Red Hat Linux platform. (Please check the manuals for your specific operating system for the correct version.) You can ascertain the version of Linux that's installed on your server by using the following command (you must have at least Update 3 installed) after logging in as the root user.

```
$ cat /etc/issue
Red Hat Enterprise Linux WS release 3 (Taroon Update 4)
Kernel \r on an \m
$
```

Operating System Patches

For your Red Hat operating system, you must have the Errata 49 kernel or higher errata patch installed. Depending on the type of your Linux installation, one of the following would guarantee this:

- kernel-2.4.9-e.49
- kernel-smp-2.4.9-e.49
- kernel-enterprise-2.4.9-e.49

You can find out your Linux version by using the *uname* command, as shown here:

```
$ uname -r
2.4.21-27.ELsmp
$
```

Since my Red Hat Linux version is 2.4.21, I clearly meet the requirement that specifies 2.4.9 with errata 49.

Software Packages

You must have the following software packages installed:

```
glibc-devel-2.2.4-32.17
glibc-common-2.2.4-32.17
gcc-2.96-128.7.2
gcc-c++-2.96-128.7.2
pdksh-5.2.14-22
openmotif21-2.1.30-12
sysstat-4.0.1-15.2-las
compat-glibc-6.2-2.1.3.2
libstdc++-2.96-128.7.2
gnome-libs-1.2.13-16
binutils-2.11.90.0.8-12.4
make-3.79.1-8
db1-1.85-7
db3-3.3.11-5
```

To determine whether a certain package is installed on your system, use the following command:

```
$ rpm -q package_name
```

For example, you can check for the *glibc* package in the following way:

```
$ rpm -q glibc
glibc-2.3.2-95.30
$
```

You can install missing packages by downloading them from Red Hat. You can install the package using the following command:

```
$ rpm -i package_name
```

Checking Kernel Parameters and Shell Limits

In addition to verifying the operating system version, you must also verify the value of certain operating system kernel parameters at the operating system level. You must also check certain shell limits.

Kernel Parameters for the Middle Tier

You might remember that I'm installing the Portal and Wireless middle tier. When I use this installation option, the OracleAS Web Cache component is automatically installed. The OracleAS Web Cache needs some special kernel requirements.

The *nofile* kernel parameter must be set to at least 65536. You can check this by using the *ulimit* command:

```
$ ulimit -Hn
65536
$
```

In our case, the value is exactly 65536, so I don't need to do anything further here. In case the value is less than 65536, add the following line to the */etc/security/limits. conf* file after logging in as the root user, and reboot the system so the new value will apply:

```
* hard nofile 65536
```

Kernel Parameters for the Infrastructure (Including the OracleAS Metadata Repository)

When you install the OracleAS Metadata Repository, which is a part of the OracleAS Infrastructure, you'll be creating an Oracle 10g database. Therefore, you must meet all the kernel requirements necessary for any standard Oracle 10g database installation.

If the values for any of the kernel parameters are higher than required, that's fine—you just can't install with lower values.

Table 2-1 shows the kernel parameters and their values that you must have, for the OracleAS Metadata Repository installation. The file column shows you the file you must edit in order to make changes in that kernel parameter.

You can find out the current values of the various kernel parameters using the commands shown in the following discussion.

To check semaphore parameters such as semms, semmmns, semopm, and semmni, use the following command (or the command: *cat /proc/sys/kernel/sem*):

```
# /sbin/sysctl -a | grep sem
```

TABLE 2-1			
	Parameter	Value	File
Values for Various Kernel Parameters	semmsl	256	/proc/sys/kernel/sem
	semmns	32000	/proc/sys/kernel/sem
	semopm	100	/proc/sys/kernel/sem
	semmni	142	/proc/sys/kernel/sem
	shmall	2097152	/proc/sys/kernel/shmall
	shmmax	2147483648	/proc/sys/kernel/shmmax
	shmmni	4096	/proc/sys/kernel/shmmni
	msgmax	8192	/proc/sys/kernel/msgmax
	msgmnb	65535	/proc/sys/kernel/msgmnb
	msgmni	2878	/proc/sys/kernel/msgmni
	file-max	131072	/proc/sys/fs/file-max
	ip_local_port_range	10000–65000	/proc/sys/net/ipv4/ip_local_port_range

The following command shows the shared memory segment sizes (shmall, shmmax, and shmmni):

```
# /sbin/sysctl -a | grep shm
```

You can check the maximum number of file handles (file-max parameter) using this command:

```
# /sbin/sysctl -a | grep file-max
```

To check the range of port numbers (parameter name ip_local_port_range), use this command:

```
# /sbin/sysctl -a | grep ip_local_port_range
```

You can change the value of the existing kernel parameters (if they are different from their recommended values), by editing the */etc/systctl.conf* file so it looks like this:

```
kernel.shmall  2097152
kernel.shmmax  2147483648
kernel.shmmni  4096
kernel.sem  250 32000 100 142
fs.file-max  131072
net.ipv4.ip_local_port_range  1024 65000
kernel.msgmni  2878
kernel.msgmax  8192
kernel.msgmnb  65535
```

To change the kernel parameters right away, without rebooting your system, use the following command:

```
$ /sbin/sysctl -p
```

Setting Shell Limits for the Oracle User

For performance reasons, you must make sure you meet the necessary shell limit requirements for the operating system user *oracle*. You must add the following lines to the */etc/security/limits.conf* file:

```
oracle           soft    nproc   2047
oracle           hard    nproc   16384
oracle           soft    nofile  2048
oracle           hard    nofile  65536
```

Make sure the following line exists in your */etc/pam.d/login* file:

```
session     required     /lib/security/pam_limits.so
```

Make changes to the Oracle user's default shell, depending on the type of shell. If you're using the Bourne, Bash, or Korn shell, add the following lines to the /etc/ profile file:

```
if [ $USER  "oracle" ]; then
  if [ $SHELL = "/bin/ksh" ]; then
            ulimit -p 16384
            ulimit -n 65536
      else
            ulimit -u 16384 -n 65536
   fi
fi
```

If you're using the C shell (csh or tcsh), add the following lines to the */etc/csh.login* file:

```
if ( $USER == "oracle" ) then
      limit maxproc 16384
      limit descriptors 65536
endif
```

All the installation restrictions discussed here are documented in the oraparam.ini and the /prereq/refhost.xml files. You may not directly edit these files, which are meant for guiding the Oracle Universal Installer.

Checking the Ports

OracleAS 10g components such as the Oracle HTTP Server, OracleAS Web Cache, and the OEM Application Server Control, use specific ports. You can let the installer choose default ports, or you can specify the ports. Note that the Oracle database you'll install as a part of the OracleAS Infrastructure runs on port 1521 by default. If port 1521 is being used by some other application, either reconfigure the application to listen on a port other than 1521, or shut the application that's using port 1521 down during the OracleAS software installation process. After the installation is over, you must reconfigure the OracleAS Metadata Repository to use a port number other than the default 1521.

You can check whether a port is being used by using the following command:

```
$ netstat -an | grep 1521
```

Using Default Port Numbers

If you want to use the default port numbers, you just have to make sure that at least one free port is available in the allotted range of port numbers for each of the OracleAS components that needs to use a port.

Using Custom Port Numbers

During installation, the Oracle Universal Installer will assign ports to the various OracleAS components. The installer will use a port number from an allotted range of ports for each component. The default port number for each OracleAS component is usually the lowest number in the allotted port range for that component. Unfortunately, sometimes these ports may end up being nondefault ports for the components. For example, the OUI may assign the port 7777 to the Oracle HTTP server, but you may wish to assign it port 80 instead. Or, you may prefer to assign the port 389 for LDAP instead of the port 3060. You can assign custom ports by using the *staticports.ini* file (you can name it differently if you wish—this is just the standard name used). Just copy and edit the default *staticports.ini* file, located in the following directory:

```
CDROM_mount_point/1012disk1/Response/staticports.ini
```

For a complete listing of the OracleAS port numbers, please refer to Appendix D, titled *Oracle Application Server Port Numbers*, in the *Application Server Administrator's Guide*.

Using the *staticports.ini* file will force the OUI to use the system administrator-specified port numbers rather than port numbers of its choice.

When you're installing the OracleAS software, in the *Specify Port Configuration Options* screen select *Manual* and provide the full path of the *staticports.ini* file there. Here's part of a typical *staticports.ini* file:

```
Oracle HTTP Server port = 7777
Application Server control port = 2000
Oracle HTTP Server Listen port = 7778
Web Cache HTTP Listen port = 80
```

In this case, the Web Cache is listening on port 80 as a front end for the OHS, while OHS itself will serve content as if it's using port 80.

You can change the port used by the OracleAS Metadata Repository and the database listener only after the installation is over.

If you don't list a component in the staticports.ini file, that component will get a default port number assigned by the installer. You can override the default installation port assignments by specifying custom port numbers in the staticports.ini file.

The portlist.ini and staticports.ini Files

After your OracleAS installation is complete, a *portlist.ini* file is created automatically in the ORACLE_HOME/install directory. The *portlist.ini* file has the same format as the *staticports.ini* file described in the previous section.

Always check the *portlist.ini* file after installation is complete to make sure that the installer assigned the port numbers you wanted for each of the OracleAS components. If you use the same port number for two components by mistake, for example, the installer will assign the second component a default port number.

The selection of ports will depend on the type of installation. For example, your port selection would be different if you've chosen to install the OracleAS Web Cache and Oracle HTTP Server together, or just the Oracle HTTP Server by itself. Also, if port 1521 (which is usually the Oracle database listener port) is being already used, you must take special actions such as reconfiguring the existing application using port 1521 to listen on a different port before starting the installation. Please refer to the Oracle Application Server Installation Guide for details on this.

Creating Necessary Operating System Users and Groups

Before you can install the OracleAS software, you must first create the necessary operating system groups and users. If you've never installed any Oracle software on your server, you must create a new *oinstall* group. Operating system groups consist of a set of users who perform related tasks and have similar privileges. Because the Oracle Universal Installer will create a new Oracle database, you must follow Oracle's guidelines regarding the creation of operating system groups for a database. For an Oracle database, Oracle recommends that you create three operating system groups for both Linux and UNIX operating systems: OSDBA, OSOPER, and ORAINVENTORY (Oracle Inventory group). The default name for the OSDBA group is *dba*, for the OSOPER group it is *oper*, and for ORAINVENTORY it is *oinstall*.

Members of the OSDBA (dba) group will have the SYSDBA Oracle database privilege, which lets them perform privileged actions such as starting up and shutting down the database. The ORAINVENTORY group (oinstall) is mandatory when you install Oracle software for the first time on any server. The Oracle Inventory group owns the Oracle inventory, which is a catalog of all the Oracle software installed on a server. All new installations and upgrades are performed by users belonging to the ORAINVENTORY (oinstall) group.

The OSOPER (oper) group is optional; you need to create it only if you plan to grant any users the OSOPER Oracle privilege to perform a limited set of administrative tasks, such as backing up databases. All database users with the OSOPER privilege will be members of the OSOPER group at the OS level.

on the job

Users belonging to the ORAINVENTORY group must be given read, write, and execute privileges on the ORAINVENTORY directory only. The group should not be given write permissions for any other directories.

Creating the Oracle Inventory Group

You (or your system administrator) need to create the Oracle Inventory group (ORAINVENTORY) only if it doesn't already exist in your system. Here's the command to create it, with the default name for the group:

```
# /usr/sbin/groupadd oinstall
```

The Oracle Installer creates the *oraInst.loc* file when you install Oracle software on a server for the first time. This file tells you the name of the Oracle Inventory group and the path of the Oracle Inventory directory. Use the following command to determine whether the Oracle Inventory group already exists on your server:

```
# more /etc/oraInst.loc
```

If the *oraInst.loc* file exists, you'll see the following, which means you don't have to create the Oracle Inventory group (oinstall):

```
inventory_loc = /u01/app/oracle/oraInventory
inst_group = oinstall
```

Creating the OSDBA Group

You must create this group only if one doesn't already exist, or if you want to give a new group of users DBA privileges in a new Oracle installation. Use the following command to create the OSDBA group:

```
# /usr/sbin/groupadd dba
```

Creating the OSOPER Group

The OSOPER group is optional; create it only if you're planning to create one or more Oracle users with limited administrative privileges. Here's how you create the OSOPER group:

```
# /usr/sbin/groupadd oper
```

Creating the oracle User

After the system administrator has created the necessary groups, he or she needs to create the all-important user that owns the Oracle software, usually named "oracle" (you can choose any name, but "oracle" is used by convention). The oracle user is the owner of the Oracle software, and this user's default or primary group will be the newly created Oracle Inventory group (oinstall). You must grant write permissions on the Oracle home directory and the inventory directory to the user oracle.

You need to install Oracle software as the *oracle user*, rather than as root. The oracle user's secondary group should be the OSDBA group (dba), and, if necessary, the OSOPER (oper) group as well. The oracle user will have a home directory like all the other users (usually something like /u01/app/oracle), under which you'll create the rest of the directory structure for holding the Oracle Database 10g server software.

on the job

Don't use the root account to install or modify Oracle software. Only the oracle user should perform any Oracle software installation operations.

Under an HP UNIX system, you can use the administrative tool SAM to create the users. In any UNIX or Linux system, you can create the users manually, with the following command:

```
$ /usr/sbin/useradd -g oinstall -G dba[, oper]
-d /home/oracle  -p  oracle_passwd oracle
```

In the preceding command,

- -g denotes the primary group of the user oracle, which is the oinstall group.
- -G denotes the secondary group, which is the dba group.
- -d denotes the home directory for the new user.
- -p denotes the password for the oracle user.

You may use the following command to set the password for the oracle user, if you wish:

```
# /usr/bin/passwd oracle
```

exam

watch   *You must give the Oracle user read, write, and execute privileges on all files and directories that are part of the Oracle Database 10g installation. The two important directories here are the Oracle Home directory, which contains the product files, and the inventory directory, which is used by the Installer.*

Note that the default home directory of the oracle user should be similar to that of the normal users of the system (usually /home/ oracle). The ORACLE_HOME directory is not meant for the oracle user; it's the location for the Oracle software binaries and similar files.

Creating Necessary Directories

In Linux and UNIX systems, a home directory is the directory that a user lands in when he or she first logs in. All home directories for a user should follow the naming convention /pm/h/u, where pm is the mount point name, h is a standard directory name, and u refers to the directory owner. For example, the /u01/app/oracle directory could be the home directory for the user named oracle.

The Directory Structure

At the root of the Oracle directory structure is the directory called Oracle base. The Oracle base directory is the top directory for all Oracle software installations. Oracle recommends that you use the form */pm/app/oracle_software_owner*. Since the default Oracle software owner is a user called *oracle*, the Oracle base directory is usually in the form of */pm/app/oracle* (e.g., /u01/app/oracle). The Oracle Installer will take this as the default Oracle base directory and install all the software under this base directory.

You can create the Oracle base directory by using the following commands (assuming that u01 is your mount point and user oracle is the Oracle software owner):

```
# mkdir -p /u01/app/oracle
# chown -R oracle:oinstall /u01/app/oracle
# chmod -R 775 /u01/app/oracle
```

The Oracle home directory is a very important directory, given that you'll install the Oracle Application Server in this directory. You can specify the Oracle home directory name and its full path during the OracleAS installation. For example, you can name your Oracle home for the Infrastructure installation "infra_10.1.2," and use the following directory: /opt/oracle/OraHome_infra_10-1_2.

It's important to note that you must install the infrastructure and the middle tier in separate Oracle homes, if you're installing them on the same computer. Here are some important points regarding an Oracle home directory:

- You can have multiple Oracle home directories on a server, with each location serving as the directory under which you install software for a separate Oracle Application Server installation.

- You must have separate Oracle Homes for the infrastructure and the middle tier.

- Generally, you can't install a new OracleAS installation into an existing Oracle home.

- You can't install OracleAS software in a non-empty Oracle home.

Oracle uses a special directory called the Oracle Inventory Directory, also known as OraInventory, to store an inventory of all the Oracle software on a server. Multiple Oracle installations can share the same Oracle Inventory Directory. You need to specify the path for this directory only the first time you install an Oracle product on a server. The usual format of this directory is as follows:

```
/oracle_base/ora_inventory
```

The first time you install Oracle software, the installer prompts for the OraInventory directory path, and creates the directory itself.

The system administrator (root) must also create the Oracle base directory, which acts as a top-level directory for Oracle software installations, and its ownership must be assigned to the oracle user. Assuming you choose the standard /u01/app/oracle directory as your Oracle base directory, you can create it and assign the necessary ownership and file permissions with these commands:

```
# mkdir -p /u01/app/oracle
# chown -R oracle:oinstall /u01/app/oracle
# chmod -R 775 /u01/app/oracle
```

During the installation, you must set the ORACLE_BASE environment variable to specify the full path to this directory (/u01/app/oracle).

As mentioned previously in this chapter, the Oracle home directory is the key directory where the installer actually installs all the Oracle Application Server executables.

on the job *You don't have to explicitly create the Oracle home directory; the installer prompts you for a symbolic name as well as the directory location for it. The installer automatically creates this directory and assigns the Oracle user the necessary privileges.*

Setting the Environment

Before you can start the actual software installation, you need to log in as the user *oracle* and set a number of environment variables. Although all of the environment variables can be set manually, you are better off editing the default shell startup file, which, on my Red Hat Linux server, is the *.bash_profile* file in the home directory of the oracle user (the /home/oracle directory by default). By editing the shell startup file, you will ensure that the environment will always be set appropriately each time you log in. You can check the value of the environment variables with the *env* command. Here are the main environment variables that you need to set:

on the job *Your environment variables may be slightly different from the ones listed here, depending on your operating system and its version. Always check the operating system-specific installation guides—it's well worth the effort to read them. The specifics in this chapter are based on a Red Hat Linux operating system.*

■ ORACLE_BASE   The ORACLE_BASE variable is the starting directory for all Oracle installations. All the software files and other files are placed in directories underneath the ORACLE_BASE directory. In our example, the directory is /u01/app/oracle.

■ TMP and TMPDIR   You can use the TMP and TMPDIR environment variables to set alternative temporary directory locations, if you don't have necessary free space in the /tmp directory. Make sure you have at least 1GB of free space in the directory you're assigning the TMP variable. Make sure the oracle user has the write permission so the installer can write to this directory. Here's how you can set the TMP variable:

```
$ export TMP =/tmp1
```

■ PATH   The PATH variable should be set to the following:

```
$ export PATH = $ORACLE_HOME/bin:/usr/bin:/usr/ccs/bin:
/etc:/usr/binx11:/usr/local/bin
```

The PATH, CLASS_PATH, SHLIB_PATH, and the LD_LIBRARY_PATH environment variables mustn't contain any references to preexisting Oracle home directories. To avoid any errors, you must unset the TNS_ADMIN environment variable as well. If you have a *tnsnames.ora* file currently in the /etc or the /var/opt/oracle directory, move or rename the file. You must also unset the ORA_NLS and LD_BIND_NOW variables.

on the **job**   *If there are other Oracle products installed on the server, you must unset the ORACLE_HOME and ORACLE_SID variables, to avoid confusion with those installations during OracleAS 10g installation.*

■ DISPLAY   The DISPLAY environment variable should be set to the following, with localhost serving as your server's symbolic name:

```
$ export DISPLAY=localhost:0.0
```

If you want to use the IP address instead of the symbolic name for your machine, just substitute your server's IP address for its symbolic name, as shown here:

```
$ export DISPLAY=172.16.15.14:0.0
```

Test the display by using the *xclock* command, as shown here:

```
# xclock &
```

If your display is set correctly, you should see a clock in your terminal window.

Sometimes, you'll run into problems when you are trying to read the CD containing the Oracle software because of display issues. For example, you may get the error "Cannot open display." The system administrator may then have to use the following command to get rid of the problems:

```
$ xhost +server_name     (OR xhost +)
```

You can also use the *xhost localhost* command, as shown here:

```
# xhost localhost
localhost being added to access control list
```

on the
Ø o b

It may be a good idea to incorporate as many of the environment variables as possible in the shell startup file in the oracle user's home directory. This way, when you log in as the oracle user, the variables will already be in force in your shell.

Edit the oracle user's profile file, which is the /home/oracle/.bash_profile file in Linux systems, as follows:

```
umask 022
ORACLE_BASE=/u01/app/oracle
PATH=$PATH:$ORACLE_HOME/bin
LD_LIBRARY_PATH=$ORACLE_HOME/lib
export PATH LD_LIBRARY_PATH
```

Note that you should use a new directory to install your Oracle Application Server, unless you're just adding a new component to an existing middle-tier installation.

Editing the /etc/hosts File

You can edit the */etc/hosts* file to specify the location of the default Identity Management realm and the host name for the OracleAS Single Sign-On feature. You can alternatively specify the Identity Management realm during the installation in the appropriate window ("Specify Namespace in Internet Directory"). When you specify a distinguished name (DN) during the installation, it will be used as the namespace by the Oracle Internet Directory within which to administer the users and groups in the OID.

The Oracle Universal Installer uses the */etc/hosts* file to suggest the default namespace for identity management. If you wish to edit the /etc/hosts file to specify the default Identity Management realm, you can do so by using the following format:

```
ip_address      fully qualified hostname      short_hostname
```

Here's an example:

```
122.21.66.89   testhost.testdomain.com      testHost
```

There is an alternative way to change the default namespace for identity management rather than editing the */etc/hosts* file as shown in the preceding example. You can use the OUI_HOSTNAME command-line parameter as an additional argument when you invoke the Oracle Universal Installer, as shown here:

```
$ /staging/Disk1/runInstaller OUI_HOSTNAME=testhost.testdomain.com
```

Installing from CD-ROM vs. Installing from the Hard Drive

OracleAS software is available in both CD-ROM and DVD-ROM format. The system administrator must mount the CD-ROM or the DVD-ROM, using the steps stated here. First, issue the following command, to determine whether the CD-ROM drive is already mounted, after inserting the first disk into the disk drive:

```
$ ls /mnt/cdrom
```

If you see the contents of the CD-ROM, your CD-ROM is already mounted. If it isn't, you must mount it using the following command:

```
$ mount /dev/cdrom /mnt/cdrom
```

You can install the OracleAS 10g software directly from the CD-ROMs or DVD-ROM. However, if you plan on performing multiple OracleAS installations, you're better off copying the CD-ROM or DVD-ROM contents to disk and installing from there.

If you want to copy the installation files to disk, you'd need 1.9GB of disk space if you're copying from the CD-ROMs, and about 1.6GB if you're copying from the DVD-ROM. In order to copy the installation files to disk, first create a staging directory, which is simply called *staging* in the following example. Underneath this directory, create three subdirectories named Disk1, Disk2, and Disk3. Once you create this directory structure, here's how you'd copy the three CD-ROMS to the three directories, one disk at a time:

```
$ cp -pr /cdrom_mount_point/10.1.2disk1/* /staging/Disk1/
$ cp -pr /cdrom_mount_point/10.1.2disk2/* /staging/Disk2/
$ cp -pr /cdrom_mount_point/10.1.2disk3/* /staging/Disk3/
```

When you want to start the OracleAS installation, you invoke the Oracle Universal Installer GUI using the *runInstaller* executable in this way:

```
$ /staging/Disk1/runInstaller
```

And here's how you'd copy the DVD-ROM contents to disk:

```
$ cp -pr /dvd_mount_point/application_server /staging/
```

The *runInstaller* executable, which you use to start the Oracle Universal Installer, is located in the Disk1 directory. When you want to start the OracleAS installation, you invoke the Oracle Universal Installer using the *runInstaller* executable in this way:

```
$ /staging/Disk1/runInstaller
```

Where to Install

There is no requirement that you must install the infrastructure and the middle tier on separate computers, although, for performance reasons, Oracle recommends using separate computers. Really, the choice depends on how powerful your servers are, in terms of the CPU speed and number of processors and the size of the RAM. If you have a fast enough computer with a large RAM, there's no reason why you can't get good performance from installing both tiers of OracleAS 10g on a single computer.

The OracleAS Metadata Repository is contained in the Oracle database that's part of the OracleAS Infrastructure.

CERTIFICATION OBJECTIVE 2.04

Installing the OracleAS Infrastructure

As explained in Chapter 1, you must install the OracleAS Infrastructure first before you install the OracleAS Middle Tier. This is because some of the components of the infrastructure, specifically the Oracle Internet Directory and the Metadata Repository, are prerequisites for some middleware components. So, let's start with the installation of the OracleAS Infrastructure first.

e x a m

w a t c h *If you're not installing OracleAS Clusters or the Identity Management features and you're using the J2EE and Web Cache middle-tier installation option, you don't need to install the OracleAS Infrastructure. You need the OracleAS Metadata Repository for a J2EE and Web Cache installation type, if use an OracleAS cluster managed through a database repository. You also would need the OracleAS Identity management component, which is part of the Infrastructure, if you plan on using the Oracle Single Sign-On feature in a J2EE and Web Cache installation.*

You don't need to create the OracleAS Infrastructure first, under the following conditions: If you're chosen the J2EE and Web Cache option (the other option is Portal and Wireless) during the middle-tier installation and you aren't using the OracleAS Clusters or the Identity Management features, you can omit the installation of the OracleAS Infrastructure completely. You can always install the OracleAS Infrastructure later on and hook up the already installed J2EE and Web Cache Application Server instance with the infrastructure. You may note here that associating an OracleAS instance with the infrastructure is the same as making the OracleAS instance a part of an OracleAS Farm.

OracleAS 10g Infrastructure Installation Types

When you install the OracleAS 10g Infrastructure, some common components are always installed by default. These are the following:

- Oracle HTTP Server
- Oracle Application Server Containers for J2EE
- Oracle Enterprise Manager (Application Server Control)

In addition to these three base or common components, there are two important OracleAS 10g Infrastructure components—the OracleAS Metadata Repository and Identity Management.

The OracleAS Metadata Repository

The OracleAS Metadata Repository is a collection of schemas in the Oracle database that are used to store data belonging to the various OracleAS 10g components. The OracleAS Metadata Repository of course, is situated in the Oracle Database 10g instance that's created to hold the repository data. You may also use an existing Oracle database for this purpose, instead of having the Oracle Universal Installer create a new database instance for you during the OracleAS installation. The OracleAS Metadata Repository consists of the following three types of metadata: product metadata, Identity Management metadata, and Management metadata. Each of these components is briefly explained here:

- *Product Metadata schemas,* used by OracleAS components such as OracleAS Portal and OracleAS Wireless.
- *Identity Management schemas,* used by the Identity Management components— the OID, OracleAS Single Sign-On, and OracleAS Certificate Authority.
- *Management schemas* used by components such as Distributed Configuration Management (DCM), which are used primarily for configuration management.

Although not all types of OracleAS installations require the Metadata Repository, the following installation types do require the Metadata Repository:

- Identity Management component installation, for the identity management schema.
- J2EE and Web Cache installations that are part of an OracleAS Cluster require a Metadata Repository for the DCM schema.
- Portal and Wireless installations, for Product Metadata schemas.
- Business Intelligence installations, for Product Metadata schemas.

Note that you have a choice between two types of repositories: a database-based repository or a file-based repository. A database-based repository, of course, is stored in an Oracle 10g database. A file-based repository, on the other hand, doesn't need a database—it's stored directly in operating system files on disk.

Identity Management Components

Identity Management components provide the directory management, security, and user management functions. Identity Management consists of the following components:

- Oracle Internet Directory
- OracleAS Single Sign-On
- Oracle Delegated Administration Services
- Oracle Directory Integration and Provisioning
- OracleAS Certificate Authority

on the

Job

You can use an existing Oracle Internet Directory instead of choosing to create a new OID during the OracleAS installation. To do this, you must not select the "Oracle Internet Directory" option in the "Select Configuration Options" screen presented to you during the OracleAS installation.

The Installation Choices

As you know by now, the Oracle Application Server consists of two basic tiers: the Middle Tier and the Infrastructure. The middle tier is where all your applications are deployed, and it's the job of the infrastructure to provide the necessary services for the middle tier. Note that a single infrastructure installation can serve multiple middle-tier installations. When you install the OracleAS, you must install the infrastructure and the middle tier separately. Therefore, you have to run the Oracle Universal Installer twice to complete the entire installation, which consists of the infrastructure and the middle tier.

You start with the installation of the infrastructure first, because the middle tier depends on the services provided by the infrastructure. If you're just installing the J2EE and Web Cache installation type, however, note that you don't have to use an infrastructure. In this case, the installation of the infrastructure is purely optional.

When you install the OracleAS 10*g* Infrastructure, you are given the following choices as possible installation types:

- Identity Management and the OracleAS Metadata Repository
- Identity Management
- OracleAS Metadata Repository

No matter which infrastructure installation type you choose, the following components are always installed:

- The Oracle HTTP Server
- OC4J
- OEM Application Server Control

w a t c h *If you want to create the OracleAS Metadata Repository in an existing database, you must use the OracleAS Metadata Repository Creation Assistant.*

The ability to create the Identity Management and OracleAS Metadata Repository separately gives you the option of creating them on separate computers. Whenever you tell the Oracle Installer to install the OracleAS Metadata Repository, either by itself or along with the Identity Management component, the installer creates a new Oracle Database 10*g* database to store the repository. You can also install the OracleAS Metadata Repository in an existing Oracle database, by using the Oracle Application Server Metadata Repository Creation Assistant.

Order of Installation

If you plan on installing both the OracleAS Metadata Repository and the Identity Management components on the same computer, the installer will automatically install them in the correct order. However, if you are installing the two components of the infrastructure on different computers, you must follow a prescribed order, as explained here:

- First install the Oracle AS Metadata Repository. This option will create a brand new Oracle Database 10g database that will contain the Metadata Repository. The Identity Management services can then use this repository.

- Install the Identity Management components in the second step. Once you create the OID, the installer registers it with the Metadata Repository you created in the first step.

What if You Create Just the Metadata Repository?

You can install just the OracleAS Metadata Repository by itself, without installing the OracleAS Infrastructure with it. The installer will create a new Oracle Database 10g database and populate it with the OracleAS Metadata Repository schemas. However, the installer won't prompt you to name this instance. Neither the Oracle HTTP Server nor the OEM Application Server Control are started after the installation (the Application Server Control isn't installed). You can manage this instance as you would a regular Oracle Database instance only with the help of the OEM Database Control tool.

Note that it is possible to create the OracleAS Metadata Repository by itself, without the infrastructure.

Some Installation Issues

Before you start the installation, you must be aware of some important issues regarding the OracleAS Infrastructure installation architecture.

- If you didn't configure a component during installation, by selecting the component in the "Select Configuration Options" screen, for example, you can always configure it after installation. However, you can configure all infrastructure components except the OID after the initial OracleAS installation. You can configure the OID only during installation by the Oracle installer.

- You can install the OracleAS Metadata Repository in an existing or a new database. If you want to use an existing database, you must use the Oracle Application Server Metadata Repository Creation Assistant.

- You don't have to install the OracleAS Metadata Repository in a database. You can choose the option of installing it in the file system.

■ You can use an existing OID instead of creating a new one, as long as you have a version 9.0.4 or later version OID.

■ You can install the Identity Management and the OracleAS Metadata Repository on separate computers.

■ You can install multiple OracleAS Metadata Repositories to increase performance. When you have multiple repositories, different components in your OracleAS topology can use different metadata repositories.

Installing the OracleAS Infrastructure

You can install the OracleAS Infrastructure using the Oracle Universal Installer. If you have already copied the contents of the installation CD-ROMs or the DVD-ROM on your file system, you can invoke the Oracle Universal Installer from there. In my case, I log in as the user *oracle* (not as root!) and invoke the Oracle Universal Installer by using the following command:

```
$ /stage/Disk1/runInstaller
```

on the **job**

The Oracle Universal Installer is a standard installation tool for Oracle products such as databases and the Application server. The installer is GUI based, and provides installation and configuration options during installation. The installer automatically detects current environment variable settings and configuration parameter values. You can use the same installer for uninstalling the Oracle Application Server software.

If you're using the Oracle Application Server media and are installing directly from it, you can just mount the media (CD-ROM or DVD-ROM) and run the Oracle Universal Installer directly from there. Here's the complete installation procedure for the OracleAS Infrastructure component of the Oracle Application Server:

1. The first screen is the **Welcome** screen. Click **Next.**

2. The next screen is the **Specify Inventory Directory** screen. You'll see this screen only if this is your first Oracle installation on a server. The Oracle Inventory Directory stores the inventory of all Oracle products created by the Installer on a server. Therefore, this directory will already exist if you've installed other Oracle products before on this server. You must enter the full path of the Oracle Inventory Directory, called OraInventory. Here's an example:

```
/opt/oracle/orainventory
```

Note that you must also specify the operating system group name that has write permissions on the inventory directory, which is usually named *oinstall*, as explained previously in this chapter. Click **Next.**

To ensure that the user performing the installation can write to the Oracle Inventory Directory, the Installer invokes the *group window,* where you must specify the group to which the user belongs (oinstall, in our case).

3. The Installer will prompt you to run a script called *orainstRoot.sh,* which grants permissions on the inventory directory to the group you specified for the user. If this is the first installation of Oracle products on your server, you, or someone, who usually is your System Administrator, must run the *orainstRoot.sh* script as the root user. You must perform this action as the root user, because you'll be writing to a directory owned by the root. The *orainstRoot.sh* script is located in the OraInventory directory. Click **Next** after the script finishes running.

4. The **Specify File Locations** window is next. Enter a name like OH_INFRA_ 10_1_2 as the Oracle home name. Specify a full path to the directory under Destination Path, as shown in the following example:

```
/opt/oracle/infra_10_1_2
```

Click **Next.**

5. The **Select a Product to Install** window is next. Select the OracleAS Infrastructure 10g option and click **Next.**

6. In the next window, **Select Installation Type,** you're presented three installation type choices:

   ■ *Identity management and OracleAS Metadata Repository*   This is the option you'll choose to install a complete OracleAS Infrastructure on this host machine. This means that the installer will install both the Identity Management services, as well as a brand new Oracle Database 10g version database to hold the Metadata Repository. You mustn't choose this option under the following circumstances:

      ■ If you don't want one of the two components to be installed on the same server, you must not select this option.

      ■ You may already have an existing Oracle database in which you want to create the Metadata Repository.

If you choose the third option, the Application Server Control tool isn't installed, since you aren't creating any Oracle Application Server components—you're merely creating an Oracle database.

- ■ *Identity Management* You choose this option if you want to add on the Identity Management services so that you can install the OracleAS Single Sign-On and the OracleAS Certificate Authority components, for which this is a prerequisite. However, you must already have created the OracleAS Metadata Repository.

- ■ *OracleAS Metadata Repository* This option will create the Metadata Repository as part of a new Oracle 10g database.

    The second and third choices are useful later on, when you want to add one of those components to an existing OracleAS Infrastructure installation, or when you want to install the Metadata Repository (Oracle database) and the Identity Management components on separate hosts. In this case, since you're installing the infrastructure with both the Identity Management and the Metadata Repository components on the same server, select the first choice, Identity Management and Metadata Repository. Click **Next.**

7. The **Confirm Pre-Installation Requirements** window is next. Verify that you've met all the installation requirements by selecting all the checkboxes shown. Click **Next.**

8. The **Select Configurations Options** window is next. The following components are grayed out, because they're automatically installed:

    - ■ OracleAS Metadata Repository (includes the Oracle Database 10g database)
    - ■ Oracle HTTP Server
    - ■ OracleAS Containers for J2EE

        Select the following options, by clicking the checkboxes next to each of them.

    - ■ Oracle Internet Directory
    - ■ OracleAS Single Sign-On
    - ■ OracleAS Delegated Administration Service
    - ■ OracleAS Directory Integration and Provisioning
    - ■ OracleAS Certificate Authority (OCA)

        You can leave the High Availability and Replication option out at this time. Click **Next.**

9. The **Specify Port Configuration Options** page is next. If you want the installer to automatically select the ports for the various components that need to be assigned a port, check the *Automatic* option. If you'd rather specify the ports yourself using the *staticports.ini* file described previously, choose the *Manual* option. Click **Next.**

10. The **Specify Namespace in Internet Directory** window is next. You must specify a location (namespace) that will serve as the default Identity Management Realm. You can either choose the default namespace by selecting the *Suggested Namespace* option, or choose the *Custom Namespace* option to specify your own location—for example, dc = acme, dc = com. Click **Next.**

11. The **OracleAS Certificate Authority** screens are next.

    ■ **Specify OCA Distinguished Name** window is next. Click **Next** after accepting the Typical DN, or entering your own Custom DN and click **Next.**

    ■ **Specify OCA Key Length** window is next. You select the key length used in the algorithms used by the OracleAS Certificate Authority to sign all of its certificates. Click **Next.**

    ■ **Specify OCA Administrator's Password** window is next. After specifying the OCA administrator's password and confirming it, click **Next.**

12. Next are a set of Oracle Database Screens, which are described in the following sections.

    The following three screens ask you to **Specify Database Configuration Options:**

    ■ *Global Database name (SID)*   This will be the name of the new Oracle database to be created later, for holding the Metadata Repository. You'll use the database name to connect to the Metadata Repository.

    ■ *Database Character Set*   Use this to choose the default database character set.

    ■ *Database File Location*   You can specify the database file location here.

    ■ After specifying the database character set and database file location, click **Next.**

13. Use **Specify Database Schema Passwords** screen to specify the passwords for the database schemas such as SYS and SYSTEM. Click **Next.**

14. The **Specify Instance Name and ias_admin Password** screen appears next. The instance name is the name for the OracleAS Infrastructure instance

that will be installed. Make sure that the instance name contains only alphanumeric characters and the _ (underscore) character. For example, you can name your infrastructure instance as follows:

```
infra_10_1_2
```

The user ias_admin is the administrative user for the Infrastructure instance. Each OracleAS instance must be given a different password for this ias_admin superuser account, though for convenience you could set them all to the same value. Enter a password for the ias_admin user and confirm it, before clicking **Next.**

on the job

The password you specify for the ias_admin user is the same one you'll use later on for the Portal Administrator (portal_admin) and the OID administrator (oidadmin).

15. The **Summary** screen is next, and after verifying your installation options, click **Install.**

16. The **Install Progress** screen shows the progress of the OracleAS Infrastructure installation. You'll have to run the *root.sh* script when prompted by the Run root.sh dialog box from a different shell, as the root user. The *root.sh* script, located in the instance's Oracle home directory, will create entries that will help automate the Oracle database startup upon a server bootup. Click **OK** after running the *root.sh* script.

    The **Configuration Assistants** screen shows the progress of the installation of the various configuration assistants, each of which will configure and start the various OracleAS components you selected earlier.

17. Finally, you'll see the **End of Installation** screen stating that the installation of the OracleAS 10g Infrastructure was successful. Note that the **End Of Installation** screen shows the URLs to access the following:

    ■ Oracle HTTP server

    ■ Oracle Application Server Welcome page

    ■ Application Server Control to manage the Oracle Application Server instance you just created

    Click **Exit** to quit the Oracle Universal Installer and end the OracleAS Infrastructure installation.

on the **job**

You can review the contents of the last screen of the installation process, which includes the URLs for the OracleAS Welcome page and the Application Server Control home page, in the file $ORACLE_HOME/install/setupinfo.txt.

Accessing the OracleAS Infrastructure

Now that you've installed the OracleAS Infrastructure, you are ready to install the middle tier. Before you do, however, confirm that the installation process installed everything correctly, by accessing the various components that were installed, as explained in the following subsections.

W a t c h

Note that all the components you configured during the installation process are automatically started up, as long as you've configured *them to use ports higher than 1024. If not, you have to start the components manually.*

Accessing the OAS Welcome Page

To access the OracleAS Welcome page, go to http://Your_ServerName:7777. If you aren't sure which HTTP port number to use, you can always refer to the *portlist.ini* file in the $ORACLE_HOME/install directory.

Application Server Control

To manage the OracleAS infrastructure through the OEM Application Server Control, go to http://MyServerName:1810 (or 1811). The port numbers 1810 and 1811 are the default port numbers for the Application Server Control belonging to the first two OracleAS instances on a given server node. The first OracleAS instance on a node will use the port number 1810 for the EM daemon; the second instance will take the 1811 port number, and so on. Of course, if those port numbers are in use by other applications, an alternative port will be used for the Application Server Control. Figure 1-2 shows the Oracle Application Server Control home page. You can administer one or more instances of OracleAS with the Application Server Control.

You can also get to Application Server Control through the Enterprise Manager link on the OracleAS Welcome page.

Regardless of whether you directly use the Application Server Control URL or use the Enterprise Manager link to access the Application Server Control, you'll be prompted for the ias_admin password, as shown in Figure 2-2.

Note that a farm is automatically created for you when you install the OracleAS Infrastructure. The Farm page is the entry point to the OEM Application Server Control. In Chapter 1, Figure 1-3 shows the Application Server Control Farm page. Click the infra_10.1.2 link (you'll again be prompted for the username and password; enter the same ias_admin username and password you used earlier to get here), which will take you to the Application Server home page.

on the **job**

The OracleAS component port numbers are available in the setupinfo.txt file, which is created in the /Oracle home/install directory.

OID Server

You can connect to the OID Server by first clicking on your infrastructure instance name on the Farm Page of the Application Server. Scroll to the middle of the page, to the section (table) titled System Components, shown in Figure 2-3.

Click the OID server link, which will take you to the OID Server home page, as shown in Figure 2-4. You can verify that the OID server is up and running, as well as the port number it's running on. You'll need this port number information when you later install the middle-tier components that use the infrastructure.

on the **job**

By default, the passwords for the OracleAS components are set to be the same as the password for the OracleAS instance password.

The Application
Server Control
System
Components
Table

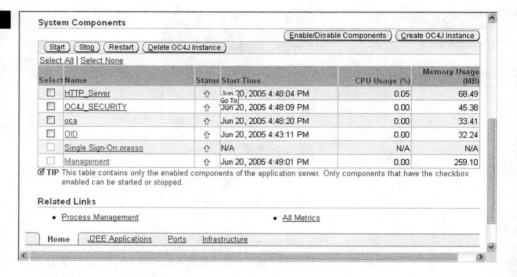

The Oracle
Internet
Directory Server
Home Page

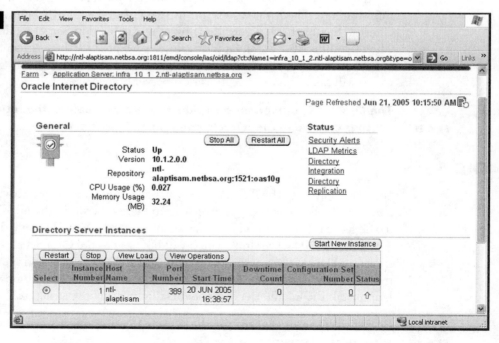

SSO Server

From the Application Server home page, click the **Single Sign-On :orasso** link in the System components table. Under the Related Links page, click the **Administer via Single Sign-on** Web Application link. Click the Login link on the upper right-hand corner of the SSO Server home page. You'll see the SSO Server home page, shown in Figure 2-5. Enter *orcladmin* as the username and the administrative user password you chose during the installation of the OracleAS infrastructure.

Post-Installation Tasks

After the OracleAS Infrastructure has been successfully installed, you can set the ORACLE_HOME, PATH, and the ORACLE_SID environmental variables. Here are some examples:

```
$ export ORACLE_SID=infra
$ export ORACLE_HOME=/u01/app/oracle/product/oracleas_home1
$ export PATH=$PATH:/$ORACLE_HOME/bin
```

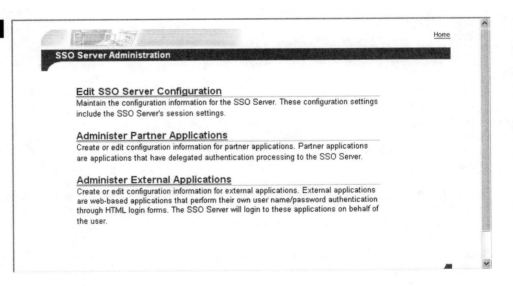

FIGURE 2-5

The SSO Server Home Page

Determining the Component Port Numbers

During the middle-tier installation, or later on, you may have a need to look up the port numbers being used by various OracleAS components. You can find out the port numbers currently assigned to the various components in the following ways:

- You can look up the *portlist.ini* file mentioned earlier in this chapter. The *portlist.ini* file is located in the $ORACLE_HOME/install directory.

- You can use the Application Server Control to look up the port numbers. In the home page, click the Ports link. This will display a page listing all the ports currently in use, as well as the allowable port ranges for each of the OracleAS components.

You must also check that the Oracle listener service is running and that it shows the name of your infrastructure database (for the repository). The following output from a Windows system shows that the listener is running OK and that the Metadata Repository database (oas10g in our case) is running and will accept requests for connections.

```
C:\Documents and Settings\salapati>lsnrctl status
LSNRCTL for 32-bit Windows: Version 10.1.0.3.0 - Production on 20-JUN-2005
16:40:12
Copyright (c) 1991, 2004, Oracle. All rights reserved.
Connecting to (DESCRIPTION=(ADDRESS=(PROTOCOL=TCP)(HOST=ntl-alaptisam.netbsa.org
)(PORT=1521)))
STATUS of the LISTENER
Alias                     LISTENER
Version                   TNSLSNR for 32-bit Windows: Version 10.2.0.0.0 - Beta
Start Date                14-JUN-2005 14:41:21
Uptime                    6 days 1 hr. 58 min. 52 sec
Trace Level               off
Security                  ON: Local OS Authentication
SNMP                      OFF
Listener Parameter File C:\oracle\product\10.2.0\db_2\network\admin\listener.ora
Lisener Log File C:\oracle\product\10.2.0\db_2\network\log\listener.log
Listening Endpoints Summary...
(DESCRIPTION=(ADDRESS=(PROTOCOL=ipc)(PIPENAME=\\.\pipe\EXTPROC1ipc)))
(DESCRIPTION=(ADDRESS=(PROTOCOL=tcp)(HOST=ntl-alaptisam.netbsa.org)(PORT=1521)))
(DESCRIPTION=(ADDRESS=(PROTOCOL=tcp)(HOST=ntl-alaptisam.netbsa.org)(PORT=8080))
(Presentation=HTTP)(Session=RAW))
(DESCRIPTION=(ADDRESS=(PROTOCOL=tcp)(HOST=ntl-alaptisam.netbsa.org)(PORT=2100))
(Presentation=FTP)(Session=RAW))
```

```
Services Summary...
Service "PLSExtProc" has 1 instance(s).
  Instance "PLSExtProc", status UNKNOWN, has 1 handler(s) for this service...
Service "emrep.netbsa.org" has 1 instance(s).
  Instance "emrep", status READY, has 1 handler(s) for this service...
Service "oas10g.world" has 1 instance(s).
  Instance "oas10g", status READY, has 3 handler(s) for this service...
The command completed successfully
C:\
```

If you need to log on to a component by using your browser, but don't know the port number to use for that component, you can always go the $ORACLE_HOME/ install directory and look up the *portlist.ini* file, which shows port numbers for all installed OracleAS 10*g* components on a host.

OracleAS Components reserve the following ports at install time. As a post-installation step, you can reconfigure a component to use a different port, but the changes you make won't be visible in this file. Here are the contents of a typical *portlist.ini* file:

```
[System]
Host Name = ntl-alapatisam.netbsa.org
[Ports]
Oracle HTTP Server port = 7777
Oracle HTTP Server Listen port = 7777
Oracle HTTP Server SSL port = 4443
Oracle HTTP Server Listen (SSL) port = 4443
Oracle HTTP Server Diagnostic port = 7202
Java Object Cache port = 7001
Oracle Notification Server Request port = 6004
Oracle Notification Server Local port = 6101
Oracle Notification Server Remote port = 6201
Log Loader port = 44001
Enterprise Manager Agent Port = 1832
Application Server Control RMI port = 1851
DCM Discovery port = 7101
Application Server Control port = 1811
Oracle Internet Directory port = 389
Oracle Internet Directory (SSL) port = 636
Oracle Certificate Authority SSL Server Authentication port = 4402
Oracle Certificate Authority SSL Mutual Authentication port = 4403
Enterprise Manager Console HTTP Port (oas10g) = 5500
Enterprise Manager Agent Port (oas10g) = 1833
```

Starting and Stopping the OracleAS Infrastructure

You must start and stop the various infrastructure components in a specific order. Here's how you **start** the OracleAS infrastructure:

1. Start the Oracle listener by issuing this command:

   ```
   $ lsnrctl start
   ```

2. Start the Oracle database where the Metadata Repository is stored, in this way:

   ```
   $ sqlplus /nolog
   SQL> connect sys/sys_passwd as sysdba
   SQL> startup
   SQL> exit
   ```

3. Start the OracleAS Infrastructure instance with this command:

   ```
   $ opmnctl startall
   ```

4. Start the Application Server Control console in this way:

   ```
   $ emctl start iasconsole
   ```

   If you need to manage the repository database, you can also start the Database Control with this command:

   ```
   $ emctl start dbconsole
   ```

To **stop** the OracleAS Infrastructure, use the following steps:

1. Stop the Application Server Control by using this command:

   ```
   $ emctl stop iasconsole
   ```

2. Stop the OracleAS Infrastructure instance process this way:

   ```
   $ opmnctl stopall
   ```

3. Stop the Metadata Repository Oracle database with the following command:

   ```
   $ sqlplus /nolog
   SQL> connect sys/sys_passwd as sysdba
   SQL> shutdown immediate
   ```

You don't have to shut down the Oracle listener service, especially if you're using it for other Oracle databases!

Installing the OracleAS Middle Tier

Because it is the middle tier of the OracleAS where applications are deployed, you must select the middle-tier type based on your application requirements. As was explained in Chapter 1, you have to select the type of middle tier from the following two types:

- J2EE and Web Cache
- Portal and Wireless

Note that the two options in the foregoing list are true of the OracleAS 10.2 Release. In the OracleAS 10.1 Release, you had an additional choice of middle-tier type—Business Intelligence and Forms, which isn't offered any longer.

For our example, I chose the **Portal and Wireless** installation option. The Portal and Wireless option automatically includes the J2EE and Web Cache components, in addition to the Portal and Wireless specific components. Here are the components in the Portal and Wireless middle-tier type:

- Oracle HTTP Server (default)
- OracleAS Containers for J2EE (default)
- OracleAS Web Cache
- OracleAS Application Control (default)
- OracleAS Portal
- OracleAS Wireless

on the ** job**

You'll have a separate Oracle HTTP Server and OC4J component for the infrastructure and the middle-tier installations.

The first four components in the component list shown here, are also part of the J2EE and Web Cache middle-tier type. The final two components are exclusive components of the Portal and Wireless middle-tier type.

Note the following things about the relationship between the middle-tier and the infrastructure installations:

■ The Portal and Wireless middle-tier type requires the OracleAS Infrastructure somewhere on your network. Ideally, it should be on a separate computer, but you can install the middle tier on the same machine as the infrastructure.

■ In the OracleAS 10.1 Release, the middle-tier type Business Intelligence and Forms also requires the OracleAS infrastructure.

■ If you are installing the J2EE and Web Cache middle tier, you don't need the OracleAS Infrastructure. You can always choose to create the OracleAS Infrastructure later on and associate a preexisting J2EE and Web Cache middle tier with it.

■ If you intend to use the Single Sign-On feature, you must have already installed OracleAS Identity Management.

■ If you plan on using database-managed OracleAS Clusters, you must install the OracleAS Metadata Repository.

■ If you choose the J2EE and Web Cache installation type, you don't have to have the OracleAS Infrastructure.

■ If you don't install the OracleAS Infrastructure, remember that you can't make use of the LDAP directory (Oracle Internet Directory) and the Oracle Single Sign-On features.

on the
j o b

Of the two middle-tier options available to you in OracleAS 10.2.0, the Portal and Wireless option is the more comprehensive installation type. You must choose this option if you aren't sure which middle-tier type you must install. You can start with the J2EE and Web Cache option, if you wish, and expand this later to a Portal and Wireless option. Of course, you must be prepared for the additional Oracle licensing your installation option entails.

Checking the Installation Requirements

You follow a similar preinstallation routine for the middle tiers as you do for the infrastructure installation. You've already created the necessary UNIX groups and users. You set up the Linux (or UNIX) environment in the same way, as regards the various environmental variables such as DISPLAY, which ensures that the Oracle Installer runs properly and by making sure that the host name is configured correctly.

The Middle-Tier Installation Process

I summarize the steps in the OracleAS middle-tier installation, starting with the invocation of the Oracle Universal Installer.

1. Start the installation by invoking the Oracle Installer, in this way:

   ```
   $ ./runInstaller
   ```

2. The Oracle Universal Installer **Welcome** page appears first. Click **Next.**
3. The **Specify File Locations** window is next. Select an Oracle Home name and provide the full directory path for it. Click **Next.**
4. In the next window, **Select a Product to Install,** you'll see three choices:

   - Oracle Application Server 10*g*
   - OracleAS Infrastructure 10*g*
   - OracleAS Development Kits 10*g*

   You've already installed the OracleAS Infrastructure components in the previous section. You now need to install the middle-tier components that are used for deploying applications. Choose the first option, Oracle Application Server 10*g,* which is also known as the *OracleAS Middle-Tier* option and click **Next.** The middle tier helps you deploy applications over the Internet and includes the Oracle HTTP Server, OC4J, Web Cache, Portal and Wireless.

5. In the **Select Installation Type** window, choose the second option, *Portal and Wireless.* As I explained earlier, this option includes the automatic installation of J2EE and Web Cache components as well by default. You must have already installed the OracleAS Infrastructure before you can choose the Portal and Wireless middle tier.

on the **Job**

If you're installing OracleAS 10.1, you'll have three options available in the Select Installation Type window. These are J2EE and Web Cache, Portal and Wireless, and Business Intelligence and Forms. In OracleAS 10.2, which is what I'm using in this book, you have only the first two options. You can install the Business Intelligence and Forms components separately, if you wish.

6. The **Confirm Pre-Installation Requirements** page is next. Confirm that you meet the stated requirements by selecting all checkboxes presented to you on this page. Click **Next.**

7. In the **Select Configuration Type** window, check the last two components, OracleAS 10*g* Portal and OracleAS 10*g* Wireless. The first three components listed in the page — the Oracle HTTP Server, OC4J, OracleAS Web Cache are always automatically configured. This window will enable you to specify which middle-tier components you want to be installed and started automatically after the completion of the installation. Click **Next.**

8. In the next page, **Specify Port Configuration Options,** choose *Automatic*, unless you want to customize the port number selection by using the *staticports.ini* file. Click **Next.**

9. Middle-tier components such as the OracleAS Portal need the Identity Management Services provided by the Oracle Internet Directory (OID). Note that you've already installed the Identity Management Services as part of the OracleAS Infrastructure installation in the previous section. In the **Register with the Internet Directory** page which is next, provide the server name where your OID instance is running, along with the port number the OID is using. You must enter either your OID Superuser username (cn=orcladmin) or your Single Sign-On username (if you've configured it) and the password, on the **Specify OID Login** page. Click **Next.**

10. On the **Select OracleAS 10***g* Metadata Repository page, provide the connection string for the Oracle database that hosts your Metadata Repository. Actually, the installer fills in the connection string information for you automatically, if you chose to create the repository in a new database. Click **Next.**

11. The next window is named **Specify Instance Name and ias_admin Password.** You must supply a unique *instance name* for this middle-tier OracleAS instance, for example, PW_10_1_2 (for the Portal and Wireless middle tier which I'm installing here). Again, remember that there's a separate OracleAS instance for each OracleAS installation. If there are multiple middle-tier instances on the same computer, you must provide unique names for all of them.

on the **job**

You can scale up from the basic J2EE and Web Cache installation type to the Portal and Wireless installation type after the middle-tier installation is completed.

You must also provide a *password* for the administrative user for this new instance, who is called ias_admin. Confirm the ias_admin user password and Click **Next.**

> **You use the username ias_admin to connect to and manage the OracleAS instance.**

12. In the **Summary** page, confirm the components you are installing and click **Install.** You can return to a previous window by clicking the **Back** button. The Install window will appear and show the progress of the installation. Once the installation of the software files is over, the **Configuration Assistants** window appears. **Configuration Assistants** will configure and start each of the components that you selected earlier.

13. Once all the components have been configured (this will take a while), the **End of Installation** page appears; it indicates whether the installation was completely successful or if some of the components weren't started successfully. Figure 2-6 shows the **End of Installation** page. You can scroll

---

FIGURE 2-6

The End of Installation Page

End of Installation

The installation of Oracle Application Server 10g was successful, but some optional configuration assistants failed, were cancelled or skipped.

Please remember...

```
http://ntl-alaptisam.netbsa.org:7779


----------------------------------------
Use the following URL to access the Oracle Enterprise Manager Application Server
Control:


http://ntl-alaptisam.netbsa.org:1814
The following information is available in:
C:\OraHome5\install\setupinfo.txt
```

Click the Release Information button to view current release information.

(Release Information...)

(Help)   (Installed Products...)   (Back)   (Next)   (Install)   (Exit)

ORACLE

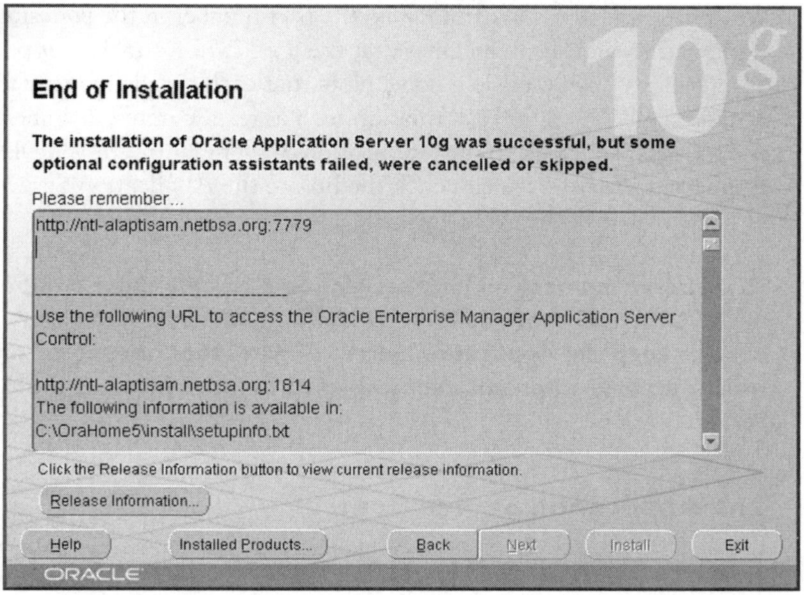

down this page and note the URLs for the Application Server Control and the Oracle HTTP Server. You can get the same information later on by looking up the $ORACLE_HOME/install/portlist.ini file. Click **Exit** to leave the Oracle Universal Installer.

Accessing and Verifying the Middle-Tier Components

Once the middle-tier installation has successfully completed, it's time to access each of the components, thus making sure that they're all running as they are supposed to. Let's see how you access each of the main components, in the following sections.

The Application Server Welcome Page

You can get to the Oracle Application Server by using the following URL:

```
http://your_ServerName:port
```

Usually, port 7777 is used for the port number for the Oracle Application Server Welcome page, and you can look up the port number in the *portlist.ini* file, as explained previously. Remember that the port 7777 is the default port only for the first OracleAS instance on a node. Note that each Oracle Home will have it's own *portlist.ini* file. You'll find information such as release notes, documentation links, and a Quick Tour link to the Application Server Control. If you wish to manage the Application Server, you can click the link to the Application Server Control on the right-hand side of the Welcome page.

To conserve memory on your server, start up only those components of the OracleAS that you'll really need. In addition, know that you don't have to keep the Application Server Control tool running all the time; start it up only when you really need to use it to monitor the Application Server.

The Application Server Control

You can navigate to the various home pages of the Application Server Control, as explained in the following sections.

The Farm Page   The Application Server Control interface, including the Welcome page, the various home pages, and so forth, are identical across all types of OracleAS instances. When you log into the Application Server Control by using the URL http:yourServerName:port, you'll go to the Farm page, which looks identical to the infrastructure instance's Application Server Control Farm page.

The Application Server Control Home Page   You can go the home page of the Application Server Control by clicking on the link pointing to the OracleAS middle-tier instance under the heading *Standalone Instances,* on the Farm page. A standalone OracleAS instance will always be part of an OracleAS Farm, but not part of an OracleAS Cluster.

Component Home Pages   During the middle-tier installation, several OracleAS components are installed. You can see the components list in table form in the middle part of the Farm page, as shown in Figure 2-7.

Application Server Ports Page   From the Application Server Control home page, you can go to the Ports page and the J2EE Applications page by clicking on the appropriate tab. Figure 2-8 shows the Ports page, which shows the component

FIGURE 2-7
The System Components Page of the Application Server Control

System Components

(Enable/Disable Components) (Create OC4J Instance)

(Start) (Stop) (Restart) (Delete OC4J Instance)

Select All | Select None

Select	Name	Status	Start Time	CPU Usage (%)	Memory Usage (MB)
☐	home	⇧	Jul 10, 2005 9:02:43 PM	0.00	28.14
☐	HTTP_Server	⇧	Jul 4, 2005 7:30:10 PM	0.21	56.32
☐	OC4J_Portal	⇧	Jul 10, 2005 9:02:13 PM	0.04	42.88
☐	OC4J_Wireless	⇩	Unavailable	Unavailable	Unavailable
☐	Portal:portal	⇩	N/A	N/A	N/A
☐	Web Cache	⇧	Jul 4, 2005 4:22:48 PM	0.03	37.28
☐	Wireless	⇩	Unavailable	Unavailable	Unavailable
☐	Management	⇧	Jul 8, 2005 12:50:28 PM	0.00	252.72

⌖ TIP This table contains only the enabled components of the application server. Only components that have the checkbox enabled can be started or stopped.

Related Links

- Process Management
- All Metrics

FIGURE 2-8

The Ports Page

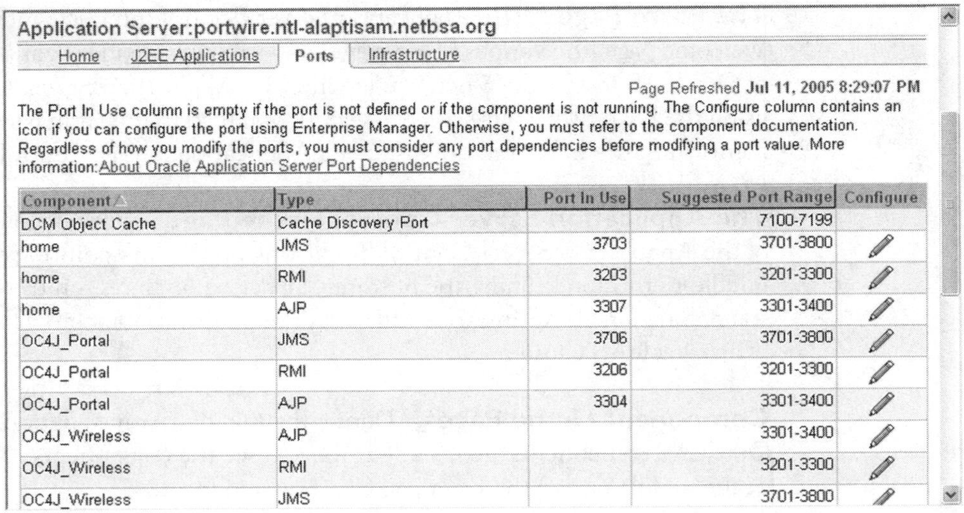

Application Server:portwire.ntl-alaptisam.netbsa.org

| Home | J2EE Applications | Ports | Infrastructure |

Page Refreshed **Jul 11, 2005 8:29:07 PM**

The Port In Use column is empty if the port is not defined or if the component is not running. The Configure column contains an icon if you can configure the port using Enterprise Manager. Otherwise, you must refer to the component documentation. Regardless of how you modify the ports, you must consider any port dependencies before modifying a port value. More information: About Oracle Application Server Port Dependencies

Component △	Type	Port In Use	Suggested Port Range	Configure
DCM Object Cache	Cache Discovery Port		7100-7199	
home	JMS	3703	3701-3800	✎
home	RMI	3203	3201-3300	✎
home	AJP	3307	3301-3400	✎
OC4J_Portal	JMS	3706	3701-3800	✎
OC4J_Portal	RMI	3206	3201-3300	✎
OC4J_Portal	AJP	3304	3301-3400	✎
OC4J_Wireless	AJP		3301-3400	✎
OC4J_Wireless	RMI		3201-3300	✎
OC4J_Wireless	JMS		3701-3800	✎

name, the ports being used by each component, and a list of the suggested range of ports for each component. You can change port settings from the Ports page.

J2EE Applications Page   The J2EE Applications page displays all J2EE applications that are successfully deployed on the Oracle Application Server instance. From here, you can go to the Application home page for each J2EE application and monitor application performance. You can also go to the OC4J home page for the OC4J instance running the application. There are separate OC4J home pages for each OC4J instance, for example, OC4J_Portal, OC4J_Wireless, and so on. From the OC4J home page, you can configure the OC4J Server, deploy new applications, and monitor application performance.

OracleAS Portal

To access the OracleAS Portal, enter the following URL in your Web browser:

```
http://hostname.domain:port/pls/portal
```

Figure 2-9 shows the Portal Welcome page, which is actually titled Portal Builder. On the left hand side of the Portal Welcome page, there's a Login link to the

FIGURE 2-9

The OracleAS Portal Welcome Page

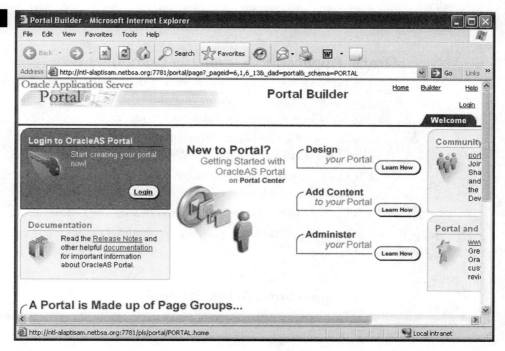

OracleAS Portal. Your OracleAS Portal username will be *portal,* and the password the same as the one you used for the ias_admin user account.

If you've used the Business Intelligence and Forms middle-tier installation option (available only in OracleAS 10g Release 1, not in OracleAS 10g Release 2), then you can also verify the OracleAS Reports Services and the OracleAS Forms Services home pages.

✔ TWO-MINUTE DRILL

Oracle Application Server 10g Components

❑ OracleAS 10g product set consists of the Oracle Application Server which consists of core components including the OracleAS Middle Tier, the OracleAS Infrastructure, and the OracleAS Developer Kits.

❑ There are two middle-tier installation types available in OracleAS 10.2: *J2EE and Web Cache* and *Portal and Wireless*.

❑ OracleAS Infrastructure consists of Identity Management Components and the OracleAS Metadata Repository.

❑ Identity Management Components include the OID and Single Sign-On.

❑ OracleAS Metadata Repository is contained in an Oracle database or in the file system.

Oracle Application Server Topology

❑ The infrastructure and middle-tier components can be installed on the same or different host machines.

❑ You can install an instance of the Infrastructure on one machine and several middle-tier instances on another machine.

❑ You can install the OracleAS Metadata Repository and the Identity Management components on the same or different machines.

❑ You can install the Metadata Repository in an existing database or in a new Oracle database.

Installing OracleAS 10g

❑ You can use the Oracle Universal Installer tool to install the OracleAS software.

❑ You can check the installation requirements manually or by using the *runInstaller* command.

❑ When you select the Portal and Wireless installation option, OC4J and the OracleAS Web Cache are automatically installed.

❑ You can either let the installer choose default ports for the components or specify your own port numbers.

❑ You use the *staticports.ini* file to specify port numbers.

❑ After the OracleAS installation completes, a file called *portlist.ini* is automatically created.

❑ If you have never installed any Oracle products on the server, you must create the Oracle Inventory (oinstall) group before the installation of OracleAS software.

❑ You must also create the Oracle Inventory directory if you're installing Oracle products for the first time on a server.

❑ The *oraInst.loc* file contains the location of the Oracle Inventory Directory.

❑ You must use separate Oracle homes for the infrastructure and the middle-tier installation.

❑ You must unset the ORACLE_HOME and ORACLE_SID variables before installing OracleAS.

Installing the OracleAS Infrastructure

❑ You must install the OracleAS Infrastructure before installing the OracleAS Middle Tier.

❑ If you're going to choose the J2EE and Web Cache installation option, you don't need to install the OracleAS Infrastructure first.

❑ The Oracle HTTP Server, OC4J, and the Application Server Control are always installed as part of the infrastructure installation.

❑ The Metadata Repository and Identity Management are the two basic components of the OracleAS Infrastructure installation.

❑ The Metadata Repository contains the product metadata schemas, identity management schemas, and the management schemas.

❑ Identity Management components primarily consist of the OID, OracleAS Single Sign-On, and the OracleAS Certificate Authority.

❑ By default, the installer creates a new Oracle database to host the Metadata Repository.

❑ You must use the OracleAS Metadata Repository Creation Assistant, if you want to create the Metadata Repository in an existing Oracle database.

❑ If you're creating both the Metadata Repository and the Identity Management components on the same machine, the installer will install them in the correct order automatically.

❏ If you're installing the Metadata Repository and the Identity Management components on different servers, you must install the Metadata Repository first.

❏ All infrastructure components except the OID can be configured after the OracleAS Infrastructure installation.

❏ An OracleAS Farm is automatically created when you install the OracleAS Infrastructure.

❏ To start the OracleAS Infrastructure instance, you must first start the Oracle database listener, and then the Oracle database hosting the OracleAS Metadata Repository. You must then use the commands *opmnctl startall* and *emctl start iasconsole*, in that order.

Installing the OracleAS Middle Tier

❏ The two middle-tier installation options in OracleAS 10.2 are *J2EE and Web Cache* and *Portal and Wireless*.

❏ The main components of the Portal and Wireless option are OC4J, OracleAS Web Cache, OracleAS Portal, and OracleAS Wireless.

❏ There are three types of Application Server Control home pages: the Farm page, the Application Server Control home page, and the Component home pages.

❏ The Application Server Control also has a Ports page and a J2EE Applications page.

SELF TEST

1. To log into the Single Sign-On (SSO) home page, you use the following username/password combination:

   A. orcladmin/the password you specified during the installation of SSO

   B. ias_admin/the password you specified during the installation of SSO

   C. sso_admin/welcome1

   D. orcladmin/orcladmin

2. After the initial OracleAS Infrastructure and Middle-Tier installation has completed, you can configure all of the following components except one:

   A. OracleAS Wireless

   B. Oracle Internet Directory

   C. OracleAS Portal

   D. OracleAS Web Cache

3. You can install the OracleAS Metadata Repository (choose two).

   A. Only in a new database

   B. Only in an existing database

   C. In an existing database or a new database

   D. In the file system

4. You must use the OracleAS Metadata Repository Creation Assistant in order to create:

   A. A new Oracle database

   B. The OracleAS Metadata Repository in a new database

   C. The Identity Management and the OracleAS Metadata Repository components together

   D. The OracleAS Metadata Repository in an existing Oracle database

5. The Metadata Repository contains:

   A. Product metadata schemas, identity management schemas, and the management schemas

   B. Product metadata schemas, identity management schemas, and Web cache schemas

   C. OID, product metadata schemas, and identity management schemas

   D. Oracle Wireless, Oracle Portal, and the OID

6. When would you not need to install the OracleAS Infrastructure?

    A. When you're installing OracleAS Clusters

    B. When you're using Identity Management features

    C. When you're not using an OracleAS Farm

    D. When you're using a J2EE and Web Cache middle-tier installation option

7. Which of the following shows the correct order of installation, supposing that you are going to install all the identity management services?

    A. Install the OracleAS Middle Tier, install Identity Management, and install OracleAS Metadata Repository.

    B. Install OracleAS Metadata Repository, install the OracleAS Middle Tier, and install Identity Management.

    C. Install OracleAS Metadata Repository, install Identity Management, and install the OracleAS Middle Tier.

    D. Install OracleAS Metadata Repository, install the OracleAS Middle Tier, and install Identity Management.

8. After the installation, how do you find out which ports have been assigned to the various OracleAS components?

    A. Use the Application Server Control Ports page.

    B. Use the *portlist.ini* file.

    C. Use the *opmnctl* command.

    D. Use the portconfig XML file.

SELF TEST ANSWERS

1. ☑ **B.** You use the ias_admin username and the password you specified for it during the installation to log into the SSO Server.
   ☒ **A, C,** and **D** are incorrect because they don't use the ias_admin username.

2. ☑ **B** is correct because you can't configure the OID after the installation.
   ☒ **A, C,** and **D** are incorrect because you can configure all components except the OID after the installation.

3. ☑ **C** is correct because you can install the OracleAS Metadata Repository in an existing or a new database. **D** is also correct because you can also create the repository in the file system without using an Oracle database at all.
   ☒ **A** and **B** are wrong because although they are true, they are not the only way to install the OracleAS Metadata Repository.

4. ☑ **D** is correct because you use the OracleAS Metadata Repository Creation Assistant only if you're creating the Metadata Repository in an existing database.
   ☒ **A, B,** and **C** are wrong because in all these cases, the Metadata Repository is automatically created by the Oracle Universal Installer.

5. ☑ **A** is correct because the Metadata Repository contains the product metadata schemas, identity management schemas, and the management schemas.
   ☒ **B, C,** and **D** are wrong because they don't contain the three correct schemas listed under alternative A.

6. ☑ **D** is correct. If you're using a J2EE and OracleAS Web Cache Middle-Tier installation type, you don't need the OracleAS Infrastructure.
   ☒ **A** is incorrect because you'll need the infrastructure if you're installing OracleAS Clusters. **B** is incorrect because you'll need the infrastructure if you're planning to use the identity management features. **C** is incorrect because even standalone instances that aren't part of an OracleAS farm can use the infrastructure.

7. ☑ **D** is correct. You must first create the Oracle Metadata Repository, because several of the identity management components use the information stored in the Oracle database to perform their functions. The middle tier follows the installation of the infrastructure, although you may not need an infrastructure in case you're installing just the J2EE and OracleAS Web Cache components.
   ☒ **A, B,** and **C** are incorrect because they don't show the correct order of installation.

8. ☑ **A** and **B** are correct. A is correct because you can find a complete list of current port assignments as well as the allowed port ranges for each component in the Application Server Control Ports Page. **B** is correct because you can use the *portlist.ini* file to look up current port assignments for the various OracleAS components.

    ☒ **C** and **D** are wrong because neither is a way to find out correct port settings.

3

Managing Oracle Application Server 10g

T his chapter focuses in detail on the most important OracleAS management tools. The most important tool in terms of day-to-day management of OracleAS is the Web-based Application Server Control. The Oracle Process Management and Notification interface helps you manually start and shut down OracleAS components, using the *opmnctl* command-line tool. It's important to understand that the Application Server Control uses *opmnctl* behind the scenes to manage the OracleAS components. You can use either the OEM Application Server Control or *opmnctl* to manage your OracleAS components.

In this chapter I explain how to start up and shut down the Application Server Control interface. I show you how to start up and shut down an OracleAS instance or a component using both the Application Server Control and the *opmnctl* tool. I also show how to access the various home pages of the Application Server Control. In addition, I discuss the *dcmctl* tool, which you use to invoke the Distributed Configuration Management service (DCM). You can use DCM to replicate common configuration information to all the members of an OracleAS cluster. DCM also helps you make backups of your configuration files, so you can replace them if necessary. I also briefly describe the *dynamic monitoring service* (DMS), which is used to collect OracleAS performance data.

CERTIFICATION OBJECTIVE 3.01

Oracle Process Management and Notification Server

Oracle Process Management and Notification Server (OPMN) performs most of the process management for the OracleAS instance. OPMN is one of the three key shadow processes used by OracleAS instances to monitor, coordinate, and manage the various components of the OracleAS instance. The other two key shadow processes are the Distributed Configuration Management (DCM) and Dynamic Monitoring Service. The DCM and DMS processes are discussed further along in this chapter. You use OPMN to manage and monitor the runtime processes of various OracleAS components. OPMN is installed and configured during the middle-tier and the infrastructure installation. You manage all OracleAS component processes with OPMN, except two: the OracleAS Metadata Repository and the

Application Server Control. OPMN manages the various processes as well as facilitates communication among them.

OPMN Components

OPMN tracks the health of the various OracleAS components. If one of the components becomes unavailable, OPMN automatically restarts the component. OPMN uses the Metadata Repository data to find out which components it should start and monitor. If an OracleAS component depends on a second component for its functioning and the second component goes down, OPMN lets the first component know about this. For example, the Oracle HTTP Server passes requests from Java applications on to the OC4J component (through OHS's *mod_oc4j* module). If the OC4J process dies for some reason, OPMN will automatically let the mod_oc4j module know about this fact, so it can stop sending additional requests until the OC4J process starts up again. Thus, OPMN plays a critical role in the functioning of an OracleAS instance. OPMN consists of the following three components.

Oracle Process Manager

The Oracle Process Manager (PM) is a centralized process management mechanism that manages all the OracleAS processes. You can see the list of all processes managed by the PM in the *opmn.xml* file. The Application Server Control also uses the PM to manage various OracleAS processes.

Oracle Notification Server

The Oracle Notification Server (ONS) transports notifications for failure, recovery, startup, and related events among the various OracleAS components. Through the ONS, the PM is able to:

- Find out when a process has completed initialization and is ready to receive requests.
- Find out what ports are being used by the various processes.
- Find out runtime process information.

on the **Job**

OPMN automatically restarts OracleAS processes that die or become unresponsive.

Process Manager Modules

The Process Manager (PM) modules are in charge of the component specific process management; they relay process information returned by the PM modules serving some other OracleAS components, whether from the same OPMN server or from other OPMN servers.

OPMN manages all the OracleAS components except the Metadata Repository and the Application Server Control.

OPMN Event Scripts

You can use *custom event scripts* that set off an event when a particular OPMN component starts, stops, or crashes. Event scripts help you supply configuration information to OPMN, gather trace details, and send notifications. Here are the three OPMN event types available to you:

- Pre-start
- Pre-stop
- Post-crash

Debugging OPMN

You can use OPMN's *debug command* to generate output you can use to confirm the status of the various OPMN processes, as well as to provide information to Oracle Support personnel diagnosing any OPMN problems. Use the *opmnctl debug* command to verify the status of an Oracle Application Server process and to determine whether any actions are pending. This command generates output that can be used in conjunction with Oracle support personnel to diagnose your OPMN problem.

The syntax for the *opmnctl debug* command is:

```
opmnctl [<scope>] debug [comp=pm|ons] [interval=<secs> count=<num>]
```

The opmnctl Command-Line Tool

You use the OPMN tool with the *opmnctl* command-line utility. The other way to use OPMN is through the Application Server Control Console, which uses OPMN to perform its process management tasks. The *opmnctl* executable is located in the

ORACLE_home/opmn/bin directory. With *opmnctl,* you can start and stop the OPMN and the various processes it manages.

The opmnctl Options

You can use the *opmnctl* command-line utility with several options, as shown here:

```
$ opmnctl
usage: opmnctl [verbose] [<scope>] <command> [<options>]
verbose: print detailed execution message if available
Permitted <scope>/<command>/<options> combinations are:
 scope      command                           options
 -------    ---------                         ---------
            start                             - Start opmn
            startall                          - Start opmn & all managed processes
            stopall                           - Stop opmn & all managed processes
            shutdown                          - Shutdown opmn & all managed processes
[<scope>]   startproc   [<attr>=<val> ..] - Start opmn managed processes
[<scope>]   restartproc [<attr>=<val> ..] - Restart opmn managed processes
[<scope>]   stopproc    [<attr>=<val> ..] - Stop opmn managed processes
[<scope>]   reload                            - Trigger opmn to reread opmn.xml
[<scope>]   status      [<options>]          - Get managed process status
[<scope>]   dmsdump     [<attr>=<val>&..] - Get DMS stats
            ping        [<max_retry>]        - Ping local opmn
            validate    [<filename>]         - Validate the given xml file
            help                              - Print brief usage description
            usage       [<command>]          - Print detailed usage description
$
```

Note that the start, stop, stopall, and startall commands don't have to be issued with any scope parameter, because they start or stop the entire OPMN component stack. However, when you're starting or stopping an individual component—for example, the WebCache component, which has two distinct processes, the WebCacheAdmin and WebCache processes—you may not want to always start and stop both the processes. You can specify the scope of the start or stop command for components with multiple processes by specifying whether the component itself— that is, all is processes—should be stopped or started, or just a specified process belonging to that component. Also, when you start or stop an individual component or a process that belongs to a particular component, you use the startproc, restartproc, and stopproc parameters to start, restart, and stop the component or one of its constituent processes.

Here's an example that shows how to use the scope parameter to specify that only the WebCacheAdmin process of the WebCache component should be stopped:

```
$ opmnctl startproc process-type=WebCacheAdmin
```

To stop both the processes of the WebCache component, you change the scope to ias-component, from process-type, as shown here:

```
$ opmnctl startproc ias-component=WebCache
```

Using the opmnctl Utility

Before the *opmnctl* utility can manage and monitor processes, you must make sure that the OPMN itself is started first. You can use the *opmnctl status* command to find out the status of the opmn processes. Here's an example showing that the main OPMN process itself is down:

```
$ opmnctl status
Unable to connect to opmn.
Opmn may not be up.
$
```

exam

ⓦ**atch**   *You can start the main opmn process by using either the opmnctl start or the opmnctl startall command.*

You can then use the *opmnctl* utility with just the *start* option, which will start just the opmn main process.

```
$ opmnctl start
opmnctl: opmn started
$
```

Once the main OPMN process starts, your *status* command will work, as shown here in the case of a middle-tier OracleAS instance:

```
$ opmnctl status
Processes in Instance: portwire.ntl-alaptisam.netbsa.org
-------------------+--------------------+---------+---------
ias-component      | process-type       |    pid | status
-------------------+--------------------+---------+---------
LogLoader          | logloaderd         |    N/A | Down
DSA                | DSA                |    N/A | Down
HTTP_Server        | HTTP_Server        |    N/A | Down
dcm-daemon         | dcm-daemon         |    N/A | Down
```

```
WebCache         | WebCache          | N/A | Down
WebCache         | WebCacheAdmin     | N/A | Down
OC4J             | home              | N/A | Down
OC4J             | OC4J_Portal       | N/A | Down
wireless         | performance_server| N/A | Down
wireless         | messaging_server  | N/A | Down
wireless         | OC4J_Wireless     | N/A | Down
$
```

You can use the *opmnctl* utility with the *startall* option to start all managed processes:

```
$ opmnctl startall
opmnctl: starting opmn and all managed processes...
opmnctl: starting opmn and all managed processes...
=======================================================
opmn id=ntl-alaptisam:6204
    8 of 8 processes started.
ias-instance id=portwire.ntl-alaptisam.netbsa.org
+++++++++++++++++++++++++++++++++++++++++++++++++++++++
$
```

Now you can use the *status* option to check the status of the managed processes, first for the OracleAS infrastructure, as shown here:

```
$ opmnctl status
Processes in Instance: infra_10_1_2.ntl-alaptisam.netbsa.org
-------------------+--------------------+---------+---------
ias-component      | process-type       |     pid | status
-------------------+--------------------+---------+---------
LogLoader          | logloaderd         |     N/A | Down
DSA                | DSA                |     N/A | Down
HTTP_Server        | HTTP_Server        |    3772 | Alive
dcm-daemon         | dcm-daemon         |    5344 | Alive
OC4J               | home               |     296 | Alive
OC4J               | oca                |    7624 | Alive
OC4J               | OC4J_SECURITY      |     472 | Alive
OID                | OID                |    1676 | Alive
$
```

If the Oracle database containing the Metadata Repository isn't up, or if the Oracle listener process isn't up, then the OID service, which needs the Metadata Repository, can't start. If the OID service fails to start, services such as the OracleAS Certificate Authority, which use the OID, won't start either.

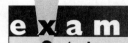

Use the same *opmnctl status* command to show the status of the OracleAS Portal
and Wireless middle tier:

```
$ opmnctl status
Processes in Instance: portwire.ntl-alaptisam.netbsa.org
-------------------+--------------------+---------+---------
ias-component      | process-type       |     pid | status
-------------------+--------------------+---------+---------
LogLoader          | logloaderd         |     N/A | Down
DSA                | DSA                |     N/A | Down
HTTP_Server        | HTTP_Server        |    9796 | Alive
dcm-daemon         | dcm-daemon         |    6284 | Alive
WebCache           | WebCache           |    8112 | Alive
WebCache           | WebCacheAdmin      |    4120 | Alive
OC4J               | home               |    7476 | Alive
OC4J               | OC4J_Portal        |    6116 | Alive
wireless           | performance_server |    2248 | Alive
wireless           | messaging_server   |    5812 | Alive
wireless           | OC4J_Wireless      |    4384 | Alive
$
```

Note two things in the foregoing process status report:

■ Make sure you're looking at the right OracleAS instance by looking at the
first line, where the instance name is reported (portwire_10_1_2.ntl-alaptisam
.netbsa.org).

■ The logloader and the DSA components are usually not up. You can bring them
up later on. The logloader compiles log messages from log files into a common
repository, and you can start it later if you want to use it. The DSA is the
OracleAS Guard server. If you are using OracleAS Guard, you can start this
after installation.

You can stop all opmn processes using the following command:

```
$ opmnctl stopall
opmnctl: stopping opmn and all managed processes...
$
```

You can also start and stop *individual components* of OracleAS, using the following commands:

```
$ $ORACLE_home/opmn/bin/opmnctl startproc ias-component=component
$ $ORACLE_home/opmn/bin/opmnctl stopproc ias-component=component
```

Here's an example that shows how you can start a single component, the HTTP_Server:

```
$ opmnctl startproc ias-component=HTTP_Server
opmnctl: starting opmn managed processes...
$
```

In the following example, the HTTP server is down, as shown by the following command:

```
$ opmnctl status
DSA                 | DSA                 |     N/A | Down
HTTP_Server         | HTTP_Server         |     N/A | Down
...
$
```

You can restart just the HTTP Server component using the *opmnctl startproc* command:

```
$ opmnctl startproc ias-component=HTTP_Server
opmnctl: starting opmn managed processes...
$opmnctl status
Processes in Instance: portwire.ntl-alaptisam.netbsa.org
-------------------+-------------------+---------+---------
ias-component      | process-type      |     pid | status
-------------------+-------------------+---------+---------
LogLoader          | logloaderd        |     N/A | Down
DSA                | DSA               |     N/A | Down
HTTP_Server        | HTTP_Server       |    5788 | Alive
...
$
```

Note that if your HTTP Server fails to come up sometimes, you may see the following error:

```
pid file c:/orahome_4/apache/apache/logs/httpd.pid overwritten -
```

You can just remove the *http.pid* file and the Apache Server will start with no problems.

The httpd.pid *file stores the process number of the OHS parent process, and you must delete this file if the OHS server isn't shut down in an orderly fashion.*

The ability to start an individual component, or even a subcomponent, is very handy when one or two components or subcomponents fail to start up, as shown here:

```
------------------------------------------------------------------
ias-component/process-type/process-set:
    wireless/OC4J_Wireless/default_island
Error
--> Process (pid=4384)
    failed to start a managed process after the maximum retry limit
    Log:
    C:\OraHome_4\opmn\logs\wireless~OC4J_Wireless-default_island~1
$
```

You can also start, stop, and restart the individual processes through the Application Server Control interface, which is explained in the next section.

In the preceding case, a subcomponent of the Wireless component — OC4J_ Wireless component — has failed to start. In my case, this happened because the opmnctl tool couldn't start up this component within the allocated time. You can run the following command in circumstances like this to start an individual component or subcomponent:

```
$ opmnctl startproc process-type=OC4J_Wireless
opmnctl: starting opmn managed processes...
$
```

You can *restart* a running process using the following command:

```
$ $ORACLE_home/opmn/bin/opmnctl restartproc ias-component=component
```

The Application Server Control Interface

Oracle Enterprise Manager (OEM) 10g Application Server Control is a Web-based tool to manage and monitor the OracleAS components. Note that there is a separate Application Server Control for each OracleAS instance. Thus, the infrastructure instance will have its own Application Server Control interface, and each middle-tier instance will have a separate Application Server Control. Using the Application Server Control interface, you can do the following:

- Manage OracleAS Clusters.
- Manage and monitor Application Server components.
- Diagnose the performance of application components.
- Configure the components.
- Deploy applications.
- Manage security.

There is no special installation procedure for the Application Server Control, because the software for it is automatically installed as part of the Oracle Application Server installation. After you create a new Oracle Application Server instance, the Application Server Control will be running on the server automatically.

Application Server Control and the Management Agent

The Management Agent performs the job of fetching data for the Application Server Control. Each Application Server Control has a separate Management Agent. The Management Agent is automatically started when you start the Application Server Control Console. You can check the management agents for the infrastructure and the middle-tier Application Server Control instances by using the *emdctl* utility. If you're using a Windows server, make sure that you first set the EMDROOT environment variable to the Oracle home location. Here's how you check the status of the agent using the *emdctl* utility:

```
C:\OraHome_4\BIN>set EMDROOT=C:\ORAHome_4
C:\OraHome_4\BIN>emdctl status agent
   Response From Agent: running
Agent Version    : 10.1.0.3.0
OMS Version      : Unknown
Protocol Version : 10.1.0.3.0
Agent home       : C:\OraHome_4
Agent binaries   : C:\OraHome_4
Agent Process ID : 11612
Agent Process ID : 11612
Agent URL        : http://ntl-alaptisam.netbsa.org:1833/emd/main/
Started at       : 2005-07-07 10:35:24
Started by user  : SYSTEM
Last Reload      : 2005-07-07 10:35:24
Last successful upload                      : (none)
Last attempted upload                       : (none)
Total Megabytes of XML files uploaded so far :    0.00
Number of XML files pending upload          :       0
Size of XML files pending upload(MB)        :    0.00
Available disk space on upload filesystem   :   48.23%
C:\OraHome_4\BIN>
```

If the management agent isn't running, as shown below, you must use the *emctl* utility (not the *emdctl* utility) to start the Application Server Control Console, which will automatically start the management agent as well. Unlike in the case where you're using the OEM Grid Control, you don't have to start (and stop) the Management Agent separately.

```
C:\emdctl status agent
Error connecting to http://ntl-alaptisam.netbsa.org:1833/emd/main/
C:\OraHome_4\BIN>
```

You can find the status of the Management Agent only with the help of the *emdctl* utility. You can't start the agent with it. As was mentioned earlier, there's no need for you to start or stop the Management Agent when you use the Application Server Control. The agent is started and stopped automatically with the Application Server Control Console. You can check whether the management agent is ready by using a URL with the following format:

```
http://your_server.your_domain:port/emd/
```

Figure 3-1 shows that the Management Agent is running. This means that you'll be able to log into the Application Server Control Console.

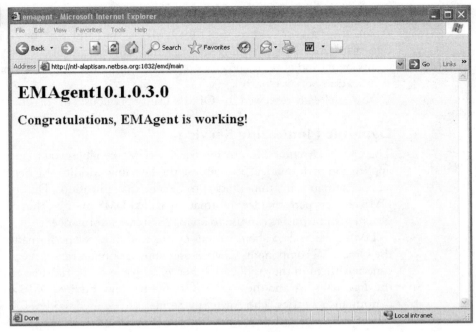

FIGURE 3-1

The Management
Agent Status

Grid Control

Make sure you understand the distinction between the Application Server Control and the Grid Control. The Application Server Control is linked to a particular Oracle Application Server instance. Each Oracle Application Server will have a single Application Server Control. The Oracle Enterprise Manager 10*g* Grid Control (or just Grid Control), on the other hand, lets you centrally manage your entire system, including databases, servers, and application server instances.

Application Server Control is already installed, configured, and ready to run out-of-the-box when you create a new Oracle Application Server instance. Grid Control, on the other hand, requires a specialized installation of its software. After you install Grid Control on the server from where you intend to manage your enterprise, you must install a Management Agent on each of the servers you want to monitor.

How the Application Server Control Does Its Job

The Application Server Control uses the following technologies to perform its many managing and monitoring functions.

OPMN

Application Server Control uses the OPMN to start and stop the Application Server instances. It's the OPMN that gathers information about the status of the components and provides process control and monitoring information to the Application Server Control.

You've already reviewed the OPMN utility previously in this chapter.

Dynamic Monitoring Service

The Oracle Dynamic Monitoring Service (DMS) enables you to measure application performance. You can use the Dynamic Monitoring Service API to add performance instrumentation to OracleAS applications. During runtime, DMS collects performance information, called DMS metrics, that developers and system administrators can use to analyze system performance.

DMS collects data about various events as well as the performance metrics for the OracleAS components. DMS stores application metrics in memory, and you can view them in the Application Server Console or use runtime tools such as the *dmstool* utility and the *AggreSpy* servlet to view and save DMS application performance metrics. The AggreSpy Servlet can be used to view OC4J metrics only if you're using the OC4J in standalone mode, without the Oracle Application Server. You can find out the various options available with the *dmstool* utility by typing in *dmstool −help* at the command line. You may turn off the DMS tool if your system is straining to service the peak load work, because the DMS isn't absolutely essential for the running of the OracleAS instance.

Distributed Configuration Management

Distributed Configuration Management (DCM) helps you manage configuration information for the OracleAS instance and its components. It is DCM that facilitates the creation and management of OracleAS Clusters and OracleAS Farms. DCM provides the following capabilities:

- Manages configurations among OracleAS instances that share a common Metadata Repository (OracleAS Farm).

- Enables you to deploy an application in an instance and have it propagated automatically to all the other instances in an OracleAS Cluster.

- Enables a configuration change in one instance to be automatically propagated to all the instances in an OracleAS Cluster.

- Manages the various configuration versions.

OracleAS implements the DCM as the DCM daemon and you can use it in two ways: using the Application Server Control or using the *dcmtl* utility.

DCM manages a repository, called the DCM Repository, to help you manage multiple OracleAS instances, by storing the OracleAS instance, Cluster, and Farm topology information. DCM also stores configuration information for the various OracleAS components, such as the Oracle HTTP Server, OC4J, and OPMN, in its repository. DCM is also in charge of keeping track of all J2EE applications deployed by the various Application Server instances.

A DCM Repository can be maintained in the following two formats, and you can access either one through the *dcmtl* utility:

- The OracleAS Metadata Repository can store the DCM Repository as a schema.
- The DCM Repository could also be saved in a file in the middle-tier OracleAS instance. The file is stored in the $ORACLE_home/dcm/repository directory.

When you register a middle-tier OracleAS with the OracleAS Metadata Repository, by default, the OracleAS Metadata Repository stores the DCM data.

You manage DCM through the Application Server Control. You can also use the *dcmtl* ($ORACLE_home/dcm/bin/dcmtl) utility from the command line to configure the OracleAS instances. In order to use the utility, you must be logged in as the operating system user that installed OracleAS. Once you use the *dcmtl* tool to make configuration changes, you must restart the OracleAS instance for those changes to take effect.

Here are some common *dcmtl* command options:

- **listcomponents**   Lists the OracleAS instance components.
- **resysncInstance**   Gets the latest configuration information *from* the Metadata Repository. Note that the resysncInstance command will overwrite the component's configuration files with the current information from the Metadata Repository. If you've damaged your existing httpd.conf configuration file, for example, you can use this command to restore the httpd.conf file to its predamaged state.
- **updateconfig**   Sends the latest configuration information *to* the Metadata Repository. Be aware that the execution of the updateConfig command overwrites the Metadata Repository data with the information in the configuration files you updated. You must run this command if you've updated your configuration files such as the *httpd.conf* file, for example. Otherwise, the Metadata Repository won't have the updated information from the manually edited httpd.conf file.

The *resysncInstance* and the *updateConfig* commands help synchronize the configuration information in the configuration files (e.g., httpd.conf) and the Metadata Repository, as shown here:

- ■ **createComponent**   Creates a new OC4J instance.
- ■ **createcluster**   Creates an OracleAS Cluster.
- ■ **joincluster**   Joins an OracleAS instance to a Cluster.
- ■ **deployapplication**   Helps deploy an application.
- ■ **getState**   Returns the state of OracleAS Components. If you use the command without any arguments, it will return the status of all the OracleAS components. The syntax is as follows:

```
getState [-i instance_name] [-cl cluster_name] [-co component_name]
```

For example, to get the state of the component HTTP_Server, you'd type this:

```
$ dcmctl getState -co HTTP_Server
```

You can use the *–v* (for verbose) flag when you use the *dcmtl* command to get detailed output about the command's operation. By typing in dcmtl help, you can review all the options you can choose when using the *dcmtl* tool. In addition to using the *dcmtl* utility from the command line, you can also use a batch script to execute multiple *dcmtl* commands from within a *dcmtl* shell. You start a *dcmtl* shell by using the following command:

```
$ dcmtl shell
```

For example, you can incorporate several *dcmtl* commands in a file called implement.sh and pass the file name as an argument to the *dcmtl* shell, as shown here:

```
$ dcmtl shell –f implement.sh
```

on the job

Make sure you invoke the dcmtl utility from the correct software directory, because the setting of the ORACLE_home variable doesn't guarantee that you're using the dcmtl executable from the correct OracleAS installation.

Note that you can control any OracleAS instance in an OracleAS Farm using the *dcmtl* command from any of the Oracle homes, by specifying the OracleAS instance name as part of the command.

The Application Server Control Console

The Application Server Control Console is the standard administrative console for accessing the Application Server Control in order to perform most everyday management and monitoring functions. The Application Server Control is part of the OracleAS installation. Of course, you may also use the more comprehensive Grid Control to manage not just the OracleAS instances but the entire enterprise, including Oracle databases. The Application Server Control Console consists of the following processes:

- **Emagent**   This is the process for the Oracle Management Agent.
- **Perl**   This is the Management Watchdog Process, which monitors the Management Agent and the Application Server Control Console.
- **Java**   This is the actual process that runs the Application Server Control Console.

Capabilities of the Various Management Tools

You've reviewed the three main OracleAS management tools—the Application Server Control, DCM, and the OPMN. As you know, the Application Server Control relies on the DCM and the OPMN to perform its tasks. However, you can use all three tools, depending on the task at hand. Table 3-1 summarizes the capabilities of these three tools.

TABLE 3-1   Capabilities of the Various OracleAS Tools

Capability	DCM	OPMN	Application Server Control
Starting and stopping instances and components	NO	YES	YES
Starting and stopping OracleAS Clusters	NO	YES	YES
Creating OC4J Instances	YES	NO	YES
Creating and joining OracleAS Clusters	YES	NO	YES
Deploying applications	YES	NO	YES
Checking status of instance and components	YES	YES	YES

From viewing Table 3-1, it's apparent that the OPMN tool serves primarily to start and stop and check the status of the instance and its components. The DCM is mostly concerned with the creation and joining of clusters, deployment (and undeployment) of applications and the like, although you could use the command option getState to get the operational status of the OracleAS components. Of course, the Application Server Control uses both of these technologies for its functioning; therefore, it can perform both types of tasks.

CERTIFICATION OBJECTIVE 3.03

Additional OracleAS 10g Tools

Oracle provides two other tools in an "as is" condition, for your use. Oracle disclaims all warranties and won't be liable for any damages incurred by or in connection with the use of these tools.

The OracleAS Hi-Av Tool

OracleAS Hi-Av Tool (iHAT) shows you a real-time view of the entire system and displays all processes managed by a set of one or more OPMN servers, including useful performance metrics about each process obtained from the DMS. According to Oracle, the tool should run on any platform that supports Java 1.4.1 and has been tested on Windows, Solaris, and Linux platforms.

You can download the OracleAS Hi-Av Tool from the following Web site: http://www.oracle.com/technology/products/ias/ias_utilities.html.

Once you download the Java jar file, go to the command line and invoke iHAT this way:

```
$ java —jar ihat.zip <host>:<port>
```

You can get the port number from the *opmn.xml* file, located in the $ORACLE_home/opmn/conf directory. The port number specified for the request attribute of the port element is what you need to specify. Here's an example on a Windows server:

```
$ java -jar ihat.jar ntl-alaptisam.netbsa.org:6007
```

To see the complete options available, use the following command:

```
$ java —jar ihat.jar -help
```

Figure 3-2 shows the iHAT Tool in action.

There are two types of formats in which you can use the Hi-Av Tool—grid view and instance view. The *grid view* is the default view, and shows a live picture of all OracleAS components configured in the opmn.conf file for all the OracleAS instances discovered in your system. The grid view thus gives you an overall picture of your system. To drill down to an individual instance, click on the appropriate node. The iHAT tool uses the *instance view* to show the management topology of the system. The units of management are the OracleAS instance, the OracleAS component, process type, and process set. The instance view also shows the process PID and various performance metrics of the process. The additional *routing view* shows the relationships between the Oracle HTTP Server and OC4J.

FIGURE 3-2

The OracleAS
Hi-Av (iHAT)
Tool

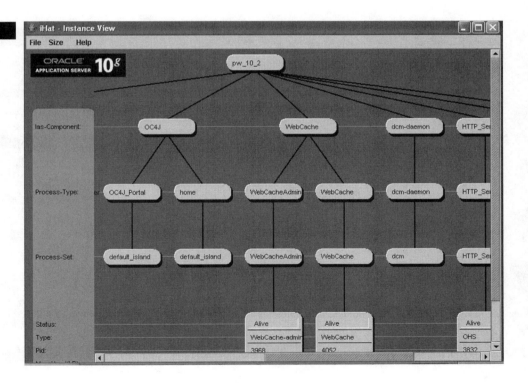

The Application Server Control Topology Viewer

The Application Server Control–based Topology Viewer, shown in Figure 3-3, provides you a graphical, real-time view of all OracleAS processes managed by OPMN, including performance statistics for each OracleAS component. You can invoke the Topology Viewer by clicking on the *Topology* link on any Application Server Control page. The Topology Viewer provides a quick view of the relationships among the various components of the Oracle Application Server, as well as those among multiple OracleAS instances. Using the Topology Viewer, you can view all the instances in a Farm, including clusters and their members. You can perform the following tasks using the Topology Viewer:

- Review the status of components.
- Start and stop the OracleAS processes.
- Monitor OracleAS performance.
- Drill down to various OracleAS component home pages.

FIGURE 3-3

The OracleAS
Topology Viewer

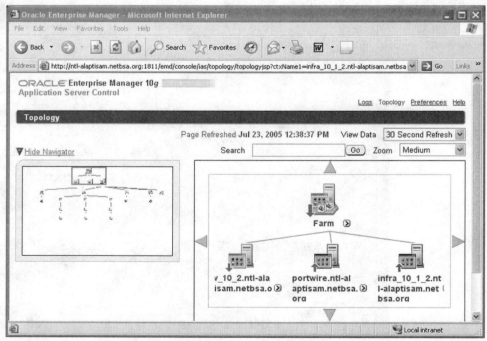

The Application Server Control Home Page

The Application Server Control home page in the Application Server Control is the starting point for managing a single instance of the Oracle Application Server. From here, you can perform the following tasks:

- View a selected set of performance metrics.
- View the status of the Oracle Application Server.
- Get detailed information about all the application server components.
- Find out how each component is performing individually and how it's affecting the OracleAS performance itself.
- Change the configuration of OracleAS components applications.

Starting Up and Shutting Down the Application Server Control

You start up and shut down the Application Server Control using the *emctl* utility, located in the $ORACLE_home/bin directory. You can use the *emctl* utility with several options, as shown here:

```
$ emctl
Oracle Enterprise Manager 10g Application Server Control Release 10.1.2.0.0
Copyright (c) 1996, 2004 Oracle Corporation. All rights reserved.
Usage::
   Oracle Enterprise Manager 10g Application Server Control commands:
       emctl start| stop| status iasconsole
       emctl set password <old ias_admin password> <new ias_admin password>
       emctl secure iasconsole
       emctl config iasconsole port [portNumber]
       emctl config iasconsole rmiport [portNumber]
       emctl config agent credentials [<Target_name>[:<Target_Type>]]
       emctl config agent port [portNumber]
$
```

on the **job** *The ias_admin password is stored in encrypted format in the jazn-data.xml file, located in the ORACLE_home/sysman/j2ee/config/ directory. If you forget the ias_admin password, you can edit this file to reset the password.*

You can perform the following tasks with the *emctl* utility:

■ Start, stop, and check the status of the Application Server Control.

■ Configure the Application Server Control port and agent credentials.

■ Reset the ias_admin user's password. You supply the initial password of the ias_admin super user during the installation process. After installation, you can use the emctl tool to change the password.

In order to access the Application Server Control through your Web browser, you must first start up the Application Server Control Console. As was explained earlier, you'll have a separate Application Server Control for each of the two OracleAS instances—the infrastructure and the middle tier. You must make sure you set the ORACLE_home environment variable correctly before you start each of the consoles. Once you set the ORACLE_home variable correctly, issue the following command to start the Application Server Control Console:

```
$ emctl start iasconsole
Oracle Enterprise Manager 10g Application Server Control Release 10.1.2.0.0
Copyright (c) 1996, 2004 Oracle Corporation. All rights reserved.
http://ntl-alaptisam.netbsa.org:1811/emd/console/aboutApplication
Starting Oracle Enterprise Manager 10g Application Server Control...
The Oracleoracleas2ASControl service is starting...................
The Oracleoracleas2ASControl service was started successfully.
$
```

on the
j o b

Make sure you set the ORACLE_home variable correctly, before starting and stopping the Application Server Control Console with the emctl utility. Otherwise, you may unwittingly be starting and stopping the wrong Application Server Control!

You must start the Application Server Control Console for the infrastructure and the middle tier separately, as each has its own separate OracleAS instance. Make sure you start both the Consoles from their respective Oracle homes.

To stop the Application Server Control Console you use the following command (again, make sure you've set the ORACLE_home variable correctly, before using the command):

```
$ emctl stop iasconsole
Oracle Enterprise Manager 10g Application Server Control Release 10.1.2.0.0
Copyright (c) 1996, 2004 Oracle Corporation. All rights reserved.
```

```
http://ntl-alaptisam.netbsa.org:1813/emd/console/aboutApplication
The Oracleoracleas4ASControl service is stopping.......
The Oracleoracleas4ASControl service was stopped successfully.
$
```

You can check the current status of the Application Server Control Console using the following command:

```
$ emctl status iasconsole
Oracle Enterprise Manager 10g Application Server Control Release 10.1.2.0.0
Copyright (c) 1996, 2004 Oracle Corporation. All rights reserved.
http://ntl-alaptisam.netbsa.org:1813/emd/console/aboutApplication
Oracle Enterprise Manager 10g Application Server Control is running.
---------------------------------------------------------------
Logs are generated in directory C:\OraHome_4/sysman/log
$
```

Sometimes, you may wish to change the Application Server Control port number. The following example shows how to do this. In this case, I'm changing the port number from 1811 to 1820. Of course, the new port number must be available, for this command to succeed.

```
$ emctl config iasconsole port 1820
Oracle Enterprise Manager 10g Application Server Control Release 10.1.2.0.0
Copyright (c) 1996, 2004 Oracle Corporation. All rights reserved.
http://ntl-alaptisam.netbsa.org:1811/emd/console/aboutApplication
Oracle Enterprise Manager 10g Application Server Control
configuration update succeeded.
$
```

Accessing the Application Server Control

Once you've started the Application Server Control Console using the *emctl* utility, you can access it through your Web browser by entering the following URL:

```
http://application_server_instance_host:<port>
```

In my case, this becomes

```
http://localhost:1811/
```

on the **!**
()o b   *If your Application Server Control Console isn't started, you can't access the*
Application Server Control.

The Oracle installer assigns the OEM Application Server port number during the Oracle Application Server installation. The default port number for the first OracleAS instance on a node is 1810; for the second instance, it is 1811; and so on. You confirm the port number by looking in the *ORACLE_home*/Apache/Apache/setupinfo.txt file.

Figure 3-4 shows the Farm page for the OracleAS Infrastructure instance. Note the main components of the infrastructure instance:

Figure 3-5 shows the System Components Table in the Application Server home page of the OracleAS middle-tier instance. Note the main components in the middle tier:

- HTTP Server
- Web cache
- Portal
- Wireless

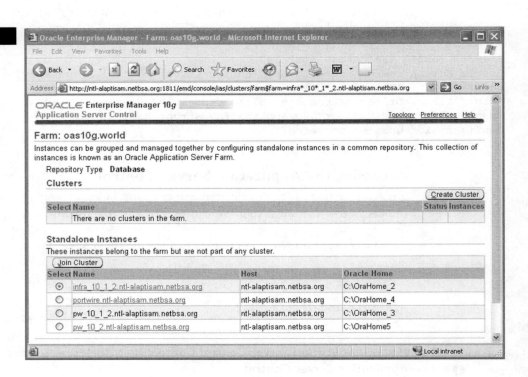

FIGURE 3-4

The OracleAS Farm Page

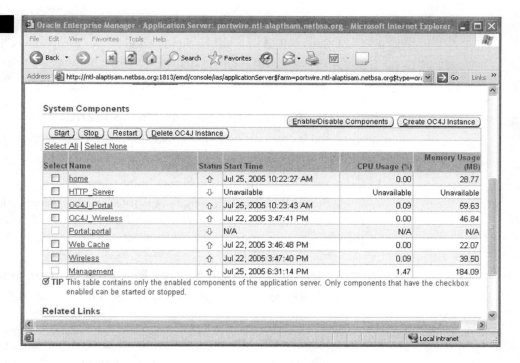

FIGURE 3-5

The OracleAS
Middle-Tier
Instance Home
Page

The corresponding System Components Table in the Application Server home page for the OracleAS infrastructure instance will show the following components:

- HTTP Server
- OC4J_Security
- OID

Managing the Application Server Instances

You can start, stop, and restart the Application Server instances through the Application Server Control tool. A summary of the steps you need to take is given in the following subsections.

Starting the Application Server Components

The previous section showed how to start the various Application Server components using the *opmnctl* utility. You can also start and stop the various components through the Application Server Control. Here are the steps:

1. Go to the Application Server Instance home page.
2. Click **Start All** to start all the Application Server components listed in the System components table, in the middle of the home page. You can start all enabled components but not any disenabled ones.

Stopping the Application Server Components

You can stop the individual components (all except the management component) in the following way:

1. Go to the Oracle Application Server home page.
2. Click **Stop All.** All system components listed in the System components table are stopped, except the management components. Of course, you use the *opmnctl* command to stop OPMN itself.

Restarting the Application Server Instance Components

To restart the Oracle Application Server and all of its components, follow these steps:

1. Go to the Oracle Application Server Instance home page.
2. Click **Restart All**. All components that are *currently running* will be restarted. If a component is down currently, it won't be started automatically by the **Restart All** command. Disabled components won't be automatically started either.

Obtaining Information about the Host Computer

You can check the host server performance by following these steps:

1. Navigate to the OracleAS Instance home page.
2. Click the name of your host server in the General section.

You'll be in the Host home page, where you can review various aspects of its performance.

The Application Server Control Home Pages

You can think of the Application Server Control as consisting of two components: the Application Server Control Console and the Enterprise Manager home pages. The Console, of course, makes everything possible—it enables access through the

Web browser and provides access to the Enterprise Manager home pages. The home pages provide a quick high-level view of the OracleAS environment and let you drill down to get detailed performance and diagnostic information.

Application Server Control provides the OEM home pages to enable you to manage the Oracle Application Server at different levels, such as the following:

- A single component of the application server instance
- A single application server instance
- An Application Server Cluster

You can manage the Oracle Application Server at the component, instance, and cluster level.

The Application Server Control Console provides you the following home pages, each designed to help you manage the Application Server at a particular level:

- The Application Server Farm page helps you manage all the OracleAS instances that are part of an OracleAS Farm. You can manage all OracleAS instances that belong to a single repository from here.
- The Application Server Instance home page is used for managing an entire Application Server instance. You can get to this page from the OracleAS Farm page.
- The Application Server Component home page is used for managing, monitoring, and configuring a single component of the Application Server (e.g., the Oracle HTTP Server). You can drill down to this page from the OracleAS Instance home page.

The three Application Server home pages are examined in the following subsections.

The OracleAS Farm Page

The OracleAS Farm page, shown in Figure 3-4, will be your default start page when you invoke the Application Server Control, under the following two conditions:

- When you install one or more components that require the use of the OracleAS Infrastructure
- When more than one OracleAS instance uses a common configuration repository

The Application Server Control gets its information from the DCM repository, and if that repository information indicates that the OracleAS instance is part of a

farm, then the entire farm is displayed. You can review the $ORACLE_
home/config/ias_properties file and look for the *InfraStructureUse=true* line,
to confirm this.

on the **Ö**ob

*The common configuration repository for an OracleAS Farm could be a
database-based Metadata Repository or a file-based repository.*

You can monitor and manage a single Application Server instance, or an entire
application server Cluster, using the OracleAS Farm page. You can also perform the
following tasks using the Farm page:

- Create and manage new OracleAS Clusters.
- Drill down to the OracleAS Instance home page for any instance.

The OracleAS Instance Home Page

You can use the Application Server home page, shown in Figure 3-6, to perform the
following tasks:

FIGURE 3-6

The Application
Server Home
Page

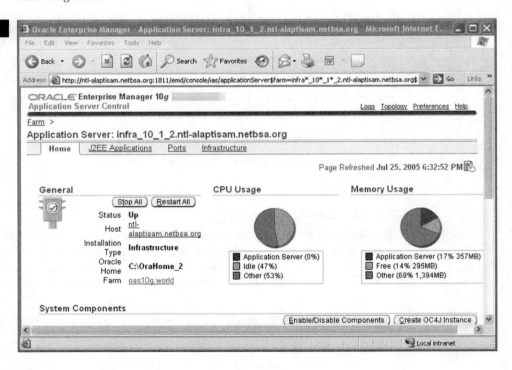

- Start and stop the Application Server instance. However, the recommended way to start and stop the OracleAS instance is by using the *opmnctl* utility, as explained previously in this chapter.
- Monitor the overall performance of the Oracle Application Server.
- Review the status and performance of the various components of the Oracle Application Server.
- Configure the OracleAS components.

on the
job

An OracleAS instance's status is shown as "down" when any of the enabled components is down, even if all the other components are running.

The following list shows how you can navigate around the Application Server home page:

- Click **J2EE Applications** to view the applications deployed across all the OC4J instances within this Oracle Application Server.
- Click **Ports** to view and modify the ports used by the various Oracle Application Server components.
- Click **Infrastructure** to configure Identity Management, Grid Control Management, or OracleAS Farm Repository Management.
- Click **Enable/Disable Components** to choose whether the components appear in the list of system components and whether you can start them and stop them as part of a server wide *Start All* or *Stop All* directive.
- Click **Logs** to search the Oracle Application Server log files.
- Click **Topology** to use the Topology Viewer, which provides a graphical view of the Application Server configuration in the OracleAS Farm.

The Application Server home page contains the *System components* table, which lists all the components of that OracleAS instance. You can check the status of the components from the System Components table. By selecting an OracleAS component in the System Components table, you can get the home page for that component.

The OracleAS Component Home Page

The component pages could vary for the various components, but it will contain the following common elements:

■ A general information section showing the current status of the component

■ Performance information such as CPU and memory usage

■ Component-specific details—for example, the HTTP Server home page contains a virtual hosts tab, and the OC4J home page shows all deployed applications

■ Links to configuration pages for the individual components

CERTIFICATION OBJECTIVE 3.04

The Correct Startup and Shutdown Sequence

When you have both an infrastructure and one or more middle-tier instances, you must stop and start the various parts of the OracleAS framework in a particular order. For example, if you don't start the Oracle database that contains the Metadata Repository, the OID can't function, and all the components that rely on the OID will, of course, fail to work. Let's look at the startup and shutdown sequence in the following subsections.

The Startup Sequence

Here is the correct order of starting the various parts of the OracleAS framework:

1. Make sure that the listener for the Metadata Repository database is running. If not, start it.

2. Start the Oracle database hosting the Metadata Repository.

3. Start the OracleAS Infrastructure instance with the *opmnctl startall* command.

4. Start the Application Server Control interface belonging to the OracleAS Infrastructure instance, using the *emctl start iasconsole* command.

5. Start each of the OracleAS middle-tier instances using the *opmnctl startall* command.

6. Start each of the middle-tier instances Application Server Control, using the *emctl start iasconsole* command.

The Shutdown Sequence

When you have both an infrastructure and one or more middle-tier instance, this is the correct order in which you stop the various components:

1. Stop each of the middle-tier instance's Application Server Control Console, using the *emctl stop iasconsole* command.

2. Stop each of the OracleAS Middle-Tier instances using the *opmnctl stopall* command.

3. Stop the Application Server Control Console belonging to the OracleAS Infrastructure instance, using the *emctl stop iasconsole* command.

4. Stop the OracleAS Infrastructure instance with the *opmnctl stoptall* command.

5. Stop the Oracle database hosting the Metadata Repository using the following command from SQL*Plus:

```
SQL> shutdown immediate
```

6. Make sure that the listener for the Metadata Repository database is stopped, using the following command:

```
$ lsnrctl stop
```

✓ TWO-MINUTE DRILL

Oracle Process Management and Notification Server

❑ OPMN performs the process management in the Oracle Application Server.

❑ All OracleAS components except the Metadata Repository (database) and the Application Server Control are managed by the OPMN.

❑ OPMN consists of three components: Oracle Process Manager (PM), Oracle Notification Server, and the PM modules.

❑ Oracle Process Manager is the centralized process mechanism for all the OracleAS components and uses the *opmn.xml* configuration file. The Oracle Notification Server carries message notifications among the OracleAS components.

❑ The PM modules are responsible for component-specific process management.

❑ OPMN event scripts sets off an event when a particular OPMN event starts, stops, or crashes.

❑ You debug OPMN commands using the *opmnctl* debug command.

❑ You use the *opmnctl* command with the *startall*, and *stopall* options to start and stop all OPMN processes.

❑ You must use the opmnctl tool to start and stop the infrastructure and middle-tier OPMN processes separately.

The Application Server Control Interface

❑ There is a separate Application Server Control Console for each OracleAS instance.

❑ You can use the Application Server Control Console at the instance, component, and cluster levels.

❑ You can use the Grid Control to manage all the OracleAS instances.

❑ You can diagnose component performance, configure the components, and deploy applications through the Application Server Control Console.

❑ The Management Agent fetches data for the Application Server Control.

❑ The Management Agent is automatically started when you start the Application Server Control using the emctl tool.

❑ You use the *emctl start iasconsole* and *emctl stop iasconsole* commands to start and stop the Application Server Control Console.

❑ The *emdctl* utility lets you find out the status of the Management Agent.

❑ The Application Server Control uses the OPMN to start and stop the OracleAS instances.

❑ The Oracle Dynamic Monitoring Service (DMS) enables you to measure application performance.

❑ Distributed Configuration Management (DCM) helps you manage and propagate configuration for multiple OracleAS instances belonging to an OracleAS Farm.

❑ DCM also lets you propagate applications to other instances in an OracleAS Cluster.

❑ You can store the DCM Repository in an OracleAS Metadata Repository or in the file system.

❑ You use the *dcmtl* utility to manage the DCM.

❑ You use a *dcmtl* shell to execute several *dcmtl* commands at once.

❑ The Application Server Control Console consists of the Emagent, Perl, and Java processes.

❑ You can use the Hi-Av tool in three formats: grid view, instance view, and the routing view.

❑ The OracleAS Topology Viewer provides a graphical, real-time view of all OracleAS processes.

❑ You have access to three types of home pages in the Application Server Control: the Application Server Farm page, the Application Server Control home page, and the Application Server Component home page.

❑ The Farm page is the default home page when you use one or more OracleAS instances that need to use the infrastructure, or when multiple OracleAS instances use a common configuration repository.

Additional OracleAS 10g Tools

❑ OracleAS Hi-Av Tool (iHAT) provides a real-time view of the entire system and displays all processes managed by a set of one or more OPMN servers.

❑ There are two types of formats in which you can use the Hi-Av Tool — grid view and instance view.

❑ The *grid view* shows a live picture of all OracleAS components.

❑ The *instance view* shows the management topology of the system.

❑ You can use the Topology Viewer to get a graphical, real-time view of all OracleAS processes.

The Correct Startup and Shutdown Sequence

❑ You must start and stop the individual OracleAS components in a certain order.

❑ You must first start the OracleAS Metadata Repository database.

❑ The Oracle listener process must be started next.

❑ The OracleAS infrastructure must be started next.

❑ Start the Application Server Control Console belonging to the OracleAS Infrastructure instance.

❑ Start the OracleAS Middle-Tier instances.

❑ Start the Application Server Control Consoles belonging to the OracleAS Middle-Tier instances.

❑ To shut down the OracleAS framework, reverse the preceding sequence.

SELF TEST

1. The management agent performs the following task:
   - A. Starts and stops the Application Server Control.
   - B. Fetches data for the Application Server Control.
   - C. Manages the Application Server Control Console.
   - D. Monitors the Application Server Control Console.

2. Which set of home pages does the Oracle Application Server have?
   - A. Farm page, Instance home page, and Component home page
   - B. Farm page, Cluster page, and Component home page
   - C. Farm page, Server home page, and Component home page
   - D. Farm page, Group home page, and Component home page

3. What is the job of the PM modules?
   - A. To carry notifications to the Oracle Notification Server
   - B. To perform component-specific process management
   - C. To perform component-specific project management
   - D. To start the OPMN process

4. To start the WebCacheAdmin process, which of the following commands would you use?
   - A. opmnctl startproc WebCacheAdmin
   - B. opmnctl ias-component=WebCacheAdmin
   - C. opmnctl startproc ias-component=OC4J_Wireless
   - D. opmnctl startproc process-type=WebCacheAdmin

5. Which of the following is the correct startup sequence for an OracleAS infrastructure instance?
   - A. Start Database, start Application Server Control, opmnctl start
   - B. Start Application Server control, Start Database, opmnctl startall
   - C. Start Database, opmnctl start, Start Application Server Control
   - D. Start Database, opmnctl startall, Start Application Server Control

6. What does the Oracle Dynamic Monitoring Service (DMS) do?

   A. Monitors application performance.

   B. Monitors OracleAS Instance performance.

   C. Monitors the OID performance.

   D. Monitors the Application Server Control performance.

7. Which of the following helps in the creation and management of OracleAS Clusters and Farms?

   A. DMS

   B. DCM

   C. OPM

   D. EMS

8. Application Server Control consists of the following set of processes:

   A. emagent, Perl, and Java

   B. Perl, Java, and OC4J

   C. emagent, Perl, and DCM

   D. emagent, Java, and DCM

9. Which one of the following can you *not* do with the help of the *opmnctl* utility?

   A. Start and stop instances and components.

   B. Start and stop OracleAS Clusters.

   C. Create OC4J Instances.

   D. Check status of instance and components.

10. Which of the following tools lets you change the ias_admin user's password?

   A. dcmtl

   B. emctl

   C. opmnctl

   D. emdctl

SELF TEST ANSWERS

1. ☑ **B** is correct because the management agent's job is to fetch data for the Application Server Control.
   ☒ **A, C,** and **D** are incorrect because the management agent isn't involved in the management of the Application Server Control Console.

2. ☑ **A** is correct because the three home pages are the Farm page, the Instance home page, and the Component home page.
   ☒ **B, C,** and **D** are wrong because they are missing one of the home pages mentioned in the correct answer.

3. ☑ **B** is correct because the PM modules perform component-specific process management.
   ☒ **A** is wrong because the Oracle Notification Server carries the notifications to the PM modules, not the other way around. **C** refers to project management instead of process management, so it's wrong. **D** is wrong because the PM modules aren't used in OPMN process startup and shutdown.

4. ☑ **D** is correct because it uses the process-type clause with the opmnctl command. Because the WebCacheAdmin is a process that's a part of the WebCache component, you must use the process-type clause here, not the ias-component clause.
   ☒ **A** is wrong because it uses the *startproc* clause without the *process-type* clause. **B** is wrong because it's missing the startproc clause, and also because the ias-component clause is used for starting an entire component, not a process that's only a part of the component (WebCacheAdmin is a part of the WebCache process). **C** is wrong because it uses the ias-component clause instead of the process-type clause.

5. ☑ **C** is correct because you start the three services in that order.
   ☒ **A, B,** and **D** are wrong because they show the wrong sequences.

6. ☑ **A** is correct because the Oracle Dynamic Service monitors application performance, with default as well as customizable performance metrics.
   ☒ **B, C,** and **D** are wrong alternatives because DMS has nothing to do with monitoring the OID, the OracleAS instance, or the Application Server Control performance.

7. ☑ **B** is correct because Distributed Configuration Management (DCM) helps in creating OracleAS Clusters and Farms.
   ☒ **A** is wrong because DMS is concerned with application performance metrics. **C** and **D** are wrong because they specify nonexistent services.

8. ☑ **A** is correct because the Application Server Control consists of those three processes.
    ☒ **B, C,** and **D** are wrong because they're missing one of the three processes listed by the correct answer.

9. ☑ **C** is correct because you can't create an OC4J instance with the help of the *opmnctl* utility. You create OC4J instance with the Application Server Control or with the DCM tool (*dcmtl*).
    ☒ **A, B,** and **D** are wrong because you can perform all of those tasks through the *opmnctl* utility.

10. ☑ **B** is correct because you change the *ias_admin* user's password with the *emctl* utility.
    ☒ **A, C,** and **D** are wrong because you can't change the ias_admin user's password with any of these three utilities.

Part II

Access Control and Identity Management

4

Managing the Oracle Internet Directory

T his chapter deals with the Oracle Internet Directory (OID), which is Oracle's implementation of a Lightweight Directory Access Protocol (LDAP). I first briefly discuss the basic concepts behind the use of directories and also explain LDAP. I then explain OID and show how to use various management tools to support OID in your organization.

CERTIFICATION OBJECTIVE 4.01

Directories and the LDAP

Large organizations these days have both internal and Web-based applications to manage. It quickly becomes an administrative nightmare to manage users and their privileges on all these various applications. Centralized directories are increasingly being seen as the best way to manage multiple systems within an organization. A directory lets you organize information so it's easy to find. Directories can be offline or online. For example, organizations maintain phone and address books for their employees in directories. They may also create directories for storing corporate white papers.

Online directories enable efficient searching and are easily updateable. You can include various types of information in an online directory, including both security information and partner-related information. An online directory can be used for tasks such as helping an employee find information about other employees, locating a user's mail server, and storing users' credentials and privileges information. A database application can use the directory to find out about a user's roles and privileges. Directories are cost effective and fast and serve as centralized integration points for applications and services.

Although a directory is similar to a database, there are fundamental differences, which are summarized here:

■ A directory is primarily designed to handle large amounts of simple information such as phone numbers and addresses. A typical transactional relational database, on the hand, is geared toward processing large transactions using huge amounts of data, sometimes with several intermediate data processing steps.

- Unlike a database, which stores data in the form of rows in a table, a directory stores data in the form of *entries*, each of which has a number of attributes and values for the attributes.

- A directory is a hierarchical database optimized for reading and retrieving data, unlike a relational database, which is usually used for both retrieving data as well as intensive writing of transactions.

- Directory servers are designed to be location independent, serving the same information no matter which server you query the directory from. Database servers, unless they are distributed databases, are located on a specific server.

LDAP

Organizations end up with a large number of special-purpose directories, each with a different organization of information. This makes it quite hard to synthesize the information contained in the various directories. There is a high cost attached to managing a large number of disparate directories, with the risk of encountering inconsistent data, as well as a high risk of security breaches, because key information is scattered over many directories. This leads to the need for a centralized directory based on uniform standards, in order to support the entire organization's needs.

Lightweight Directory Access Protocol (LDAP) is a standard protocol that facilitates directory access and provides a common language for LDAP clients and servers to communicate. LDAP is a popular industry standard, and Oracle has its own implementation of this standard. Information that has been managed in multiple systems and formats can be brought under one umbrella using a directory service such as LDAP. You can replace all your tnsnames.ora files on clients and manage user connectivity, authorization, and security with the help of the LDAP directory services. The LDAP directory can provide solid password policy management, data privacy, data integrity, and strong authentication and authorization protocols.

When users are registered and maintained in an LDAP repository, they are referred to as *shared schemas* or *schema-independent users*. When an LDAP-registered user connects to a specific database, the database will ask the LDAP server for confirmation of the user's identity and the roles that should be assigned to the user upon connection. Thus, in a database with several hundred users for a certain application, you need to create only one schema to manage the application. The individual user will be registered in the centralized directory, and when the user connects to the database, he or she will be assigned this common schema.

LDAP is a lightweight implementation of the International Standards Organization (ISO) X500 standard for directory services. Because it requires very little client-side software, it's an ideal protocol for Internet applications. The latest version of LDAP, Version 3, was adopted as an Internet standard in December of 1997. You can simplify directory management with LDAP, because it provides the entire organization with an identical standards-based interface to deal with an extensible directory service. A summary of the benefits provided by an LDAP-based directory service is given in the following paragraphs.

By the consolidation of enterprise-wide data, instead of multiple special-purpose directories, you end up with a single LDAP-based directory. This both reduces administrative overhead and enhances data security, by reducing the duplication of sensitive data.

An LDAP-based directory is mainly meant for the reading of data by large numbers of users, unlike a database, which usually has a large number of transactions that include updating and inserting data. Using LDAP you can cache and index the data to improve performance. Here's a summary of the key benefits gained by using LDAP-based directories:

- *Distributed servers*   You can replicate versions of LDAP servers among multiple servers, thus providing high availability of the directory server.
- *Standards based*   LDAP provides standard interfaces for C and Java and supports PERL, TCL, Python, PHP, VB, and other commonly used programming languages.
- *Scalability*   LDAP servers are highly scalable.
- *Security*   LDAP has built-in authentication mechanisms as well as means to ensure secure transmission of data.

LDAP Components

In a traditional database, data is stored in the form of rows in a (relational) table. An LDAP directory doesn't use tables. It instead uses a hierarchical tree—called a *Directory Information Tree* (DIT)—to store its data, which are in the form of *entries*.

You uniquely identify each entry in the DIT of an online directory by a *distinguished name* (DN). The DN tells you exactly where an entry is situated in the directory hierarchy (directory information tree).

Entries consist of *attributes*, which are the properties that define each entry. For example, an entry called *persons* may have attributes such as first name, last name, title, address, and phone number. You can define an entry's structure with the help of an *object class*, which is a set of attributes. Each entry in the directory is assigned an object class—some of the properties of an object class can be optional, whereas others are mandatory. Thus, each entry is also an instance of an *object class*. Of course, if two entries are assigned the same object class, they'll be sharing an identical set of attributes.

Entries

The set of information pertaining to a directory object is called an entry. A directory object could be an employee or a shared network resource, for example. As mentioned earlier, you use a distinguished name (DN) to uniquely identify a directory entry. A distinguished name of an entry consists of all the names of the parent entries, all the way to the root entry. You can tell where exactly a certain entry is in the directory hierarchy with the help of its distinguished name. The *directory information tree* (DIT) is thus simply a tree-like structure made up of all the DNs of the entries.

Let's say you have an employee named Sam Alapati working in the Sales division of the Generalco Company's UK office. The employee Sam Alapati can be located as follows in the Generalco Company's DIT. Note that, by convention, you start with the lowest directory information tree component on the left, the next higher component next, and so on, until you move up the common node or the *root* entry.

```
dn=cn=Sam Alapati,ou=Sales,c=uk,o=GeneralCo
```

In the preceding the common name (cn) of the employee is Sam Alapati. Sam Alapati works in the Sales organization unit (ou). The country (c) is UK, and the organization (o) name is GeneralCo. Employee Sam Alapati will have his attributes, such as email address, jpeg photo, and so forth under the Sam Alapati entry.

If you also have another employee with the same name working in the finance division of the GeneralCo company's US office, that employee's entry would look as follows, again starting from the common root node at the top of the inverted tree structure:

```
dn=cn=Sam Alapati ou=finance c=us o=GeneralCo
```

The distinguished name (dn or DN) of an entry uniquely identifies each entry in the Directory Information Tree. Thus, the following two DNs refer to two different entries in the GeneralCo organization:

```
dn=cn=Sam Alapati ou=sales c=uk o=GeneralCo
dn=cn=Sam Alapati ou=finance c=us o=GeneralCo
```

A *relative distinguished name* (RDN) is the lowest and the most granular component in a DN, with no qualifying entry names underneath it that address it. In the case where dn = cn = Sam Alapati, ou = sales, c = uk, o = generalco, the RDN is cn = Sam Alapati. The RDN for the entry right above Sam Alapati's RDN is ou = sales and the RDN for the next higher entry is c = uk. A DN, then, is nothing but a chain of related RDNs, with each RDN being separated by a comma. By using the DN of an entity, you can easily identify its exact location in the overall DIT of an organization.

Attributes

Attributes are specific information items attached to an entry. For example, the entry Sam Alapati in the previous examples might have attributes such as title, phone number, address, jpeg photo, and so on. You can have two types of OID LDAP attributes: those that are application specific, and those that are primarily meant for operational purposes. Let's look at the two types of LDAP attributes briefly.

Operational Attributes   Operational attributes provide information about the operation of the OID. The OID automatically creates these attributes when you add entries to it, to help you in searching for them later on. Here are some of the important operational attributes:

- *creatorsName*   Name of the person who created the entry
- *createTimestamp*   When the entry was created
- *modifersname*   Name of the person who modified the entry
- *modifyTimestamp*   When an entry was modified

Application Attributes Application attributes are created and maintained by the OID users for their directory usage and have nothing to do with the operation of the OID itself. For example, the Title, Street, and TelephoneNumber attributes are typical application attributes used in the OID.

Table 4-1 shows some common LDAP entity attributes. Oracle Internet Directory implements all standard LDAP attributes. Note that all attributes must follow a specific syntax. For example, you must use a string of numbers with the appropriate spaces and hyphens for the TelephoneNumber attribute.

Because various applications, including third-party applications, can use the OID directory, you should use only well-known attributes in the various RDNs that are part of the DIT structure of an organization. Following are some of the commonly used attributes for applications that use the OID:

- *c* A country's name
- *dc* A DNS domain name component
- *o* An organization's name
- *ou* Name of an organizational unit

Attribute Type	Attribute String	Description
authPassword	pw	Authentication password
commonName	cn	Common name for an entry (e.g., John Smith)
company	co	Name of the company
country	c	Name of the country
domainComponent	dc	DN of a component in a Domain Name System (e.g., dc = uk, dc = acme, dc = com)
organization	o	Name of the organization (e.g., o = mycompany)
organizationalUnitName	ou	Name of an organizational unit (e.g., Marketing)
Owner	owner	DN of the person who owns the entry (e.g., cn = John Smith, ou = Finance, o = Acme, c = uk)
Surname	sn	Last name of a person
mailAlternateAddress		Alternate mailing address

TABLE 4-1 Common LDAP Attributes

Some attributes have *options*, meaning that you can specify multiple values for the same attribute. For example, if an employee has two addresses, you can use the address attribute's options feature to store both the addresses, to better help you in searching for and comparing attributes.

on the job

Oracle Internet Directory caches common entries in the cache memory, thus enhancing the performance of OID operations.

Object Classes

An *object class* is a named *group* of attributes. You assign attributes to an entry by assigning an object class to the entry. Thus, an entry is an instance of an object class. An object class has a set of *mandatory* attributes and could have some *optional* attributes as well. You don't have to supply values for the optional attributes.

Let's say you are defining a new entry, which needs attributes like commonName (cn) and surname (sn). The organizationalPerson object class includes both of these attributes as mandatory attributes. The organizationalPerson object class also includes the optional attributes telephoneNumber, uid, streetAddress, and userPassword. Thus, you have to provide values only for the two mandatory attributes of the organizationalPerson class—commonName and surname. You aren't required to submit values for the other optional attributes of the organizationalPerson class. A *subclass* is an object class derived from another object class called the superclass—organizationalPerson is a subclass of the object class person. The object class *person*, for example, *is* the superclass of the object class *organizationalPerson*. A subclass inherits all the superclass attributes.

Directory Naming Contexts

A *directory naming context* is a subtree of a DIT that resides entirely on one directory server. The directory naming context must begin at an entry that serves as the top of the subtree and extends downward to the leaf entries. A directory naming context could be a single individual entry, or, of course, the entire DIT. Note that to enable users to discover specific directory-naming contexts, you publish those naming contexts in OID (i.e., insert these entries) by using either the Oracle Directory Manager or the ldapmodify utility.

It's common to use a domain name-based schema to represent your DIT. Using the domain-name scheme, the root of a DIT can be expressed as the following, for example:

```
dc=us,dc=somecompany,dc=com
```

CERTIFICATION OBJECTIVE 4.02

Oracle Internet Directory

Oracle Internet Directory (OID) is an Oracle application that's part of Oracle's Identity Management infrastructure that provides enterprise-wide security services. However, OID isn't a security product but rather an enterprise data management product. The other main components of the Identity Management infrastructure are features such as Oracle Delegated Administration Service, OracleAS Single Sign-On, and OracleAS Certificate Authority. OID is a general-purpose directory service that lets you manage user and network information. It uses the LDAP Version 3 as the foundation, but adds high performance and availability features to it.

OID provides directory services to both the Oracle database and OracleAS 10g. OID is a powerful product that can support millions of entries and a high number of user accesses on a single OID directory node because it's based on the powerful Oracle Database 10g version database. In addition, you can also use Oracle's Real Application Clusters to enhance scalability and availability. You can provide the following three levels of user authentication in an Oracle Internet Directory:

You must be aware that OID is primarily a data management mechanism that happens to store security data, rather than a security tool, although it's part of the Oracle Identity Management infrastructure.

- ■ Password based
- ■ Anonymous
- ■ Secure Sockets layer (SSL), with the help of certificates

OID provides the following security benefits:

- ■ Using SSL's cryptographic capabilities, OID ensures data integrity during transmission.
- ■ Using SSL's data encryption capabilities, OID ensures data confidentiality.
- ■ Using algorithms such as the MD4 algorithm, OID ensures password protection.
- ■ OID provides support for access control for reads, writes, and updates of individual attributes for OID entries.

Although you can place the OID in any Oracle database, Oracle Corporation recommends strongly that you place it in a dedicated Oracle database. You can locate this database either on the same server as the OID installation or on a different server.

How Oracle Internet Directory Works

Let's trace the way the OID processes a user's search request for an entry in the DIT:

1. If the user uses SSL, then the user's search request is SSL encrypted; otherwise it's sent in clear text.
2. Whether the user issues the command through the Oracle Directory Manager or a command line tool, ultimately a C function in the C API is invoked.
3. The C API uses the LDAP protocol to send a request to a directory server instance to connect the user to the OID.
4. The OID Server authenticates the user, a process known as *binding*. The server also checks the Access Control Lists (ACLs) to ascertain that the user is authorized to perform the search.
5. The directory server converts the search request from LDAP to Oracle Call Interface (OCI)/Oracle Net Services and sends it to the Metadata Repository, located in the Oracle Database.
6. The Oracle Database retrieves the information that was requested and passes it to the OID server using Oracle Net. The OID server will then pass the information to the client using LDAP, again using the C API.

Security Benefits of OID

OID enables secure directory information management by providing the following types of user authentication:

- Anonymous
- Password based
- Certificate based, using the secure sockets layer (SSL)

The OID stores two types of credentials: passwords to authenticate users to the OID and passwords to authenticate users to the various Oracle components.

OID protects user passwords using the MD4 algorithm, which is a one-way hash function that produces a 128-bit hash. You can also use other encryption algorithms besides the MD4, which is the default encryption algorithm for the OID.

In addition to providing for the types of user authentication described in the foregoing list, OID provides the following security features:

- *Access control*   You can control the users' accesses at a fine-grained level by controlling their ability to read, update, or insert data at the attribute level.
- *Data integrity and confidentiality*   By using SSL's secure message digest, OID ensures that data hasn't been tampered with (deleted or updated) during its transmission. By using SSL encryption procedures, OID protects unauthorized reading of data.
- *Centralized storage of user's authentication credentials*   OID can store the passwords for authenticating users to the directory itself as well as the passwords for authenticating users to other Oracle components.

Note that users can store non-Oracle authentication credentials if the non-Oracle applications are directory enabled.

Hosted and Non-Hosted Environments

OID can be used in two different environments. The first, known as a *hosted* environment, is one in which an enterprise hosts the OID for other enterprises. The hosting enterprise is known as the *default subscriber,* and the enterprises that use the host's OID services are called *subscribers.* The host enterprise's OID administrator may grant limited domain or application-specific administrative privileges to the subscriber users.

A *non-hosted* environment has only a single default subscriber, which is the host itself. OID exists to serve just the hosting enterprise, and there aren't any subscribers. The non-hosted environment is known as the default subscriber.

Default Directory Information Tree

Upon installation of the OID components, there's a default *schema* and a default *Directory Information Tree* (DIT) that are also created automatically so that you can administer various Oracle components. The *directory schema* contains information about how data is organized in the DIT. It contains *metadata* for object classes, attributes, matching rules, and syntax.

A directory schema helps reduce the duplication of data and contains the following:

- Rules about the kinds of objects you can store
- Rules for how directory servers and clients treat information during various operations
- Help applications to maintain the integrity and quality of the data stored in the directory
- Help applications to access and modify directory objects

You can change the default DIT later on, to suit your enterprise's needs. During installation, the following items are installed by the Oracle Universal Installer:

- *Base Schema Objects*   These are the basic object classes and attributes that the OID needs to use.
- *Root Oracle Context*   This contains product-specific information about all the enterprise-wide Oracle products.
- *Default Identity Management Realm*   An Identity Management realm limits the scope of identity management policies. All users within an Identity Management realm in an organization are managed by identical identity management policies. By default, all Oracle products use the default Identity Management realm. There is one default Identity Management realm in the OID, and all Oracle products initially make use of that realm.
- *Identity Management Realm–Specific Oracle Context*   This contains the Oracle component data that is specific to a particular Identity Management realm.
- *Default Password Policy*   This is the set of password policies applicable to all the users under an Identity Management realm.

OID Architecture

The OID service is implemented as an application running on an Oracle database. OID server processes use standard Oracle Net services to talk to the database, and clients communicate with the OID service using the standard LDAP protocol. An OID node is a set of processes that performs the work of the OID, including receiving client requests for data and providing the data to them. An OID node consists of the following components:

■ *The OID Directory Server Instance*   One or more OID directory instances are connected to the Oracle database, also called the directory store, which is the collection of OID data.

■ *The Oracle Database*   The OID repository or store of data is maintained in an Oracle database.

In addition to the two basic components of the Oracle Internet Directory Node — the OID directory server instance and the Oracle database — you may also have an optional Oracle Directory Replication Server. The oracle to ensure continuous availability of data Oracle Directory Replication sends changes to the replication server in other OID servers.

In addition, the OID node needs the OID Monitor utility that controls the OID server processes, and the OID Control utility, which you use to start and stop the OID Server processes. The various OID components are presented in the following subsections.

The OID Directory Server Instance

Every OID node has to have at least one OID Directory Server instance running. A node can have several OID directory server instances connected to the same repository database. The OID directory server instance is the workhorse of OID, and it performs the following functions:

■ Listen for LDAP client requests for connections to OID on specific TCP/IP ports.

■ Connect to the Oracle database and retrieve information from there.

■ Return the retrieved information to the client that requested it.

The OID directory server instance has the following components:

■ The OID Listener and Dispatcher Process (the OID Listener and Dispatcher process listens to client requests for connections to the OID server)

■ Oracle Directory Server Processes

■ Database connections

Note the following things about the Directory Server instance:

■ There can be multiple Directory Server instances on a node, each of them using a different port to service user requests.

■ Each Directory Server instance has one dispatcher process.

■ Each Directory Server instance has one or more server processes.

Oracle Net Services are used for connections among the OID Control Utility, the OID Monitor, and the Oracle Directory Server instance, and the LDAP is used for connections between the Oracle Directory Manager (and the Oracle Directory Replication Server) and the Oracle Directory Server instance.

Architecture of the Directory Server Instance   I briefly describe the architecture of an OID Directory Server instance in this section. OID Listener/ Dispatcher listens for requests from LDAP clients at a specified port. Each OID server instance must have one dispatcher process.

The Oracle Directory *Server processes* perform the directory work involved by connecting the database (Metadata Repository). You can configure the Directory Server to use multiple server processes, although the default number of server processes is one (1). The number of server processes created is determined by the configuration parameter ORCLSERVERPROCS.

Each of the server processes maintains a *database connection*. The configuration parameter ORCLMAXCC determines the number of database connections from each server process, and the default value is two (2). The server process connects to the database server using the Oracle Net Services listener/dispatcher service to talk to the Oracle database.

The Oracle Directory Replication Server

The optional Oracle Directory *Replication Server*'s job is to replicate data between OID servers. You use the Oracle Directory replication server to provide continuous availability of data. Each OID node can have a single replication server. The replication server copies data from the primary OID on one node, also called the "supplier," to the secondary OID on a different node, called "consumer." The replication server on the supplier node will propagate the data to the replication server on the consumer node.

Note that the OID server replication is in fact implemented with database replication over Oracle Net, and the replication process has nothing to do with LDAP. Also remember that the replication can work one way or in both directions.

The Oracle Database Repository

All OID data is stored in the Metadata Repository database, which is part of the OAS infrastructure.

The OID Monitor Utility

The OID Monitor utility manages the OID server (and the replication server) processes by monitoring and terminating processes when necessary. All actual commands to start and stop the OID Server processes are issued through the OIDCTL utility, but the OID Monitor utility interprets and processes those commands. The activities of the OID monitor are logged in the $ORACLE_HOME/ldap/oidmon.log file. When an OID server process dies abnormally, the OID monitor restarts it as well. You issue the actual OID server management commands through the OID Control (OIDCTL) utility, but it's the OID Monitor utility that interprets and processes those commands.

The OIDCTL Utility

You manage the OID server instance, including the starting and stopping of the instance, by issuing commands through the OIDCTL utility. The OIDCTL utility communicates with OIDMON by sending messages to the OID server tables. It's important to understand that you don't actually start or stop anything with OIDCTL directly. You merely use the utility to instruct OIDMON to start or stop the OID server instance.

Configuration Parameters for the OID Instance

The configuration parameters for an OID server instance are stored in a configuration set entry, also known as the *configset entry*. The start command for the OID server refers to the configuration set entries when it starts the OID instance. The default configuration set entry is known as *configset0*. You can create customized configuration set entries later on if you so wish.

Managing OID

As mentioned earlier, you can start and stop the OID server processes through the OIDCTL utility. However, it's the OIDMON utility that actually performs the actions you specify through the OIDCTL utility. In addition to these, the following additional management tools are available:

- OID command-line tools
- Bulk tools
- LDAP command-line tools
- Oracle Directory Manager

In the following sections, let's learn how to use the various tools to manage an OID instance.

The OID Command-Line Tools

There are two main OID command-line tools: OIDMON and OIDCTL. As explained previously, the OID monitor interprets and processes the OIDCTL commands you must use to bring the OID Server instance up or down. So, let's start with an explanation of how to manage the OIDMON utility before looking at the OIDCTL tool.

Using the OIDMON Utility

In order to connect to an OID server to read data, first the OID Server instance must be started. Because the OIDMON utility performs the actual work of managing the OID instance, this means that you must start the OID Monitor prior to starting the instance. Thus, the proper sequence for starting the OID server instance is as follows:

- Start the OID Monitor process first, using the OIDMON utility.
- Start the OID server instance process next, using the OIDCTL utility.

You can't connect to an OID server without an OID server instance up and running.

If there is heavy user load, you can start multiple OID Server instances, all serving a single Oracle Directory Server. Each of the instances must use a separate port.

If you wish to shut down the OID server instance, you must reverse the preceding steps:

- Stop the OID server instance.
- Stop the OID Monitor process.

The OIDMON Utility   You use the command line executable *oidmon* to start and stop the OID Monitor process. Here's the syntax of the oidmon utility:

```
$ oidmon
usage: oidmon [connect=cc] [host=hostname] [sleep=nn] start | stop
options:
    connect=cc    The tnsname of the database to connect to for start/stop.
                  If connect string is not provided, it set by default to the
                  value of ORACLE_SID environment variable.
    host=hostname  Name of the (logical) host.
                   Defaults to hostname where oidmon is started.
    sleep=nn      The time interval in seconds at which the Monitor
                  monitors OID servers. If sleeptime is not provided,
                  it is set by default to 10 seconds.
    start | stop Start or Stop the Monitor.
o
```

Starting and Stopping the OID Monitor As you can see, the first three parameters—*connect*, *host*, and *sleep*—are *optional*. Thus, you can start and stop the OID Monitor on your server (using default net service name and host and sleep parameters) in this way:

```
$ oidmon start
$ oidmon stop
```

on the job

You must stop the OID Monitor only if you're shutting down the LDAP service altogether. If you have any OID directory or replication server instances running, you must leave the OID Monitor process running.

In the case of both starting and stopping the OID Monitor process, note that you won't get back any message on the command line after executing the command—you simply get the OS prompt back, indicating that the start or stop command was successfully carried out.

The OIDCTL Utility

It's through the OIDCTL utility that you issue your actual management commands to start and stop the OID server instance. You must make sure that the OID Monitor process is running before you start the OID server instance. Here's the syntax of the OIDCTL utility:

```
$ oidctl
usage: oidctl connect=cc server=ss instance=nn [host=hostname]
              [configset=cc] [flags=ff] start | stop
options:
connect=cc     The tnsname of the database to connect to for start/stop.
server=ss      The name of the OID server to be started/stopped.
               Server names must be either oidldapd/oidrepld/odisrv
instance=nn    The numerical value of the instance to be started/stopped.
               Instance value is mandatory for OIDLDAPD/OIDREPLD/ODISRV.
               Instance value MUST be < 0 and >= 1000.
host=hostname  Name of the (logical) host,
               where OID server to be started/stopped.
configset=cc   The numerical value of the configuration set to be used
               ONLY while starting a OID server.
               Configset value MUST be <= 0 and >= 1000.
flags=ff       The flags needed ONLY while starting the OID server.
               If the flags consist of UNIX-style keywords, then,
               those keyword-value pairs MUST be separated by spaces.
$
```

e x a m

ⓦ a t c h *Only the server and instance arguments are mandatory when you issue either the stop or the start commands.*

Note the following additional points about the syntax of the OIDCTL command:

- The *connect* attribute points to the net service name of the OracleAS Infrastructure database, which stores the OID data.

- The *server* attribute specifies the name of the OID server to be started or stopped.

- You can also use the *−p* attribute (not shown) to specify the port number for the OISD server instance. The default port number is 389 for non-SSL-enabled usage and 636 for SSL-enabled usage.

- You can use the additional *debug* attribute (not shown), to specify the debug level during instance startup.

- As you can see from the foregoing syntax output, you use the *configset* and *flags* parameters only when starting the OID server instance.

The OPMN monitors all OracleAS components, including the Oracle Internet Directory. However, it's important to understand that OPMN isn't directly aware of the OID Server instances, because it's aware only of the OIDMON. **OPMN directly starts and stops as well as monitors only OIDMON. OIDMON in turn is directly responsible for the starting, stopping, and monitoring of the OID Server instance.**

Starting an OID Server Instance

Here's a typical way you specify the OIDCTL utility to start an OID server instance:

```
$ oidctl connect=OID2 server=oidldapd instance=2 configset=3 debug 1024 start
```

Stopping an OID Server Instance

You use the same OIDCTL utility with which you started your OID server instance, to stop it as well. Again, server and instance are the *two mandatory attributes* that you should provide when you wish to stop an OID server instance. Here's an example that shows how to stop a running OID server instance:

on the job **The OID Monitor must be running before you issue the command to stop the OID server instance.**

```
$ oidctl connect=OID2 server=oidldapd instance=2 stop
```

The foregoing command will stop the OID server instance 2, connected to the repository database named OID2.

on the job **The instance number you provide in the oidctl stop command must specify a running OID server instance.**

Process Control of OID

In Chapter 3 you learned about OPMN and its command line interface, the opmnctl utility. OPMN works as a daemon process that continuously monitors all OracleAS component processes, including the OID. The OPMN installed in the

OracleAS infrastructure will monitor the OID, which is also part of the OracleAS Infrastructure. So, as is the case with all the other OracleAS components, you use the opmnctl utility to start and stop the OID component as well. Here's how you use the three tools, opmnctl, oidmon, and oidctl in relation to the management of the OID:

- The opmnctl utility is used to start the OID Server.
- The OIDMON process performs the process control of the OID Server instance(s).
- The oidctl utility is useful for performing tasks such as configuring additional OID Server instances.

Although you can start and stop the OID Server instance with the help of the oidctl utility, as was shown in the previous section, the *recommended way* to do so is through the opmnctl utility. The OPMN will communicate with the OIDMON to start, stop, and monitor the OID Server instances. Here are the ways you can use the opmnctl utility to start and stop the OID Server instance:

```
$ opmnctl startall
$ opmnctl startproc ias-component=OID
```

When you use the opmnctl utility to start the OID Server, OPMN will issue an *oidmon start* command internally, transparent to you. This will result in the starting of not just the OIS Server instance, but also any configured replication directory instances along with the Oracle Directory Integration and Provisioning server instance. Note that when you start the OID Server instance through OPMN, the OPMN process will ensure that the OIDMON process is running at all times. If OIDMON goes down for some reason, OPMN will automatically bring it up again.

When you plan to shut down the OID Server, the recommended approach is to use the opmnctl utility, in one of the following ways:

```
$opmnctl stopall
$opmnctl stopproc ias-component=OID
```

When you use either of the two commands listed here, OPMN will issue an internal *oidmon stop* command, which shuts down the OID Server instance, as well as the replication server and Oracle Directory Integration and Provisioning server instances.

OID Command-Line Tools for Managing Entries and Attributes

You can use the Oracle Directory Manager or the Oracle Application Server Control GUI-based tools to manage your OID. However, you also can use several command-line tools to manage data stored in the OID. The two types of command-line tools available to you—LDAP command-line tools and bulk tools—are discussed in the following subsections.

A Brief Introduction to LDIF Files

Before you start looking at the various OID command-line tools, let's review some general information about the LDAP Data Interchange Files (LDIF) that you need to employ when using the command-line tools.

LDIF Files

LDIF files are text files in a special format that you use to exchange data between LDAP servers. As you are aware by know, OID is one such LDAP directory. You must adhere to some special formatting rules when using LDIF files. For example, you terminate each line in an LDIF file with a line feed. You can have the following types of lines in an LDIF file:

- *Directive lines* are lines that don't begin with either a space or hash symbol (#) and specify data for an entry or an operation.
- *Continuation lines* start with a space and denote that the line is a continuation of the preceding line.
- *Blank lines* help separate entries.
- *Comment lines* begin with a hash (#) symbol.
- *Separator lines* start with a dash (-) and denote the end of an operation.

Your LDIF entry sequence must adhere to the Directory Information Tree (DIT), in a top-down fashion. List the child entries underneath the parent entries. All the attributes or object classes that you use for an entry must already exist in the schema.

LDIF files follow a specific format, shown here:

```
dn: distinguished_name
changetype: add|delete|modify|modrdn|moddn
attribute_type: attribute_value
...
objectClass: object_class_value
```

In the LDIF standard format, this is what the individual items stand for:

- *dn* refers to the *distinguished name* of the entry and all the information under the dn line, until you encounter a space, belonging to that entry. Note that you can refer to the distinguished name in either lowercase letters as here (dn) or in uppercase (DN). Here's an example of a dn:

```
dn: cn=Sam Alapati,ou=Sales,dc=company,dc=com
```

- *Changetype* refers to the operation you wish to perform on an entry—for example, add, delete, or modify a line.
- *Attribute_type* refers to a certain attribute type such as a cn and the value assigned to that attribute type. Here's an example, where the attribute_type is cn and the value is Sam Alapati:

```
cn: Sam Alapati
```

- *Objectclass* as an attribute refers to the entry's object class. You can have multiple objectclass directives. Here's one example:

```
objectClass: person
```

An LDIF File Example

Here's a simple example that shows a typical LDIF file format:

```
dn: cn=Sam Alapati,ou=Sales,o=Generalco, c=US
changetype: add
cn: Sam Alapati
sn: Alapati
mail: salapati@us.generalco.com
telephoneNumber: 999-999-9999
photo: \$ORACLE_HOME\emp\photos\salapati.jpg
objectClass: organizationalPerson
objectClass: person
objectClass: top
```

Note that the first line shows the DN of the entry. You can see that I'm adding this entry, because the second line shows that *changetype* is "add." You then have a series of *attribute:value* pairs, with the attributes being cn, sn, mail, telephoneNumber, and photo. You end the entry for Sam Alapati in this case with three different objectclass values for the entry in this example. To denote the end of the LDIF entry, you use a blank line at the very end.

To delete the entry you just added, you merely have to specify the DN of the new Sam Alapati entry and use "delete" as the value for the changetype directive:

```
dn: cn=Sam Alapati,ou=Sales,o=Generalco, c=US
changetype: delete
```

Modifying the DN of an Entry

Because the DN of an entry uniquely fixes the location of a particular directory entry in the DIT, modifying the DN of any entry will move the entry to a different node of the DIT. In order to modify rather than delete the DN for an entry, you use the changetype *moddn*. You must also provide the new RDNs where necessary. That is, you must provide the new parent DN for the user whose DN is being modified. In the following example, the entry Sam Alapati's department has changed from Sales to Finance. You now modify the new DN you had created earlier (dn: cn = Sam Alapati, ou = Sales, o = Generalco, c = US), to reflect this, as shown here:

```
dn: cn=Sam Alapati,ou=Sales,o=Generalco, c=US
changetype: moddn
newsuperior: ou=Finance,o=Generalco, c=US
```

Note the use of the *newsuperior* directive, which lets you specify the new parent DN for the Sam Alapati entry, whose original RDN was ou = Sales, o = Generalco, c = US. The new parent RDN is ou = Finance, o = Generalco, c = US.

LDAP Command-Line Tools

LDAP command-line tools let you directly create and update OID data stored in the Metadata Repository. You can modify both the OID entries as well as their attributes either by using standard files or files written in the *LDAP Data Interchange Format* (LDIF). The most common command-line tools for managing LDAP entries and their attributes are discussed in the following subsections.

ldapadd You use the *ldapadd* command, which works as an *LDAP Data Add Tool*, to add entries to the OID directory one entry at a time. The ldapadd command has the following syntax (I omitted several arguments that aren't mandatory, to keep the command example simple).

```
ldapadd [arguments] -f filename
```

The −f attribute provides the name of the LDIF file. Here's an example:

```
ldapadd -p 389 -h myhost -f myown.ldif
```

ldapaddmt You use the *ldapaddmt* command, a *multi-threaded LDAP Data Add Tool*, to add several entries to the OID concurrently. The *ldapaddmt* command is very similar to the *ldapadd* command in that you can use it to add entries, their object classes, attributes, and values to the directory. It is different from the *ldapadd* command in that it supports multiple threads for concurrently adding OID entries. Here's the syntax for the *ldapaddmt* command (again, simplified):

```
ldapaddmt -T number_of_threads -h host -p port -f filename
```

In the following example, the *ldapaddmt* command is given five threads to concurrently process the entries in the file testentries.ldif:

```
ldapaddmt -T 5 -h node1 -p 3000 -f testentries.ldif
```

ldapbind The *ldapbind* command works as an Authentication validation Tool, when you attempt to authenticate a client/user to a directory server. Here's the syntax for the *ldapbind* command, with three mandatory attributes: host (-h), binddn (-D), and password (-w). The *host* attribute refers to the host name (or IP address) of the OID server. The *binddn* attribute is the DN of the OID server user whom you are attempting to bind to the directory—for example, dn = cn = orcladmin—and the password attribute refers is the user password to bind to the directory.

```
ldapbind -h oid_hostname -D "binddn" -w password
```

Here's an example showing you how to use the *ldapbind* command:

```
ldapbind -h mycompany.com -D "cn-orcladmin" -w password -p adminpasswd
```

ldapcompare You use the *ldapcompare* command, which is classified as an Attribute Comparison Tool, to check whether an entry contains a specific attribute value. The tool helps you compare an attribute value you specify on the command line to the attribute value in the OID entry for that attribute. Here's the syntax for the *ldapcompare* command:

```
ldapcompare -h oid_hostname -D "binddn" -w password -a attribute_name -b
"basedn" -v "attribute_value"
```

Several of the attributes you pass with the *ldapcompare* command are optional (and aren't shown). However, the −v attribute is mandatory, because you pass the attribute value you wish to compare to the OID entry, with the −v attribute (-v "*attribute_value*").

The following is an example that shows how you to use the *ldapcompare* command to check whether an entry for the person named Sam Alapati has the title "DBA":

```
ldapcompare -h myhost.company.com -D "cn=orcladmin" -w password -p 389 -a
title -b "cn=Sam Alapati,ou=Sales,o=IMC,c=US" -v "DBA"
```

ldapdelete   You use the *ldapdelete* command, which is an LDAP *Data Deletion Tool*, to delete OID entries. The *ldapdelete* command enables you to remove entire entries from the directory that you specify in the command line. The *ldapdelete* command has the following syntax:

```
ldapdelete [arguments] ["entry_DN" | -f input_filename]
```

Here's an example that deletes an entry on the host named myhost.

```
ldapdelete -p 389 -h myhost "ou=EuroSInet Suite, o=IMC, c=US"
```

ldapmoddn   The *ldapmoddn* command, an LDAP command belonging to the LDAP *DN/RDN Modification Tool* category, enables you to modify the DN or RDN of an entry, rename an entry or a subtree, or move an entry or a subtree under a new parent. Here's the simplified syntax with only the required attributes:

```
ldapmoddn -h oid_hostname -D "binddn" -w password \
-b "base_dn" {-R "new_rdn"|-N "new_parent"}
```

For example, you can use *ldapmoddn* in the following way, to modify the RDN of the entry Mary Smith. The RDN for Mary Smith is changed from the current parent node dc = Americas to the new parent node, dc = India.

```
ldapmoddn -h myhost.company.com -D "cn=orcladmin" -w password -p 389 \
-b "cn=Mary Smith,dc=Americas,dc=IMC,dc=com" -N "dc=India,dc=IMC,dc=com"
```

ldapmodify The *ldapmodify* command, belonging to the LDAP *Data Modification Tool* category, lets you create, update, and delete attribute data for an entry, using an LDIF format file you supply as the input. Here's the syntax for this command, showing only the required attributes:

```
ldapmodify -h oid_hostname -D "binddn" -w password \
{-f ldif_filename | -X dsml_filename}
```

And here's an example showing how you can use your own LDIF file, in this case named *modify.ldif*, to update entry attribute data. You must make sure that the file you supply is a properly formatted LDIF file.

```
ldapmodify -h myhost.company.com -D "cn=orcladmin" -w password -p 389 -f
/home/myfiles/modify.ldif
```

ldapmodifymt Using the *ldapmodifymt* command, which falls into the category of a *Multi-Threaded LDAP Data Modification Tool,* you can modify several OID entries concurrently. The *ldapmodifymt* command is very similar to the *ldapmodify* command, but runs in a multi-threaded mode, thus enabling you to modify several entries simultaneously. The syntax of this command is very similar to that of the *ldapmodify* command, as shown here:

```
ldapmodifymt -h oid_hostname -D "binddn" -w password\
-T number_of_threads {-f ldif_filename | -X dsml_filename}
```

As you can see, the only change between the *ldapmodify* and the *ldapmodifymt* commands is that the latter has an extra attribute, -T, which stands for the number of threads you wish to specify for the simultaneous processing of entries.

ldapsearch You use the *ldapsearch* command, which is classified as an *LDAP Search Tool,* to search for specific OID directory entries. Again, you can specify several attributes with the *ldapsearch* command, but here's the modified syntax showing only the required attributes:

```
ldapsearch -h oid_hostname -D "binddn" -w password -b "basedn" {-s base|one|sub}
{"filter_string" [attributes]|-f input_file}
```

Here's an example that shows how to use the *ldapsearch* command to search for all OID entries where the staffnumber attribute is less than or equal to 50:

```
ldapsearch -p 389 -h sun1 -b "ou=hr, o=acme, c=us" \
-s subtree "staffnumber>=50"
```

Using Bulk Tools

When you have a large number of directory entries to add, delete, or modify, *bulk tools* rather than the LDIF command-line tools are the way to go. There are three main bulk tools: a bulk deletion tool called *bulkdelete*, a bulk loading tool called *bulkload*, and a bulk modification tool called *bulkmodify*. There is also a data export tool called *ldifwrite*, which helps you load data from the OID into an LDIF-formatted file. Each of these tools is discussed in the following subsections.

bulkload   The *bulkload* command is a *bulk loading tool* that uses the Oracle SQL*Loader utility to load large numbers of entries into the OID. The input file you provide must be in the LDIF format. The bulk loading operation goes through several distinct phases to load the data: the process of checking the entries to make sure they're valid, the generation of intermediate files to help load the data, and finally, the actual loading of the data itself. In addition, there's an index creation stage after the load is completed. If the load fails for some reason, the original data is put back in place by the bulk loading tool.

Here's the syntax for using the command:

```
bulkload.sh -connect connect_string {-check -file_name ldif_file} | \
{-generate -file_name ldif_file [-restore]} | {-load } | -recover | -index}
```

Here's an example showing how to use the bulk loading tool (bulkload):

```
bulkload.sh -connect orcl -check -generate -load ~/testfiles/data.ldif
```

bulkmodify   Use the *bulkmodify* command, which works as a *bulk modification tool*, when you want to modify a large number of directory entries fast. Here's the syntax for this command:

```
bulkmodify -c connect_string -b "base_dn" {-a attr_name |\
-r attr_name} -v attr_value
```

The −a parameter shows the name of the single attribute you wish to add (-a) or replace (-r). The −v parameter provides the single attribute value you wish to add or replace. Here's an example:

```
bulkmodify -c orcl -b "c=US" -a telephoneNumber\
-v "972-580-2564" -f "manager=Anne Smith"
```

Note the optional –f attribute, which stands for a filter string containing only a single attribute. If you don't specify a value for the –f parameter, it defaults to objectclass = *.

bulkdelete   The *bulkdelete* command is a bulk deletion tool that lets you quickly delete an entire subtree of the OID directory information tree (DIT). Here's the syntax for this command, with the two required parameters:

```
bulkdelete.sh -connect connect_string -base "base_dn"
```

The –base attribute shows the DN of the subtree you want to delete—for example, "dc = company, dc = com." Here's an example showing how to use this command to delete the OracleContext subtree:

```
bulkdelete.sh -connect mydb -base "cn=OracleContext"
```

ldifwrite   The *ldifwrite* tool is a *data export tool* that lets you convert OID information into an LDIF-formatted file. After writing the OID information to an LDIF file, you can then use the file to load data into a new replicated directory or an alternative OID node for backup purposes. Note that you can use the *ldifwrite* command along with the *bulkload* tool. Here's the syntax:

```
ldifwrite [-c connect_string] -b "basedn" -f file_name [-E character_set]
[-t num_threads]
```

Note that the connect string (-c) is optional, because without it, by default you'll connect to the database name that you specify by using the $ORACLE_SID environment variable. The –f parameter needs the path and file name of the LDI file you'll be getting, and the –b parameter shows the base DN of the subtree that you're outputting to the LDIF file. Here's an example:

```
ldifwrite -c otherdb -b "ou=India, o=orient, c=us" -f test1.ldif
```

The Oracle Directory Manager

The Oracle Directory Manager (ODM) is the main GUI-based tool that enables you to manage the data in the OID server. The OID Directory Manager connects to a running Oracle Directory instance and lets you manage the OID contents. ODM lets you perform most OID administrative tasks. However, note that the ODM can't start and stop the OID Monitor (oidmon) or the OID Server instances—you must use the OIDMON and OIDCTL utilities for that. You can also use LDAP command-line tools to perform some other OID-related tasks that you can't perform using ODM.

on the job

You can use a single ODM instance to connect to and manage multiple OID server instances.

It's important to remember that you don't use the Oracle Directory Manager to perform OID instance management tasks such as starting and stopping the directory monitor, directory server, or directory replication server instances; rather you use it to manage the OID data.

Oracle Directory Manager Capabilities

The main function of the Oracle Directory Manager (ODM) is to maintain and administer OID data. You can perform the following data management tasks with ODM:

- Configure directory server instance parameters.
- Connect to a directory.
- Control access to OID entries.
- Search, view, and maintain object classes, entries, and their attributes.
- Manage replication nodes.

on the job

You can't start or stop the OID directory monitor process, the directory server instance, or the directory replication server instance through the OID Directory Manager interface; you can only maintain and administer OID data through it.

Starting the Oracle Directory Manager

You just specify the name of the ODM executable, *oidadmin*, at the operating system prompt in a UNIX/Linux system, to start the ODM GUI interface. On a Windows server, go to Programs => Oracle_Home => Integrated Management Tools => Oracle Directory Manager. Click on Oracle Directory Manager to get to the Oracle Directory Manager interface. Make sure you set your DISPLAY variable correctly when running the ODM on a UNIX server. Note that in order to log into the ODM, you must have an OID instance running.

To use the ODM, you must first connect to an OID server. Figure 4-1 shows the response from the OID when you first start the ODM.

You must first specify an active OID server name, along with the port on which it's running, in order to connect to the ODM. When you click OK in the displayed alert, the Directory Server Name Manager will appear. Click ADD on the right-hand side to add a new directory server name. You can use the dialog box that appears to specify a valid directory server name and the port number it's running on (default is 389). Once you do this correctly, the Oracle Directory Manager Connect Dialog box will appear, as shown in Figure 4-2. You have to enter the following pieces of information in the ODM Connect Dialog Box:

Prompt for a
Directory Server
Connection
before Using
ODM

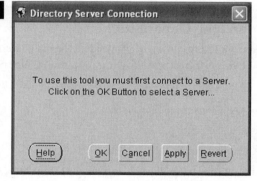

The ODM
Connect Dialog
Box

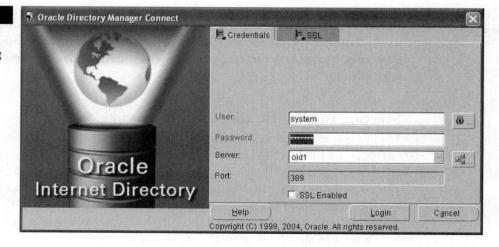

You must use a directory user name, not the Oracle database system username credentials, when connecting to the ODM.

■ *User* You can log in as an anonymous user by leaving the user and password fields blank. If you've already created users, you can log in using the DN for the username—for example:

```
cn=sam,ou=st,ou=mycompany,c=us
```

If you wish to log in as an administrator, you must enter the superuser's name, *orcladmin*.

■ *Password* The superuser orcladmin's password is the same password you specified for the ias_admin user during installation.

■ *Server* Enter the name of the server on which the OID server instance is running.

■ *Port* Enter the port number, which is 389 by default.

■ *SSL Enabled* If you have access to an SSL-enabled port, you can stipulate that all communications be made over the Secure Sockets Layer (SSL). SSL enables data transmission in an encrypted format. By choosing the SSL-tabbed page, you can connect to the OID server using SSL and must provide the SSL location, which indicates the location of the user's wallet. In addition, you must specify the SSL password, which is the wallet password, and the type of SSL authentication. Authentication types could include no certificates (encryption only), one-way certification, or two-way certification.

Once you successfully enter this listed information, the Oracle Directory Manager GUI will appear, as shown in Figure 4-3.

Connecting to Additional Directory Servers by Using Oracle Directory Manager

You can connect to multiple directory server instances simultaneously and view or modify the data, schema, and security for each of the directory servers. You'll see all the servers listed in the navigator pane under *Oracle Internet Directory Servers*. To connect to another OID Server instance, select **Oracle Internet Directory Servers** in the Navigator pane and choose **New.**

FIGURE 4-3 The Oracle Directory Manager

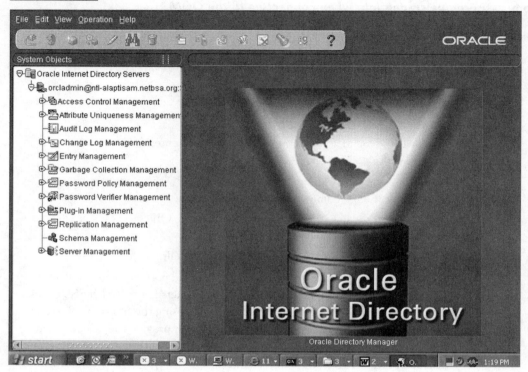

Navigating in the ODM

As Figure 4-3 shows, you can use the Menu Tool bars or the tree-like Navigation Pane to navigate in the ODM interface. When you log into the ODM, you'll see the Oracle Directory Servers in the Navigation Pane, and you can expand this tree to see all of its subcomponents. These subcomponents include the following:

- Entry management
- Access control management
- Password policy management
- Replication management

■ Schema management
■ Server management

Disconnecting from an OID Server

When you log into the ODM, you can see all the OID servers you're currently connected to by clicking on the Oracle Internet Directory Servers item in the Navigation Pane. Figure 2-4 shows that there's a single Oracle Internet Directory Server managed by the ODM. There are two tabs, **Connected Servers** and **Server List,** on the right-hand side. By right-clicking an OID server name and selecting the **Disconnect** option, you can stop a running OID instance. You can also disconnect from an OID server instance by using the **Disconnect** icon, which is the first icon in the toolbar.

When you exit from the ODM, all connections between the ODM and the OID instance are terminated.

Routine OID Administration at a Glance

Oracle Internet Directory routine administration tasks are described in the following subsections:

Managing Attributes

You can add, delete, or modify attributes with command-line tools as well as ODM. By changing the attributes, you'll only be changing the object class definitions, not the actual directory entries themselves.

Managing Entries

You can add, delete, and modify director entries with LDAP command-line tools, as well as ODM. You can import bulk data files using command-line tools. You can view the DIT hierarchy of entries through the ODM.

Managing Object Classes

You can manage object classes in the OID with the help of the ODM.

Managing Security

You can set up an Access Control Policy (ACP) point. You can also set up SSL through the help of the Single Sign-On server.

OID Log Files

The $ORACLE_HOME/ldap/log directory is the default directory where all OID logs are sent. The log directory includes the following types of log files:

- OID monitor log files (oidmon.log)
- OID Directory Server logs (oidldapd*.log)
- OID Replication Server logs (oidrepld*.log)
- Bulk load log files (*.log)

CERTIFICATION OBJECTIVE 4.03

Identity Management and the OID

Identity management refers to the creation and management of OID entries such as application users, devices, processes, and applications that form the enterprise environment. In addition to the entities belonging to your organization, identity management also deals with users outside the organization, such as customers and extraneous applications such as Web services, which interact with your enterprise.

Benefits

Here's a summary of the main benefits of using identity management in an enterprise:

- Store passwords and other security credentials in a secure, centralized place.
- Easily manage application user roles and permissions.
- Personalize enterprise applications such as Portals for various users.
- Manage security policies and authorization rules centrally, thereby enhancing security.
- Reduce administrative costs through centralization and automation.
- Enhance accuracy of security-related data.
- Access multiple applications, thus accelerating application deployment and increasing productivity.

- Reduce administrative costs through centralization and automation.
- Enhance user self-management capabilities within an organization.

on the Job

OID lets you maintain single-user identities by storing user information required by all applications managed by the OID server (Single Sign-On feature). In addition, OID stores all configuration information for all OracleAS components and applications, which enables the OID administrator to grant users various administrative privileges on the OracleAS components.

You can create enterprise identities and manage the shared properties of these identities through a single enterprise-wide console. Using Oracle's Identity Management infrastructure, you can perform the following identity management tasks relating to enterprise identities and groups:

- Create enterprise entities as well as groups of enterprise identities.
- Manage identities in various enterprise services by performing tasks such as account creation, account suspension, and account deletion.
- Manage policies associated with the identities, including authorization and authentication policies, and manage the delegation of privileges to the identities.

CERTIFICATION OBJECTIVE 4.04

Oracle Identity Management

OID, which was discussed in the first part of this chapter, is used to store directory data, and it manages this with the help of the Oracle database on which it's implemented. OID's job is to provide LDAP-compliant directory services. However, OID is but a part, albeit the most important part, of a wider Oracle Identity Management infrastructure, called *Oracle Identity Management*. Oracle Internet Directory acts as a shared repository for the Oracle Identity Management infrastructure. Besides the OID-based LDAP directory services, Oracle Identity Management provides a comprehensive set of identity services, including single sign-on, security certificates, delegated and self-service administrative capabilities, and directory and provisioning integration. Oracle Identity Management provides *distributed security*, not only for the Oracle Application Server, but for other Oracle products as well.

The Identity Management Process

You can simply summarize identity management as a process that defines user identities and manages them in an enterprise environment. Here's what the identity management process entails:

- Provisioning and coordinating user identities
- Managing user roles, credentials, and privileges
- Administering the delegation of responsibility to users
- Ensuring secure deployment of applications
- Arranging for user self management of passwords and preferences
- Providing single sign-on access
- Making possible automated application provision

Thus, identity management would involve routine tasks such as creating enterprise users, modifying or deleting those users, and managing their privileges. Don't forget that besides managing enterprise users, identity management also involves the management of outside entities such as customers and suppliers, network entities, and Web services, as well.

Oracle Identity Management System Components

Oracle Internet Directory is at the heart of Oracle's Identity Management infrastructure, but is far from being its only component. Oracle's Identity Management infrastructure consists of the following components:

- Oracle Internet Directory
- Oracle Delegated Administration Services
- Directory Provision Integration Service
- Directory Integration
- OracleAS Single Sign-On
- Oracle Certificate Authority

A fully functional identity management system has several requirements. Oracle provides a set of features and services that address each of these requirements for an identity management system. In the following text, I list the important identity management requirements and show how OracleAS 10g provides services to manage each of the key components by providing corresponding services for each of the requirements:

- *LDAP Directory Services* These are for storing and managing user and group information. Oracle Internet Directory provides the LDAP directory services and acts as the store for enterprise users and group information.

- *Directory Integration platform and application user provisioning* First, you'll need both a provisioning framework to link to the enterprise provisioning system (e.g., your human resources application). In addition, you need a *directory integration platform* to help integrate the centralized identity management directory with existing application-specific directories or the current enterprise directory you might be using. The Oracle Directory Integration and Provisioning feature takes care of both directory integration and application user provisioning for you.

- *User and application administrator management of directory information* The Oracle Delegated Administration Services (DAS) feature enables users or application administrators to manage their OID information directly without your intervention. You can delegate selective access rights either to the administrators or to the users directly.

- *Single sign-on access to Oracle and third-party Web applications* You'll need a runtime model for user authentication, so users don't have to provide their credentials for accessing each of the applications they use. The OracleAS Single Sign-On feature provides single sign-on access to both Oracle and non-Oracle applications.

- *Generation and publication of public key infrastructure (PKI) security certificates to support strong authentication methods* OracleAS Certificate Authority can issue, revoke, renew, and publish certificates to support PKI-based authentication.

The Oracle Internet Directory enables all types of Web applications to use the OracleAS Single Sign-On feature, whereby you log in only once to OracleAS in order to access any of the applications. OID acts as the storage location for all the SSO Server data. The OID thus stores all the user information needed by various applications and helps maintain a single-user identity for the users. Through OID, you can easily manage this single-user identity that is applicable to applications across the enterprise.

In addition to storing user information, OID also stores configuration information for various OracleAS components and applications. Using this information, OID determines the administrative privileges to be granted to various users to manage the various components.

Identity Management and the OracleAS Infrastructure

There are two main areas where any applications you deploy against the Oracle Identity Management infrastructure will interact with the OracleAS infrastructure: user *authentication* and user *authorization*. When users access an application, the OracleAS infrastructure uses the identity management infrastructure services to perform the validation of the user credentials. For example, the OracleAS Single Sign-On feature might help validate a user's credentials by providing encrypted browser cookies.

After a user has been authenticated, the user's privileges must be checked to ensure that the user can perform the actions she intends to perform. Again, information managed by the identity management infrastructure comes in handy to perform the user authorization. For example, J2EE applications use the OracleAS Java Authentication and Authorization Service (JAAS) Provider (OracleAS JAAS Provider), to tap into the user access and user roles information stored in the OID, which is a key component of the Oracle Identity Management infrastructure.

The Identity Provisioning Flow

Application provisioning involves the provisioning of users, groups, and roles in the Oracle Identity Management infrastructure. You can either use administrative tools to manually provision these entries, or you can use provisioning integration to automate the provisioning process.

Once you deploy the OracleAS Identity Management infrastructure, your first step is to define the identity management security policies you wish to use. Security policies control the data users and applications can access, and the OID stores these policies as access control lists (ACLs). You manage the access control lists using the Oracle Directory Manager.

The OID also provisions the various enterprise users, gathering the data through various means such as the OID self-service console, other directories, or bulk loading tools that were described earlier in this chapter. The OID also helps you manage the groups and roles in the enterprise, besides the enterprise users.

When an application needs to deployed against the Oracle Identity Management infrastructure, you must first grant the application administrator necessary privileges to use the OID administration tools. Using these tools, the application administrator will then create the OID entries to support their applications.

Use of Identity Management by Various Oracle Technology Stacks

Each of the various Oracle technology stacks, such as the Oracle Application Server, the Oracle Database, Oracle E-Business Suite, and the Oracle Collaboration Suite, uses its own set of security models and related policies. However, they all depend on the Oracle Identity Management infrastructure to implement their security policies. For example, the Oracle Database depends on the identity management infrastructure to manage enterprise roles, virtual private databases, and the Oracle Label Security feature. Similarly OracleAS depends on the identity management infrastructure for JAAS roles, for example. Oracle Email, a component of the Oracle Collaboration Suite, uses the OID to manage user preferences and address books.

The Delegated Administration Services (DAS) feature of the Oracle Identity Management infrastructure enables the various Oracle technology stacks to manage user preferences and similar things on their own. The various stacks also use the Oracle Directory Integration and Provisioning feature to automate the provisioning of user accounts and roles.

Oracle Directory Integration and Provisioning

Oracle Directory Integration and Provisioning helps an enterprise integrate its applications and other directories with OID. It helps keep the OID data consistent with the data in applications and other connected directories. For example, an organization would like to keep the OID data update its information automatically when the data in its human resources database changes, due to the addition and removal of employee entries. If the company uses the OracleAS Portal, then it would like the Portal to be automatically notified of changes made in the OID.

The Oracle Directory Integration and Provisioning framework consists of two services:

- *The synchronization integration service*, which keeps all connected directories consistent with the OID. A connected directory concept is relevant to the Oracle Directory Integration and Provisioning environment and refers to directories that require full synchronization between the Application Server Certificate Authority and themselves. For example, a company's human resources database falls under the category of a connected directory. Note that the connected directories may also include non-OID LDAP directories (e.g., the Microsoft Active Directory).

■ *The provisioning integration service*, which sends notifications to target applications such as the OracleAS Portal, when user and group entries change in the OID.

You've already learned the basics about the OID earlier in this chapter. You'll learn about directory integration, application user provisioning, and delegated administration further on in this chapter.

Oracle Identity Management enables you to create enterprise users (enterprise identities) and provide them centralized and secure access to enterprise applications. You do this by using Oracle Identity Management components to perform the following tasks:

■ Create enterprise-wide entities and groups of entities through OID.

■ For the enterprise users, provision services such as account creation, suspension, and deletion.

■ Manage authentication and authorization of various security and authorization policies related to the enterprise users.

■ Delegate administrative and other privileges to the enterprise users.

Note that you can also use Oracle Identity Management as a general-purpose identity-management solution for user-written and third-party enterprise applications.

Oracle Internet Directory Metadata

The OID server relies on *directory metadata* when it's creating directory objects and while processing incoming LDAP requests. Directory objects are collections of object classes, attributes, and matching rules. OID uses the following types of metadata:

■ *Directory Schema*   The directory schemas contain the objects classes, attributes, and matching rules that are supported by OID, and OID uses the schema definitions while creating directory objects.

■ *Access control policy point (ACP)*   Access control points are used to determine whether users are authorized to perform certain operations in the directory.

■ *Root DSE entry*   Also known as DSE-Specific entry, the root DSE entry contains attributes that store information such as naming contexts DNs, that pertain to the directory server, not the users.

■ *Privilege Groups*   These are groups that are used in access control policy evaluation to determine whether users have access to the policy.

■ *Special Directory Entries*   Special directory entries include the following:

    ■ Catalog entries, which contain information about indexed attributes in the underlying database. The directory uses the information during directory searches

    ■ Common entries, which contain information about hosted companies, including the hosted company DN, user search base, and nickname

    ■ Plug-in event–related information

    ■ Entries for storing information about encryption and verifier attribute types

    ■ Entries to store information about user password credential–related polices that the Directory Server should implement

Identity Management Realms

You use the concept of an Identity Management realm to delimit the enterprise area over which you define and enforce identical identity management policies. An Identity Management realm is defined as an "entity or organization that subscribes to the services offered in the Oracle product stack" (Oracle Internet Directory Administrator's Guide). The Identity Management realm is designed to capture the *deployment intent* in the directory metadata. All directory-enabled applications will use the OID to obtain realm properties, such as password policies for the realm. In addition, the Identity Management realm serves to set identity management policies for users and groups.

An Identity Management realm is represented as an OID directory entry and is associated with a special object class. An Identity Management realm consists of three things:

■ A collection of *enterprise identities* (e.g., all employees of a company working in a certain country)

■ A set of *identity management policies* that include the following:

    ■ *Directory structure and naming policies* that customize the directory structure and specify where identities are located and how they are identified

    ■ *Authentication policies* to specify authentication methods and protocols

    ■ *Identity management authorizations* to control access to privileged services and delegate administration when necessary

■ A *collection of groups,* which are the aggregation of identities, to simplify the enforcement of the identity management policies

You can typically identify an Identity Management realm by using *one* of the following:

■ Fully qualified LDAP DNs (distinguished names)

■ Unique global identifiers

■ Simple enterprise names

Because you can define multiple Identity Management realms within the Oracle Identity Management infrastructure, you can use separate identity management policies (e.g., different password policies) in each realm. The directory entry that serves as the root of the Identity Management realm determines the *scope of the identity management policies* defined in the realm, and by default, the scope is the entire DIT under the root of the Identity Management realm. Note that an Identity Management realm is represented as a normal directory entry that has a special object class associated with it.

Each Identity Management realm has a separate realm-specific administrator, with complete control over that Identity Management realm.

Identity Management Policies

Identification management policies used within an Identity Management realm include the following:

■ *Directory structure and naming–related policies,* which let you customize deployment directories and the location of the various entities

■ *Authentication policies,* which let you dictate specific authentication methods and protocols

■ *Authorization policies,* which let you control access to various services

The Default Identity Management Realm

In simple terms, an Identity Management realm is a location in the OID where all the user and group context is stored. When installing the OracleAS instance, you must select a value for the infrastructure domain. The default Identity Management realm will come configured for your use, and it will be set for the domain you chose. Typically, you'll have a default Identity Management realm, then, looking like this (dc stands for domain component):

```
dc=acme,dc=com
```

The default users will be located in the following container:

```
cn=users,dc=acme,dc=com
```

The default groups will be in the groups container:

```
cn=groups,dc=acme,dc=com
```

In most deployments, you won't need anything beyond this default Identity Management realm to manage users and applications in your enterprise. Although you have all users and groups aggregated under the single default Identity Management realm, you can use DAS to delegate administration to the users.

You'd want to think about creating additional Identity Management realms only in the following situations:

- You have disparate sets of applications.
- You have different schema definitions.
- You need to use separate password policies for the entries.
- You have different user communities, such as employees and customers.

In order for any Oracle component to use the Identity Management infrastructure, it first of all needs an Identity Management realm that delineates the scope of the Identity Management policies. During the OID installation, the default Identity Management realm is automatically created. Various Oracle components use the default Identity Management realm to locate users, groups, and policies when no other realm is explicitly specified for that particular component. The default Identity Management realm is mandatory, and there can only be one default realm per OID instance.

During the OID installation, the Oracle Universal Installer creates a default DIT structure based on your domain information (abc.xyz.com, for example) and creates the default Identity Management realm (the domain name schema is an option). This default Identity Management realm is part of the global DIT. If you have the Oracle Installer set up the DIT based on domain names, then the default Identity Management realm will use domain components (dc) as part of its DN. For example, if you are installing the OracleAS on a computer named *oidserver.us.greatcompany. com*, then the *root of the Identity Management realm* that's automatically created, will be *dc = us, dc = greatcompany, dc = com*.

Note that it's entirely possible to just use the default DIT thus created, without ever configuring the Root Oracle Context, which is defined next.

Oracle Context

An *Oracle Context* is a directory entry that stores policies and metadata pertaining to a specific Identity Management realm. The OID directory entry *OracleContext* is the *Root Oracle Context* created under the default Identity Management realm during the OID installation, and contains a pointer to the default Identity Management realm. The Root Oracle Context is a special entry in the OID and is created right underneath the root of the Identity Management realm. For example, in the previous section you learned how the Identity Management realm came to have the distinguished name *dc = us, dc = greatcompany, dc = com*. The Oracle Context associated with this default Identity Management realm will have the distinguished name

```
cn=OracleContext,dc=us,dc=greatcompany,dc=com.
```

During the installation of the OracleAS instance, OID will create the Oracle Context that's associated with the default Identity Management realm, to store all realm-specific policies and metadata. This Oracle Context will have the following DN:

```
cn=OracleContext,dc=us,dc=mycompany,dc=com.
```

Oracle software will use the Oracle Context to detect the realm-specific policies and metadata. In addition, OID creates a directory structure in the default Identity Management realm to enable the various Oracle components to locate the various identities. For example, all users will be located in the container cn = users, right under the root of the Identity Management realm, for example, cn = users, dc = us, dc = mycompany, dc = com. For groups, the corresponding distinguished name will be cn = groups, dc = us, dc = mycompany, dc = com.

The OID will also create an administrator for the Identity Management realm under the users container—for example, cn = orcladmin, cn = users, dc = us, dc = mycompany, dc = com. Finally, the OID will create default authentication policies (e.g., the default directory password policy) and identity management authorizations (e.g., user and group creation privileges).

The *Root Oracle Context* is used by all Oracle products to store their product specific information, and it contains the following items:

- The deployment-specific DIT design, including user and group naming and placement
- The identity management policies associated with this realm, including naming and containment policies
- Realm-specific information specific to Oracle applications

The Root Oracle Context includes both *site-wide information* and a *discovery mechanism*. Site-wide information comprises metadata pertaining to various Oracle components and includes information such as default users and their profiles, default passwords, and access policies and the default configuration settings for the Oracle components.

The discovery mechanism–related information is stored in the Identity Management realm and contains details about how the various Oracle components find out subscriber details in the OID. The discovery mechanism includes the following types of information (note that subscriber and Identity Management realm are interchangeable terms):

- *Subscriber Search base (OracleSubscriberSearchBase)* This is a common point in a hosted environment for all Oracle products to locate a subscriber. In a non-hosted environment, this points to the parent of the default subscriber.
- *Subscriber Nickname (OracleSubscriberNickNameAttribute)* This attribute contains the nickname of the subscriber, to be used when searching for that subscriber under the subscriber searchbase.
- *Default Subscriber (OracleDefaultSubscriber)* This attribute value refers to the default subscriber node.

Identity Management Realm–Specific Oracle Context

There can be only one default Identity Management realm in the OID. However, you can have multiple Identity Management realms. In each of the Identity Management realms, you can have an Oracle Context specific to that realm, called the *Identity Management Realm–Specific Oracle Context*. Each of these Identity Management Realm–Specific Oracle Contexts will have the following common entries:

- Identity Management realm user-naming and location policies
- Oracle Component information that's specific to a particular Identity Management realm

■ Mandatory authentication attributes

■ A discovery mechanism for the Oracle components to use when searching for subscriber-related information—for example, the Oracle common user node *OracleCommonGroupSearchBase*

■ A default password policy for the Identity Management realm

■ Privilege assignments for the Identity Management realm

■ An access policy to prevent unauthorized access from other Identity Management realms

■ Application-specific data for that realm, including authorization information

There are some *common entries* in the Identity Management Realm–Specific Oracle Context to help locate users and groups:

■ *User Search Base (OracleCommonUserSearchBase)*   All users are placed under the node specified by the User Search Base.

■ *User Nickname Attribute (OracleCommonUserNickNameAttribute)*   You use the nicknames specified here when searching for a user under the User Search Base.

■ *Group Search Base (OracleCommonGroupSearchBase)*   You'll find all the groups under the Group Search Base node.

■ *User Object Class (OracleCommonUserObjectBase)*   This attribute contains the list of object classes (e.g., *person, orcluser*) used to create user entries under that subscriber tree.

e x a m

w a t c h   *The default Identity Management realm configuration for Oracle products includes just the default Identity Management realm and all Oracle components serve users in that realm. Thus having common Identity Management policies for all users is the default.*

For example, if an ASP is hosting an OID-enabled application that is shared by several client companies, each client company will have its own subscriber. If a user logs onto the application, the application itself will use the search base attributes listed here to find the correct subscriber information, in order to validate the user's identity and privileges. Thus, the same username can be used in the same application, but by different subscribers.

The Default Schema and Directory Information Tree

During the installation of the OID by the Oracle Universal Installer, the following DIT components are installed:

- *Base schema elements* These include the basic attributes and object classes required by the OID.
- *Root Oracle Context* This is the directory containing common Oracle component information.
- *Default Identity Management realm* This is the mandatory identity realm used by various Oracle components. Oracle components use the default identity realm to locate users, groups, and policies when no other realm is explicitly specified for a component.
- *Identity Management Realm–Specific Oracle Context* This is the Oracle context specific to each Identity Management realm.
- *Default Password Policy* This contains the password policy for all users.

Directory Schemas

A directory schema safeguards the integrity of directory-stored data and reduces duplication by specifying rules about the types of objects you can store in the OID, and how the directory server and other clients can use that information during various operations. The metadata, such as object classes and attributes relating to how exactly the OID organizes data in the DIT, are stored in a modifiable entry called the *subentry* (named subSchemaSubentry), which is a special class of OID entry.

Oracle Application Server Administration Model

During the OID installation, the installer creates an OID administrative user called OID superuser (cn = *orcladmin*), who is privileged to perform any operation inside the OID. The orcladmin user helps bootstrap the OracleAS initial deployment. The superuser has full access to all OID directory information. The default user name of the superuser is *orcladmin*. The superuser uses the Oracle Directory Manager to perform several administrative actions, because that user can't log in through the Single Sign-On Server at this point.

You can change the OID administrator (Orcladmin) password by using the ODM or the OID Self Service Control.

Delegation of OID Administration

During the OID installation, the OID superuser *orcladmin* creates the default DIT. The superuser delegates administration of the Oracle Context to the Oracle Context administrators. The Oracle Context administrators delegate the administration of OracleAS to OracleAS administrators. The OracleAS administrators can install and start all OracleAS components. The OracleAS administrators can delegate user and group administration tasks to users and application group administrators.

You can have multiple administrators in OID, with each administrator managing a different *domain*. There is a directory role for each domain:

- *OID global administrator role* has privileges over the entire OID server.
- *Domain administrator* or subscriber-specific role has domain-wide privileges only, granted by the OID global administrator.
- *Application administrators* manage an application's data and delegate rights on the application data to the users.

Access Control and OID

Because OID stores application access control information in various entries and attributes, you can control user access to applications by defining access policies on the access related entries/attributes. You can implement access control at two levels in an OID:

- *User level* By specifying application policies, you can control a user's privileges to perform specific operations with application data.
- *Administrator level* You can use OID to manage all access control policies for applications and specify which administrators or users can manage these access policies.

The iASAdmins Group

The *iASAdmins* group is created in the Oracle Context, with the distinguished name (DN) *cn = iASAdmins, cn = groups, <Oracle Context DN>*. The OracleAS administrator must be a member of the iASAdmins group in OID to configure the various OracleAS components. In order for a user to administer an OracleAS component that user must be a member of the iASAdmins group as well.

Standalone Modes

In a standalone OID installation, the OracleAS administrator starts the initial OracleAS instance using the default orcladmin account. The administrator can later delegate OracleAS administration to other users by adding them to the iASAdmins group in OID.

Shared Mode

In a shared OID installation, where OID is used for other applications in addition to OracleAS, the OracleAS administrator should get the equivalent of the iASAdmins group privileges from the OID administrator orcladmin.

Managing Users and Groups

In the following subsections, OID user and group management concepts are explained.

Managing Users

Even if a user has access to multiple applications in the enterprise, there's only a single entry in OID representing that user's identity. OracleAS users are represented as *user objects* in OID. OID provides necessary user and group information to the various OracleAS components by granting certain privileges to the following *administrative groups*.

Authentication Service   The DN for the Authentication Service is cn = authenticationServices, cn = groups,<Oracle context DN>. Members of this group can compare the passwords presented by a user with the one stored for them in the OID.

User Security Admin   The User Security Admin has the DN cn = oraclUser SecurityAdmins, cn = groups,<Oracle Context DN>. Members of this group can read, compare, and reset user passwords in OID.

User Proxy Privilege   The DN for the User Proxy Privilege group is cn = userProxyPrivilege, cn = groups,<Oracle Context DN>. Membership in this group grants Oracle products the privilege to proxy on behalf of end users.

Adding Users to Groups   By default the OID superuser and the subscriber context superuser have user and group administration privileges. However, the administrator can grant user and group administration privileges to other OID users by adding those users to certain privilege groups, as explained subsequently.

By adding users to certain groups, the OracleAS administrator can delegate user management privileges to users. Here are the three groups you can add users to, so as to delegate user management to users:

- *The User Create Group* enables a user to create users. The DN for this group is cn = orclDASCreateUser, cn = groups,<Oracle context DN>.
- *The User Edit Group* lets a user edit other users' properties. The DN for this group is cn = orclDASEditUser, cn = groups,<Oracle context DN>.
- *The User Delete Group* membership enables a user to delete users. The DN for this group is cn = orclDASDeleteUser, cn = groups,<Oracle context DN>.

Managing Groups

By adding users to certain groups, the OracleAS administrator can delegate *group management* privileges to certain users. Here are the three groups you can add users to, so as to delegate group management privileges:

- *The Create Group* enables a user to create groups. The DN for this group is cn = orclDASCreateGroup, cn = groups,<Oracle context DN>.
- *The Edit Group* lets a user edit the group properties. The DN for this group is cn = orclDASEditGroup, cn = groups,<Oracle context DN>.
- *The User Delete* group membership enables a user to delete groups. The DN for this group is cn = orclDASDeleteGroup, cn = groups,<Oracle context DN>.

Password Policy Management

OID password policies ensure that password creation and maintenance follows predetermined rules, such as the password expiration policies. When you install OID, the installer creates common default password policies for each subscriber in an Identity Management realm, using the auxiliary object class *pwdpolicy*, which contains password-related attributes such as *pwdMaxAg( )*, *pwdMinLength( )*, and *pwdMaxFailure( )*. You must use the same object class later on to create a password policy. The *userPassword* attribute of the user entity is related to these password polices. In order to enforce the password policy you must set the *oraclcommonusersear chbase* in the common entry attribute of the user.

You can view and modify the values of the default password policy object attributes through ODM. In addition, you can use command-line tools as well to perform the two tasks. You can use *ldapsearch* to look up password policies, and *ldapmodify* to modify password policies. Please see the previous discussion of the *ldapsearch* and *ldapmodify* to find out how to use these tools to search for and modify directory entries.

on the **job**

*If you use the bulk tools **ldapbind** or **ldapcompare**, the OID server enforces the password policies. Any password changes you make through **ldapadd** or **ldapmodify** must meet the password policy requirements as well.*

During the OracleAS installation, a password policy is created using the pwdpolicy auxiliary object class. In order to create a password policy, you must use this object class.

CERTIFICATION OBJECTIVE 4.05

Delegated Administrative Service

In an OID, you can use Delegated Administrative Service (DAS) to delegate certain administrative tasks (e.g., maintaining user and group entries to subscriber administrators and application end users), thus making possible site-based directory data management. DAS uses predefined services called *Delegated Administrative Services*, which perform the actual directory operations on behalf of users. DAS relies on the *proxy user* feature to perform services on behalf of the users, and represents a single set of services for managing application-related OID data. DAS makes it possible for OID administrators to lighten their burdens by delegating routine directory administration tasks to other administrators and end users for directory-enabled applications.

on the **job**

DAS lets you store enterprise user data centrally, while distributing the administration of that data to various administrators and end users.

There are different levels of privileges you can grant to users and groups, based on your administrative level. The *global administrator* has full privileges for the entire directory and can grant the privileges to create and manage realms to *realm administrators*. The realm administrators can delegate certain privileges to the users and groups.

You can delegate the following privileges with DAS:

- Creating, modifying, and deleting users and groups
- Assigning user and group privileges
- Managing services and accounts
- Configuring DAS
- Managing OracleAS Reports and OracleAS Forms services resources

DAS includes a Web-based OID Self-Service Console, which enables you to access the directory data of an application. Using the Self-Service Console, you can do the following:

- Manage your personal information in the directory, as well as any directory data you are authorized to manage.
- If you are a *subscriber (Identity Management realm) administrator*, you can manage subscriber-level information, such as provisioning a new user or group and managing the users and groups within an Identity Management realm.
- If you are a *site administrator*, you can manage site-level information, and Identity Management realm (subscriber) level information such as creating new subscribers and changing their privileges.

Note that you can use either the OID Self-Service Console or DAS services to develop your own tools for administering application data in the directory.

Architecture of DAS

DAS uses a servlet-enabled OC4J instance together with the Oracle HTTP Server to receive client requests and process the requests with the help of LDAP data from the OID, which it compiles into an HTML page before sending it back to the client.

Various Oracle components log into the OID as proxy users, which means that they assume the identity of the end user who requires the OID information. Because numerous logins by components as proxy users pose a security risk, DAS provides centralized proxy access. When a user logs into an Oracle component, that component will log into the central Delegated Administrative Service. DAS, in turn, logs as the proxy user for the original end user and retrieves the information from the OID. Thus, when the end users or application administrators log into the OID Self-Service Console, DAS logs into the OID on their behalf as a proxy user.

You can also use DAS with OracleAS Single Sign-On feature. The first time a user accesses DAS, the Oracle HTTP Server redirects the user to the SSO server for authentication. The SSO verifies the user's credentials by comparing them with those saved in the OID and, upon successful verification, directs the user to DAS, along with an encrypted parameter to DAS containing the user's identity. DAS will then log into the OID as a proxy user, using the DN of the end user. It'll convert the LDAP results into HTML pages, before sending them back to the client browser.

Managing DAS

DAS is installed as part of the OracleAS 10g Release 2 (10.1.2) infrastructure. You can also choose to install DAS separately by itself. This enables you to install multiple instances of DAS on various servers, with all of them communicating with a single OracleAS instance.

Starting and Stopping DAS

You can start and stop DAS either from the command line or by using the Application Server Control. Both methods are discussed in the following subsections.

Using Command-Line Tools   Because DAS runs inside the OracleAS infrastructure instance, make sure that you run these commands from the OracleAS infrastructure instance. From the command line, you start and stop DAS with the opmnctl utility. To start DAS, you use the *opmnctl startall* command, and to stop it, you use the *opmnctl stopall* command.

You can also start the DAS by using the dcmtl utility, as shown here:

```
$ ORACLE_HOME/dcm/bin/dcmctl start -co OC4J_SECURITY
```

You can also stop the DAS by using the dcmtl utility, as shown here

```
$ ORACLE_HOME/dcm/bin/dcmctl stop -co OC4J_SECURITY
```

Using Application Server Control   On the Application Server Control Console, follow these steps to start and stop DAS:

- Go to the Instance home page, and scroll down to the **System Components** section.
- Select **OC4J_SECURITY.**
- In the **System Components** section, choose **Start, Stop,** or **Restart.**

Monitoring DAS

On a UNIX/Linux system, you can verify that DAS is running by checking to make sure that the Oracle HTTP server and the OC4J JVM services are running. In addition, you must verify that the DAS Web site is running. Here are steps to verify that the DAS service is running:

1. First, look for the name of the Oracle HTTP Server in the list of running processes by using the following command:

   ```
   $ ps -ef|grep http
   ```

   If you see the name of your HTTP server in the process list, then OHS is up and running.

2. Next, check whether the OC4J instance is running by issuing the following command:

   ```
   $ ps -ef|grep java
   ```

   Check for the OC4J instance in the process list that's output by the previous command. If you see that the OC4J instance is running, you're ready to make the final check to see whether the DAS Web site is running.

on the job

On a Windows server, the best way to check for DAS is to go the Application Server Control's Component table and see whether DAS is listed as running there.

FIGURE 4-4

The Oracle
Internet
Directory Self-
Service Console
Home Page

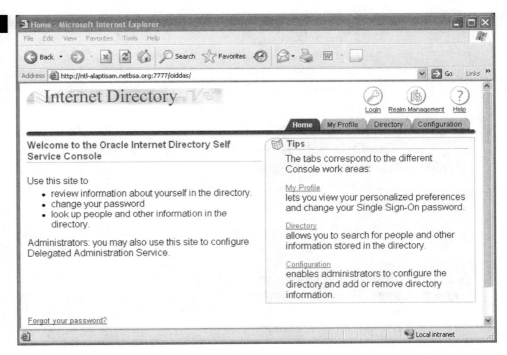

3. To verify whether the DAS Web site is running, go to the default DAS Web
   site at http://hostname.domain:7777/oiddas. Figure 4-4 shows the Oracle
   Internet Directory Self-Service Console home page.

Using the OID Self-Service Console

To log into the OID Self-Service Console, follow these steps:

1. Use the following URL to access the Self-Service console (use port 7778,
   which is the OHS listening port for the OracleAS infrastructure instance).

   ```
   http://servername:7778/oiddas/
   ```

2. Select **Login** at the top of the page, which will take you to the Oracle
   Application Server Single Sign-On window.

3. In the Single Sign-On window, you must enter your credentials. In the **User Name** field, enter your Self-Service Console user name, and in the **Password** field, enter your Self-Service Console password. The **Company** field will appear if it's a hosted service, in which case you also enter the name of your company in that field.

4. Choose **Login.**

The OID Self-Service Console Work Areas

You manage the OID with the help of the following three tabs on the home page of the OID Self-Service console, which take you to the main work areas of the console:

■ *My Profile*   Lets you view your preferences and change your Single Sign-On password.

on the
Ó o b

To change your own password, use the My Profile tab on the Console home page. To change another user's password, you must use the Directory tab and search for that user. You can then change the user's password in the Password Management section.

■ *Directory*   Lets you search for people and/other information in the OID. You can also create users or edit the user's directory information (changing the user's password, for example) once your search for a directory user is successful. You can also search for a group and manage group information from here. From the Directory work area, you can also assign privileges to users and groups as well as revoke privileges.

■ *Configuration*   Lets you configure the directory and add, remove, and modify directory information.

Creating the Default Identity Management Realm-Specific Context

You must first create the default subscriber context, which is the root entry, which contains information about the default subscriber. You create the default subscriber in this way:

1. Click on the Configuration tab on the home page of the OID Self-Service Console.

2. The Identity Management Realm page, seen in Figure 4-5, enables you to configure a new entry for the Identity Management realm. In the page, you enter the following key attributes:

■ *Login Name*   This mandatory field will be an attribute such as EmployeeNo or SSN, which helps uniquely identify the users.

on the
Job

Oracle Application Server Single Sign-On locates the user by using the Login Name attribute, when a user logs in, and looks for them under the DN you provide for the User Search Base attribute.

■ *RDN*   You must enter an RDN component for the user entry.

■ *User Search Base*   This is the DN of the entry under which the user entries for this realm are located.

■ *User Creation Base*   This is the DN of the entry under which to create users for this realm; it should be the same as the user Search Base attribute. You can create users under different contexts under the same user search base by

---

FIGURE 4-5

The Identity
Management
Realm
Configuration
Page in OID

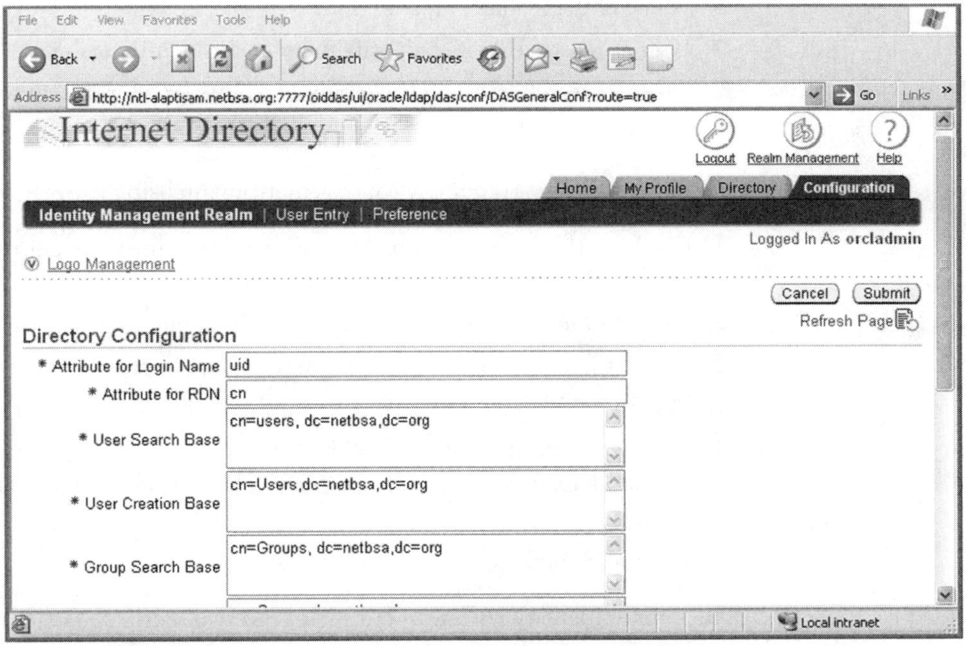

File   Edit   View   Favorites   Tools   Help

Back ▾ | Search ☆ Favorites

Address http://ntl-alaptisam.netbsa.org:7777/oiddas/ui/oracle/ldap/das/conf/DASGeneralConf?route=true   Go   Links »

Internet Directory

Logout   Realm Management   Help

Home | My Profile | Directory | Configuration

Identity Management Realm | User Entry | Preference

Logged In As **orcladmin**

Ⓥ Logo Management

Cancel   Submit

Refresh Page

Directory Configuration

* Attribute for Login Name   `uid`

* Attribute for RDN   `cn`

* User Search Base   `cn=users, dc=netbsa,dc=org`

* User Creation Base   `cn=Users,dc=netbsa,dc=org`

* Group Search Base   `cn=Groups, dc=netbsa,dc=org`

Local intranet

providing a value for this attribute that's different from that of the user search base.

- *Group Search Base* A mandatory attribute that represents the DN of the entry under which group entries for this realm are located.
- *Group Create Base* This is the DN of the entry under which you create groups for this realm.
- *Logo Management* You can also enter any necessary logos in this section.

3. Click **Submit** to save the changes you made.

Configuring an Identity Management Realm

To configure Identity Management realms using the Self Service Console, you must be either an OID administrator, or must have been given the necessary privileges. You must specify the following attributes for the Identity Management realm:

- Name of the new Identity Management realm, which is a mandatory field. The name you enter will be used to create the DN for this realm entry.
- Name of the realm contact person.
- User attributes that will identify them in the identity realm.
- The user search base and the group search base root entries in the DIT.
- Realm and product logos.

You can configure an Identity Management realm using the following steps:

1. Click on the Identity Management realm link in the upper right hand corner of the PID Self-Service Console home page.
2. The SSO login page appears. Use the *Orcladmin* username to log in.
3. In the Identity Management realm page that appears, click on the create button to create an entry for a new subscriber.
4. In the Create Identity Management realm page, select the **Configuration** tab.
5. In the Identity Management realm window, enter the values for the various fields.
6. Choose **Submit** to save your changes.

The Create Identity Management realm has two sections: Basic Information and Logo Management, where you enter the necessary information described previously, to create the new Identity Management realm.

Managing Users and Groups Using DAS

You can use DAS to manage users and groups and to assign privileges to users and groups. Let's review these three tasks briefly.

Managing User Entries

Using DAS, administrators can search for and maintain user entries.

Searching for User Entries

To search for a user entry, follow these steps:

1. Click on the Directory tab.
2. In the Search for User page, enter the user name (or the first few characters of the name) in the Search for User field.
3. Click Go.

Maintaining User Entries

Maintaining user entries involves creating, deleting, and modifying user entries. To create a user, click on the Create button in the Search for User page and enter the values in the fields shown there. You delete a user from the same page by first entering the username and then clicking the delete button. You modify a user's attributes by first selecting a user and then clicking on the Edit button.

Managing Group Entries

Using DAS, administrators can search for and maintain user entries.

Searching for Group Entries   To search for a group entry, follow these steps:

1. Click the Directory tab.
2. Click Groups on the top of the page.
3. In the Search for Groups page, enter the group name in the Search Group Name field. If you want to see all groups in the directory, leave this field blank.
4. Click Go.

Maintaining Group Entries   You can create, modify, or delete group entries in a manner analogous to that of member management, but you must use the Search for Group page to perform these tasks.

on the **j o b**

If a user account is locked, for example, due to exceeding the number of failed logins, you can unlock the user accounts within the Single Sign-On environment, by clicking on Accounts from the Search for User page. You can unlock, enable, and disable accounts from here.

Assigning Privileges to Users and Groups

You can grant users and groups privileges to create and manage users and groups, as well as to assign privileges to those two entities. You assign these privileges to a user by first searching for a user and then clicking **Assign Privilege.**

CERTIFICATION OBJECTIVE 4.06

OracleAS Portal and the Oracle Internet Directory

OAS Single Sign-On provides a single point of credential validation and controls users' access to various resources, based on their profiles. The SSO Server validates users' credentials against their profiles stored in the Oracle Internet Directory, when the users log in to the SSO server. Most portal elements have an access control list (ACL), which determines which users and groups may access the element. In addition, you can also use global privileges to grant access to all objects of a given type in a portal. The OID stores the following types of OracleAS Portal related data:

- All OracleAS Portal–specific entries
- User and group attributes

OracleAS Portal also needs to be able to access the OID data through DAS.

Caching OID Information in the OracleAS Portal

The OracleAS Portal also caches OID information to improve performance, and this information needs to be refreshed by the OID periodically to keep it up-to-date. Cached information includes the following:

- OracleAS Portal OID connection information
- Delegated Administrative Service (DAS) URLs

- User group membership information
- The IDs of privilege groups for authorization checks on various directory portlets such as the User and Group portlets

To update cached OID information, the OracleAS Portal uses the *Oracle Directory Provisioning Integration Service* of the Oracle Directory Integration Platform (DIP). The DIP service notifies OracleAS Portal so that when a portal-relevant information change is made in the OID, the relevant information is refreshed by getting the new information from OID to the portal. In order for the *Oracle Directory Provisioning Integration Service* to work, you must first make sure that the DIP service is started, by using the following command:

```
$ oidctl instance=2 server=odisrv start
```

In addition, you must subscribe OracleAS Portal to specific events in the OID—for example, user deletion. You subscribe the Portal to OID events by creating a subscription provisioning profile in the OID for OracleAS Portal. During the Portal installation, the OracleAS Portal Configuration Assistant (OPCA) creates the initial profile, and you can alter or delete this profile later on with the OPCA.

You must also make sure that directory synchronization is enabled in the OracleAS Portal. You enable directory synchronization in the Directory Synchronization section of the SSO/OID tab in the Global Setting page. You select the *Enable directory synchronization* check box here to enable synchronization of the specified data with the OracleAS Portal.

OracleAS Portal Entries in OID

The following OracleAS Portal entries are created in the OID's DIT structure:

- OracleAS Portal *default user accounts* are created in the default Identity Management realm's user container.
- OracleAS Portal *group container* is created in the default Identity Management realm's group container. The format of the Portal group container is *portal_schema_name.yymmdd.hh.mi*.
- OracleAS Portal *default groups* are created in the OracleAS Portal group container.
- OracleAS Portal application entity is created in the Root Oracle Context.
- OracleAS Portal directory synchronization subscription is created in the provisioning file of OID.

Configuring OID Settings in the OracleAS Portal

Here's how you configure OID settings in the OracleAS Portal:

1. Log into the OracleAS Portal and from the OracleAS Portal home page (Portal Builder page) click the **Administer** tab.
2. In the Services portlet, click the Global Settings link.
3. Click the SSO/OID tab.

You can configure the following Portal settings in the OID:

- *Local Group Search Base DN*   Defines the node in which the OracleAS Portal searches for existing groups.
- *Group Creation Base DN*   This is the node in the DIT under which portal groups are created through the Group portlet.

Accessing DAS from OracleAS Portal

OracleAS Portal lets you add and modify user and group information through DAS. The following three OracleAS Portal portlets let you perform various user and group management tasks using DAS:

- The User Portlet lets you create and modify users.
- The Group Portlet lets all users view it, but users who are members of the OracleDASCreateGroup can a create groups. Similarly to edit groups, one must be a member of the OracleDASEditGroup, and to delete groups, a member of the OracleDASDeleteGroup.
- The Services Portlet will take you to the OID Self Service Console.

Portal administrators can create DAS roles and assign a combination of OID and OracleAS Portal privileges to those roles.

TWO-MINUTE DRILL

Directories and the LDAP

- ❏ Directories are mainly meant for centralized storage of enterprise-wide information that's readable very quickly.
- ❏ LDAP directories store data in the form of a Directory Information Tree (DIT), which consists of various entries.
- ❏ A distinguished name (DN) in a DIT uniquely identifies an entry in a DIT.
- ❏ A DIT is made up of all the DNs of the entries in it.
- ❏ A relative distinguished name (RDN) is the most granular component of a DN.
- ❏ Attributes are specific information attributes of a DIT entry.
- ❏ An object class is a named group of entity attributes.
- ❏ A subclass is an object class derived from another object class.
- ❏ A directory naming context is a subtree of a DIT that resides entirely on a single directory server.

Oracle Internet Directory

- ❏ You can provide password-based, anonymous, and Certificate-based (using SSL) levels of user authentication in the OID.
- ❏ The MD4 algorithm is the default encryption algorithm in OID.
- ❏ OID isn't primarily a security related tool—it's primarily an enterprise data storage and retrieval system.
- ❏ Hosting enterprises are called default subscribers.
- ❏ Enterprises that use hosts for OID services are known as subscribers.
- ❏ When you install OID, a default schema and a default DIT are automatically created.
- ❏ A directory schema contains rules about how data can be organized in the DIT.
- ❏ The configuration parameters for an OID server instance are stored in a configuration set entry called the *configset* entry.
- ❏ The default configuration set entry is known as configset0.

❏ An OID node consists of an OID Directory Server instance, an Oracle Directory Repository Server, and an Oracle Database.

❏ The OID data is stored in the Metadata Repository database.

❏ The OID Directory Server instance performs all the work of the OID.

❏ The Oracle Directory Replication Server instance replicates data between OID servers. This server is optional.

❏ The primary node is called the supplier and the secondary node, the consumer.

❏ Each OID node must have at least one OID server instance running.

❏ The number of OID Directory Server instances is determined by the ORACLESERVERPROCS configuration parameter (default is 1).

❏ The configuration parameter ORACLEMAXCC determines the number of database connections from each OID Server process (default is 2).

❏ OIDMON utility manages the OID Server processes and interprets and processes OIDCTL commands.

❏ You manage OID Server instances with the OIDCTL utility.

❏ You must start the OID Monitor before you can start the OID Server instance.

❏ You must stop the OID Monitor only if you're shutting down the LDAP service altogether.

❏ You use the *configset* and *flags* parameters only when starting the OID server instance.

❏ Command line utilities let you directly create and update OID data stored in the Metadata Repository.

❏ When you want to add, delete, or modify a large number of directory entries, you use *bulk tools*.

❏ You use the Oracle Directory Manager GUI tool to maintain and administer OID data.

❏ You use the command-line utility oidadmin to start and stop the ODM GUI interface.

❏ The $ORACLE_HOME/ldap/log directory is the default directory for all OID-related logs.

Identity Management and the OID

❏ Identity management deals with the creation and management of OID entries that form the enterprise environment.

❏ OID stores user information required by the applications managed by the OID as well as configuration information for all OracleAS components.

❏ OID acts as the shared repository for the Oracle Identity Management infrastructure.

❏ Oracle Directory Integration and Provisioning consists of two services: the synchronization integration service and the provisioning integration service.

❏ Directory metadata is useful when creating directory objects and while processing LDAP requests.

❏ OID uses the following types of metadata: directory schema, access control policy point (ACP), root DSE entry, privilege groups, and special directory entries.

Oracle Identity Management

❏ Identity Management realms are designed to capture the "deployment intent" in the directory metadata.

❏ You can use multiple Identity Management realms in the OID so as to use separate identity management policies in each realm.

❏ During the OID installation a mandatory Default Identity Management realm is created.

❏ The OracleContext entry contains realm information specific to Oracle-based applications.

❏ The Root Oracle Context consists of site-wide information and a discovery mechanism.

❏ In each Identity Management realm, you have a separate realm-specific Oracle Context.

❏ The default user name of the OID superuser is orcladmin.

❏ You can have multiple administrators in OID, such as the OID global administrator, domain administrators, and application administrators.

❏ You can implement access control at the user level and at the administrative level in an OID.

❏ In order for a user to configure an OracleAS component, that user must belong to the iASAdmins group in the relevant Oracle context.

❏ The OracleAS administrator can delegate user and group management privileges to users by adding users to certain groups.

❏ Common default password policies for subscribers in an Identity Management realm are applied using the auxiliary object class *pwdpolicy*.

❏ The default value for attributes of the *pwdpolicy* object class is zero.

Delegated Administrative Service

❏ DAS is used to delegate administrative tasks to subscriber administrators and application end users.

❏ DAS relies on the proxy user feature to perform services on behalf of users.

❏ There are two types of administrators: *global* and *realm*. You can also refer to these two types of administrators as site administrators and subscriber administrators.

❏ DAS uses a servlet-enabled OC4J instance, together with the Oracle HTTP server, to receive client requests and process them.

❏ You can start and stop DAS using the Application Server Control or with the dcmtl utility.

OracleAS Portal and the Oracle Internet Directory

❏ An access control list (ACL) determines which users and groups may access a portal element.

❏ You can give grant global privileges to grant access to all objects of a given type in a portal.

❏ The OracleAS Portal caches OID information to improve performance.

❏ OracleAS Portal uses the Oracle Directory Provisioning Integration service to update cached OID information.

❏ You manage the DIP service by using the oidctl utility.

❏ You create a subscription provisioning profile in OID for OracleAS Portal, to subscribe the portal to OID events.

❏ There are three types of OracleAS portlets to help you perform user and group management tasks using DAS: the User Portlet, the Group Portlet, and the Services Portlet.

SELF TEST

1. You can use the bulk tool *ldifwrite* to accomplish which of the following tasks? (choose two)
   A. To transfer data between two directory servers
   B. To transfer data between a directory server and a database
   C. To back up directory information
   D. To modify a large number of entries in a short time

2. You can use the Oracle Directory Manager (ODM) to (choose two)
   A. Control access to an OID entry.
   B. Search and maintain attributes.
   C. Start and stop the OID Monitor process.
   D. Start and stop the OID Server instance.

3. DAS uses the following feature of OID to perform operations on behalf of users:
   A. Proxy-user feature
   B. Default Identity realm
   C. Oracle Context
   D. Single Sign-On feature

4. You start and stop DAS with the following tool:
   A. dcmtool
   B. opmnctl
   C. emctl
   D. dasctl

5. Which of the following statements is true?
   A. The DIT is the most granular component of a DN.
   B. The DN is the most granular component of a DIT.
   C. The entity attributes are the most granular components of a DIT.
   D. The RDN is the most granular component of a DIT.

6. Which of the following is the default OID encryption algorithm?

    A. MD4 algorithm

    B. MD5 algorithm

    C. MD25 algorithm

    D. MD45 algorithm

7. Which one of the following OID server configuration parameters determines the number of OID Server processes created?

    A. ORCLMAXCC

    B. ORCLCCMAX

    C. ORCLSERVERPROCS

    D. ORCLMAXSERV

8. Which one of the following could you start using the OC4J_SECURITY component of OracleAS?

    A. OracleAS Portal

    B. OID

    C. dcmtl

    D. DAS

9. Which of the following is a part of the services provided by the Directory Integration Platform service?

    A. Starts the OID.

    B. Manages the ODM.

    C. Updates OID cache information for DAS.

    D. Notifies OracleAS Portal when relevant changes are made in the OID.

10. Which of the following shows the set of valid OracleAS portlets that help you perform user and group management tasks through DAS?

    A. User, Administrator, and Group

    B. User, Group, and Management

    C. User, Group, and Services

    D. User, Administrator, and Services

SELF TEST ANSWERS

1. ☑ **B** and **C** are correct because you can use the *ldifwrite* command to write data from the OID to a database and to back up data.
    ☒ **A** is wrong because the ldifwrite tool can't transfer data directly between two OID servers. **D** is wrong because it's the *bulkmodify* tool, not *ldifwrite*, that modifies a large number of entries quickly.

2. ☑ **A** and **B** are correct because ODM is primarily designed to help control access to OID entries and to search and maintain entry attributes as well.
    ☒ **C** and **D** are wrong because you can't use the ODM to manage the OID server processes.

3. ☑ **A** is correct because DAS uses the proxy-user feature of OID to perform operations on behalf of the users.
    ☒ **B, C,** and **D** are wrong because DAS doesn't directly use these features to perform operations on behalf of the users; it's the proxy-user feature that lets it do this.

4. ☑ **B** is correct because you use the opmnctl utility t o stop DAS, along with all other OracleAS Server middle-tier components and the infrastructure.
    ☒ **A, C,** and **D** are wrong because you can't start or stop DAS with any of those tools.

5. ☑ **D** is correct. The relative distinguished name (RDN) is the most granular component of a DIT because there aren't any entities underneath a RDN.
    ☒ **A** is wrong because DIT refers to the whole OID tree structure and thus is the largest, not the smallest, component of a DIT. **B** is wrong because a DN can be composed of several RDNs, which happen to be the smallest component of a DIT. **C** is wrong because the entity attributes aren't recognized as complete components of a DIT, like a RDN or DN.

6. ☑ **A** is correct because by default, OID uses the MD4 encryption algorithm.
    ☒ **B, C,** and **D** are wrong because they point to the wrong or a nonexistent encryption algorithm.

7. ☑ **C** is correct because the ORCLSERVERPROCS configuration parameter determines the number of OID server processes that should be created.
    ☒ **A** is wrong because the ORCLMAXCC parameter determines the number of database connections from each server process, not the number of server processes. **C** and **D** are wrong because they refer to nonexistent configuration parameters.

8. ☑ **D** is correct because you use the dcmtl utility with the OC4J_SECURITY option to start and stop DAS.

☒ **A** and **B** are wrong because you can't start either the OracleAS Portal or the OID using the OC4J_SECURITY component. **C** is wrong because dcmtl is actually the utility you use to start and stop DAS.

9. ☑ **D** is correct because the Directory Integration Platform (DIP) notifies the OracleAS Portal when any portal-relevant changes are made in the OID.
☒ **A** and **B** are wrong because DIP doesn't help you manage either OID service or the ODM. **C** sounds correct, but is wrong because DIP doesn't actually update the OID cache information for DAS; it only notifies the OracleAS Portal about the changes.

10. ☑ **C** is correct because the User, Group, and Services portlets help you perform user and group management tasks though the OID.
☒ **A, B,** and **D** are incorrect because they include a nonexistent portlet.

5
Managing the Oracle HTTP Server

CERTIFICATION OBJECTIVE 5.01

Introduction to the Oracle HTTP Server

Oracle HTTP Server (OHS) is OracleAS 10*g*'s Web Server component and is based on the Apache 1.3 Web server. OHS handles client HTTP requests and can serve static and dynamic content in response. OHS supports Server Side Includes as well as providing load-balancing capabilities. As you probably know, the Apache Web server is the most popular Web server today on the Internet, hosting more Web sites than any other Web server. OHS extends the highly flexible, stable, and highly scalable Apache with several custom modules or "mods" in order to provide specialized Oracle functionality in addition to a high availability infrastructure that helps to manage process, death detection, and failover. You can also use the OHS to access several Oracle components such as Forms, Reports, and the OracleAS Portal via the Web. You can also access Oracle stored procedures through the OHS.

In the OHS directories, you'll often see a reference to Apache files. In fact, the base directory for the OHS is named $ORACLE_HOME/Apache/Apache directory. This is so because OHS is built from the basic Apache Web server, specifically, the Apache version 1.3.

Here are some of the salient features of OHS in relation to OracleAS 10*g*:

- OHS supports SSL encryption based on industry standard algorithms. The SSL capability is special to the Oracle HTTP Server and isn't a part of the standard Apache Web server's capabilities.

- OHS supports both standard authentication features of HTTP servers, storing credentials in flat files; it also supports the OracleAS Single Sign-On feature, with the help of the Oracle-supplied mod_osso module.

- Using the *virtual host* feature, OHS can service multiple domain names over a single IP address. Virtual hosting capability is part of the core Apache Web server features.

- OHJS provides support for distributed authoring and versioning (DAV), with the help of WebDav. Oracle's *mod_oradav* module provides support for this.

- OHS supports URL rewriting so users don't have to change bookmarks in order to change URLs. The support for reverse proxy capabilities makes content provided by multiple servers appear as though it were coming from the same server. URL rewriting is a part of the Apache Web server's basic features.

Important OHS Components

OHS consists of the following important components:

- *HTTP Listener*   This is based on the Apache HTTP listener; it listens to and handles incoming connection requests.
- *Modules (mods)*   The OHS modules extend the functionality of the OHS Server. There are two types of modules: standard Apache modules and OracleAS-specific modules. In addition, OHS offers enhanced versions of the standard HTTP server (Apache) modules.
- *Perl Interpreter*   The final OHS component is a persistent PERL runtime environment, enabled by the mod_perl Apache module.

Oracle HTTP Server Modules

The Apache HTTP Server contains a core set of features, which are extended by the use of dynamic shared objects called modules. Modules are loaded into the HTTP Server when the server starts, and are used for extending the basic capabilities of the Apache server. Oracle HTTP Server includes the basic Apache HTTP server modules and additionally provides specialized Oracle-specific modules. These Oracle modules enhance the HTTP server's capabilities and enable its integration with other OracleAS components. Here's a brief description of the important Oracle-provided OHS modules:

- *mod_certheaders* enables reverse proxy servers such as the OracleAS Web Cache to transfer SSL connection information to OHS, using HTTP headers. The information is transferred to the standard CGI environment variables from the certificate headers. Using certain *mod_certheader* directives, some HTTP requests can be treated as HTTPS requests.
- *mod_dms* enables performance monitoring of various components using Oracle's Dynamic Monitoring Service (DMS).
- *mod_oc4j* routes requests from the Oracle HTTP Server to the Oracle Application Server Containers for J2EE (OC4J).
- *mod_onsint* provides integration support with Oracle Notification Service (ONS) and Oracle Process Manager and Notification Server (OPMN).
- *mod_oradav* enables WebDAV clients to connect to an Oracle database and process information in various schemas. *Mod_oradav* is based on Apache's *mod_dav* module, which is how Apache implements the WebDAV specification.

The WebDAV protocol helps multiple authors to work with Web content by letting them share and edit common files.

- *mod_ossl* enables the OHS to use Secure Socket Layers (SSL), which enables the use of strong cryptography.
- *mod_osso* supports the OracleAS Single Sign-On feature.
- *mod_plsql* enables the Oracle HTTP Server to connect to an Oracle database and enables Web applications to use Oracle stored procedures, using the PL/SQL Gateway.
- *mod_wchandshake* enables the OracleAS Web Cache to automatically discover the Oracle HTTP Server.

on the job   **OHS doesn't load all the modules in the httpd.conf file automatically upon a start or restart. It dynamically loads the modules as and when they are needed.**

The Oracle HTTP Server Processing Model

Once you start the Oracle HTTP server, it listens for connection requests and passes them on to the appropriate service. The spawning of these listener processes differs in UNIX and Windows servers. In a UNIX/Linux system, the OHS control process launches several copies of itself, known as *child processes*, to listen to user's requests. The main process runs as the root user and the child processes under a less privileged user account, usually a UNIX user named "nobody." Each child process is another instance of the httpd program, as you can see from the output below.

```
[] $root 12928 1   0  Apr 11  ? 36:06 /opt/hpws/apache/bin/httpd -d
/opt/hpws/apache -k start
  awuser  7898 22238  0  May 16 ?   0:14 /opt/apache/bin/httpd -DSSL
  awuser 12653 22238  0  May 19 ?   0:12 /opt/apache/bin/httpd -DSSL
  awuser 22249 22238  0  May 16 ?   0:14 /opt/apache/bin/httpd -DSSL
  awuser 22248 22238  0  May 16 ?   0:15 /opt/apache/bin/httpd -DSSL
  awuser 22250 22238  0  May 16 ?   0:15 /opt/apache/bin/httpd -DSSL
    root 22238     1  0  May 16 ? 18:55 /opt/apache/bin/httpd -DSSL
$
```

On a Windows server, there is a multithreaded implementation of the HTTP server process, which involves a single control process and just one child process; it creates multiple threads to listen to connection requests. Thus, the child processes actually aren't separate processes but threads within a single child process.

Under both UNIX and Windows systems, the *httpd.pid* file, located in the $ORACLE_HOME/Apache/Apache/logs directory, contains the process ID of the original OHS process.

Starting and Stopping the Oracle HTTP Server

You start and stop the OHS with the help of the *opmnctl* tool, which was explained in Chapter 3. When you use the *startall* command, all OracleAS components, including the OHS, are started by OPMN. Similarly, by using the *stopall* command, you can stop all the OracleAS processes. You can also *start* just the OHS server itself using the following command:

```
$ opmnctl startproc ias-component=HTTP_Server
```

You *stop* the OHS component by using the following *opmnctl* command:

```
$ opmnctl stopproc ias-component=HTTP_Server
```

Although you can start and stop the OHS processes with the *opmcntl* command as shown here, it's best to start OHS as part of the entire component stack of the OracleAS instance, because OHS is a key component of the OracleAS instance and you may run into problems by starting and stopping just the OHS by itself. You may also reconfigure, start, and stop the OHS server from the Application Server control console.

on the **job**

You mustn't use the apachectl *script, traditionally used to start up the Apache Web server, to start the OHS.*

Oracle HTTP Server Installation and Configuration

By default, Oracle HTTP Server is installed in the $ORACLE_HOME/Apache directory on UNIX and the $ORACLE_HOME/Apache directory on Windows. The Apache directory contains subdirectories for configuring various modules. There's a subdirectory that's also named Apache under the main Apache directory, and this is the base directory of Oracle HTTP Server ($ORACLE_HOME/Apache/Apache). Each of the OHS modules such as *mod_oradav*, for example, has its own directory under the OHS home directory, which is the $ORACLE_HOME/Apache directory. Here are the important subdirectories under the $ORACLE_HOME/Apache/Apache directory:

- *bin* contains OHS binaries or executables.
- *cgi-bin* contains the CGI scripts that the OHS executes on behalf of various clients. This is the default location for the CGI scripts, but in fact, you can store them anywhere on the server.
- *logs* contains both OHS access logs and the error logs.
- *conf* contains the configuration files.
- *htdocs* contains the HTML scripts. Note that this is also just a default directory from which OHS serves all its static Web documents. Because these are easily accessible by outsiders, you must use alternative locations for storing the Web documents.

Because the htdocs directory allows access to anyone on the Web, you must keep only publicly available information in this directory.

- *include* contains header files for creating custom modules.
- *PHP* contains sample code for *mod_php* and the PHP executables.

The main Oracle HTTP Server configuration file is called *httpd.conf* and is located in the ORACLE_HOME/Apache/Apache/conf directory in UNIX and Linux based systems and the ORACLE_HOME\Apache\Apache\conf directory in a Windows system. You can manually edit the *httpd.conf* file to reconfigure the HTTP server, but Oracle recommends against your doing so. The preferred method to make configuration changes is by accessing the *httpd.conf* file using the Application Server Control Console. You must go to the Advanced Server page from the OHS home page and click the *httpd.conf* file. You can then view and edit the configuration file. Figure 5-1 shows the *httpd.conf* file in the Application Server Control Console. Note that the *httpd.conf* is only the main configuration file for OHS. However, you may include pointers to other configuration files such as the *oracle_apache.conf* file, which is used to load specified Oracle-related modules and is usually included as a file inside the *httpd.conf* file.

Remember that the recommended way to modify the OHS configuration is through the Application Server Control Console. This way, the metadata repository information will be updated automatically, unlike the case with the manual modification of the *httpd.conf* file.

Here are some important things to remember about the configuration files:

- There's one directive per line.
- Directives are case insensitive.

FIGURE 5-1

The *httpd.conf* Configuration File

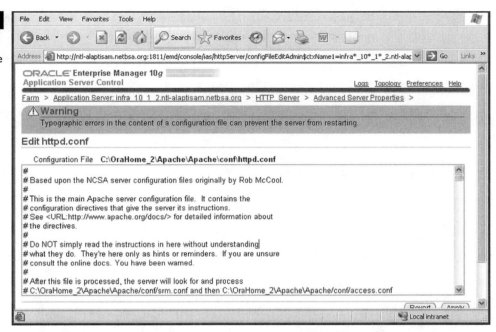

- Arguments to the directives are case sensitive.
- You can't include comments after a directive, but you can include comments on their own line by prefixing the pound (#) sign.
- Any blank lines or white spaces in between lines are ignored.

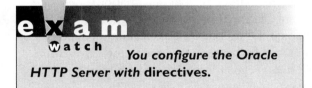

e x a m

ⓦ a t c h   *You configure the Oracle HTTP Server with directives.*

Other Server Configuration Files

The *httpd.conf* file, as mentioned, is the primary configuration file for the Oracle HTTP Server. This file contains directives as well as pointers to other configuration files. Here's a brief summary of the other configuration files:

- *mod_oc4j.conf*   This file helps you configure the *mod_oc4j* module, which carries requests from the HTTP Server to OC4J.
- *mime.types*   The *mime.types* file contains extra Internet media types to be sent to clients so they can handle file contents. You can also include the *AddType directive* in this file.

■ *oracle_apache.conf*   This is the main file for storing configuration files of all
supported modules such as *moddav* and *plsql*. Here are the typical contents of
the *oracle_apache.conf* file:

```
# Advanced Queuing–AQ XML
include "C:\OraHome_2\rdbms\demo\aqxml.conf"
# Directives needed for OraDAV module
include "C:\OraHome_2\Apache\oradav\conf\moddav.conf"
include "C:\OraHome_2\Apache\jsp\conf\ojsp.conf"
include "C:\OraHome_2\Apache\modplsql\conf\plsql.conf"
# Oracle uix
include "C:\OraHome_2\uix\uix.conf"
#OiD DAS module
include "C:\OraHome_2\ldap\das\oiddas.conf"
#Directives needed for SSO module
include "C:\OraHome_2\sso\conf\sso_apache.conf"
#Directives needed for OCM module
include "C:\OraHome_2\Apache\Apache\conf\ocm_apache.conf"
```

Note that some of the minor configuration files can be read each time a related
file or directory is requested by a client. Some files, on the other hand, are read only
once, when the OHS instance is started. These files, like the main configuration file
httpd.conf file, are called server-wide configuration files.

OHS Directives

Directives are configuration instructions that govern the behavior of the OHS
Server, and there is one directive per line in the OHS configuration files.
OHS directives let you customize the Web server for your organization's
needs. All you have to do to configure OHS is to simply make changes to the
httpd.conf file. Throughout this chapter, the various OHS configuration directives
are explained in detail. In fact, most of this chapter is devoted to the explanation
of various OHS configuration directives. A given configuration directive can't
arbitrarily be used anywhere you want. You can use each directive in a specific
context. There are four contexts in which the configuration directives can be
applied:

■ *Server config*   A directive is said to have a server config context if it can be
used only in the main server configuration file (*httpd.conf*) and not inside any
scope-limiting containers such as <Directory> and <VirtualHost>. You can't use
these directives in *.htaccess* files either.

- *virtual host*   A directive that has a virtual host context can be placed only within the <VirtualHost> containers in the server configuration files.
- *directory*   A directive in the directory context can be used in the main server configuration file, but only within the <Directory>, <Location>, and <Files> containers.
- *htaccess*   A directory that's valid in the *.htaccess* context, can be placed only inside the per-directory *.htaccess* files. Of course, depending on the override settings, the file itself may or may not be processed.

Depending on the context in which the server issues a directive, there are *three* classes of directives, as described in the following paragraphs.

Global   *Global directives* belong to the *server configuration context* and apply to the entire OHS server. All directives inside the *httpd.conf* file are global directives, except the so-called container directives (more on this later), which limit the scope of a directive to only a certain area of the OHS. For example, you may want directives in the *httpd.conf* file not to apply to the entire server but to be restricted only to particular files and directories, or only to certain hosts and URLs. You can then use the various available OHS containers such as <Files>, <Directories>, and <VirtualHost>, to limit the scope of these configuration directives. As another example, the virtual host container limits the directives inside it only to virtual hosts and not the main server. Container directives are always enclosed in start and end tags (e.g., <Virtual Host> and </VirtualHost>).

Per Server   The per-server class of directives can have a *server configuration or a virtual host context*. In the *httpd.conf* file, all directives outside the <VirtualHost> container are the per-server class directive for the main server and are in the server configuration context. Similarly, all directives inside the <VirtualHost> container are directives in the virtual host context and apply only to virtual hosts and not to the main server.

Per Directory   The per-directory class directives can belong to any of the four contexts: server configuration, virtual host, directory, or *.htaccess*. You can use these directives anywhere.

Here's the syntax for specifying a configuration directive (server level) in the *httpd.conf* file:

```
KeepAlive ON
```

The *KeepAlive* directive, which is discussed in more detail later on, enables the OHS to maintain persistent connections to the client instead of automatically closing a connection after each request by the client.

Basic Oracle HTTP Server Configuration Directives

There are several configuration directives that you can use to configure basic things such as the directories from which OHS will serve static Web documents or the directories for storing the error logs. You also have directives that help configure access control by specifying the server and port names.

When I discuss the OHS processing model subsequently in the chapter, I discuss several OHS processing-related directives, such as those that determine whether persistent browser-server connections should be maintained and for how long. Finally, in the last part of this chapter, I explain several OHS configuration directives that are applied under a limited scope instead of being applicable to the entire OHS server. I also explain some special OHS directives that limit or enable several OHS features in a later section in this chapter. In the following sections, I discuss three types of basic OHS configuration directives:

- File Location Specification directives
- Access Control directives
- Administration directives

Let's start by discussing the simple OHS configuration directives, starting with directives that let you configure the location of various OHS server files.

File Location Specification Directives

There are several important directives that govern the location of various OHS server files. The following directives can be specified in the server configuration context.

ServerRoot   The *ServerRoot* directive by default specifies the main OHS or base directory for the OHS server installation, underneath which lie the subdirectories where the binaries, log files, configuration files, and other documents such as HTML files are located. Typically, the *ServerRoot* directive points to the $ORACLE_HOME/Apache directory. The directory specified by the *ServerRoot* directive usually contains the subdirectories bin, conf, htdocs, and logs. It's important to remember that often, other configuration directives use *ServerRoot* as part of their relative path name.

```
Example: ServerRoot /usr/local/ohs
```

PidFile   The *PidFile* directive lets you specify the location of the PID file. The PID file contains the Process ID of the OHS server. If you don't begin the filename with a slash (/), the path is relative to the *ServerRoot* directory.

ScoreBoardFile   The *ScoreBoardFile* directive is an optional directive required only under some systems; it helps to set the location of a file used by the main control server process to communicate with the child processes. You can check for the presence of the *ScoreBoardFile* on your system by seeing whether an active OHS server has created this file. Usually, only Windows-based OHS implementations will have the *ScoreBoardFile*.

OHS uses a scoreboard to record communications between the parent and child processes. Some architectures may be able to maintain this "scoreboard" in memory, but some others actually require a physical file to do so. If you use this directive, OHS will create a file on disk to record the communication details. Here's how you use the *ScoreBoardFile* directive:

```
ScoreBoardFile /var/run/apache_status
```

CoreDumpDirectory   The *CoreDumpDirectory* is found only in UNIX systems and is the directory location where the OHS server will try to switch before dumping core dumps. By default, the *CoreDumpDirectory* is set to the same value as the *ServerRoot* directory. However, you must use the *CoreDumpDirectory* directive to specify a more secure location, because you don't

exam
watch
The OHS recognizes changes to the main configuration files only when you start or restart the server.

want the server, running as just any user, to be able to write to the all-important *ServerRoot* directory, which holds critical OHS binaries and configuration files in its various subdirectories.

DocumentRoot   This directory is where the HTTP Server stores and serves files from, and the default location is the *htdocs* directory, whish is relative to the *ServerRoot* directory. The directory specified by *DocumentRoot* is the main document visible to a Web browser. This directory location allows public access to all pages, so you mustn't keep sensitive information here.

Unless you use a directive such as Alias, the HTTP Server will append the requested URL's path to the document root to make the complete path to the document. Here's a simple example that illustrates this point:

```
documentRoot /usr/web
```

In the preceding example, when a user accesses http://www.myhost.com/index.html, the user will be referred to /usr/web/index.html.

Note that you must specify *DocumentRoot* without a trailing slash.

ErrorLog   The *ErrorLog* directive sets the name of the HTTP Server log file, and by default it is logs/error_log. Note that this path is relative to the *ServerRoot* directory. Thus, if the *ServerRoot* directory is specified as /usr/web/ohs, then the error log files will be located in the /usr/web/ohs/logs directory. You can also specify an alternative pathname by explicitly providing the entire pathname of the alternative directory. The two important OHS log files are the *access log* and the *error log*.

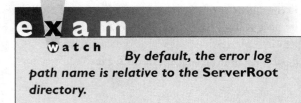

Access Control Directives

There are several important directives that relate to access control. These directives set the server and server administrator options, and they can be set for the main OHS server or a virtual host. Access control directives are useful when you want to limit the IP addresses or ports the OHS server will listen to, for example. Let's discuss the important access control–related OHS configuration directives, which are the *Listen*, *UseCanonicalName*, *ServerName*, and *Port* directives.

Listen   The *Listen* directive tells the OHS server which port and IP address combinations it should listen to for client connection requests. The syntax for the *Listen* directive is as follows:

```
Listen [IP-address:]portnumber
```

As you can see, you can specify both the IP address and the port number as arguments to the *Listen* directive. However, the IP address is only an optional argument. If you specify only a certain port number, the OHS server will listen to all requests from all IP addresses on that port. If you specify the optional port number as well as the mandatory port number arguments, the OHS server will listen to requests only from the port number and IP address combination. Here's an example:

```
Listen 192.166.14.12:80
```

The OHS server will listen to requests only from the IP address 192.166.14.12, on port 80. If you specify multiple *Listen* directives with various IP and port number combinations, OHS will accept connection requests from all the specified combinations of IP addresses and ports. Note that if you leave out the IP address, OHS will honor requests from all IP addresses, as long as they come through the specified port.

UseCanonicalName   On occasion, the OHS server needs to construct self-referential URLs—that is, URLs that refer back to the same server. When redirecting a URL to the same server (i.e., when the OHS Server has to construct a self-referential URL), it has two choices regarding the host name and port. The first option is to use the host name and port specified by users in the HTTP 1.1 header. The other way is to use the host name and port numbers specified by the *ServerName* and *Port* directives. You can choose the latter option by setting the *UseCanonicalName* setting to ON, which is the default setting for this directive. If you set the *UseCanonicalName* directive to ON, the Oracle HTTP Server will use the *Server Name* and *Port* directives to construct the canonical name for the server.

```
Example:  ServerName = www.example.com
          Port = 9090
          Canonical Name = www.example.com:9090
```

Self referential URLs may be useful when you have an intranet server, where you use short names such as www. If a user types a short name such as http://www/test (without the trailing slash), OHS will redirect it by default (*UseCanonicalName* is ON by default) to http://www.mydomain.com/test/, and the user may thus be forced to authenticate twice (if you have enabled authentication)—first to //www, and then to //www/test. If you set *UseCanonicalName* to OFF instead, OHS will redirect this self-referential URL to simply http://www/test/.

ServerName   The *ServerName* directive specifies the host name and port that the server uses to identify itself when redirecting user URLs. IF you don't specify the *ServerName* directive, the OHS server will try to perform a reverse lookup on the IP address to gather the host name information. If you omit the optional port argument for the *ServerName* directive, then OHS will use the port number specified in the incoming requests. It's a good idea to always explicitly specify the hostname and port by using the *ServerName* directive. Here's the syntax of the *ServerName* directive:

```
ServerName fully-qualified-domain-name[:port]
```

As you can see, the fully qualified domain name is mandatory, and the port specification is optional, for the *ServerName* directive. Let's say the name of the server hosting the OHS server is test.company.com. Let's say the server also has a DNS alias named www.company.com. If your goal is for the server to be always identified as www.company.com, you can do that by setting the following value for the *ServerName* directive:

```
ServerName www.company.com:80
```

Under a virtual hosting system, the *ServerName* directive inside the <VirtualHost> container specifies the host names that should be specified in the HTTP 1.1 headers to match the virtual host name.

The *ServerName* directive defines the host name for the SERVER_NAME variable used in the canonical server name for URL redirection requests.

Port   The *Port* directive sets the SERVER_PORT environment variable used in redirection requests. If you don't set the *Listen* directive, the OHS Server accepts connections and redirects to the port number specified by the *Port* directive. That is, in the absence of the *Listen* directive, the *Port* directive specifies the default port for the Web server. If you do set the *Listen* directive, however, OHS uses the *Port* directive only for redirection; this is usually the IP and port on the Web cache that sits in front of the OHS. When you use the *Listen* directive, that directive will override any port value that's been set by you, which will become the default port for redirected URLs or any other URLs generated by the Oracle HTTP Server. The port numbers OHS can use range from 0 to 65535, but all port numbers below 1024 are reserved for system use.

You can start OHS only from the root account if you choose port number 80.

Administration Directives

The following four directives determine the Oracle HTTP Server privileges.

User   The *User* directive specifies the userid that the server will assume when answering requests. The user must have privileges to access common files and execute non httpd request type code.

Group   Use the *Group* directive to specify the operating system group under which the HTTP Server will handle requests. You must create a new group for running the HTTP Server.

The User and Group directives are available only for OHS Servers running on UNIX operating systems. They aren't available on Windows operating systems.

ServerAdmin   The *ServerAdmin* directive creates an email address to be included in all error messages to the clients. Ideally, you should create a separate email address solely for this purpose.

ServerTokens   The *ServerTokens* directive specifies the amount of OHS Server details that should be revealed to the clients as part of the error messages. You can use the following four settings:

- *Prod* is the preferred setting and outputs only the server name.
- The *min* setting includes the server name and version.
- The *os* setting shows server name, the version, and the operating system.
- The *full* setting, which is the default, outputs server name, version, operating system, and compiled modules. Obviously, this default setting could be dangerous, as it reveals quite a bit of information about your Web server.

Note that both the *ServerAdmin* and *ServerTokens* directives determine the information the OHS server will present when it generates documents such as error messages. The *ServerTokens* directive also sets the value of the OHS HTTP response header field.

The directives inside the *.htaccess* file apply to the directory in which the file is located, as well as to all subdirectories that are underneath that directory. You can control the directives that can be placed in the *.htaccess* files by using the *AllowOverride* directive.

The .htaccess Files

Remember that the configuration directives placed in the *httpd.conf* file are read only upon starting the Apache Web server. Thus, there is no way you can make dynamic configuration changes by modifying the *httpd.conf* file. However, you can use a special file called the *.htaccess* file to make dynamic changes to the Web server. The configuration directives within the *.htaccess* file are read *each time* a request is made to the Web server, not each time it's started.

The directives in an *.htaccess* file apply to the directory in which you place the file and to all subdirectories underneath it. Using *.htaccess* files, you can make configuration changes solely on a per-directory basis instead of making server-wide changes. The syntax of the *.htaccess* files is similar to that of the main OHS configuration file, *httpd.conf*. The *httpd.conf* file is read-only when you start the OHS Server. Unlike the *httpd.conf* file, *.htaccess* files are read on every access to the HTTP server and the directives placed in the *.htaccess* files come into immediate effect, without a need for bouncing the server. You can also refer to the *.htaccess* files as distributed configuration files, because they enable you to make per-directory configuration changes rather than server-wide configuration changes.

Note that you can change the default name *.htaccess* by using the configuration directive *AccessFileName*. Here's an example that shows how you can use the *AccessFileName* directive to change the default *.htaccess* filename to the default file name config_dir:

```
AccessFileName config_dir
```

You can also limit the directives that are permitted in an *.htaccess* file by using the *AllowOverride* directive in the *httpd.conf* configuration file.

The *.htaccess* file's main purpose is to enable you to make a configuration change on a *per-directory* basis instead of a per-server basis. If you place some configuration directives in a text file named *.htaccess* file and place it in a certain directory, those directives will apply to that directory and its subdirectories only. Note that you can include any directive you may place in an *.htaccess* file in the main configuration file, *httpd.conf* itself, by using the <Directory> container. You use *.htaccess* files mainly to allow users without root access to alter the Apache Server configuration, albeit on a limited basis.

Note that there are disadvantages to using the *.htaccess* file for configuring the Apache server. For one thing, your Web server will take a performance hit, because Apache must look in every directory for potential *.htaccess* files when you enable *.htaccess* files by using the *AllowOverride* option (more on this directive later). For example, if you place an *.htaccess* file in the /www/htdocs/example directory, Apache must look for the *.htaccess* file in each of these locations:

```
/.htaccess
/www/.htaccess
/www/htdocs/.htaccess
/www/htdocs/example/.htaccess
```

Each time a document is requested, the Apache server must load the *.htaccess* file as well, thus hurting its performance.

In addition to the performance implications, there are security issues when you allow users to use *.htaccess* files to configure the server. Basically, you are relinquishing some control over the Web server to the users. To avoid this, you may just put the directives in the <Directory> section of your main *httpd.conf* file and avoid the use of the *.htaccess* files altogether. For example, the following two are equivalent ways of specifying the *AddType* directive, the first using the *.htaccess* file and the second using the <Directory> container.

Using the *.htaccess* file:

```
AddType text/example .exm
```

Using the <Directory> section in the *httpd.conf* file:

```
<Directory /www/htdocs/example>
AddType text/example .exm
</Directory>
```

Thus, from both the security point of view as well as the performance angle, *.htaccess* files are not a good choice for setting per-directory directives. You can use the directory container in the *httpd.conf* file itself, to set the per-directory scoped configuration directives. *.htaccess* files are mainly used to allow users limited privileges to modify certain OHS server configuration directives, without the involvement of the Web server administrator. In this sense, they do serve a valid purpose. However, when you allow users to specify OHS configuration directives, remember that you're introducing potential security vulnerabilities into your system as well. Because the OHS server has to scan all the directories and subdirectories when you use *.htaccess* files, there's a potential performance hit.

Managing Processes and Connections

There are several server configuration-level directives you can use in the *httpd.conf* server configuration file to control the number of OHS processes and other runtime server-related issues. On a UNIX server, you use the following server-level directives to manage processes and connections:

- *StartServers*   The *StartServers* directive determines the number of child server processes created with the parent control process. The default value for the *StartServers* directive is 5. Because the OHS server will dynamically adjust the number of child server processes depending on the load, you don't have to worry about setting the value for this directive, in general.

- *MaxClients*   The *MaxClients* directive determines the maximum number of simultaneous connections that will be handled by the OHS server. Any connection attempts over the *MaxClients* setting will be queued, and will be accepted once the existing connections start dropping off. The default value for the *MaxClients* directive is 150.

- *MaxRequestsPerChild*   This directive lets you specify the number of requests each child process can handle before it dies. Each child process will handle a maximum of 30 requests during its lifetime before it automatically expires. If you set the *MaxRequestsPerChild* directive to a value of 0, the child processes will not die until you reboot the OHS server. Although this may seem like a tempting thing to do, remember that you increase the risk of running out of memory, say by a child process incurring a memory leak during its (eternal) lifetime. Also, when the OHS server load drops, it's advisable to run with a smaller number of child processes than that required during the peak load times. By setting a positive value (the default *is* a positive value of 30), you guarantee that the child processes have a finite lifetime, thus matching the number of child processes with the OHS server load.

■ *MaxSpareServers* This directive specifies the maximum number of unused child server processes that must be kept running. By default, the value for this directive is a maximum of ten server processes. If there are more idle servers than that specified by the *MaxSpareServers* directive, OHS will start killing idle child processes until it reaches the *MaxSpareServers* setting.

■ *MinSpareServers* This directive specifies the minimum number of child servers that must be kept running, and the default value for this directive is 5. If there are fewer than five child server processes alive, new processes are created at an increasing rate on a per second basis, until the rate set by the MAX_SPAWN_RATE parameter is reached. Default value for the MAX_SPAWN_RATE parameter is 32.

You use the following directives in both the UNIX and the Windows systems:

■ *KeepAlive* This directive enables you to use a persistent connection, which improves the scalability of the Oracle HTTP Server. By default, the *KeepAlive* directive is set to ON, meaning persistent connections are enabled by default when you use OHS. Since HTTP connections are stateless, if you don't set this parameter to ON, a browser will need to make separate connections for each request from the server. Thus, for a Web page that contains a half a dozen images calling for .gif files, a client Web browser is forced to open a total of seven connections—one for the page and six requests for the six image files. Making multiple connections to satisfy the client request as shown here will increase the latency due to the time it takes to establish all the connections. By letting the *KeepAlive* directive remain at its default ON setting, your Web server performance will be dramatically higher, because latency will drop due to the need for fewer connections. Of course, there is an inherent tradeoff in using the *KeepAlive On* setting, because this way your server will have the burden of managing more persistent connections than if you had set the *KeepAlive* directive OFF.

on the
Job

*You must keep the **KeepAlive** directive set to OFF if you're using OracleAS Clusters.*

■ *KeepAliveTimeout* This directive determines the number of seconds the OHS Server waits for a connection request following the first connection, before terminating the connection.

- *MaxKeepAliveRequests* This directive determines the number of requests allowed per connection, when you set the *KeepAlive* directive to ON. Default value is 0, which means that there is no limit to the number of requests that are allowed. You must set *MaxKeepAliveRequests* at a high value to make OHS perform efficiently.
- *ThreadsPerChild* This directive controls the number of simultaneous requests for connections. It is applicable only to a Windows server.

CERTIFICATION OBJECTIVE 5.02

Managing the Oracle HTTP Server

You can manage the Oracle HTTP Server through the Application Server Control, or with the help of command-line tools.

Managing from the Command Line

The two command-line tools you use to manage OHS are *opmnctl* and *dcmtl*. You can start, restart, *and* stop the Oracle HTTP Server along with the rest of the OracleAS components using the opmnctl utility, or just the Oracle HTTP Server by itself. Here's how you start and stop the OHS server using the opmnctl command-line utility, which is located in the $ORACLE_HOME/opmn/bin directory:

```
$opmnctl startproc ias-component=HTTP_Server
$opmnctl stopproc ias-component=HTTP_Server
$opmnctl restartproc ias-component=HTTP_Server
```

You can also use the dcmtl utility to configure the Oracle HTTP Server instance.

Always use the opmnctl command-line tool to start, stop, and restart the Oracle HTTP Server to avoid potential problems caused by the inability *of the configuration infrastructure to communicate with server processes. You shouldn't use the apachectl utility to manage the OHS.*

Using the Application Server Control to Manage OHS

You can view the status and a brief performance report of the Oracle HTTP Server in the Application Server home page, shown in Figure 5-2. To get to the home page of the Oracle HTTP Server, go to the System Components table of the relevant OracleAS instance and click the HTTP_Server link. From the HTTP Server home page, you can click links to view the status metrics, module metrics, and the response/load metrics. You can also view the error log for the HTTP Server by clicking the Error Log link.

Go to the System Components table section of the Application Server Control to find where you can start, stop, and restart the OHS server. You can also stop and start the OHS using the *Stop All* and *Start All* buttons on the Application Server Control home page.

You can use the Application Server Control to conveniently manage the OHS and modify the default configuration settings. You've already seen how you can start, stop, and restart the OHS Server using the Application Server Control. Let's briefly examine the various OHS management features in the Application Server Control.

FIGURE 5-2	

The Oracle
HTTP Server
Home Page

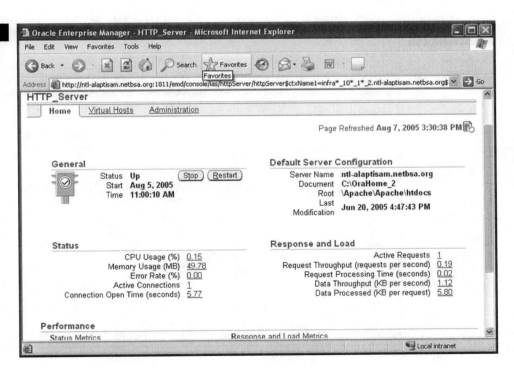

Editing the httpd.conf File

You can edit the *httpd.conf* file by following these steps:

- On the Application Server home page, select Oracle HTTP Server from the System Components table and click the HTTP_Server link.
- On the HTTP Server home page, click the Administration tab.
- Click the *Advanced Server Properties* link in the HTTP_Server Administration page.
- In the Advanced Properties page, click the *httpd.conf* link, to edit that file.

Figure 5-3 shows the Advanced Server Properties page. You can view and modify several OHS configuration files from this page, including the *httpd.conf* file and the *oracle_apache.conf* file, which helps configure the Oracle-specific HTTP parameters.

Although you can modify the *httpd.conf* file manually, the advantage in editing the file using Application Server Control is that the configuration changes are effected immediately, because the OHS server is automatically bounced when you

FIGURE 5-3

The Advanced Server Properties Page

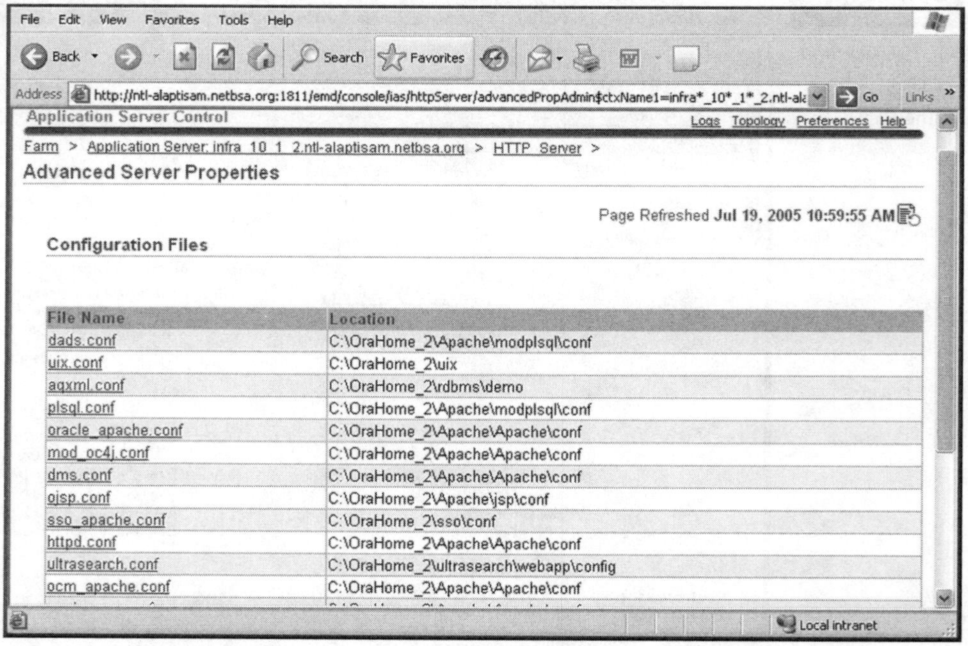

modify the configuration. Also remember that if you do decide to manually edit the *httpd.conf* file, be sure to issue the following *dcmtl* command at the command line:

```
$ dcmtl updateconfig -v
```

When you issue this command, the Metadata Repository is updated with the configuration changes you make by manually editing the *httpd.conf* file. The −v option gives you detailed information (verbose) about the results of executing the command. Make sure that you execute the *dcmtl* command in the appropriate OracleAS instance home directory. You can't guarantee that you're issuing the command in the right environment by merely setting the ORACLE_HOME environment variable. You must be in the correct ORACLE_HOME location to make sure you're running the command for the appropriate instance.

Monitoring the Oracle HTTP Server

You can view the following types of Oracle HTTP Server metrics using the Application Server Control.

Status Metrics   The OHS Status metrics show you a summary of the memory usage, CPU usage, connection rates, and error rates for the server.

e x a m

w a t c h   *Oracle recommends that you use the Application Server Control page to modify the Oracle HTTP Server configuration, rather than directly edit the httpd.conf file.*

Response and Load Metrics   Response and Load Metrics provide an overall picture of server performance. The Response metrics show the average number of requests submitted and the length of time the server took to respond to the users' requests. The Load metrics show the average number of bytes of data processed with the requests. Of course, large loads will result in a slower response time.

Module Metrics   The module metrics for the HTTP Server show the current response times for the various HTTP modules.

Server Properties Page

You can view and modify basic OHS settings from the Server Properties page, which can be reached in the following way:

1. Navigate to the relevant Application Server Control HTTP Server home page.
2. Click the Administration tab, which will take you to the Administration page.
3. On the Administration page, click Server Properties.

Here's a brief summary of the Oracle HTTP Server settings you can view and modify from the Server Properties page:

General Settings

In the General section of the Server Properties page, you can view general OHS settings. You an also modify the following settings from here:

- *Document root location*   You can specify a relative path or an absolute path for the document root location, with the relative path being relative to the *ServerRoot* directory specified in the configuration file.
- *Administrator E-Mail*   All error messages to users contain the Administrator E-mail address to be used by the HTTP Server.
- *User and group settings*   You can modify the initially chosen values for the user and group directives in the *httpd.conf* configuration file.
- *Listener addresses and ports*   Using this section, you can do the following:
  - Change the default port setting for the HTTP Server.
  - Add, remove, or change a current listening address or port.

Note that the Listening Addresses/Ports table contents are the same as the contents of the *Listen* directive in the OHS Server configuration file (*httpd.conf*).

Error Log and Access Log Settings

You can view the error logs and the access logs and change their settings from the Logging section of the Server Properties page. You can perform the following tasks from here:

- Change an error log or access log filename or location.
- Set the logging level for the error logs.
- Set the IP Address Translation type.
- Add and remove an access log file.
- Change the log format of an access log file.

Client Request Handling Settings

The Client Request Handling Settings section shows information about various client request settings, such as the following:

- *Maximum Requests Processed Simultaneously* You use this to limit the number of simultaneous user requests, and the value seen here is the same as the settings specified for the *MaxClients* directive (UNIX) and the *ThreadsPerChild* directive (Windows).

- *Request Timeout* This value is the same as the *Timeout* directive setting.

- *Limit Requests Handled by Each Child Server Process* This value is the same as the setting of the configuration directive *MaxRequestsPerChild* on UNIX hosts and is unavailable on Windows hosts.

Client Connection Settings

The Client Connection Settings section shows you various client connection settings such as the following:

- *Allow Multiple Requests per Connection* This value is equivalent to the setting for the *KeepAlive* directive.

- *Connection Timeout* This specifies the number of seconds an idle connection will remain open, and its value is equivalent to the *KeepAliveTimeout* directive setting.

- *Limit Requests per Connection* This specifies the maximum simultaneous requests per connection, and its value is equivalent to the setting of the *MaxKeepAliveRequests* directive.

Using Oracle HTTP Server Log Files

As mentioned previously, all OHS Server log files are stored in the $ORACLE_HOME/Apache/Apache/logs directory. Here's a summary of the different types of log files in this directory:

- *httpd.pid file* There is a single *httpd.pid* file, in which the OHS Server stores the process ID (PID) of the parent server process. The PID is usually a four-digit number, and you may need it for restarting or terminating the parent process on a UNIX system. You can change the name of this file using the *PidFile* directive described previously.

■ *error_log*   The error log contains OHS Server errors, and you can change the name of this file with the *ErrorLog* configuration directive. The error log is a critical file, because it's the first place you look when you have OHS Server performance problems. Here's a typical line in the error_log file on a Windows server:

```
[Mon Jul 18 16:24:13 2005] [error] [client 172.16.14.15]
 [ecid: 1121721846:172.16.14.15:5940:7412:3,0]
mod_plsql: /pls/orasso/htp.p HTTP-503 ORA-12154 Proxy log On failed.
Please verify that you have specified correct connectivity information
 i.e. username, password & connect-string in the DAD
```

on the **job**   ***You can access the error logs and the access logs using Application Server Control by going to the Server Properties page from the Oracle HTTP Server home page.***

■ *access_log*   This file contains a detailed account of all accesses to the OHS Server, including items such as the remote host name, remote user, time, request, bytes transferred, and so forth. You can change the name of this file using the *TransferLog* server level configuration or the virtual host directive. You use the same arguments for TransferLog as for Custom Log. However, you can't specify the log format explicitly. You also can't specify conditional logging of client requests. OHS simply determines the log format by using the last used *LogFormat* directive settings that didn't define a nickname. If no other format is specified, the Common Log Format (CLF) is used.

The access log information is vital in generating server usage reports. Here's a sample line from an error_log file:

```
172.16.14.15 - - [10/Nov/2005:11:51:24 -0500]
"GET /ohs_images/figure1.gif HTTP/1.1" 200 18752
```

For every 10,000 requests, the access log grows by about 1MB. If your access log gets very big, you shouldn't try to remove it or move it. You should, instead, reset the log files by first moving the log file and then telling the OHS Server to reopen the log file, as shown here:

```
$ mv access_log access_log.old
$ kill -1 'cat httpd.pid'
```

This two-step procedure will keep the access log size under control, and it backs up the access files at the same time.

- *ssl_engine_log and ssl_request_log* These error logs contain messages from the SSL connection requests. The files are created when you start OHS in the SSL mode, and the *SSLLog* directive is enabled in the server or virtual host configuration.

By default, all log files are in the standard Common Log Format (CLF), but you can change the format using the *LogFormat* and *CustomLog* directives, and you can control both the content of the log file and its format. The CLF format is:

```
LogFormat "%h %l %u %t \"%r\" %>s %b" common
```

The preceding CLF format corresponds to the following:

```
host ident authuser date request status bytes
```

The LogLevel Directive

The *LogLevel* directive in the *httpd.conf* configuration file determines the verbosity of the error messages in the various error logs you saw earlier. By changing the *LogLevel* directive setting, you control the output in the log files. Here are the possible settings for the *LogLevel* directive:

- *Emerg* refers to a system emergency, where immediate action is needed.
- *Crit* refers to a critical condition.
- *Error* is an error condition.
- *Warn* is a warning condition.
- *Notice* is a normal but noteworthy event.
- *Info* refers to an informational message.
- *Debug* is a debugging message.

Note that setting the error logging level to *Notice*, *Informational*, or *Debug* typically produces numerous trivial informational messages.

CERTIFICATION OBJECTIVE 5.03

OHS Configuration Directives

As was mentioned previously in this chapter, you can classify OHS directives into classes or groups based on the *context* in which they can be used. A context indicates where in the server's configuration files a directive is considered *legal*. You can have directives that have either a server configuration, a virtual host, a directory, or an htaccess context. Remember that all directives are legal only in their specified contexts—if you use them in the wrong contexts, you'll get errors or the HTTP Server may even fail to start. You've learned about the key administrative and other OHS configuration directives earlier. Let's delve a little deeper into the application of the OHS configuration directives in various contexts and see how the OHS merges the directives when necessary.

The Server Configuration Context

The *server configuration context* applies to all directives inside the *httpd.conf* file unless they are part of any type of a *container*. Containers are arbitrary *sections* of the OHS that limit the scope of the OHS configuration directives—for example, to only a certain directory, file, or URL. This means that the scope of server context directives that fall within a container will be limited to the containers' sphere of influence.

If you place any OHS directive in the *httpd.conf* file, it will automatically apply to the entire OHS Web server. However, there may be cases in which you want certain directives to apply only to part of the server. You use OHS containers to limit the *scope* of the configuration directives. The most important of these containers are the <VirtualHost>, <Directory>, <DirectoryMatch>, <Files>, <FilesMatch>, <Location>, and <LocationMatch>. For example, a directive placed within the container tags <Files> and </Files> within the *httpd.conf* file will apply only to a certain file system. Similarly, you can limit the scope of a directive to a certain URL, by enclosing the directive within the container tags <Location> and </Location>. Containers thus help you to configure the OHS server at a decentralized level. Virtual hosting is a feature by which the OHS Web server serves multiple Web sites simultaneously. By using the <VirtualHost> container, you can limit the scope of a configuration directive to a certain Web site only.

Here are the various OHS containers, which are denoted by opening and closing tags before and after their names within the *httpd.conf* file. Remember that any directives that don't fall into one of these containers will apply to the entire server.

- *<VirtualHost>* You can use the <VirtualHost> directives to serve multiple Web sites from a single server. This Virtual Host context specifies that a directive can appear inside <VirtualHost> containers in the server configuration files. The virtual host section's directives apply only to specific virtual hosts identified by a specific IP address–IP port pair. I'll explain the <VirtualHost> container in the section titled Virtual Host Context, later in this chapter.
- *<Directory> and <DirectoryMatch>* These containers or sections contain directives applicable to particular directories.
- *<File> and <FileMatch>* These containers or sections contain directives applicable only to certain files.
- *<Location> or <LocationMatch>* These containers or sections contain directives applicable to particular URLs.

The various OHS container directives are examined in more detail in the following subsections. Note that the container directives always have HTML-type opening and closing tags surrounding the directives they enclose, as, for example, in <Directory>, </Directory>.

Virtual Host Context

OHS can serve multiple Web sites simultaneously, using a feature known as *Virtual Hosting*. If you place directives inside a <VirtualHost> container, they will apply only to requests from specific Web sites. The virtual host context specifies that a directive can appear inside <VirtualHost> containers in the server configuration files. The virtual host section's directives apply only to specific virtual hosts identified by a specific IP address–IP port pair. Virtual hosts and the use of the <VirtualHost> container are explained in more detail later in this chapter, in the section on virtual hosting.

Directory Context

Web servers can serve static and dynamic content, with most of the static content being stored on the server (corresponding to the default htdocs directory) and the dynamic content being generated on the spur of the moment, usually with the help of data from databases, for example. Containers help you configure the serving of both static and dynamic Web pages. You use configuration containers to modify the configuration of either particular physical locations in your file system, or particular locations in the Web space. The file system is the physical view of your disks as it appears to the operating system. The Web space, on the other hand, is how your site appears to the Web server and your clients. A path such as /dir may appear to a client as /usr/local/apache/htdocs/dir. Note that there may not be a one-to-one correspondence mapping between the Web space and the file system, because a dynamic Web page my not be present anywhere on the file system; instead, it may be generated with the help of database input, for example.

The <Directory> and <Files> directives are *file system–related containers*, which apply directives to selected parts of the file system on the server. The <Location> and <LocationMatch> containers aren't file system related. These are *Web space containers* and are put in to change the configuration for (usually dynamic) Web space content only.

You choose between the file system–based containers and the Web space–related containers (URL based), depending on where the objects are located. If the objects are loaded on your file system, use the <Directory> and <Files> (and <DirectoryMatch> and <FilesMatch) containers. If, instead of the file system, the objects are from elsewhere, as is the case when you generate dynamic Web pages from a database, use the <Location> and <LocationMatch> directives. Don't use the <Location> directive to limit access to file system objects; the restrictions you specify can be circumvented because a file system location doesn't have a one-to-one correspondence with a Web space (URL) location.

<Directory>

The <Directory> container can contain any directory context directives that apply to a named directory and its subdirectories. You may use a full path to a directory or a wildcard string (? matches a single character and * matches any sequence of characters). Note the following:

- <Directory /> operates on the whole file system.
- <Directory dir> refers only to absolute directories.
- <Directory/home/*public_html> points to the public_html sub directory under any directory in the /home directory.
- You can't nest <Directory> containers inside each other.

Note that although you can't nest <Directory> containers inside each other, you may refer to nested directories in the document root.

If more than one directory section in the *httpd.conf* file matches the directory containing a document, Apache will apply the directives to all of the directory sections! Apache will apply the directives to the shortest directory first and then process through all the directory sections, ending with the longest directory match. In addition, any *.htaccess* file directives are applied as and when Apache finds them during this process.

Here's an example with multiple directory sections. In this example, the document *test.html* is in the /home/www/dir/ directory.

```
<Directory />
AllowOverride none
</Directory>
<Directory /home/>
Allowoverride FileInfo
</Directory>
```

OHS will process the directory directives in the following order:

■ AllowOverride None (this will disable all *.htaccess* files).

■ AllowOverride FileInfo (for the directory /home).

■ Look for and apply the *FileInfo* directives in /home/.htaccess, /home/www/.htaccess and /home/www/dir/.htaccess in that order.

on the **job**

A directive that's valid in the directory context can be used inside <Directory>, <Location>, and <Files> containers in the server configuration files, subject to some restrictions.

<DirectoryMatch>

The *DirectoryMatch* directive is very similar to the *Directory* directive, with the difference that the Web server will accept regular expressions as arguments as shown in the following example, which matches directories starting with web and ending with a number from 1 to 0:

```
<DirectoryMatch "/web[1-9]/">
```

<Files>

The <Files> directive is a container directive that matches files instead of directories and is similar to the <Directory> and <Location> directives. The <Files> directive is used to control access by filenames. The directives inside this section can be applied to all files matching the specified filename. Note the following:

- <Files> sections are read after the <Directory> sections and the *.htaccess* files are read.
- <Files> sections are read before the <Location> sections.
- You can nest <Files> sections inside <Directory> sections.

The *filename* argument can include a filename or a wild-card string, where ? matches any single character, and * matches any sequence of characters. You can also use extended regular expressions by adding the ~ character, as shown here:

```
<Files ~ "\.(gif|jpe?g|png)$">
```

Although the example shows the use of regular expressions to match filenames, the <FilesMatch> container is more appropriate in such cases.

In the following example, the directives within the <Files> and <Files> tags fall into the Files container, and they deny access to any file on your server that's named secret.html, no matter where it is on the server:

```
<Files secret.html>
Order allow,deny
Deny from all
</Files>
```

If you want to restrict access to only certain files within a directory, you can do so, by combining the <Files> and <Directory> containers. The following example shows this:

```
<Directory /var/web/dir1>
<Files secret.html>
Order allow,deny
Deny from all
</Files>
</Directory>
```

The preceding combination means that the client will be denied access to all of the following files:

```
/var/web/dir1/secret.html
/var/web/dir1/subdir2/secret.html
/var/web/dir1/subdir3/secret.html
Any file named secret.html under the /var/web/dir1/ directory.
```

<FilesMatch>

This is the counterpart of the <DirectoryMatch> directive, which enables you to control access by filename. Unlike the <Files> directive, it accepts regular expressions to match filenames.

```
Syntax: <FilesMatch regex> ... </FilesMatch>
Example: <FilesMatch "\.(gif|jpe?g|png)$">
```

<Limit>

You use the <Limit> directive to restrict enclosed access control directives only to certain HTTP methods. By default, the Web server imposes access controls on all access methods, which is as it should be. Using the *Limit* directive, you can specify that only the listed HTTP methods fall under the purview of access controls. Any access method that isn't listed with the *Limit* directive won't have any access restrictions. Here's an example:

```
<Limit POST>
Require valid-user
</Limit>
```

In the example, the access control restriction is imposed only where the POST method is used. All other methods are unrestricted or unprotected by these access control restrictions, which apply only to the POST method. Because the POST method lets users write to the server, the *Limit* directive requires the users to be authenticated as valid users.

<LimitExcept>

You use the <LimitExcept> container to restrict access controls to all HTTP methods except the named methods. You use <LimitExcept> and </LimitExcept> to enclose a group of access control directives that will apply to any HTTP access method not listed inside the container. Thus, <LimitExcept> is the opposite of a <Limit> container, and you can use it to control both standard and nonstandard methods of access.

To prevent unknown access methods from evading access control restrictions, you should use the *LimitExcept* directive, which imposes access restrictions on all access methods except those specified in the *LimitExcept* directive, as shown here:

```
<LimitExcept POST>
Require valid-user
</LimitExcept>
```

In this example, the access control directive enclosed in the *LimitExcept* directive (Require valid-user) applies to any HTTP access method except the POST access method.

e x a m

ⓦ a t c h

You must always use the <LimitExcept> container in preference to <Limit> when restricting access, because a <LimitExcept> section provides complete protection against arbitrary and unknown access methods.

<Location>

You use the <Location> directive to specify that the directives in a block be applied only to the stated URLs and not a physical directory. Thus, the scope of the <Location> directives is limited by URLs and not physical directories. Note the order in which the various configuration sections (containers) are read upon starting the Oracle HTTP server:

1. <Directory>
2. .htaccess files
3. <Files>
4. <Location>

Note that you can use regular expressions with the tilde character and wildcard directories with the <Location> directive.

Make sure you aren't using the <Location> container to control access to physical files or directories. The <Directory> container controls access to the physical directories and files. If you use the <Location> container directives to control access to directories and files, your access controls could be easily sidestepped, because more than one URL can point to the same physical directory. You must use the <Location> container only to apply directives to content that doesn't live in your file

e x a m

ⓦ a t c h

If you use the <Location /> specification instead of just <Location>, your configuration directives in that container will apply to the entire server.

system. If the content is actually located in the file system, you must use the <Directory> and <Files> containers to apply configuration directives to that content.

The URLs affected by the <Limit> directive may use wildcards, with ? matching a single character, and * matching any sequences of characters. You may also use regular expressions by adding the ~ character.

<LocationMatch>

The <LocationMatch> directive is similar to the <Location> directive, but it lets you specify all types of regular expressions. Note that the <Location> directive lets you use only regular expressions with the tilde character and wildcard directories. In the following example, the <LocationMatch> directive matches the URLs contained in either the /hr/data or the /finance/data string.

```
<LocationMatch "/(hr|finance)/data">
```

.htaccess Context

The *.htaccess* context applies to the *.htaccess* files in which you can place any directory to limit the directive to that directory only. Although a directive that is valid in the *.htaccess* context appears inside per-directory *.htaccess* files, it may or may not be processed, depending on the value of the *OverRides* directive.

What Are Block Directives?

A *block directive* specifies *conditions* under which the directive will take effect. Thus, block directives aren't scope based, but rather depend on whether the HTTP Server will take its directives into account when starting up, based on some condition holding true or false. You can use block directives to limit directives to work only on certain virtual hosts, directories, or files. There are two block directives: <IfModule> and <IfDefine>.

<IfModule>

You use the <IfModule> directive to mark those directives that are processed only if a certain module is present and is available in the OHS server. The stated module can be made available to OHS in either of two ways. It can be statically compiled into the OHS server, or you must make the module dynamically available by compiling the module and placing a LoadModule line in the *httpd.conf* file. The LoadModule line must appear before the <IfModule> directive.

Here's an example using the <IfModule> directive that comes into effect *only* for the mod_user_dir.c module:

```
<IfModule mod_userdir.c>
UserDir public_html
</IfModule>
```

Any URL whose path starts with a tilde would be mapped to UserDir, provided the mod_userdir.c module exists. Otherwise, the <IfModule> directive has no effect.

<IfDefine>

As you're probably aware, in the Apache HyperText Transfer Protocol (HTTP) server program, the httpd daemon, when run as a standalone process, creates child processes or threads to handle user service requests. You normally don't invoke the httpd daemon directly, but rather do so through using the *apachectl* utility on Apache systems, and the opmnctl utility in Oracle HTTP Server.

The directives within an <IfDefine> section are processed only if the enclosed *test* is evaluated to be true; otherwise, everything between the two <IfDefine> section markers is *ignored*. The <IfDefine> directive uses the parameter-name argument given on the httpd command line via the –D parameter. Note that the <IfDefine>directive is thus used for conditionally processing directives, based on the evaluation of the conditions that prevail when the OHS server is started. OHS will apply the directives within the <IfDefine> directive only if the stated parameter is defined on the httpd command line. In the following example, requests will be redirected to alternative sites only if you start the OHS server with the httpd –DclosedForNow option.

```
<IfDefine ClosedForNow>
Redirect / http://otherserver.example.com/
</IfDefine>
```

By using the parameter-name specification, you can reverse the test and process directives within the <IfDefine> sections if the parameter name isn't defined.

Note that containers can't include other containers, with the exception of the *Limit* directive and the Files container. You can include a Files container in a Directory container. You can place any directive inside a Limit or LimitExcept container, as long as the *Limit* or *LimitExcept* directive is placed within a container that conforms to these directives. You can include all the other container types inside a <VirtualHost> container.

Merging Containers and Contents

The Oracle HTTP Server merges multiple directives in a very particular order, with directories being searched from the top down, as shown here:

- Directories inside (non-regular expression) directory containers and *.htaccess* directives are processed simultaneously. The *.htaccess* directories, if they are allowed, will always override the *Directory* container directives.
- Next to be applied are the DirectoryMatch containers and the Directory containers.
- *Files* and *FilesMatch* container directives are merged simultaneously next.
- *Location* and *LocationMatch* directives are applied simultaneously last.

Each group is processed in the order it appears in the *httpd.conf* file, except for the <Directory> containers. The <Directory> containers are processed from the shortest directory component to the largest directory component. For example, OHS will process /usr/web/dir before it processes /usr/web/dir/sub_dir. If more than one <Directory> container refers to the same directory, they are processed in the order in which they appear in the *httpd.conf* file.

Directives inside the <VirtualHost> container are applied after the corresponding directives from the main server are applied. This allows virtual host configuration directives to override the main server configuration settings.

The following example shows how containers are merged, when all the containers are applied to a particular client request. The merging starts at 1 and ends at 5.

```
<Location />
5
</Location>
<Files f.html>
4
</Files>
<VirtualHost *>
<Directory /a/b>
2
</Directory>
</VirtualHost>
<DirectoryMatch "^.*b$">
3
</DirectoryMatch>
<Directory /a/b>
1
</Directory>
```

The following example shows that although you placed some access restrictions, given that the <Location> container is evaluated last, your access restrictions specified in the <Directory> container don't actually apply.

```
<Location />
Order deny,allow
Allow from all
</Location>
# <Directory> section's directive
# will be ignored since <Location> is processed after this
<Directory />
Order allow,deny
Allow from all
Deny from hacker.example.com
</Directory>
```

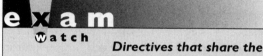

ⓦatch   *Directives that share the same scope will be merged in the order they are found.*

Note that the *VirtualHost* container directives are processed after the main server configuration directives. This allows the virtual host directives to take precedence over the main server directives.

The Oracle HTTP Server processes all section groups in the order in which they appear in the configuration files, with one exception. The Directory container (<Directory>) sections are processed from the shortest directory component to the longest. Here are some things to remember:

■ Use the <Directory> or <Files> directives to match objects at the file system level.

■ Use the <Location> directive to match URLs.

■ The <Location> container is always processed last.

Virtual Hosting

Virtual hosting is the maintenance of multiple Web sites on a single machine. For example, you may run both www.mycompany1.com and www.mycompany2.com Web sites from the same server. You can define IP-based or name-based virtual hosts using the *VirtualHost* directive. IP-based virtual hosts have different IP addresses for each Web site. Name-based virtual hosts run multiple names on a single IP address.

You use the <VirtualHost> container to enclose a set of directives that apply only to a named virtual host. You may place any directive that can be used in a virtual host context in the virtual host container. When OHS receives a client request for a document that's on a virtual host, OHS will use the configuration directives for that virtual host's virtual host container. Using the <VirtualHost> container directive, you can specify the following alternative directives to the main HTTP server:

- *ServerAdmin*
- *ServerName*
- *DocumentRoot*
- *ErrorLog*
- *CustomLog*

Here's how you use the <VirtualHost> directive to specify additional hosts:

```
<VirtualHost     www.myhost1.com>
DocumentRoot /usr/virtual/htdocs/info
ServerName       www.myhost1.com
ErrorLog         /usr/virtual/h1/logs/error_log
</VirtualHost>
<VirtualHost     www.myhost2.com>
DocumentRoot     /usr/virtual/htdocs/finance
ServerName       www.myhost2.com
ErrorLog         /usr/virtual/h2/logs/error_log
</VirtualHost>
```

The foregoing example uses a name-based virtual hosting system. Here's an example showing a virtual host that's IP based:

```
<VirtualHost     172.14.12.14    205.123.33.199>
ServerName       www.myhost.com
ServerAdmin      Webmaster@myhost.com
DocumentRoot     /docs/myhost/www
ErrorLog         /docs/myhost/logs/error_log
TransferLog      /docs/myhost/logs/access_log
</VirtualHost>
```

exam
ⓦatch   *Name-based virtual hosting   hosting means that you'll have an IP means that you'll have multiple Web sites   address for each Web site. for each IP address, and IP-based virtual*

IP-Based Virtual Hosts

You must provide a different IP address for each IP-based virtual host, either by setting up your machine within multiple physical network connections, or by using virtual interfaces called "ip aliases." You can run multiple httpd daemons to support the different IP-based virtual hosts, or you can continue to use the default setup of a single httpd daemon. In our examples in this section, the single httpd daemon mode is assumed.

You can configure multiple hosts on a single server, using a separate *VirtualHost* directive for each virtual host. You *can't use* the following HTTP Server directives in a *VirtualHost* directive, because they can be used only in the server configuration context:

- *ServerType*
- *StartServers*
- *MaxSpareServers*
- *MinSpareServers*
- *MaxRequestsPerChild*
- *BindAddress*
- *Listen*
- *PidFile*
- *TypesConfig*
- *ServerRoot*
- *NameVirtualHost*

Here's an example showing how you use the <VirtualHost> container to set up different configuration values for the *ServerAdmin, ServerName, DocumentRoot, ErrorLog,* and *TransferLog* or *CustomLog* configuration directives for the two virtual hosts defined here:

```
<VirtualHost 10.0.0.1>
ServerName www.newco.com
ServerAdmin webmaster@mail.newco.com
DocumentRoot /groups/newco/www
ServerName www.newco.com
ErrorLog /groups/newco/logs/error_log
TransferLog /groups/newco/logs/access_log
</VirtualHost>
```

```
<VirtualHost 10.0.0.2>
ServerName www.citygroup.org
ServerAdmin webmaster@mail.citygroup.org
DocumentRoot /groups/citigroup/www
ServerName www.citigroup.org
ErrorLog /groups/citigroup/logs/error_log
TransferLog /groups/citigroup/logs/access_log
</VirtualHost>
```

Name-Based Virtual Hosts

In an IP-based virtual hosting system, each virtual host will need a separate IP address, because the virtual host uses the IP address to determine which host to serve. This forces you to have multiple IP addresses, one for each virtual host you wish to set up. When you use name-based virtual hosting, the HTTP Server expects the client to supply the hostname as part of the HTTP header information. This way, several hosts can share a single IP address.

It's very simple to configure name-based virtual hosting. All you need to do is to configure the DNS server to map host names to their correct IP addresses and then configure OHS so it can recognize the multiple host names. Name-based virtual hosting means you'll need fewer hard-to-acquire IP addresses. Unless you have strong reasons for doing so, you should use name-based virtual hosting. Following are some of those reasons:

- If you're supporting some obsolete clients, you may find that they aren't compatible with name-based virtual hosting.
- You may not be able to use name-based virtual hosting with some SSL secure servers.
- There are some operating system and network bandwidth management techniques that can't distinguish between hosts unless they are on distinct IP addresses.

You must use the *NameVirtualHost* directive to designate the IP address on the server that will accept requests for the name-based virtual hosts. If you want any or all IP addresses on the server to be used, you must provide * as the argument to the *NameVirtualHost* directive. Make sure that the IP address you specify is associated with a network interface on the server. You must provide a port argument (*:80, for example) if you intend to use multiple ports.

Once you do specify the *NameVirtualHost* directive, you must specify a <VirtualHost> block for each of the virtual hosts you wish to serve. You provide arguments to the <VirtualHost> directive that are similar to those you use for the *NameVirtualHost* directive. You need at least the following two directives inside each <VirtualHost> directive:

- The *ServerName* directive to designate the host to be served
- The *DocumentRoot* directive to indicate the directory where the host's contents are stored

In the following example, originally you have the domain www.mydomain.com. You now wish to add the virtual host www.myotherdomain.com, pointing to the same IP address. Here's how your *httpd.conf* file will look:

```
NameVirtualHost *:80
<VirtualHost *:80>
ServerName    www.mydomain.com
ServerAlias mydomain.com *.mydomain.com
DocumentRoot  /www/mydomain
</VirtualHost>
<VirtualHost *:80>
ServerName    www.myotherdomain.com
ServerAlias mydomain.com *.mydomain.com
DocumentRoot  /www/myotherdomain
</VirtualHost>
```

The *ServerAlias* directive inside the first <VirtualHost> block, shown as follows, indicates that the name inside is an alternative name that clients can use to access the same Web site.

```
ServerAlias domain.com *.com.
```

Once you specify the <VirtualHost> directive in the manner shown in the preceding example, all requests for hosts in the domain.com domain will be served by the virtual host www.domain.com You must make sure that you configure your DNS server to map the names to an actual IP address on your server.

on the job *Any configuration directives set in the main server context (that is, outside the <VirtualHost> container) will be used only if they are not overridden by any virtual host settings.*

When a client connects to the Web address, the HTTP server will first check whether the client is the IP address specified by the *NameVirtualHost* directive. If so, the server will check for a matching IP address in one of the <VirtualHost> sections and look for a matching *ServerName* or *ServerAlias* for the requested host name. If it can't find any matching host names, it uses the first listed virtual host that matches the IP address. In order to provide a special configuration for client requests that don't match any of your virtual hosts, all you have to do is put that configuration in the first <VirtualHost> container in the *httpd.conf* file.

The first listed virtual host is the *default virtual host*. When an IP address matches the *NameVirtualHost* directive, the HTTP Server will not use the *DocumentRoot* for the main server.

Using Special Configuration Directives

In addition to the many OHS configuration directives you have learned about so far, Oracle HTTP Server provides two special directives, *Options* and *AllowOverride*, which you can use to allow or disable several features of the Oracle HTTP Server.

Options

You use the *Options* directive to configure the server features available in a directory. In other words, you enable or disable specific HTTP server features with the *Options* directive. You thus can use the *Options* directive to control what programmers can and can't do with a directory The syntax of the *Options* directives is as follows:

```
Options [+|-]option [[+|-]option] ...
```

If you set the *Options* directive to None, no extra features are enabled whatsoever.

All The All option means that all options are allowed, and this is the default parameter for the *Options* directive. The only exceptions are the *MultiViews* directive, which isn't allowed by default. Of course, any mutually exclusive directives such as *Includes* and *IncludesNoexec* won't be allowed together.

ExecCGI   If you want CGI scripts to be allowed, you must set this parameter. The only exception is for directories defined with *ScriptAlias*.

FollowSymLinks   This parameter allows the HTTP Server to follow symbolic links for files or directories. However, this parameter doesn't affect the contents of the Location container.

SymlinksIfOwnerMatch   This is a more limited version of the `FollowSymLinks` parameter; it allows the HTTP Server to follow symbolic links only if the target file (or directory) and the symbolic link are owned by the same user.

Includes   The `Includes` parameter controls the execution of server-side includes (SSI).

IncludesNOEXEC   The `IncludesNOEXEC` parameter allows server-side includes but won't allow CGI script execution via the `#exec` and `#include` commands.

Indexes   This parameter will return a listing of the directory contents when a URL maps to a directory and there's no index file associated with the *DirectoryIndex* directive.

MultiViews   The option will allow content-negotiated multiple views.

If multiple options are applicable to the same directory, the options aren't merged. OHS will use the most specific options and ignore the rest. However, if you prefix all the options under the *Options* directive with a + or − sign, OHS will merge the various options. The options you specify with the + sign will be added to the current options being used, and those you prefix with the − sign will be removed from the currently operative options.

Here's an example showing the use of the *Options* directive without the + and − symbols:

```
<Directory /web/docs>
Options Indexes FollowSymLinks
</Directory>
<Directory /web/docs/test>
Options Includes
</Directory>
```

As you can see, only the Includes option will be used for the /web/docs/test directory. This means that I'm replacing the set of options for the /web/docs/ directory (Indexes, FollowSymLinks) with the single Includes option, for the /web/docs/test directory. If instead, I want to add the Includes option to the existing option FollowSymLinks and not use the Indexes option, I can do so by using the + and − symbols, as shown here:

```
<Directory /web/docs>
Options Indexes FollowSymLinks
</Directory>
<Directory /web/docs/test>
Options +Includes -Indexes
</Directory>
```

AllowOverride

Whereas the *Options* directive lets you enable and disable features, the *AllowOverride* directive lets you exercise an even finer-grained control over several HTTP Server features. As you can recall, the per-directory configuration files, called *.htaccess* files, supplement the main OHS server configuration file, *httpd.conf*. The *AllowOverride* directive determines which of the directives in a directory *.htaccess* file can override the server configuration. The HTTP Server will consider any *.htaccess* file in a directory as though they were in a Directory container.

The AllowOverride directive applies only to Directory containers.

Directives in lower Directory containers will have preferences over directives in the higher directories. The default setting or the *AllowOverride* directive is ALL, which enables the overriding of all directives. The HTTP server will merge the directives in all *.htaccess* files at the same level. Here are the other options for the *AllowOverride* directive:

- AuthConfig
- FileInfo
- Indexes
- Limit
- Options
- None

Here's an example showing how to use the *AllowOverride* directive:

```
AllowOverride AuthConfig Indexes
```

Directory Indexing

As you have learned, `Indexes` is one of the parameters you can use with the *Options* directive. You use the `Indexes` option to tell the HTTP Server whether it should produce an HTML page when a directory is requested. You add indexes to the list of options in this way:

```
Options +Indexes
```

You have several options when a user requests a directory rather than a file:

- The HTTP Server can return a default file: You can use the *DirectoryIndex* directive, which follows, to specify the default file:

```
DirectoryIndex index.html index.htm
```

In the foregoing example, the server will first try to return the index.html and then the index.htm file.

- An HTML page of the directory contents can be generated and sent back
- A "permission denied" error can be issued
- A "file not found" error can be issued, as shown here:

```
DirectoryIndex index.html /cgi-bin/error404.cgi
```

If you enable `Indexes` and none of the resources specified with the *DirectoryIndex* directive are found, by default the HTTP Server will generate an index of the directory. To avoid this default behavior, you must specify a non-relative URL as the (last) option for the *DirectoryIndex* directive, as illustrated in the preceding example.

Directory Listings

You may not want all users to have access to backup files and files such as the .profile and the .cshrc files. To prevent all files from showing up in file listings, you use the *IndexIgnore* directive. Any files you specify as options for the *IndexIgnore* directive will not appear in file listings. Here's a simple example:

```
IndexIgnore .??* *~ *# *.bak HEADER* README*
```

The following are the results of using the *IndexIgnore* directive in the above manner:

- All backup, header, and readme files are not listed.
- Any filename that starts with a dot and is longer than three characters is ignored.

Once you eliminate a file from being listed, through the **IndexIgnore** *directive, that file can no longer be reinstated as part of a file listing.*

Response Handling

When the Oracle HTTP Server encounters an error while processing a user's request, it first logs the error in the *error_log* file and then sends an error message to the client. Using the *ErrorDocument* directive, you can customize the Oracle HTTP Server's response in the form of an HTML document.

When the Oracle HTTP Server encounters an error, it can do one of the following four things:

- Send a simple hard coded message.
- Send a custom message.
- Redirect to a local URL-path.
- Redirect to an external URL.

By default, the Oracle HTTP Server will choose option 1 when it encounters errors. Since this means that the user will get an ugly error message, you must choose one of the options and customize the response of the Web server to error conditions. You can use the *ErrorDocument* directive to configure one of the other three options. You can specify an HTTP error-response code and a URL or a message when you use the *ErrorDocument* directive. Local URL paths start with a slash (/) relative to the *DocumentRoot*, or a full URL, if it's external. The HTTP Server can also provide a message to be displayed by the browser. Here are some examples:

```
ErrorDocument 500 http://foo.example.com/cgi-bin/tester
ErrorDocument 404 /cgi-bin/bad_urls.pl
ErrorDocument 401 /subscription_info.html
ErrorDocument 403 "Sorry can't allow you access today"
```

You can also use the special value *default*, to specify the simple hardcode message by the HTTP Server, as shown here. Doing this will ensure that the simple hardcoded message will be restored, instead of inheriting an existing *ErrorDocument* value.

```
ErrorDocument 404 /cgi-bin/bad_urls.pl
<Directory /web/docs>
ErrorDocument 404 default
</Directory>
```

Expires Header

The Expires header in a document determines when a document becomes out of date. Using the *ExpireActive* directive, you can turn the sending of the Expires header on and off.

on the Job

The mod_expires module controls the Expires header.

Using Aliases

The *Alias* directive maps URLs to file system locations. The file system location can be a file or a directory, as indicated in the syntax for the *Alias* directive shown here:

```
Alias URL-path file-path|directory-path
```

Using the *Alias* directive, you can store documents in directories other than the directory specified by the *DocumentRoot* directive. Here's an example:

```
Alias /image /ftp/test/image
```

In the preceding example, a client request for the http://myserver/image/foo.gif file will return the file /ftp/test/image/foo.gif. Here's another example, showing how you can create an entire virtual path structure to hide the underlying file system:

```
Alias /pub  /public
Alias /pub/users /home/users/pub
Alias /pub/users/john /support/staff/john/public
```

on the
job

If you include a trailing / on the url-path, the server will require a trailing / in order to expand the alias.

You can also specify additional <Directory> sections, which cover the destination of aliases. Because OHS checks aliases before it checks the <Directory> containers, only the destinations of the aliases are affected. Here's an example:

```
Alias /image /ftp/test/image
<Directory /ftp/test/image>
Order allow,deny
Allow from all
</Directory>
```

If you've already specified access control for the /ftp/test/image directory, using the *Alias* directive as shown here will modify the access settings for that directory and its subdirectories.

If you're creating aliases to directories outside the directory specified by *DocumentRoot*, you must ensure that the server has access to the target directory.

AliasMatch

The *AliasMatch* directive works similar to the way the *Alias* directive does, but it uses standard regular expressions instead of simple prefix matching. If the regular expression matches the URL-path, any parenthesized matches are substituted into the given string and used as a filename. Here's an example, which shows how the *AliasMatch* directive activates the /icons directory:

```
AliasMatch ^/icons(.*) /usr/local/apache/icons$1
```

A reference to the icons directory in a URL will be redirected to the real icons directory.

ScriptAlias

The *ScriptAlias* directive works like the *Alias* directive, with the difference that it marks the target directory as containing CGI scripts to be executed by the mod_cgi's cgi-script handler. URLs will be mapped to scripts beginning with the second

e x a m
ⓦ a t c h   *Using ScriptAlias is the
only way to enable the execution of CGI
scripts without specifying the ExecCGI
option, and therefore is useful if you
have a policy of not permitting users to
execute their own CGI scripts.*

argument, which refers to a full path name in the local file system. Here's an example:

```
ScriptAlias /cgi-bin/ /web/cgi-bin/
```

In the foregoing example, a request for `http://myserver/cgi-bin/foo` would result in the HTTP server's running the script /web/cgi-bin/foo.

Access Restriction Directives

Often times, you may find it necessary to control access to the server, based on certain characteristics of a client request. For example, you may wish to restrict requests based on client's host name, IP address, or some other characteristic. You can use special access control directives in the <Directory>, <Files>, and <Location> containers, as well as in the *.htaccess* files, to restrict access to particular parts of the OHS server.

There are three types of access control directives you can use to restrict access by users. You use the *Allow* and *Deny* directives to determine which users are allowed or denied access to the server. A third access directive, *Order*, determines the default access state, as well as determining the way the *Allow* and *Deny* directives will interact. Note that the access restrictions apply to all access methods such as GET, POST, and PUT. However, by enclosing directives inside the <Limit> directive, you can restrict requests using only certain access methods.

The all-important access directives are examined in some detail in the following subsections.

Allow

Using the *Allow* directive, you can control which host can access an area of the server. You can control access by specifying host names or IP addresses or by some other client characteristics captured through the environmental variables.

You always use the keyword *from* when using the *Allow* directive (*Allow from . . .*), if you choose to specify the value for the *Allow* directive, as shown here:

```
Allow from all
```

All hosts are allowed access to your server, unless you restrict them by configuring them with the *Deny* and *Order* directives, which are discussed in the following subsections. Here's an example showing how to use the *Allow* directive. By using this directive, you are allowing access from the host with the IP number 10.1.2.3.

```
Allow from 10.1.2.3
```

Deny

The *Deny* directive restricts access to the server based on the host name, the IP address, or environment variables. The syntax and the arguments for the *Deny* directive are similar to those of the *Allow* directive. Here's an example:

```
Deny from 10.1.2.3
```

The *Deny* directive here refuses client requests to the OHS server from the IP address 10.1.2.3.

Order

It's possible to use both *Allow* and *Deny* directives together on a Web server. To avoid a conflict between these two directives, you must have some way to specify the precedence rules for applying the *Allow* and *Deny* directives. Using the *Order* directive, you control the default access state for the Web server, as well as the order in which the server will apply the *Allow* and *Deny* directives.

The *Order* directive could take the following values (both values are part of the Order specification):

- *Deny, Allow* OHS will evaluate the *Deny* directives before the *Allow* directives. By default, access is allowed to all clients. A client who *doesn't match a Deny directive or matches an Allow directive* is allowed access to OHS.
- *Allow, Deny* OHS evaluates the *Allow* directives before the *Deny* directives. By default, access is denied to all clients. A client who *doesn't match an Allow directive or matches a Deny directive* will be denied access by OHS.

In the following example, only the hosts in the oracle.org domain are allowed access, and all the other hosts are denied access.

```
Order Deny,Allow
Deny from all
Allow from oracle.org
```

In this example, all hosts in the oracle.org domain are allowed access, except for the hosts in the test.oracle.org subdomain. The latter group is denied access by the

Deny directive (Deny from test.oracle.org). All hosts that aren't in the oracle.org domain are denied access, because by default, the *Allow, Deny* order means that access is denied to the OHS server.

```
Order Allow,Deny
Allow from oracle.org
Deny from test.oracle.org
```

In this example, I use the same domains and sub domains as before for the *Allow* and *Deny* directives, but *reverse the order to Deny, Allow*.

```
Order Deny,Allow
Allow from oracle.org
Deny from test.oracle.org
```

Now, all hosts are allowed access to the OHS server, because although the *Allow* and *Deny* directives are listed in that order, *Deny* will be evaluated first. OHS evaluates the *Allow* directive last, and this will override the *Deny* directive, which specifies that requests from the test.oracle.org subdomain will be denied. Not only will all hosts in the oracle.org domain be allowed access (inasmuch as the *Allow* directive specifies that), but all hosts from any domain are allowed access, because the default access state of Deny< Allow is to allow access.

Obtaining the HTTP Server Status

You can use the Status module, which lets you check OHS Server performance statistics though an HTML page. You use the *Location* directive, to specify whether you want to allow the generation of server status reports from a specific IP address (or symbolic machine name). In the *Location* directive, for the Allow from attribute, you must provide the IP address/machine name, as shown in the following example:

```
<Location /server-status>
   SetHandler server-status
   Order deny,allow
   Deny from all
   Allow from ntl-alapatisam.netbsa.org
</Location>
```

FIGURE 5-4

The HTTP Server
Status Page

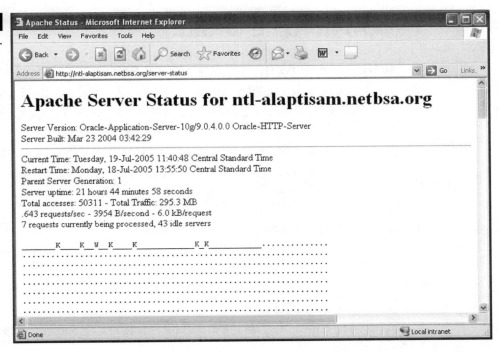

The *Location* directive shown in the foregoing example allows server status reports only for browsers from the ntl-alapatisam.netbsa.org domain.

Once you set up the *Location* directive as shown here, you can access the server status reports using the following URL:

```
http://servername:port/server-status
```

Figure 5-4 shows the server status page for the HTTP Server.

TWO-MINUTE DRILL

Introduction to the Oracle HTTP Server

❑ The Oracle HTTP Server (OHS) is based on the Apache 1.3 Web Server.

❑ The following three OHS components run within a single OHP process: the HTTP listener, the modules, and the Perl Interpreter.

❑ OHS modules extend the functionality of the OHS server.

❑ There are two types of OHS modules: standard Apache modules and OracleAS specific modules.

❑ In a UNIX/Linux system, the main http process runs as the root user and the other processes under a less-privileged user.

❑ On Windows server, there's a multithreaded implementation of the HTTP Server processes, with a single control process and a child process.

❑ The httpd.pid file contains the process ID of the parent server process.

❑ You must not keep sensitive information in the *htdocs* directory.

❑ The main configuration file of the Oracle HTTP Server is called the *httpd. conf* file.

❑ The recommended way to modify the OHS configuration is through editing the *httpd.conf* file through the Application Server Control Console.

❑ The *httpd.conf* file is a server configuration file, read only when you start or restart the Oracle HTTP Server.

❑ The *httpd.conf* file contains directives, which are configuration instructions as well as pointers to other configuration files.

❑ The "other" configuration files include the mod_oc4j.conf, mime.types, and the oracle_apache_conf file.

❑ There are three types of directives: server-level, container, and per-directory directives.

❑ The default name of the per-directory configuration file is *.htaccess*.

❑ You control the directives that can be placed in the *.htaccess* file by using the *AllowOverride* directive.

❑ Directives are always applied in a hierarchical manner.

❏ If you set *UseCanonicalName* to ON, the HTTP Server will use the *ServerName* and *Port* directives to construct the canonical name for the server.

❏ If you don't set the *Listen* directive, the *Port* directive specifies the default port.

❏ If you set the *Listen* directive, the *Port* directive is used only for redirection.

Managing the Oracle HTTP Server

❏ You use the *opmnctl* and *dcmtl* command-line utilities to manage the Oracle HTTP Server.

❏ You can edit the *httpd.conf* file from the Application Server Control Console.

❏ When you modify the *httpd.conf* file using the Application Server Control Console, the HTTP Server is bounced automatically.

❏ The error_log file contains OHS error messages, and you can change the name of this file with the *ErrorLog* directive.

❏ The access_log contains a detailed account of all HTTP Server access.

❏ If the error_log grows too big, you should reset the log file rather than try to remove it (or move it).

❏ By default, all HTTP log files are in the Common Log Format (CLF).

OHS Configuration Directives

❏ You can classify directives into various classes, based on the following types of contexts: Server config, Virtual directory, Directory, and *.htaccess*.

❏ Server Config context directives can't be used in the <Directory> or <VirtualHost> containers or in the *.htaccess* files.

❏ Directives in the *.htaccess* file are applied in the order in which they appear.

❏ Global directives are applicable only outside of container directives.

❏ You can use per-directory class directives anywhere.

❏ Container directives limit the scope of a directive.

❏ Containers can't be included in another container, except the <VirtualHost> container.

❏ Block directives specify the conditions under which a directive will take effect.

❏ Virtual host directives take precedence over the main server directives, since virtual host directives are processed later.

❏ Directory containers are processed from the shortest component to the longest.

❏ Virtual hosting is the maintenance of multiple Web servers on a single machine.

❏ You can define IP-based or name-based virtual hosts using the *VirtualHost* directive.

❏ Under name-based hosting, there are multiple Web sites for each IP address.

❏ Under IP-based virtual hosting, you'll have a separate IP address for each Web site.

❏ The *NameVirtualHost* directive is required when you configure name-based virtual hosts.

❏ You use the *Options* directive to specify features that the HTTP Server will allow.

❏ The default parameter for the *Options* directive is `All`, meaning that all options are allowed by default.

❏ The *AllowOverride* directive determines which of the directives in a directory *.htaccess* file can override the server configuration.

❏ You use the *IndexIgnore* directive to prevent all files in a directory from showing up in file listings.

❏ The *Alias* directive lets you store documents in directories other than that specified by the *DocumentRoot* directive.

❏ The *AliasMatch* directive works like the *Alias* directive but uses standard regular expressions instead of simple prefix matching.

SELF TEST

1. You can change the name of the *.htaccess* file in a directory in your path, with the help of which of the following directives?

   A. *AccessFileName*

   B. *ChangeAccessFile*

   C. *AccessNameFile*

   D. *AccessConfig*

2. The *AllowOverride* directive is valid only in

   A. Server containers

   B. Virtual Hosts

   C. Directory containers

   D. File containers

3. The *IndexIgnore* directive

   A. Prevents users from finding backups of CGI scripts.

   B. Is not a good idea because users can find backups of CGI scripts.

   C. Helps list all available files.

   D. Keeps users from seeing any file listing at all.

4. The default name for the per-directory configuration file is

   A. *.access*

   B. *.htaccess*

   C. *httpd.conf*

   D. *osso.conf*

5. Which of the following can be used by specifying the *AllowOverride* directive?

   A. *.htaccess* files

   B. Directories

   C. Containers

   D. Server log files

6.   The Oracle HTTP Server processes all section groups in the order in which they appear in the configuration files, with the exception of

A.   The <Files> container

B.   The <FilesMatch> container

C.   The <Location> container

D.   The <Directory> container

7.   What's the difference between the *Alias* and *AliasMatch* directives?

A.   *AliasMatch* uses standard regular expressions instead of simple prefix matching.

B.   *AliasMatch* uses simple prefix matching instead of standard regular expressions.

C.   *AliasMatch* allows the use of CGI scripts.

D.   Only *AliasMatch* allows you to create aliases outside of the directory specified by *DocumentRoot*.

8.   If you set *UseCanonicalName* directive to ON,

A.   The HTTP server will use only the *Port* directive.

B.   The HTTP server will use only the *ServiceName* directive.

C.   The HTTP server will use neither the *Port* nor the *ServiceName* directives.

D.   The HTTP server will use the *Port* and *ServiceName* directives.

SELF TEST ANSWERS

1. ☑ **A** is correct. If you want to call your *.htaccess* file by a different name, you can do so by using the *AccessFileName* directive.
   ☒ **B** and **C** are incorrect because they refer to nonexistent directives. **D** is incorrect because the *AccessConfig* directive doesn't allow you to change the *.htaccess* filename.

2. ☑ **C** is correct. The *AllowOverride* directive is valid only in the <Directory> containers.
   ☒ **A, B,** and **D** are incorrect because the *AllowOverride* directive can't be used in those containers.

3. ☑ **A** is correct because you use the *IndexIgnore* directive to keep users from accessing various files, including the backups of CGI scripts.
   ☒ **B** is incorrect because users can't find backups of CGI scripts when you use the *IndexIgnore* directive. **C** is incorrect because the *IndexIgnore* directive helps you prevent all available files from being listed. **D** is incorrect because users can see all files that you don't restrict with the *IndexIgnore* directive.

4. ☑ **B** is correct because *.htaccess* is the default name for the per-directory configuration file.
   ☒ **A** is incorrect because *.access* is a made up filename. **C** and **D** are incorrect because they are configuration files for the HTTP Server and for the SSO Server.

5. ☑ **A** is correct because you use the *AllowOverride* directive to control the contents of the *.htaccess* files.
   ☒ **B, C,** and **D** are incorrect because the *AllowOverride* directive isn't meant to control the contents of those three entities.

6. ☑ **D** is correct because in the case of the <Directory> container, the HTTP Server processes from the shortest directory to the longest, not in the order they appear in the configuration files.
   ☒ **A, B,** and **C** are incorrect because they are all processed in the order in which they appear in the configuration files.

7. ☑ **A** is correct because the *AliasMatch* directive uses standard regular expressions instead of simple prefix matching for filenames.
   ☒ **B** is incorrect because the *AliasMatch* directive uses regular expressions, not prefix matching. **C** is incorrect because *AliasMatch* has nothing to do with CGI scripts. **D** is incorrect because the *AliasMatch* doesn't give you the right to create aliases outside the directory specified by the *DocumentRoot* directive.

8. ☑ **D** is correct because the HTTP Server will use both the *Port* and *ServiceName* directives when you set the *UseCanonicalName* directive to ON.

☒ **A, B,** and **C** are incorrect because the HTTP Server will use the values specified by both the *Port* and *ServiceName* directives.

6

Single Sign-On, SSL, and OracleAS Certificate Authority

OracleAS Single Sign-On

OracleAS Single Sign-On is a component of the OracleAS Infrastructure. More specifically, it's a part of the Identity Management component of the OracleAS Infrastructure. The OracleAS Single Sign-On Server enables a user to log in to multiple applications registered with the Oracle Application Server with a single username and password. Oracle Application Server Single Sign-On retrieves the user information from the Oracle Internet Directory. Once the Single Sign-On Server authenticates a user, that user can log in to all the applications for which that user is registered. For the security administrator, this is wonderful, because management time and effort to administer user accounts and passwords is drastically reduced. It also enhances security across the enterprise as users don't have to juggle a multitude of usernames and passwords for the multiple applications they need to access.

Once you register an application with OracleAS Single Sign-On, a user's identity is validated by the OracleAS Single Sign-On only once, no matter how many Oracle Application Server applications the user invokes later on. This feature reduces administrative costs and management time, provides enhanced enterprise security, and makes it easier for users, who now have to remember only a single username and password instead of a multitude of them.

OracleAS Single Sign-On Server Components

OracleAS Single Sign-On Server has the following components that enable it to perform its tasks.

OracleAS Single Sign-On Server

The OracleAS Single Sign-On (SSO) Server uses the Oracle database, the Oracle HTTP Server, and the OC4J Server to let you securely log into multiple applications. As its name indicates, the key function of the Single Sign-On Server (which is a set of programs running in the Oracle database, OHS and OC4J) is to enable users to gain access to multiple applications by authenticating only once. The Single Server Sign-On Server enables you to uses its "authenticate once, log in many times" feature in two types of application, which are described in the subsequent text.

Oracle Internet Directory and the Identity Management Infrastructure

The Oracle Internet Directory (OID) is the repository for all Single Sign-On–enabled user accounts and passwords. Besides the OID, OracleAS Single Sign-On also uses the other components of the Oracle Identity Management Infrastructure (see Chapter 4), which include Oracle Directory Integration and Provisioning, Oracle Delegated Administration Services, and OracleAS Certificate Authority.

All the account and password information necessary for the operation of the Single Sign-On Server is stored in the Oracle Internet Directory. The OracleAS Single Sign-On feature uses the OID data to authenticate users by itself and retrieves the necessary OID credentials information to let individual applications authenticate users.

Partner Applications

Partner applications are applications that run on the Oracle Application Server, such as the OracleAS Portal, OracleAS Discoverer, and Oracle Delegated Administration Services. These applications delegate their authorization functions to the Single Sign-On Server. The partner application is, however, responsible for determining whether a Single Sign-On authenticated user is indeed authenticated to access the application. Once a user logs in to the Single Sign-On Server, an authentication module called *mod_osso* enables the partner applications to accept the user information that's authenticated by the Single Sign-On Server instead of authenticating the user credentials by themselves (partner applications, that is).

The SSO Server's repository contains all pertinent information for the partner applications, which includes the following:

- Application ID
- Home URL
- Success URL
- Logout URL

on the **job**

If you can log in to one partner application through the Single Sign-On Server, you can log in to all partner applications registered with that server.

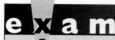

External Applications

External applications control their own authentication without delegating it to the Single Sign-On Server by requesting user account names and passwords when a user logs into the application. The application, and not the Single Sign-On Server, is responsible for user authentication. For example, Yahoo!Mail requires you to fill in your user credentials inside an HTML form.

on the
o b
Single Sign-On credentials are stored in the OID, and the SSO Server authenticates users against these credentials.

Single Sign-On comes into the picture when an application chooses to let the Single Sign-On feature store (in an encrypted format) and retrieve user application credentials such as account names and passwords in the Metadata Repository when they log into the Single Sign-On server. Under this arrangement, a user logs into the Single Sign-On Server and the Server will then use the sign-on user name to retrieve the application name or password to log the user into an application. The user usually uses the *Remember My Login Information For This Application* checkbox upon the user's first login to the application through the Single Sign-On Server.

mod_osso

The Oracle HTTP module, *mod_osso*, enables the Oracle HTTP Server to act as a partner application to the OracleAS Single Sign-On Server and authenticate the other partner applications. Using *mod_osso* vastly simplifies the authentication process, because the *mod_osso* module, running on the OHS, acts as the sole partner application to the Single Sign-On Server. After it authenticates a user logging in to the OracleAS Single Sign-On, *mod_osso* sends the following header values to the applications so they can authorize the user:

- User name
- User DN

- User GUID
- Language and territory

Single Sign-On Authentication Flow

As mentioned previously, the *mod_osso* module enables the Oracle HTTP Server to act as a partner application for the OracleAS SSO Server.

on the job

Any application that obtains user identities from the mod_osso module is automatically Single Sign-On enabled.

Users access the Single Sign-On Server indirectly by first entering the URL of a partner application such as the OracleAS Portal, which invokes the Single Sign-On login screen. Once a user has been authenticated by the SSO server, the user accesses all other partner applications and external applications without the need for reauthentication.

Accessing Partner Applications

I briefly describe how a user gains access to a *partner* application in this section.

- A user attempts a login to a partner application.
- The *mod_osso* module–enabled Oracle HTTP server redirects the user to the Single Sign-On Server.
- The Single Sign-On Server verifies the user's credentials in the Oracle Internet Directory.
- After verifying the user credentials, the Single Sign-On Server sends them to the partner application.
- The partner application serves the content request by the user's browser.

Accessing External Applications

To access an *external* application, select an application from the list of external applications offered by the External Applications portlet in the OracleAS Portal home page. Once you select a particular application, the application login procedure is initiated.

Here are the authentication steps when you're authenticating to an external application for the first time:

■ The login procedure of the external application will determine whether there are any credentials for the user in the single sign-on password store. If so, it tries to authenticate the user with those credentials. Otherwise, it will prompt the user for the password credentials.

■ The user enters the username and password credentials. By selecting the *Remember My Login Information* check box in the login screen, the user can save these credentials in the password store for use the next time around.

■ If the user elects to save the login credentials, the server then creates a login form with the user's credentials and sends it to the client browser with instructions to post it to the external application.

■ The client browser submits the login form to the application and successfully logs in the user.

Of course, if you don't choose to save your credentials in the password store, you must provide the username/password information each time you want to log in to the external application. If you do save your credentials, on subsequent attempts to log in to an external application, the SSO Server will retrieve your credentials and construct the login form for submitting to the external application's login processing routine. Otherwise, the authorization process is exactly the same as described for the first-time authentication.

Changing Passwords

You'll see a "change password" screen when your password is about to expire. You can still continue to log in under the old password for a grace period. If you wish, you can cancel the "change password" dialog box and continue with your login.

If a user wants to change a password during a normal time (other than a password expiration time), regular users can do it through the Oracle Delegated Administration Services, which lets authorized users perform user and group management tasks. You can access DAS this way:

```
http://host:port/oiddas/
```

Note that DAS and OracleAS Single Sign-On usually have the same host name. You must use https instead of http if you are using SSL. You don't need to enter a port number if you're using the default port 80 for non-SSL and 443 for SSL-based connections.

Here's the sequence of events in the authentication process:

- When a user tries to access a partner application, the application will look for a partner application cookie in the user's Web browser.
- If there's no partner application cookie, the user is redirected to the SSO Server.
- The SSO Server provides a login page for the user. If the username/password combination is authenticated based on the stored values in the OID, the SSO Server will then set an SSO cookie in the user's browser. This cookie will help identify the user to the SSO Server.
- The SSO Server will then redirect the user to the partner application with authentication tokens to verify that the user has valid credentials to log in.
- The partner application will now set a cookie in the user's Web browser.

Further requests for logging in to the same or different applications don't bring up a new login page. The HTTP Server uses the *mod_osso* cookie to log in the user now.

CERTIFICATION OBJECTIVE 6.02

Configuring and Managing the SSO Server

Unlike the case with most of the applications that are part of the OracleAS stack, you don't directly start and stop the SSO server. Because the Single Sign-On Server needs both the Oracle HTTP Server and the OC4J instance in order for it to run, when you start or stop either the Oracle HTTP server or the OC4J instance, you automatically start and stop the SSO server as well. Let's briefly review how to start and stop the OracleAS SSO Server from the command line and through the Application Server control.

Command Line

As you learned in Chapter 3, you use the command-line utility *opmnctl* to start and stop the Oracle HTTP Server and the OC4J instance. Here's the important thing you need to remember: Because the OracleAS Single Sign-On Server requires *both* the Oracle HTTP Server as well as the OC4J instance to be running, whenever you start or stop either of these two, you'll automatically start and stop the Oracle SSO Server. Therefore, you can use the following commands to start the SSO Server.

```
$ opmnctl startproc process-type=ohs
$ opmnctl startproc process-type=OC4J_SECURITY
```

Either of the following commands will stop the OracleAS SSO Server:

```
$ opmnctl stopproc process-type=ohs
$ opmnctl stopproc process-type=OC4J_SECURITY
```

Of course, assuming that that all the infrastructure components are located in the same Oracle Home, you can start and stop the Oracle HTTP Server, the Single Sign-On Server, OC4J, and Oracle Internet Directory with a single command using the *opmnctl* utility as shown here:

```
$ ORACLE_HOME/opmn/bin/opmnctl startall
$ ORACLE_HOME/opmn/bin/opmnctl stopall
```

Using the Application Server Control

You can also use the System Components table in the Oracle Application Server for the appropriate OracleAS instance, and you can start, restart, or stop the Oracle HTTP Server and the OC4J instance. Again, you use the OC4J_SECURITY component to start and stop the SSO server. Figure 6-1 shows the Systems Components table of the OracleAS Infrastructure instance. Note that you don't have the option of directly selecting the Single Sign-On Server in order to stop and start the Server instance. You must start and stop the SSO Server by selecting either the HTTP Server or OC4J_SECURITY and clicking start or stop.

Single Sign-Off

Just as you log in only once through the SSO Server and access several partner applications through it, you can also log out of all active partner applications by logging off the current application you are in. Simply click log out in the current partner application, to go to the single sign-off page, from where you can log out simultaneously from all partner applications you're logged into.

However, external applications don't let the Single Sign-On Server control the logging out process. You must log out of each of the external applications yourself.

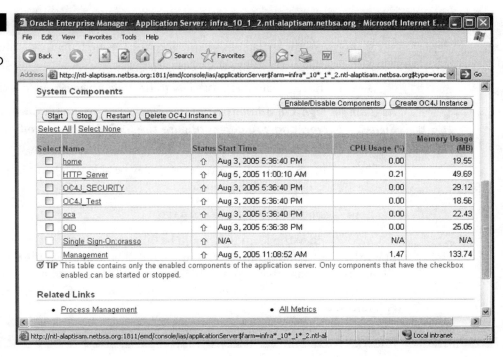

FIGURE 6-1

Starting and
Stopping the SSO
Server through
the Application
Server Control

Creating the Single Sign-On Administrator

The OracleAS SSO administrator has complete privileges on the SSO Server,
including the privileges to perform the following tasks:

■ Configuring the SSO Server

■ Administering partner and external applications

Unlike several other superusers in OracleAS 10g, you must *create the Single
Sign-On administrator* after the OracleAS Infrastructure installation, using the
orcladmin OID superuser account. To create a new SSO administrator, you have to
log in as the orcladmin user and make that user a member of the iASAdmins group
(using the Directory Manager).

on the
job

*You can create the OracleAS Single Sign-On administrator account using the
orcladmin account, which is the name of the OracleAS administrator.*

The steps for creating a new SSO administrator are as follows:

1. Log in as the orcladmin superuser to the Oracle Directory Manager.
2. Go to *Entry Management* => *cn=OracleContext*=>*cn=Groups*=>*cn=iASAdmins*.
3. Add the new administrator's DN to the *uniquemembers* field and click Apply.

on the **!** **job**

As a Single Sign-On administrator, you have full privileges on the Single Sign-On Server, and you can configure the SSO Server as well as administer both partner and external applications.

The OracleAS SSO Administrator will now be able to log in to the SSO home page using the following URL format:

```
http://hostname:port/pls/orasso
```

Once you click the login link, you'll be taken to the Oracle AS SSO login page. Enter the SSO administrator's credentials and click Login. On the Oracle AS SSO administration page that appears, click on the SSO Server administration link to start administering the SSO Server. Figure 6-2 shows the OracleAS Single Sign-On Administration Page.

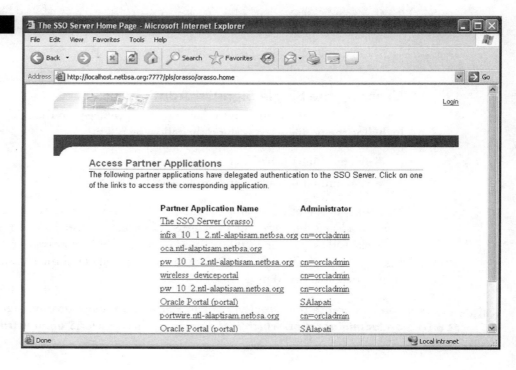

FIGURE 6-2

The OracleAS SSO Administration Page

Configuring the OracleAS SSO Server

You can configure the OracleAS SSO Server after first logging in to the server. After you log in, select SSO Server Administration. On the page that appears next, click the *Edit SSO Server Configuration* link. From the configuration page, you can modify the following:

- Single sign-on session duration length for a user
- Choice of automatic verification that the IP address of the browser matches the IP address provided to the SSO Server in the authentication request

Administering Partner and External Applications

As explained previously, partner applications and external applications are two of the important components of the OracleAS Single Sign-On Server. Let's briefly review the administration of the two types of applications that you can add to the OracleAS Single Sign-On Server.

Partner Applications

As you may recall, an application that delegates its authentication functionality to the OracleAS Single Sign-On Server is called a partner application. A partner application can be any Web-based application. All partner applications are registered with the OracleAS Single Sign-On Server by integrating them with the *mod_osso* module.

The various applications that are part of the OracleAS instance, such as the OracleAS Portal and the OracleAS Web Cache, are automatically registered with the OracleAS Single Sign-On Server when you install the OracleAS instance. This is done indirectly by registering the *mod_osso* module, with which the partner applications are integrated. On a UNIX platform, you use the *ssoreg.sh* script to manually register the *mod_osso* module with the OracleAS Single Sign-On Server in order to register a partner application. To accomplish this on a Windows Server, you use the *ssoreg.bat* batch file. You may want to manually register the *mod_osso* module under the following circumstances:

- When the configuration file for the OracleAS Single Sign-On Server (*osso.conf*) is corrupted or lost
- When you change host names or port number of the Oracle HTTP Server
- When you enable the SSL feature on the OracleAS Single Sign-On Server after the initial installation of the OracleAS instance
- When you run the single sign-on registration tool, you create a new *osso.conf* file

Using ssoreg The syntax for the *ssoreg.sh* and the *ssoreg.bat* script contains the same parameters. The syntax of the UNIX script, *ssoreg.sh,* is given here:

```
$ORACLE_HOME/sso/bin/ssoreg.sh
-oracle_home_path orcl_home_path
-site_name site_name
-config_mod_osso TRUE
-mod_osso_url mod_osso_url
[-virtualhost]
[-update_mode CREATE | DELETE | MODIFY]
[-config_file config_file_path]
[-admin_info admin_info]
[-admin_id adminid]
```

Here's an explanation of the various parameters in the *ssoreg.sh* script:

■ *oracle_home_path* You must specify the complete home path for the OracleAS middle tier instance home.

■ *site_name* This shows the hostname and port of a partner application—for example, *myapp.mydomain.com.*

■ *config_mod_osso* You must set it to TRUE to register the application with *mod_osso* and generate a new *osso.conf* file.

■ *mod_osso_url* This is the URL for the partner application, in the following format:

```
http://application.domain:port
```

If the Oracle HTTP Server is using port 80 for regular HTTP connections, or port 443 for HTTPS connections, you can ignore the port number in the mod_osso_url parameter.

■ *Virtualhost* This is an optional parameter that you use only if you want to register a virtual host with the OracleAS Single Sign-On Server.

■ *update_mode* This is an optional parameter used to create, delete, or modify the partner registration record.

■ *config_file* This indicates the location of the *osso.conf* file for any virtual hosts you may configure.

By default, ssoreg creates a file with the name osso.conf in the ORACLE_HOME/Apache/Apache/conf/osso directory.

■ *admin_info* This is used to provide the name of the *mod_osso* administrator.

■ *admin_id* This is used to provide additional information (e.g., the email address) about the administrator.

Here's an example that shows how to use the *ssoreg.sh* script:

```
$ ssoreg.sh -oracle_home_path $ORACLE_HOME -site_name
host.mydomain.com -config_mod_osso TRUE-mod_osso_url http://myhost.mydomain.com
```

You must restart the Oracle HTTP Server after running the *ssoreg.sh* script.

Using Application Server Control to Create Partner Applications

You can create partner applications from the Application Server Control Console, using the following steps:

1. Go to the OracleAS SSO Server Administration page by clicking the link at the bottom of the SSO home page.

2. Click the *Administer Partner Applications* link.

3. To add a new partner application, click the *Add Partner Application* link.

External Applications

External applications are Web applications that don't delegate their authentication tasks to the OracleAS Single Sign-On Server. By configuring an application as an external application you enable it to be single sign-on–enabled without changing the application's interface.

You use the *Administer External Applications* link on the SSO Server Administration page to add, edit, or delete external applications. Once you add an external application to the OracleAS Single Sign-On Server, you use the external application's link in the Administer External Applications page to log in to that application. You'll be then asked to authenticate yourself to the external application through the pop-up window that appears. In order to automatically log in to the external application the next time, you click the *Remember My Login Information For This Application* checkbox on the external application login page.

The information stored in the password store is used to construct the login document that's posted by the client browser to the external application, as explained previously in this chapter, thus simulating a normal login routine.

Monitoring the SSO Server

You can monitor the OracleAS SSO Server easily through the Application Server control. Log into the OracleAS infrastructure instance and go to the System Components page. Click the *Single Sign-On: Orasso* link. Figure 6-3 shows the SSO Server Monitoring home page, which you can use to monitor the server load and user activity. There are four sections in this page:

■ *General*   Provides information about the status and the start time of the SSO Server and the connect string for the database that hosts the SSO Server.

■ *Last 24 Hours Status Details*   Provides information about all logins during the past 24 hours, including the number of successful and unsuccessful logins.

■ *Login Failures During the Last 24 Hours*   Shows the IP addresses and failure times for each user.

FIGURE 6-3

The SSO Server Monitoring Home Page

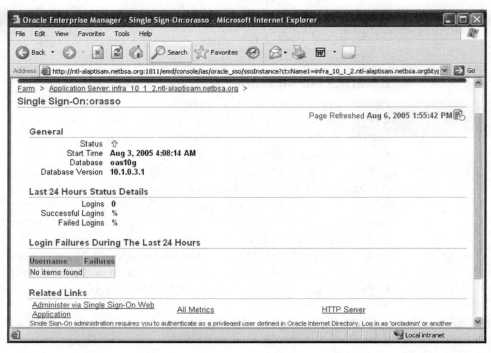

The *Related Links* section contains three links:

- *Administer Via Single Sign-On Web Application*   This links to the home page for OracleAS Single Sign-On and enables you to administer all partner applications that have delegated authentication to the SSO Server.
- *All Metrics*   The All Metrics page lists all performance metrics pertaining to the SSO Server, such as the following:
  - Login server metrics for the past 24 hours
  - Most failed login users' metrics
  - Login server metrics for the past hour
  - Response metrics
- *HTTP Server*   This takes you to the Oracle HTTP Server home page.

Accessing the SSO Server from OracleAS Portal

During the installation of the OracleAS instance, the OracleAS Portal is automatically added as a partner application for OracleAS Single Sign-On. The OracleAS Portal is thus one of the partner applications that you'll see listed in the OracleAS SSO home page. You can also access the SSO Server from OracleAS Portal as well. To access an external application registered with OracleAS SSO, the OracleAS Portal must be a partner application to OracleAS SSO.

CERTIFICATION OBJECTIVE 6.03

Using the Secure Sockets Layer

Secure Sockets Layer (SSL) is a well-known communications protocol that enables you to send messages securely across the Internet. You can use SSL to provide secure communication among the various OracleAS components and between the OracleAS components and external browsers. SSL uses certificates to authenticate users' identities. SSL is an industry-standard protocol for secure network communication, and OracleAS 10g supports SSL versions 2 and 3, as well as TLS version 1. SSL ensures secure communication by using three important concepts: *Encryption, Data Integrity,* and *Authentication.* Let's briefly review these important concepts.

■ Encryption algorithms such as AES, RC4, and 3DES permit a message to be read only by its intended recipient. During the initial SSL handshake, the client and server decide on the encryption algorithms to use during the transmission of messages.

■ Data integrity ensures that the recipient of the message receives the original message without its being tampered with in any way. SSL uses a *message digest*, which contains hashed messages produced by using hash functions, to compare different messages and determine whether they match. If the message digests don't match, it's possible that data tampering has occurred.

on the
Ĵob

Public key encryption is the only safe method to implement data security over the Internet.

■ Authentication is the process of verifying that the server and client are indeed who they claim to be. SSL uses digital identities called certificates to authenticate the identity of the server and the client.

In the OracleAS, SSL lies between the Oracle HTTP Server and the TCP/IP Layer and handles encryption and decryption tasks when users connect using secure connections (https, as against the usual http). Oracle's SSL implementation is done through the *mod_ossl* module, which supports SSL Version 3.0. The *mod_ossl* module provides the following services:

■ Certificate management using Oracle wallets

■ Encryption using RSA or DES standards

■ Integrity checking of messages using the MD5 or SHA checksum algorithms

■ Multiple access checks to authorize clients

Private and Public Key Cryptography

Cryptography is the process of encryption and decryption of messages and is at the heart of SSL, because SSL encryption is used to provide the data encryption, data integrity, and authentication features. Cryptography uses text- or number-based keys known only to the sender and the recipient, to scramble the original message. Each key consists of a binary number, typically from 512 to 2048 bits. The smaller the number of bits, the weaker the encryption. Thus, 2048 bits provides a higher degree of encryption than 512 bits. Data is encrypted by algorithms that combine the key bits with the original data bits. SSL uses two types of cryptography: *private key cryptography* and *public key cryptography*.

Private Key Cryptography

Private key cryptography is also known as *symmetric key cryptography*; it involves the use of the same key by both parties to secure messages that are sent and received. The secret key is securely distributed to both parties and stored by them. A major problem with symmetric keys is the secure transmission and protection of the common key used by the two parties. In addition, because a separate key is required for each pair of people, a large number of keys must be maintained.

Public Key Cryptography

Private key cryptography has the inherent problem that it's difficult to ensure the secure storage and transmission of the common key between the two parties involved in the communication of messages. *Public key cryptography* uses public and private *key pairs* and provides a secure distribution method for the key pair. In this method, also called an *asymmetric encryption* scheme, the public and private keys are entirely different. Furthermore, each entity maintains only a single pair of keys—one public and the other private. The public key is used to encrypt the message. Each entity keeps its private key secret and publishes the public key to everyone. Other entities use this public key of the first entity to encrypt messages they send. The receiving entity uses its private key to decrypt the message. The public and private keys are related mathematically, so if you encrypt with one, you can decrypt only with the other.

on the job

In a private/public key pair encryption scheme, the public key is distributed whereas the private key required for decryption is not shared.

Only a party that holds the associated private key can decrypt the encrypted messages. Here's how the public and private keys are dealt with in OracleAS 10*g*:

■ The private key algorithm, which is used to decrypt the message along with its credentials, is securely stored in an encrypted container called *Oracle Wallet*.

■ The public key algorithms offer encryption but have no built-in security communication mechanism, because they don't verify the identity of the parties using them. For this reason, a third-party certificate authority (CA), trusted by both the communicating parties, is used to authenticate the parties. The certificates issued by the CA contain an entity's name, the public key, and related security credentials, including the CA name, the CA signature, and the certificate effective dates. Certificates verify the user's right to use a public key, thus preventing unauthorized interceptions by third parties.

Digital Certificates

Digital certificates (also called digital IDs) help identify the authenticity of a user and the user's eligibility to use an encryption key by binding the user identity to a pair of encryption keys. Digital certificates contain information such as the following:

- Name of the issuer, also called the Certificate Authority
- Owner's name and the owner's public key
- Expiration date of the public key
- Serial number of the certificate
- Digital signature of the certificate issuer

Digital Signatures

Digital signatures involve the following steps:

1. First, a message digest is created by processing the message text through a message algorithm.
2. The individual sending the message encrypts the message digest using his or her private key, thus turning the message into a digital signature that can be decrypted only by using the public key of the sender.
3. The individual receiving the message decrypts the digital signature and creates a new message digest.
4. The values of the new message digest are checked against the value of the first message digest to make sure that the message wasn't tampered with.

Note that any doubts about the validity of a digital signature (certificate) can be resolved by querying the certificate issuer itself, which must identify itself with a digital certificate. You can thus work up the chain until you reach a "trusted" certificate issuer.

A Typical SSL Session

When a server and a client use the SSL protocol, the initial phase, known as the "handshake" phase, is limited to the authentication of the server (and the client, if necessary), through the exchange of a series of messages and the establishment of the cryptographic keys to be used for the data transmission. Once this phase concludes successfully, the actual data transfer phase commences.

on the
()ob

When using SSL with HTTP, the Web browser requesting a page from a server uses the HTTPS protocol, instead of the HTTPS protocol.

Here's a summary of how a client and a server communicate using the SSL protocol:

1. The Web browser uses the HTTPS protocol instead of the normal HTTP protocol when accessing the SSL-enabled server. The initial message to the server includes a list of encryption algorithms the client can use along with the random number employed in generating the keys. The client includes information about the cipher suite, which is the set of encryption, data integrity, and authentication algorithms used during the transmission of data between the client and the server.

2. The server responds by sending a message back to the client, informing the client as to which cipher suite it will use, as well as the random number it will use for the encryption.

3. The server also sends a digital signature (a certificate) to the client, thus verifying that it's the right server.

e x a m
ⓦatch

A cipher suite is a set of encryption protocols that specify the type of certificate to be used (RSA or DSS), the type of symmetric encryption to be used (RC4, RC2, IDEA, DES, or 3DES) and the type of signature algorithm to be used (MD5 or SHA). For example, the cipher suite SSL_RSA_EXPORT_WITH+RC4_40_MD5 uses RSA for authentication, RC4_40 for encryption, and MD5 as the hashing algorithm.

4. The client uses the server's certificate to authenticate the server, by using the server's public key to verify that the server is the same as the one that signed the certificate. The client also verifies that the certificate was sent by a trusted CA.

5. The client generates a random value called a "pre-master secret" and encrypts it with the server's public key before sending it over to the server.

6. The server retrieves the random value using its private key.

7. Using the pre-master secret random numbers known to both parties, the client and server calculate the keys they will use in the session, which are the following (symmetric keys are used to encrypt and decrypt data):

   ■ Encryption keys that the client and the server use to encrypt data before transmitting it to the other party

   ■ Keys that the client and the server use to create a message digest of the data

8. Using the keys they generated, the client and server send a confirmation message, called a "Finished" message, to each other. To ensure that the previous "*handshake*" messages weren't tampered with, the two sides verify that those messages match the messages in the Finished message.

9. Once the server and client confirm that the messages are secure by checking the contents of the Finished message, they transfer data using the encryption keys and the cipher suite they agreed on during the initial negotiations.

on the **0ob**

By default, none of the OracleAS components are configured for SSL during the installation of OracleAS 10g.

Requirements for Using SSL

To use SSL in OracleAS, you must satisfy the following requirements:

■ You must provide a certificate and an Oracle Wallet for your Web site.

■ Clients will need certificates also, if you plan on authenticating them.

■ You must configure relevant OracleAS components such as the Oracle HTTP Server to use SSL.

CERTIFICATION OBJECTIVE 6.04

Oracle Wallet Manager

Oracle Wallets are *logical containers* used to store security credentials such as certificates and public/private key pairs. You can store an Oracle Wallet in the OID itself or on your file system. The Oracle Wallet Manager is a GUI interface you use to manage the Oracle Wallets. Using the Oracle Wallet Manager, you can create Oracle Wallets, private keys, and certificate requests: you can download certificates into the Oracle Wallet, upload certificates to the OID directory, and perform other certificate-management tasks. You can use the Oracle Wallet Manager to manage security credentials on the OracleAS as well as on the Oracle database and other clients.

OracleAS components that act as SSL servers, which include Oracle HTTP Server, OracleAS Web Cache, OPMN, and Oracle Internet Directory, need Oracle Wallets, which already come with the certificate you want the server to use. You must specify the Oracle Wallet location for each of these components. For example, to configure Oracle HTTP Server for SSL, you specify the location of the Oracle Wallet using the *SSLWallet* directive.

Here's a list of the important tasks performed using the Oracle Wallet Manager:

- Generating public/private key pairs and creating certificate requests for submitting to the Certificate Authority
- Installing certificates
- Configuring trusted certificates
- Creating new Oracle Wallets and deleting Oracle Wallets
- Opening and closing existing Oracle Wallets
- Uploading and downloading certificates to and from the OID and other LDAP directories
- Importing and exporting Oracle Wallets

Default Locations for Storing Oracle Wallets

By default, in the absence of a Web cache, the wallets are stored in the $ORACLE_HOME/Apache/Apache/conf/ssl.wlt/default directory. You can specify a custom location for storing the wallets by providing either an absolute directory path or a path relative to the Oracle home directory. Here are some examples, first of an absolute and then a relative path, in both UNIX and Windows platforms.

```
/etc/wallets/testpath/wallet (UNIX)
C:\product\OracleAS\10.1.2\testpath\wallet (Windows)
%ORACLE_HOME%/testpath/wallet (UNIX)
%ORACLE_HOME%\testpath\wallet (Windows)
```

Starting Oracle Wallet Manager

On a Windows platform, you start the Oracle Wallet Manager by going to Start => Programs => OracleAS 10g Home => Integrated Management Tools => Wallet Manager. You start the Oracle Wallet Manager on a UNIX/Linux server using the following command:

```
$ owm
****DISPLAY environment variable not set!
    Oracle Wallet Manager is a GUI tool which
    requires that DISPLAY specify a location
    where GUI tools can display.
    Set and export DISPLAY, then re-run.
$ owm
```

Figure 6-4 shows the Oracle Wallet Manager GUI interface.

FIGURE 6-4	
The Oracle Wallet Manager	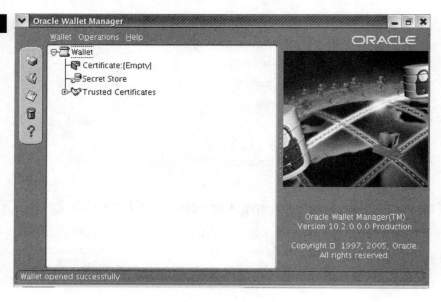

Managing Wallets

You can *create* a new Oracle Wallet by either by using the top icon on the left hand side or by clicking Wallet in the Menu at the top and selecting New from the dropdown list. Figure 6-5 shows the options under the Wallet Menu.

When you create a new Oracle Wallet, make sure you use a very strong password for the Wallet, because the Wallet credentials can be used to log into multiple database servers and application servers. You can change the Wallet passwords (with immediate effect) by selecting *Passwords* from the Wallets Menu item. The *Auto Login* Oracle Wallet Manager feature enables PKI-based access to services without a password.

on the **job**

If you want to configure single sign-on access to multiple Oracle databases, you must enable Auto Login (by default, it is disabled).

To *open* an existing wallet, select Wallet=> Open from the Menu bar. Once the wallet is opened, you'll see it displayed in the directory tree where you opened it.

You can *save* a wallet by using one of the three options shown in Figure 6-5.

■ *Save* saves the wallet after you make any changes to an open wallet.

■ *Save As* saves the open wallet in a new directory location.

■ *Save in System Default* saves an open wallet to the default directory location and makes it the wallet used by SSL.

FIGURE 6-5	
The Wallet Menu Item in Oracle Wallet Manager	

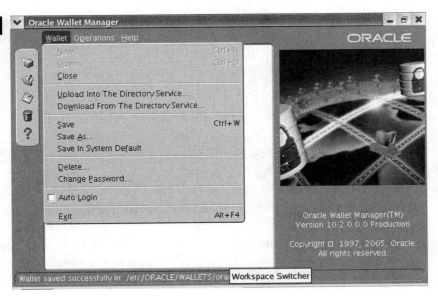

Also in Figure 6-5, you can see the message from the system indicating that the currently open wallet has been successfully saved:

```
Wallet saved successfully in: /etc/ORACLE/WALLETS/oracle
```

You can *delete* an Oracle Wallet either by selecting the Delete option under the Wallet item or by selecting the Delete icon, which is the third icon on the left-hand side. If you delete a currently open wallet, it will continue to remain in memory and will be available for wallet operations until you exit the Oracle Wallet Manager.

on the
job
You can create standard PKCS #12 wallets that use a directory on your file system to store security credentials, or create PKCS #11 wallets that can store the credentials on a hardware security module for the servers or private keys on tokens for clients.

You can *export* an Oracle wallet to a text-based PKI format. The various components such as certificate chains, trusted certificates, and private keys could be formatted according to the same or different encoding standards. To export a wallet, select Operations=> export wallet and specify the file system to save your wallet in and a file name for the wallet.

Uploading and Downloading Wallets

To upload a wallet to an LDAP directory, the target wallet must be *open* and it must contain at least one *user certificate*. You can use the directory password to upload the wallet, unless the wallet contains an SSL certificate, in which case you must use SSL. Here's a summary of the wallet uploading procedures:

1. Choose Wallet> *Upload Into the Directory Service* option. You must first save the wallet before you can upload it to the OID.

2. Choose yes to continue with the wallet upload process. At this point, the Wallet certificates are checked to see if they are using a SSL key. If at least one certificate has SSL key usage, enter the LDAP directory server name and port information here and click OK. The Oracle Wallet Manager will then use SSL to connect to the LDAP directory server. If none of the certificates are using an SSL key, enter the user's distinguished name (DN), the LDAP server host name, and the port number and click OK. The Oracle Wallet Manager will connect to the LDAP directory server using simple password authentication.

In order to download a wallet from the OID, choose wallet > *Download From the Directory Service*. The Oracle Wallet Manager will connect to the OID using simple password authentication. Because the downloaded wallets exist only in the working memory, you must explicitly save them in either the default or a new location.

CERTIFICATION OBJECTIVE 6.05

Managing Certificates

A certificate essentially binds a network identity with a corresponding public key. Oracle Wallet Manager uses two kinds of certificates: *user certificates* and *trusted certificates*.

■ User certificates are used by server applications to validate an entity's identity in a public key/private key–based message exchange. User certificates can be used by end users or applications such as Web servers; thus, a server certificate is a type of user certificate. Normally, user certificates do not validate other user certificates.

■ A trusted certificate is any certificate you trust, such as one provided by a certificate authority (CA). You can import a trusted certificate either by pasting the certificate from the email sent you by the CA or by importing it from a file.

Before you can use certificate-enabled single sign-on, you must do the following:

■ Install Oracle Internet Directory and the OracleAS Single Sign-On Server.

■ Install a valid server certificate for the Oracle HTTP Server.

■ Make sure that the client certificate's DN is the same as the user DN in the OID, or that it contains the user's nickname and, optionally, the user's realm.

---

exam

ⓦatch   *You must first install a trusted certificate from the CA before you can install a user certificate issued by that authority. When you create a new Oracle Wallet, several trusted certificates are* *installed by default. For example, trusted certificates from VeriSign, RSA, Entrust, and GTE Cyber Trust are automatically installed by the Oracle Wallet Manager when you create a new wallet.*

- Install the server certificate issuer's certificate in the client browser as a trusted certificate.
- Install the client certificate issuer's certificate on the OracleAS Single Sign-On Server as a trusted certificate.

CERTIFICATION OBJECTIVE 6.06

Enabling OracleAS Components to Use SSL

You can enable any of the OracleAS components to use the Secure Sockets Layer. Let's briefly look at how to enable SSL for key OracleAS components.

The Oracle HTTP Server and SSL

One of the common uses of SSL is the securing of HTTP communications between browsers and Web servers. The *mod_ossl* module, which supports SSL v. 3.0, is used to implement Oracle's SSL capabilities. The *mod_ossl* module provides the following services:

- Encrypted communications between the browser and the HTTP Server
- Integrity checking of communications through standard checksum algorithms
- Managing certificates using Oracle Wallets
- Client authorization using multiple checks

Configuring HTTP Server for SSL

To configure the Oracle HTTP Server for SSL certificates, you modify the following parameters in the configuration file, ssl.conf, located in the `$ORACLE_HOME/Apache/Apache/conf` file. You may also choose the Certificate Authority as a part of the configuration.

As you learned in Chapter 5, you can configure the Oracle HTTP Server by using directives to modify the OHS Server's functionality. There are quite a few special directives called the *mod_ossl* directive, which you can use when configuring the Oracle HTTP Server for SSL. These *mod_ossl* directive names are preceded by the term *SSL*. For example, the SSLVerifyClient directive specifies whether clients present certificates during the connection process. Similarly, the SSLCipherSuite specifies the cipher suite to be used by clients during the initial SSL handshake process.

To enable the HTTP Server for SSL certificates, use the following parameters in the *sso.conf* file, in the SSL Virtual Host Context section (you must also make sure that the SSLEngine parameter is turned on, as part of configuring the Oracle HTTP Server):

on the job

You can use the SSLEngine switch to enable and disable SSL for the HTTP Server.

- *SSLWallet* This provides the location of the server wallet, which contains the server's certificate, private key, and trusted certificates. The default for this parameter is OracleHome/Apache/Apache/conf/ssl.wlt/default. If you're using the Oracle Certificate Authority installed in the same home as SSL, the wallet location would be ORACLE_HOME/oca/wallet/ssl.
- *SSLWalletPassword* This is the password for the server wallet.
- *SSLVerifyClient* This parameter lets you choose the verification type for client certificates. There are three verification type choices:
  - none—SSL without certificates
  - optional—server certificate and optionally, a client certificate
  - require—both server and client certificates

Oracle recommends that you choose either *optional* or *require*. Once you've configured SSL for the HTTP Server, log in to the Oracle HTTP Server using the https protocol instead of the normal http protocol, by using the following URL:

```
https://host.domain:443.
```

Port 443 is the default SSL port for the Oracle HTTP Server. You'll be presented with a certificate when you log in and you must respond to that certificate in order to log in.

Configuring Oracle Internet Directory for SSL

The Oracle Internet Directory must store the user certificates in order for you to use certificate-based SSL authentication. The OID automatically publishes all OracleAS Certificate Authority–issued certificates, but if the certificate was

exam

ⓦatch

When using ldapmodify to publish third-party certificates, you must set the correct globalization support variable before running the tool, as shown in this example, first for the UNIX/Linux and then for the Windows server:

```
$ setenv NLS_LANG = AMERICAN_AMERICA
.UTF8 (Linux)
$ set NLS_LANG=AMERICAN_AMERICA.UTF8
(Windows)
```

issued by a third-party CA, you can upload the certificate to the OID as an LDIF file, using the command-line tool *ldapmodify*. The *ldapmodify* command-line tool, including its syntax and an example, were presented previously in this chapter.

In the following example, the certificate of user *salapati* is represented as an attribute of his entry in the directory, using the attribute type `usercertificate`.

```
dn: cn=salapati,cn=users,dc=realm1,dc=oracle,dc=com
changetype: modify
replace: usercertificate
usercertificate::MIIC3TCCAkYCAgP3MA0GCSqGSIb3DQEBBAUAMIG8MQswCQ
KY9LQtIjLnCaIJKUZmS1Qj+bhu/IHeZLGHg4TJg3O2XVA5u/VxwjLeGBqLXy2z7o3RujNKx2CVx6p/
OHk
jnw4w6KVau2hcBgC9m4kzUGhHJ9b65v/zx7dIUKyJr4RF+lJhJg4/oYXxLrYHp5NAkHP4htT0gqCXiI=
```

Configuring OracleAS SSO for SSL

The first step in configuring the OracleAS SSO for SSL is to convert all references to HTTP in the SSO URLs to the HTTPS protocol, using the *ssocfg.sh* script, located in the $ORACLE_HOME/sso/bin directory. Here's an example:

```
$ ssocfg.sh protocol new_host new_port [sso_schema_name]
```

You must specify *https* for the protocol parameter. The new_host parameter refers to the host name of the Oracle HTTP Server listener for the SSO Server. Port is the port number of the listener and sso_schema_name is the name of the SSO schema, with the default schema name being *orasso*.

Configuring OracleAS Web Cache for SSL

You can also configure the OracleAS Web Cache to use SSL and thus to receive HTTPS-based browser requests as well as to send HTTPS requests to the origin server, which is the main Web server. (That is, as opposed to a proxy server. Origin servers and proxy servers are explained in Chapter 9.) Here are the steps involved in configuring HTTPS support for the OracleAS Web Cache:

- You must create wallets to store the certificates.
- You must configure HTTPS Port and Wallet locations.
- Optionally, you can request client-side certificates.
- You can also optionally allow only HTTP requests for some URLs.

OracleAS Portal and SSL

OracleAS Portal is one of the partner applications for OracleAS SSO. Each of the components the OracleAS Portal communicates with must be configured individually to support HTTPS. Once you do this, you need to perform the following tasks to enable the OracleAS Portal to use the HTTPS protocol:

1. First secure the Parallel Page Engine (PPE), which assembles the portal pages.
2. You must add the OracleAS Portal as a partner application to the OracleAS SSO Server. You reassociate the portal to the secured SSO Server by running the Oracle Portal Configuration Assistant (OPCA) in the SSO type of the MIDTIER mode.
3. Finally, you must configure HTTPS as the protocol for communications between the OracleAS Portal and the Delegated Administrative Service (DAS).

CERTIFICATION OBJECTIVE 6.07

OracleAS Certificate Authority

OracleAS Certificate Authority is part of the Identity Management solution of OracleAS and is designed to make it easy to deploy public key certificates. Public Key Infrastructure (PKI) enables secure network transmission and supports secure email, data integrity, and digital signatures. OracleAS Certificate Authority creates and publishes X.509 V3 certificates to support PKI-based authentication methods. Earlier in this chapter you learned about the key pair method of authentication, which involves using a private and a public key to transfer information securely. A certification authority is a trusted third party that authenticates the public key owner's identity and validates the connection between the public key and a person through the creation of a certificate. Oracle Application Server Certificate Authority is one of several certification authorities such as Verisign and Thwate that provide digital certificates. The digital certificates issued by a certificate authority contain the public key and important information about the key owner and the certification authority.

When an entity wishes to send an encrypted message to another entity, it first contacts the CA and obtains a certificate that authenticates the entity and binds it to its public/private key pair. The entity then sends its encrypted message to another entity along with the digital certificate from the CA. When the CA sends out a digital certificate, it signs it using its private key. Thus anyone can use the published public key of the CA to verify the CA's signature and thus to ascertain the veracity of a certificate. Once the recipient of a message validates the certificate in this way, it can use the certificate owner's public key to send encrypted messages.

Public Key Infrastructure

A Public Key Infrastructure (PKI) consists of the following elements:

- Encryption algorithms
- Encryption keys
- Methods to distribute keys securely to enable their widespread use while maintaining secure decryption by authorized users
- Trusted entities to authenticate the ability of a user to use the keys

A PKI proves the following benefits:

- Secure and reliable user authentication, which is guaranteed by the proof of possession of the private key, which in turn is verified by the procedure that uses the public key. In addition, the CA validates the authenticity of the public key, based on the public/private key pair.

- Data integrity, which is made possible by the user of digital signatures, which involve an established public/private key pair. As you may recall, a digital signature is a coded digest of a user's message, encrypted by the user's private key. The user receiving the message can check its veracity by using the original user's public key.

- The *non-repudiation of messages* feature is enabled by the digital signatures. The use of digital signatures means that there is proof of who sent the original message, thus making it hard for senders to deny they sent the message.

- Prevention of unauthorized access to data: Because it is very difficult to derive the private key from the public key, a user's messages would be almost impossible to decrypt by someone other than the owner of the key pair.

Traditionally, organizations have relied on manually approving certificate requests, which made these PKI architectures both difficult to implement and expensive. A user had to fill in a form and deliver it to the appropriate registration authority. After the registration authority validated the user's identity, the user had to deliver the form to the certificate authority in charge of issuing the certificate, which could take weeks sometimes to review the information and issue the requested certificate. The user then needed to search for the new certificate and import it into the browser.

The OracleAS PKI removes the inconvenience and the delays inherent in traditional PKI management. Users don't need to request third-party certificates and submit them to applications and a central directory. Oracle Application Server Certificate Authority, the heart of the OracleAS PKI, provides an easy PKI solution, with a user-friendly Web interface and an integrated Registration Authority (RA).

Users submit certification requests online and get certificates right away without having to wait. The certificate is also linked automatically to the user's entry in the OID, which enables the Single Sign-On feature to authenticate users by checking their directory entries. The certificate issued by the CA can substitute for single sign-on credentials and enable access to all single sign-on applications configured for PKI.

Key Features of OracleAS Certificate Authority

OracleAS Certificate Authority (CA) provides industry-standard certificates and is integrated with the other OracleAS components such as Single Sign-On, SSL, and the LDAP-based OID. A summary of the key features of the OracleAS Certificate Authority is given in the following subsections.

Support for Open Standards

OracleAS CA supports open standards X.509 version 3 certificates, which helps in communicating with heterogeneous computing environments.

Flexible Policy

The OracleAS CA provides only a few default policy rules to restrict the certificate properties, which a site can easily configure to suit its own PKI requirements.

Hierarchical Support

OracleAS CA supports hierarchical certificate authorities, which enables a subordinate CA installation to obtain certificates from any other standards-compliant CA.

Ease of Use

Administrators can use the administrative Web interface of the OracleAS CA to manage certificate requests and to generate certificate revocation lists (CRLs). Users can use the end-user Web interface to request new certificates, check on the status of their certificate requests and save the CRL or install it in their browser.

Scalability and High Availability

Using the OracleAS and the Oracle database as the repository, OracleAS CA automatically provides scalability and high availability benefits.

Automatic or Conventional Provisioning

An application authenticating to the OracleAS Single Sign-On Server can obtain certificates using one of the following three methods:

- Having an administrator review and issue certificates
- Using the OracleAS Single Sign-On Server authentication to issue certificates to users who have been authenticated automatically by the OracleAS Single Sign-On Server

■ Implementing certificate-based authentication through the automatic provisioning of certificates by the OracleAS Certificate Authority, using OracleAS Single Sign-On Server and SSL

OracleAS PKI Management Tools

You use the following tools to manage OracleAS PKI.

Oracle Internet Directory

The OID enables PKI-based single sign-on, and the OracleAS Certificate Authority uses the OID to store certificates. The OID enables OracleAS Certificate Authority to simplify certificate provisioning by enabling it to easily publish the certificates it issues to entities contained within it. The OID enables the propagating of certificate information to all connected databases.

Users can request certificates from the OracleAS Certificate Authority, once they have registered in the OID and are authenticated through the OracleAS Single Sign-On Server. OracleAS Certificate Authority will immediately issue the certificate automatically and provision it in the OID, which enables the SSO to identify the users and fill in the required information in a user's certificate request. This enables future use of the certificate for single sign-on authentication.

The Oracle Wallet Manager

As you're aware by now, public key cryptography provides a solution to the problem that exists in private key cryptography, wherein you have to securely transmit and store the common private key that's shared between both parties in a transaction. Public key cryptography uses public/private key pairs to transmit information. The *public key* is available to all and is used to encrypt messages that can be decrypted only by someone who holds the associated *private key*.

What's an Oracle Wallet?

An Oracle Wallet is a secure (i.e., encrypted) container for storing private keys and security credentials to safeguard the identity of the client and/or the server. The Oracle Wallet Manager is a GUI tool that lets you create wallets for enterprise users. You can also use the Oracle Wallet Manager to store and retrieve wallets from the OID. The Oracle Wallet Manager can provide strong encryption using the Triple-DES (3DES) algorithm to secure the wallets.

An Oracle Wallet stores CA public keys. Although public key algorithms take care of safeguarding the message itself, you still don't know whether the identities of the communicating parties can be trusted. You must still know whether the public key used to encrypt a message does indeed belong to the person who claims to be its owner. The process of verifying the ownership of the public key is called *authentication*. A third party, called the Certificate Authority (CA), performs this authentication. The CA issues a public key certificate that contains information that includes an entity's name and the public key along with other credentials.

When a CA uses its private key to encrypt a message, a matching public key must be used to decrypt it—this verifies that the message was indeed encrypted by the CA. Because the CA public key is well known, you don't have to authenticate it each time it's accessed. The Oracle Wallets are used to store these CA public keys.

You can use Oracle Wallet Manager to acquire, use, and store digital certificates. The X.509 version 3 standard is an international standard that defines the specification of the certificates and provides these specifications for certificates. The PKCS #12 (Personal Information Exchange Syntax) standard provides specifications for certification containers. The PKCS #12 standard increases interoperability by allowing users with standard existing PKI credentials to export certificates and import them into Web browsers or into the Oracle Wallet Manager.

The Oracle Wallet Manager generates PKCS #10 certificate requests that are then submitted to the OracleAS Certificate Authority. The Oracle Wallet Manager not only enables certificate-related operations but also manages the Oracle Wallets, which act as containers for the certificates. If you don't use Oracle Wallets, you must either install the certificate permanently in your browser, making it easy for anyone to obtain it, or continuously install and deinstall the certificate. With Oracle Wallets, certificates can be read from the OID directly, thus making SSL a feasible way to communicate.

Oracle Enterprise Login Assistant

The Oracle Enterprise Login Assistant lets you open and close user wallets, thus enabling and disabling SSL-based connections. It also provides the SSO capability for the SSL-authenticated users.

Oracle Enterprise Security Manager

You use the Oracle Enterprise Security Manager to manage enterprise users and enterprise roles in the OID. Using this tool, you can create new enterprise domains, assign users to the domains, and authorize enterprise roles for those users in the enterprise domains.

OracleAS Certification Authority

OracleAS Certificate Authority provides easy-to-deploy Oracle PKI solutions at the enterprise level, and its PKI is compatible with products from leading PKI vendors such as RSA, Baltimore, and Entrust. You use the OracleAS Certificate Authority to administer and manage certificates, including the processing of requests for new certificates; verifying user credentials; and issuing, renewing, and revoking certificates. OracleAS Certificate Authority makes credential verification and authentication efficient and fast, thus enabling the speedy issuance of certificates.

OracleAS Certificate Authority is seamlessly integrated with other OracleAS products. For example, a user authenticating to the OracleAS Single Sign-On Server can easily obtain a certificate without any understanding of PKI. Using either the OracleAS Single Sign-On Server or SSL means that the user will be immediately issued a certificate rather than requiring administrative intervention for that purpose. The user can then use the certificate for transparently authenticating to the OracleAS Single Sign-On Server, thus providing increased security. In addition, the newly issued certificate is published in the Oracle Internet Directory.

OracleAS Certificate Authority Architecture and Configuration

OracleAS Certificate Authority is a part of the OracleAS Infrastructure and utilizes the OID and the OracleAS Single Sign-On Server to perform its certificate provisioning tasks. It uses the Metadata Repository of the OracleAS infrastructure to store certificates and related information. An OID-based user must be first authenticated by the SSO before the OracleAS Certificate Authority can issue a certificate to that user. To enable this, the OracleAS Certificate Authority utilizes the *mod_sso* component of the Oracle HTTP server to connect to the SSO server. When it creates a new certificate, the OracleAS Certificate Authority publishes it to the OID, and upon the deletion of a certificate, it automatically deletes the certificate entry in the OID as well.

A user automatically authenticated by the SSO and SSL will have the necessary privileges to get a new certificate or revoke an existing certificate for the same DN. A user who needs to be manually authenticated by the SSO and SSL is limited to the privileges of listing and requiring certificates.

The Registration Authority and the Certificate Authority

The OracleAS Certificate Authority consists of two main working components: the Registration Authority (RA) and the Certificate Authority (CA).

The RA is an interface between the CA and the end user and performs tasks such as the verification and certification of entity identification. The RA receives requests to issue new certificates, to renew expired certificates, and to revoke existing certificates. The RA is responsible for the verification of the requestor's identification and the requestor's privileges to use the supplied identification and public key. Upon verification of the user's credentials and privileges, the RA approves the request if everything is OK and sends the request to the CA. The RA consists of the following modules:

- *Authorization module*   Enforces the privilege requirements for the various certification-related user requests.
- *Validation module*   Validates the security certificates.
- *Policy module*   Enforces the certificate policies created by the OracleAS CA Administrator.

A user authenticated by the SSO and the SSL has automatic privileges to request new certificates or revoke old ones, as long as they use the same Distinguished Name (DN). A manually authenticated user can list or request certificates but cannot revoke them. The OID will automatically publish any created certificates and delete those that are revoked.

OCA Configuration

The configuration information for the OracleAS Certificate Authority is located in the $ORACLE_HOME/oca/conf/oca file in the XML format. Both the OracleAS Certificate Authority command-line tool *ocactl* and the policy administration module of the RA use this configuration file.

The PKI credentials and certificates are stored in an Oracle Wallet. The following types of wallets and certificates are necessary for the OracleAS Certificate Authority to function, and they both are created automatically during the installation of OracleAS Certificate Authority:

■ CA *Signing Wallet*   Contains the signing key and signing certificate of the OracleAS Certificate Authority.

■ CA *SSL Wallet*   Contains the SSL certificate and private key of the SSL server hosting the OracleAS Certificate Authority.

on the
()ob

The OracleAS Certificate Authority administrator password is stored in the password store along with the other passwords used by the OracleAS Certificate Authority and can be changed with the ocactl tool.

OracleAS Certificate Authority uses two types of passwords. The first type consists of the passwords it needs to access entities such as the OID, Oracle databases, and SSL. The second type of passwords are those it uses to protect items like the Signing Wallet and the SSL Wallet. OracleAS Certificate Authority uses an encrypted password store to keep passwords it uses, and you can change them using the *ocactl* command-line tool.

Creating a Complete Wallet

In this section, I briefly describe how to create a complete Oracle wallet. Here are the steps:

1. Create a new wallet using the Oracle Wallet Manager, as explained previously in this chapter.

2. Generate a certificate request.

3. Send the certificate request to the appropriate Certificate Authority (CA), either by copying and pasting it into an email, or by exporting the certificate request to a file.

4. The CA will send your signed user certificate accompanied by its associated trusted certificate.

5. Import the certificates into the wallet in the following order: first, import the CA's trusted certificate. If the certificate is being issued by a CA whose trusted certificate is already stored in the wallet, you can skip this step. Once you have imported the CA's trusted certificate, import the user certificate sent by the CA into the Oracle Wallet.

Before you can create an Oracle Wallet, you must know how to manage the OracleAS Certificate Authority. The starting and stopping procedures for the Certificate Authority are discussed in the following subsection.

Starting and Stopping the OracleAS Certificate Authority

You use the command-line tool *ocactl*, found in the Oracle Home/bin directory to start and stop the OracleAS Certificate Authority. First, verify that the following OracleAS infrastructure components are running:

- Oracle HTTP Server
- Oracle Internet Directory
- The *oca* process for the OC4J component of the infrastructure

Here's how you can use the *opmnctl* command to verify that the necessary OracleAS components are running:

```
$ opmnctl status
Processes in Instance: infra_10_1_2.ntl-alaptisam.netbsa.org
-------------------+--------------------+---------+---------
ias-component      | process-type       |     pid | status
-------------------+--------------------+---------+---------
LogLoader          | logloaderd         |     N/A | Down
DSA                | DSA                |     N/A | Down
HTTP_Server        | HTTP_Server        |   13168 | Alive
dcm-daemon         | dcm-daemon         |     N/A | Down
OC4J               | home               |   10696 | Alive
OC4J               | oca                |   15592 | Alive
OC4J               | OC4J_SECURITY      |   12580 | Alive
OID                | OID                |   16016 | Alive
$
```

Note that you need the OCA administrator password to use the *ocactl* utility.

On a UNIX/Linux and a Windows server, the *ocactl* utility is located in the ORACLE_HOME/oca/bindirectory. Here are the various options you can use with the *ocactl* utility:

```
$ ocactl
OracleAS Certificate Authority 10g (10.1.2)
Copyright (c) 2003, 2004, Oracle Corporation. All rights reserved.
Usage: ocactl <command>
        <command> := start
                   | stop
```

```
            |  status
            |  setpasswd
            |  generatewallet
            |  convertwallet
            |  importwallet
            |  revokecert
            |  renewcert
            |  updateconnection
            |  changesecurity
            |  set
            |  clear
            |  linksso
            |  unlinksso
            |  help
For help on a particular command, please use [ocactl help <command>]
$
```

As you can see, you can perform several management tasks relating to the OracleAS Certificate Authority using the *ocactl* utility, including stopping and starting the OCA.

Accessing the OracleAS CA Home Page

The recommended way to start the OracleAS Certificate Authority is by using the *ocactl* utility, as shown in the previous subsection. Although you can do so, for security reasons you mustn't start and stop the OCA using the Application Server Control Console. Once you start the OracleAS CA, you can access the OracleAS CA home page using the following URL:

```
https://hostname.hostdomain:ssl_port/oca/admin
```

The port number for the OracleAS CA can be found in the *portlist.ini* file.

Obtaining a Certificate   If this is the first time you're using the administration interface, you'll be asked to request a Web Administrator PKI certificate before you can start managing the OracleAS CA. An enrollment form will appear to guide you through the certificate registration process. You must enter the following details to obtain the certificate:

- Common name and email address
- Organization unit and organization
- Location, state or province, and country
- Password

Once you receive the Web Administrator certificate (it will be in the common name you specified), you must import it into your browser to start using the Web-based OracleAS Certificate Authority administration interface.

The OracleAS CA Home Page

The three tabs on the home page correspond to various OracleAS CA administrative task areas.

Certificate Management Use this tab to manage certificates, certification requests, and certificate revocation lists. You can perform the following tasks from here:

- Viewing certificate details
- Approving and rejecting certification requests
- Searching and listing issued certificates and certificate requests
- Revoking certificates
- Managing the Certificate Revocation List (CRL)

Configuration Management Use this tab to set up notifications and alerts as well as to manage certificate policies.

View Logs Use this tab to search logs.

on the Ⓙob *You can renew a user certificate within ten days of its expiration date by default. If you don't do this, the certificate will expire, and you'll have to issue a new certificate after receiving and approving a new request for it.*

Accessing OracleAS CA User Pages

To access the OracleAS CA user home page, use the following URL:

```
https://hostname.domain_anme:ssl_port/oca/user
```

The user pages are useful for finding certification requests and importing certificates and CRLs into a user's browser. Users can authenticate themselves to the OracleAS CA through the following methods:

- Single Sign-On, based on the SSO password
- Secure Sockets Layer (SSL) based on certificates
- Manually by obtaining a certificate request form, submitting it, and waiting for its approval by the OracleAS CA administrator

TWO-MINUTE DRILL

OracleAS Single Sign-On

❑ OracleAS Single Sign-On is part of the Identity Management component of the OracleAS infrastructure.

❑ Single Sign-On enables a user to log in to multiple applications by logging in once into the OracleAS SSO Server.

❑ OracleAS Single Sign-On components include the OID, Single Sign-On Server, partner and external applications, and the *mod_osso* module.

❑ Partner applications run on the OracleAS and delegate their authorization functions to the Single Sign-On Server.

❑ External applications control their own authentication instead of delegating it to the Single Sign-On Server.

Configuring and Managing the SSO Server

❑ You start and stop the OracleAS SSO Server when you start and stop either the Oracle HTTP server or the OC4J instance.

❑ You can also use the system components table in the Application Server Control Console to start and stop the OracleAS SSO Server.

❑ You can use the single sign-off page to log off from several applications at once.

❑ The OracleAS SSO Administrator has complete configuration and administration privileges on the OracleAS SSO Server.

❑ You must create the SSO administrator after installation, using the orcladmin OID super account.

❑ The SSO administrator must be a member of the iASAdmins group.

❑ Partner applications are registered with the SSO Server by integrating them using the *mod_osso* module.

❑ Single Sign-On credentials are stored in the OID.

❑ The *mod_osso* module enables the Oracle HTTP Server to act as a partner application to the Oracle Single Sign-On Server.

❑ You can use the *ssoreg.sh* script to manually register the *mod_osso* module with the OracleAS Single Sign-On Server.

❑ The *ssoreg.sh* script regenerates the *osso.conf* configuration file.

❏ The default HTTP port number is 80, and the default HTTPS port number is 443.

❏ To access an external application registered with the OracleAS SSO, the OracleAS Portal must be a partner application to the SSO Server.

Using the Secure Sockets Layer

❏ SSL uses security certificates to authenticate a user's authenticity.

❏ SSL uses three concepts: encryption, data integrity, and authentication.

❏ SSL is implemented through the *mod_osso* module.

❏ Cryptography is the process of encryption and decryption of messages.

❏ SSL uses both private key and public key cryptography.

❏ Private key cryptography is also called symmetric key cryptography and involves the use of identical keys by both parties to secure a message.

❏ Public key cryptography uses the concept of public/private key pairs. The private keys are kept secret and the public keys are published.

❏ Certificates verify the user's right to use a public key by binding a user's identity to a pair of encryption keys.

❏ The initial authentication phase of an SSL session is called the *handshake phase*.

❏ A cipher suite is a set of encryption protocols that specify the certificate type, the encryption type, and the signature algorithm to be used in the communication.

Oracle Wallet Manager

❏ Oracle Wallets are logical containers that hold certificates and public/private key pairs.

❏ The SSL Wallet directive specifies the location of the Oracle Wallet when you configure the Oracle HTTP Server for SSL.

❏ You start the Oracle Wallet Manager with the *owm* command-line utility.

❏ You must use the Auto Login feature (disabled by default) to configure single sign-on access to multiple Oracle databases.

❏ Standard PKCS #12 wallets use a directory to store the security credentials, and the PKCS #11 wallets are stored on a hardware security module.

❑ To upload a wallet, the wallet must be open and it must have at least one user certificate.

❑ Oracle Wallet Manager uses *trusted certificates* and *user certificates*.

❑ User certificates are used by server applications to validate entity identities in a public key/private key–based message exchange.

❑ A trusted certificate is any certificate that you trust, such as one provided by recognized certificate authorities (e.g., VeriSign).

❑ You must first install a trusted certificate from a CA before you can install user certificates issued by that CA.

Managing Certificates

❑ Oracle Wallet Manager uses two kinds of certificates: *user certificates* and *trusted certificates*.

❑ User certificates are used by server applications to validate an entity's identity in a public key/private key–based message exchange.

❑ A trusted certificate is any certificate you trust, such as one provided by a certificate authority (CA).

❑ You must first install a trusted certificate from the CA before you can install a user certificate issued by that authority.

Enabling OracleAS Components to Use SSL

❑ You can enable any OracleAS component to use SSL.

❑ To enable the HTTP Server for SSL you must modify the *sso.conf* file.

❑ Third-party CA issued certificates can be uploaded to the OID in an LDIF file, using the command-line tool *ldapmodify*.

❑ The first step in configuring the OracleAS SSO Server for SSL is to use the *ssocfg.sh* script to change the HTTP references to HTTPS.

❑ You must reassociate the OracleAS Portal to the secured SSO Server by using the OPCA tool.

OracleAS Certificate Authority

❑ OracleAS Certificate Authority is part of the OracleAS Infrastructure and it enables the deployment of public key certificates.

❑ A Public Key Infrastructure (PKI) consists of encryption algorithms, encryption keys, secure methods to distribute the keys, and trusted entities to authenticate users.

❑ A PKI-based digital certificate binds a private/public key pair to an identity after authenticating the identity.

❑ A digital signature helps in the nonrepudiation of messages.

❑ Applications authenticating to the OracleAS Single Sign-On Server can obtain certificates in three ways: manually, through the OracleAS SSO authentication, and through the automatic provisioning of certificates by the OracleAS Certificate Authority.

❑ OracleAS PKI management tools include the OID, the Oracle Wallet Manager, the Oracle Enterprise Login Assistant, and the Oracle Enterprise Security Manager.

❑ Newly issued certificates are automatically published in the OID.

❑ Before an OID-based user can be issued a certificate by the OracleAS CA, the user must connect to the OracleAS SSO Server.

❑ The Registration Authority component is the interface between the CA and the end user and is responsible for the verification of the certificate requestor's identification and privileges.

❑ The configuration information for the OracleAS CA is located in the $ORACLE_HOME/oca/conf/oca file.

❑ You use the *ocatctl* utility to start and stop the OracleAS Certificate Authority.

❑ You can change the encrypted passwords in the password store using the *ocactl* utility.

❑ For security reasons, you mustn't use the Application Server Control Console to start and stop the OracleAS CA.

❑ The CRL is a list of all revoked certificates.

SELF TEST

1. The `SSLEngine` parameter helps you to

   A. Configure the number of SSL engines to start.
   B. Enable or disable SSL in the Oracle HTTP Server.
   C. Enable or disable SSL in the SSO.
   D. Install the SSL option when installing the OracleAS Infrastructure.

2. You can start and stop the OracleAS Single Sign-On Server through

   A. Only the OC4J instance
   B. Only the Oracle HTTP Server
   C. Both the OC4J instance and the Oracle HTTP Server
   D. Neither the OC4J instance nor the Oracle HTTP Server

3. When you enable SSL on the Single Sign-On Server after the OracleAS installation,

   A. You must register *mod_osso* manually.
   B. You must create the *httpd.conf* file manually.
   C. You must create the *osso.conf* file manually.
   D. You must delete the *osso.conf* file manually.

4. *Asymmetric encryption* relies on

   A. Both parties having the same secret key
   B. Keeping the public key secret
   C. Publishing the private key and keeping the public key secret
   D. Publishing the public key and keeping the private key secret

5. Auto Login

   A. Must be enabled for Single Sign-On access and is enabled by default.
   B. Must be enabled for Single Sign-On access and is disabled by default.
   C. Must be disabled for Single Sign-On access and is enabled by default.
   D. Must be disabled for Single Sign-On access and is disabled by default.

6. In order for a wallet to be eligible for an upload,

   A. The wallet must not contain an SSL certificate, and the wallet should be closed.
   B. The wallet must contain an SSL certificate, and the wallet should be closed.

    C. The wallet must contain an SSL certificate, and the wallet should be open.

    D. The wallet must not contain an SSL certificate, and the wallet should be open.

7. You must

    A. First install a user certificate before you can install a trusted certificate.

    B. Install either user certificates or trusted certificates, but not both together.

    C. First install a trusted certificate before you can install a user certificate.

    D. Install the trusted certificate every time you want to install a user certificate.

8. You can use the *ldapmodify* command to

    A. Add user certificates to the OID.

    B. Add user certificates to the Oracle Wallet Manager.

    C. Modify user certificates in the OID.

    D. Add trusted certificates to the OID.

9. The three important modules of the Registration Authority in the OracleAS Certificate Authority, are

    A. Authorization, validation, and encryption

    B. Authorization, policy, and validation

    C. Validation, encryption, and policy

    D. Authorization, certification, and validation

10. OCA needs the following wallets to operate:

    A. SSL Signing Wallet and the SSL CA Wallet

    B. CA Signing Wallet and the OCA SSL Wallet

    C. OCA Signing Wallet and the OCA SSL Wallet

    D. CA Signing Wallet and the CA SSL Wallet

SELF TEST ANSWERS

1. ☑ **B** is correct because the `SSLEngine` parameter lets you enable (or disable) the HTTP server for SSL.
   ☒ **A** is wrong because the `SSLEngine` doesn't have anything to do with the number of SSL engines. **C** is wrong because this parameter is used to enable SSL in the HTTP Server. **D** is wrong because the parameter isn't used when you install the OracleAS instance.

2. ☑ **C** is correct because you start and stop the OracleAS SSO Server through starting and stopping either the OC4J instance or the HTTP server.
   ☒ **A** and **B** are wrong because they both leave out one of the ways to start and stop the OracleAS SSO Server. **D** is wrong because you can use both the OC4J instance and the Oracle HTTP server to manage the OracleAS SSO Server.

3. ☑ **A** is correct because you must register *mod_osso* manually, when you enable SSL on the Single Sign-On Server after the OracleAS installation.
   ☒ **B, C,** and **D** are wrong because you don't have to manually create or delete any of these files.

4. ☑ **D** is correct because in asymmetric encryption, you publish the public key and keep the private encryption key private.
   ☒ **A** is wrong because this is true only in symmetric encryption. **B** is wrong because the public key is published, not kept secret. **C** is wrong because it's the opposite of what must be done.

5. ☑ **B** is correct because Auto Login must be enabled for Single Sign-On access and is disabled by default.
   ☒ **A** is wrong because Auto Login is disabled by default. **C** and **D** are wrong because Auto Login must be enabled, not disabled, for Single Sign-On access.

6. ☑ **C** is correct because a wallet must contain an SSL certificate and it should be open in order for it to be exported.
   ☒ **A, B,** and **C** are wrong because they violate one or both of the conditions for exporting wallets, as explained in the correct answer.

7. ☑ **C** is correct because you must first install a trusted certificate before you can install a user certificate.
   ☒ **A** and **D** are wrong because you must install the trusted certificate first. **B** is incorrect because you can and *must* install both types of certificates.

8. ☑ **A** is correct because you can use the *ldapmodify* command to *add user certificates* to the Oracle Internet Directory.

☒   **B** is wrong because you use the *ldapmodify* tool to add user certificates to the OID, not the Oracle Wallet Manager. **C** is wrong because you use the tool to *add*, not modify, user certificates in the OID. **D** is wrong because you use the tool to add user certificates to the OID, not trusted certificates.

9.   ☑   **B** is correct because the three important modules of the Registration Authority in the OracleAS Certificate Authority are authorization, policy, and validation.
   ☒   **A, C,** and **D** are wrong because they include the wrong or nonexistent RA modules.

10.   ☑   **D** is correct because the OCA needs the CA signing wallet and the CA SSL wallet in order to function.
   ☒   **A, B,** and **C** are wrong because they refer to nonexistent wallets.

Part III

OracleAS 10g
Middle-Tier Components

7

OracleAS Portal

CERTIFICATION OBJECTIVES

The OracleAS Portal is an OracleAS middle-tier component and is installed as a part of the Portal and Wireless middle-tier installation option. The OracleAS Portal makes it possible to create and deploy Enterprise Information Portals (EIPs). An EIP not only provides access to Web content but also access to summary versions of various applications. In this chapter, our goals are to understand OracleAS Portal architecture, configuration, and administration.

CERTIFICATION OBJECTIVE 7.01

OracleAS Portal

The OracleAS Portal is a central Web-based access point to an organization's information sources as well as to its applications. An employee, for example, could use the organization's portal to access Web pages called portal pages. The employee could also use the portal as a jump-off point for various applications. The centralized nature of a portal means that portal administrators manage the portal instance for the organization and provide users with the means to access information on their own.

The Portal Hierarchy

The basic component in any portal is a portal page, which is similar to normal Web pages and can be created with input from various sources. What makes the portal page organization unique is the hierarchy within which all portal pages fall. Here's the hierarchical structure of an OracleAS Portal:

- The *portal site* is at the top of the portal hierarchy; it refers to the OracleAS Portal installation, accessible by using a unique URL.

- Next in the hierarchy is the *page group,* which is a collection of related portal pages. The page group contains additional items essential for the functioning of the portal pages, including items such as page templates and styles.

- A *portal page* occupies the next rung in the portal hierarchy and is the main thing users see when they access the OracleAS Portal. A portal page can have several *regions,* which help in providing the basic layout for the portal page. You can specify the percentage of the portal page that a certain region will occupy.

■ Finally, a region may have one or both of two types of object—*portlets* and *items*—which provide the content that's presented in a portal page.

Relationships among the OracleAS Portal Components

The relationships among the various parts of the OracleAS Portal hierarchy are discussed in the following subsections.

Page Groups

The OracleAS Portal is a collection of one or more *page groups*, each of which is a hierarchical collection of portal pages. An OracleAS Portal site can have multiple *portal groups*. The top page of each page group is termed the root page for that page group. You may create page groups based on the organizational or regional business divisions or on the particular intranet to be served.

When you install the OracleAS Portal, several default page groups are automatically created and cannot be deleted. One of these page groups is called the *Portlet Repository*; it stores all the portlets, from both local and external providers, that can be added to pages. Here's a list of some other important default page groups:

■ *Corporate pages* contain the default home page for a site.

■ *Shared objects* contain personal pages of users as well as objects that can be shared across page groups.

■ *Portal design-time pages* contain all of the OracleAS Portal pages, including the search and navigator as well as the Portal Builder page.

Portal Pages

The OracleAS Portal enables you to organize and present information from multiple data sources in a single, convenient view, called a *portal page*. When a user interacts with the OracleAS Portal, what the user sees are the portal pages, which can contain any HTML content. Each page is divided into *regions*, which determine how space is allocated to that page's portlets or items; this is how information on portal pages is published.

A page consists of two main things: a user-defined *layout* and a *content* portion, represented by portlets and items. In addition, a page has attributes about itself, called the page's *metadata*. Note that each time you display a particular page, the page is dynamically assembled based on the layout and content (portlets and/or items) associated with that page. The OracleAS Portal creates portal pages from certain base page types, which define the type of content that can go in that page.

You can create custom page types by extending the base page types and adding additional page attributes to complement the standard page attributes contained in the base page types. Some base page types in the OracleAS Portal are described in the following subsections.

Regions

A portal page can be divided into regions, say one for a banner, another for the navigation bar and yet another along the bottom for a footer. A region has a set of display and other options that control how its content is displayed. These options include such things as whether to display borders around portlets and the width and height of a region relative to the entire page.

Portlets

A portal page can contain one or more components called *portlets* that get their content from various data sources. Portal pages can be created by using browser-based wizards or built as Java Server pages.

Portlets are reusable building blocks that enable easy publishing of information and are critical components of the OracleAS Portal. By adding portlets to a user's view of the portal, you can easily deliver new content to that user. For example, you can use portlets to provide dynamic charts, tables, or graphs of data to your users. Portlets can supply new content gathered from various sources, using the OracleAS Portal instance to help publish its information in the portal. The portlet *provider* is a data source that provides the portlets.

You can create some portlets by using the *portlet creation wizard,* and others by using PL/SQL or Java. For example, you can use the Portal Creation Wizard to create form portlets that display forms and reports portlets that display customized reports. Portlets can be written in PL/SQL or Java. The OracleAS Metadata Repository database is the source for the PL/SQL portlets. Java portlets can be obtained from any location accessible from the network, including external Web providers and the OracleAS Metadata Repository. When you install the OracleAS Portal, you automatically get access to several portlets created by third-party vendors registered through Oracle's Partner Program.

The concept of a *portal provider* helps explain how information from various sources is published in the portal. Providers own the portlets and allow data from various sources to be brought into a portal page. An application or a data source can be represented as a portlet and can communicate with the OracleAS Portal through a provider. A portlet can have only one provider. A provider can serve multiple portlets at once, representing the underlying application or data source.

Items

In addition to portlets, you can use *items*, which are the other basic type of OracleAS Portal building blocks. Items are individual content entities that reside on a page in an item region. There are two types of items: content item types and navigation item types.

Portal Page Appearance

In order to provide a standard look and feel to your OracleAS Portal site, you use certain portal features such as the following:

- Templates
- Styles
- Shared objects
- Navigation pages
- Translations

Content Classification

In order to make it easier to find content in the OracleAS Portal, the content is classified according to its type. There are two content classification methods: *categories* and *perspectives*.

Categories

Categories help you classify content into different types, such as sales reports and location maps, thus enabling users to quickly locate and display various types of content. Under each category, you can have multiple subcategories as well.

Perspectives

Perspectives enable you classify content on a more fine-grained basis than classifications, enabling you to create groups across multiple categories. For example, you may have a human resources page group with perspectives such as Employees, Administrators, Sales Representatives, Accountants, and the like. Perspectives enable users to quickly display content that's applicable to them.

Prerequisites for Accessing the OracleAS Portal

The OracleAS Portal runs with the help of several other Oracle Infrastructure and Middle-Tier components. If you don't have one of the following components up and running, your attempt to access the OracleAS Portal will result in an error:

- Oracle HTTP Server
- OracleAS Web Cache
- Portal Services
- OracleAS Metadata Repository
- OC4J_Portal

on the job

The OID automatically propagates changes to the OracleAS Portal. When relevant user or group information changes in the OID, the OracleAS Portal receives notifications from the OID, based on its provisioning profile, thus keeping the portal data in step with the OID information. The provisioning profile is enabled by default, thus making the propagation of information from OID to the OracleAS Portal automatic. You can recreate the provisioning profile by using the ptlconfig tool.

In addition, you must correctly configure the OracleAS Portal DAD (Database Access Descriptor), before you can connect to the OracleAS Portal. Because the OracleAS Metadata Repository is in an Oracle database, make sure that the SQLNet listener service is running as well. If you are using the Single Sign-On feature, you must ensure that the connection configuration is done correctly between the OracleAS Portal and the OracleAS Single Sign-On Server. To fix any configuration problem, you edit the *iasconfig.xml* file to make the necessary changes, before running the *ptlconfig* script. You follow the same strategy if you're having connection issues between the OracleAS Portal and the Oracle Internet Directory.

Three-Tier Architecture

The OracleAS Portal architecture consists of *three basic tiers:* the client browser, the infrastructure tier, and the middle tier. Oracle recommends that you install these three tiers on separate servers for performance and availability reasons, although it's possible to run them on the same server.

The Client

The client uses the HTTP or the HTTPS protocol to send requests to the OracleAS Portal instance, traversing through firewalls and proxies to do so. The client browser may be redirected to the Single Sign-On Server for authentication.

Infrastructure Tier

The infrastructure tier consists of the Oracle HTTP Server, OracleAS Single Sign-On, Oracle Internet Directory, and the OracleAS Metadata Repository. Let's briefly look at how some of the OracleAS infrastructure components interact with the OracleAS Portal.

The OID is used for provisioning users and groups for the OracleAS Portal and stores all user and group information. Object and page privileges of the users are stored in the OID as well, thus enabling fast lookups of those privileges. The OracleAS Portal uses Delegated Administrative Services (DAS) to enable users to directly access the OID.

The Oracle Directory Integration Platform will automatically propagate relevant changes in the OracleAS Portal to the Oracle Internet Directory.

Users are redirected to the OracleAS Single Sign-On for redirection, if you've configured the OracleAS Single Sign-On authentication. SSO will verify the user credentials by sending LDAP-based requests to the OID.

The OracleAS Metadata Repository, another OracleAS Infrastructure component, stores the access control lists (ACLs) for portal objects. The OracleAS Metadata Repository stores these and other OracleAS Portal–related data in a special schema called the PORTAL schema. As you learned in Chapter 2, the OracleAS Metadata Repository consists of a set of schemas that contain the metadata for all OracleAS components. The OracleAS Portal is one of those components, and it accesses the metadata during its run-time operations.

Middle Tier

The middle tier consists of the OracleAS Web Cache, the Oracle HTTP Server, Oracle Application Server Containers for J2EE, and other OracleAS components. The OracleAS Web Cache, for example, helps optimize the throughput of the OracleAS Portal, by servicing user requests from its cache when it's possible to do so. As you've seen earlier, if the OracleAS Web Cache has the requested portal page in its cache, it will service the request itself, instead of sending it to the origin HTTP server and the Parallel Page Engine.

on the
j o b

Although all three tiers of the OracleAS Portal—the client tier, the infrastructure tier, and the middle tier—can be run on a single machine, the Oracle Corporation recommends that you use separate servers for each of the three tiers.

OracleAS Web Cache   The OracleAS Web Cache improves OracleAS Portal performance by trying to service the request from previously cached pages. If the page isn't found in the Web cache, the client request is forwarded to the origin HTTP server.

The Parallel Page Engine   The Parallel Page Engine (PPE) runs as a Java servlet within OC4J and accepts URL requests through the *mod_oc4j* plugin of the Oracle HTTP Server. The PPE is at the heart of the OracleAS Portal runtime engine and is in charge of creating runtime portal pages. You can have multiple PPEs to improve the performance of the OracleAS Portal. The PPE builds portal pages for display by first retrieving the metadata relating to the page layout from the Portal Repository. The PPE then requests all the providers to return the portlets they service and adds these portlets to the portal page structure it already created.

on the
j o b

The OracleAS Portal will dynamically assemble and format a page each time a user requests one, unless full-page caching is used, in which case the pages are served right from the cache itself.

Providers   Portal providers serve to link the data sources and the OracleAS Portal pages through the use of portlets. Providers contribute the real support for the portlets being displayed on each portal page. The OracleAS Portal comes ready with several built-in providers. Furthermore, you can create other providers should you need them. There are two types of providers: Web providers and database providers:

Web providers gather information available on the Web, such as stock quotes and local news, and send it to the OracleAS through portlets, using SAP-based messages over the HTTP protocol. Because Web providers use SOAP (Simple Object Access Protocol), they can be written in any language.

Database providers provide portal content by using data stored in the Oracle database (used as the OracleAS Portal Repository); this content must be written in the PL/SQL language.

The PPE makes requests to both the database providers and the Web providers through HTTPS. It uses *mod_plsql* when dealing with database providers, and SOAP-based message protocol over HTTP/S when dealing with Web providers. The OracleAS Web Cache uses an invalidation-based cache methodology, whereby a requested URL is deemed correct when it can be serviced from its cache until the URL has been invalidated.

Provider groups contain a set of providers sharing common features and thus simplify the organization of multiple providers. Provider groups can contain only those providers that are accessed via the Federated Portal Adapter.

Ultra Search   Ultra Search is an Oracle text-based application that supports crawling, indexing, and searching of heterogeneous repositories such as databases, Web servers, and email mailing lists.

How OracleAS Portal Assembles Pages

When a client requests a portal page, the OracleAS Portal dynamically assembles and formats the page based on the page's assigned portlets and layout elements. However, if *full page caching* is employed, pages are served out of the cache instead of being dynamically assembled. A portal page can display content from the Metadata Repository, or content from an external provider.

The OracleAS Portal Cache is different from the OracleAS Web Cache. The portal cache is a file-based cache for storing portal pages and portlets. You can use the portal cache to enforce validation or expiry-based caching. There are two kinds of portal caches. The portal *content cache* stores OracleAS Portal contents such as page metadata and database and Web portlets. The portal *session cache* stores the session information for the portal users. The portal contents and session cache content are both stored usually in the $ORACLE_HOME/Apache/modplsql/cache directory, in the file *cache.conf*. You can configure various parameters for the portal cache, such as the total cache size and the maximum time a cached file can be stored in the cache.

If OracleAS Portal performance is slow, check to make sure that caching hasn't been disabled. Make sure that the PlsqlCacheEnable parameter is set to ON in the cache.conf file described previously and that this parameter has been configured correctly as well.

Note that there is a separation of page content and presentation, inasmuch as the content is drawn from various sources through portlets managed by providers, and the presentation elements (page definitions) such as layout and look and feel are retrieved from the Oracle Metadata Repository.

Following is a brief summary of how OracleAS's various components contribute to the creation and delivery of a portal page. I include the OracleAS Web Cache in the component mix, because you *must use* the OracleAS Web Cache if you want to run the OracleAS Portal. Note that the key to understanding the following process is to know the difference between having a fully cached portal page and assembling a new page from cached and non-cached data. If a user's request for a portal page can be satisfied by getting it from the OracleAS Web Cache without accessing the OracleAS Portal, the OracleAS Portal isn't used. OracleAS Portal and Parallel Page Engine come into the picture only if the portal pages can't be served from the OracleAS Web Cache. The process for the creation and delivery of a portal page is as follows:

1. A client browser requests a portal page by sending a URL to the Oracle HTTP Server. This request is actually first received by the OracleAS Web Cache.

2. OracleAS Web Cache forwards the client's request for the portal page to the Oracle HTTP Server.

3. The Oracle HTTP Server sends the request to the OracleAS Portal services, because the request is for a portal page, not a regular HTML document. As described previously in this chapter, the PPE is in charge of overseeing the creation of a portal page from the various sources of information available.

4. The Parallel Page Engine (PPE) retrieves the portal *page definition* (which contains information about the layout of the page as well as the portlets that are a part of the page), by first trying to get it (the page definition) from the Oracle Web Cache. If the page definition isn't found in the OracleAS Web Cache, it checks the OracleAS Portal Cache as well. If there's no page definition stored in either cache (Web cache or the portal cache), the OracleAS Metadata Repository generates a page definition from data in the Portal Repository (actually a special default portal page group), which is usually located in the Metadata Repository.

5. The PPE will *parse* the page definition next, and if there is a *fully cached portal page* in the OracleAS Web Cache, it will return the page to the client by way

of the OracleAS Web Cache. If the OracleAS Web Cache doesn't hold a fully cached page that matches the page definition, the PPE will have to build a new page using the following methodology:

   a.   The PPE checks whether the necessary portlets for a portal page are already cached in either or both the OracleAS Web Cache and the portal cache itself. If there's a cached copy of the portlets, the PPE contacts the appropriate provider for validation of the cached copy.

   b.   If a cached copy of the requested portlet content isn't in either one of the two caches, the PPE sends a request to the appropriate provider that owns the portlet(s) to execute that portlet and send the content to the portal page.

6.   Web providers return the validated portlet — or a newly generated content for the portlet — to the PPE using the HTTP (or HTTPS) protocol. Database (DB) providers return the same using either of the HTTP (or HTTPS) or SOAP protocols.

7.   The PPE aggregates all the content it receives from the various providers into the portal page and sends it to the OracleAS Web Cache.

8.   The OracleAS Web Cache sends the portal page to the client browser that made the initial request for that page.

CERTIFICATION OBJECTIVE 7.02

Managing the OracleAS Portal

You can manage and configure the OracleAS Portal by using the Application Server Control Console, as well as through various portal configuration scripts. The Application Server Control Console is used as the main administrative tool for the OracleAS Portal. You can perform the following administrative and configuration-related tasks using the Application Server Control Console:

- Enabling and disabling components
- Administering clusters
- Starting and stopping services
- Viewing logs and listening ports
- Performing real-time monitoring

In the following subsections, various aspects of OracleAS Portal management and monitoring are reviewed.

OracleAS Portal Administrative Services

The OracleAS Portal framework provides administrative services such as the following:

- Access to monitoring and configuration tools
- OracleAS Single Sign-On Server
- Directory integration
- Web caching
- Security
- Migration of content between Portal instances
- Monitoring the OracleAS Portal instance performance

Note that the portlets on a portal page contain dialog boxes that let you perform such tasks as managing users and groups, setting up security and search features, and administering the portal and the database. You can perform administrative tasks using the following methods:

- *Administrative Portlets* let you perform most of the administrative and configuration tasks. You must log in as a portal Administrator to perform these tasks.
- You can perform certain administrative tasks only through the *Application Server Control*.
- You use *configuration scripts* that are installed during the OracleAS installation to configure certain aspects of the OracleAS Portal.

In the following subsections, let's learn how to monitor and manage the OracleAS Portal using the various methods just mentioned.

Using Administrative Portlets

You can log in to the OracleAS Portal instance by using the following URL:

```
http://hostname.domain:port/pls/portal
```

For example, if your port is the default port, 7777, you'll use the following URL:

FIGURE 7-1

The OracleAS
Portal "Portal
Builder" Page

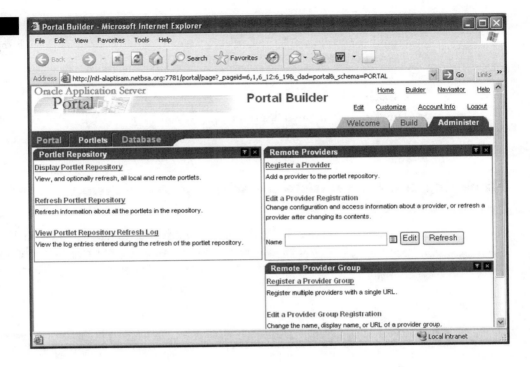

```
http://hostname.domain:7777/pls/portal
```

Log in as the user PORTAL, using the password for the original *ias_admin* account
that you provided during the OracleAS instance installation process. Note that
the OracleAS Portal instance uses the OracleAS Web Cache HTTP listen port.
However, if you wish, you can change the OracleAS Web Cache HTTP listen port.

Once you log into the OracleAS Portal instance, you'll see the *Portal Builder
page*, as shown in Figure 7-1. There are three tabs on this page: *Welcome, Build, and
Administer*. Click the Administer tab, to start administering the OracleAS Portal
instance. There are three subtabs on the Portal Administer page, and these are
explained briefly.

Portal

The portlets available in this subtab let you perform such tasks as managing users
and groups, configuring instance settings, and administering other OracleAS
services such as Delegated Administrative Service (DAS) and the OracleAS
Web Cache.

Portlets

From here you manage the *Portlet Repository*, which contains information about the portlets and the registered providers.

Database

The database subtab helps you manage database tasks such as creating schemas and roles and monitoring database information.

Managing the Portal Instance with the Application Server Control

You use the Application Server Control interface to manage the OracleAS Portal instance. You can access the portal instance by first going to the OracleAS middle-tier instance and then to the System Components page. There are two OracleAS Portal–related system components, as shown in Figure 7-2.

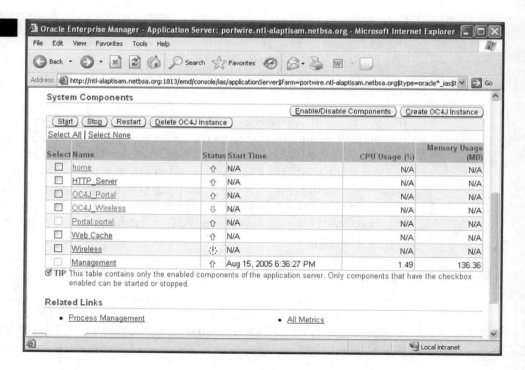

FIGURE 7-2

The System Components Page with the Portal Entries

By clicking the OC4J_Portal link, you can reach the OC4J Server home page. OC4J_Portal is the OC4J instance containing OracleAS Portal–related Web applications (e.g., Parallel Page Engine). The OC4J Server Portal home page provides a single view of the instance and a launching point for administration of the various elements in the J2EE application environment. The OC4J Server home page is used to:

- Configure the OC4J Server instance.
- Administer services and resources such as data sources and security.
- Monitor the availability, usage, and performance of the server and applications.

The Portal:portal link takes you to the OracleAS Portal instance home page. You monitor the Portal instance from this home page. You also monitor the various OracleAS Portal components such as the Oracle HTTP Server, *mod_plsql*, and OracleAS Web Cache from the OracleAS Portal home page. Figure 7-3 shows the OracleAS Portal home page.

FIGURE 7-3

The OracleAS Portal Home Page

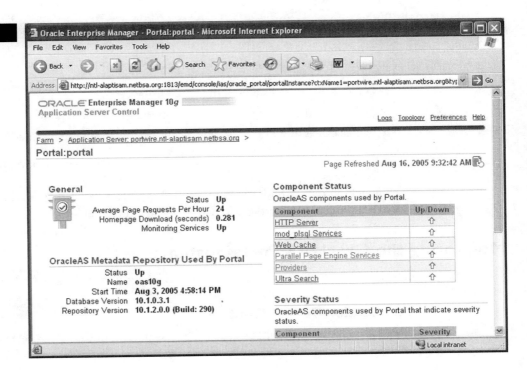

The OracleAS
Portal Welcome
Page

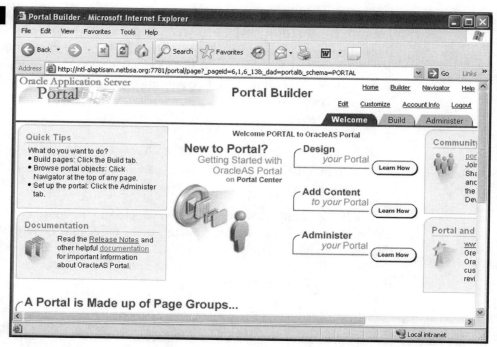

You can do the following from the OracleAS Portal home page:

- Check the overall status of the Portal instance.
- Check on the Portal instance's usage of the Metadata Repository.
- Check the status of the OracleAS components the portal instance needs to use.

You can make changes in the Portal Web Cache settings by clicking the Portal
Web Cache Settings link under the Administration sections.

By clicking the Portal End User Default Homepage, you can go to the Welcome
page of the OracleAS Portal instance, as shown in Figure 7-4.

Monitoring the OracleAS Portal Instance

The following tools and services can be used to monitor the OracleAS Portal instance.

Application Server Control

Using the Application Server Control, you can perform the following portal-related
management and monitoring tasks:

- Stopping and starting the OracleAS Portal instance
- Viewing logs
- Viewing metrics
- Configuring settings

OracleAS Portal Logging Service

By using the Log Registry records in the Services portlet, you can register objects and actions for which the OracleAS Portal Logging service should collect logging information. The data is logged in the Activity Log tables.

OracleAS Portal Activity Reports

There are several Activity Log views that let you analyze the data in the Activity Log tables. OracleAS Portal lets you create Activity reports based on the Activity Log views.

mod_plsql Performance Logging Service

The *mod_plsql* performance logging service enables you to collect performance statistics about user requests to the OracleAS Portal.

OracleAS Portal Performance Reports

Using the Performance Reporting scripts located in the $ORACLE_HOME/portal/admin/plsql/perf directory, you can generate performance reports based on the data collected by the *mod_plsql* performance logging service.

CERTIFICATION OBJECTIVE 7.03

OracleAS Portal Schema, User, and Group Management

Note that all the groups discussed here are located in the OID directory information tree (DIT) under the following distinguished name (DN):

```
cn=<portal_group_container>,cn=Groups,dc=MyCompany,dc=com.
```

Default OracleAS Portal Schemas

The OracleAS Portal components are mostly installed in the Oracle database, with a few items being installed in the OracleAS Middle Tier. When you install the OracleAS Portal, the following *default database schemas* are created in the OracleAS Metadata Repository:

- **PORTAL** This is the main database schema for the OracleAS Portal and contains the OracleAS database objects and code. By default, the database schema is always named PORTAL during standard OracleAS Portal installations, and you must perform a custom install if you want to give it a different name.

on the **job**

The PORTAL schema is the product schema for the OracleAS Portal.

- **PORTAL_PUBLIC** The PORTAL_PUBLIC schema is used as a default database mapping account so that a light-weight portal user can access the Oracle database as a valid database user and execute various PL/SQL code elements. PORTAL_PUBLIC is the *default* OracleAS Portal access schema. You can create a *custom* OracleAS Portal access schema, grant it the necessary database privileges from the application product schema (the PORTAL schema) and map certain portal users to the new schema, if you wish, by performing a custom installation of OracleAS Portal.

- **PORTAL_DEMO** This is an optional schema that contains the OracleAS Portal demonstration code.

- **PORTAL_APP** This schema is meant for the authorization of external JSP applications.

During the OracleAS installation the Portal schema passwords are stored in the OID; you can *retrieve them* using the Oracle Directory Manager. You can *change the passwords* by using the Application Server Control and clicking the Change Schema Password link in the Metadata Repository section of the Infrastructure tab in the middle-tier OracleAS instance.

Managing Portal Users

Because user and group information is stored in the OID, the portal administrator uses the Delegated Administrative Services (DAS) interface to enter user and group information in the OID. You can access DAS directly or through the OracleAS Portal Builder page.

o n   t h e   **j o b**

OracleAS Portal users are Single Sign-On (SSO) users.

Before you learn how to add and manage users to the OracleAS Portal, it's a good idea to learn about the default portal users first.

Default Portal Users

When you install the OracleAS Portal, the following four default portal users are created:

- *PORTAL*   The PORTAL user is the superuser for OracleAS Portal and has all the available global privileges in the OracleAS Portal. The password for the PORTAL user is what you supplied during the OracleAS installation.
- *ORCLADMIN*   This account is similar to the PORTAL account and is created for the use of the OracleAS administrators. Note that this orcladmin account is a portal user and is different from the orcladmin OID superuser account.

- *PORTAL_ADMIN*   This is a user with limited administrative privileges (e.g., schema creation and management). The PORTAL_ADMIN account doesn't confer privileges to perform database work. This account is meant mostly for a limited domain administrator who manages portal pages and user accounts.

e x a m

⊛ a t c h   *The password for the orcladmin, portal, and portal_admin accounts is the same as the one you provided for the ias_admin user account during OracleAS installation.*

- *PUBLIC*   The PUBLIC user account is used for unauthenticated access to the OracleAS Portal. After the user logs in using the PUBLIC user account, the username changes to the username by which the user can be authenticated.

Creating Users

The portal administrator can create new users by using the User portlet, which enables the administrator to specify the following information:

- Username and password
- Job-related information
- Photograph in GIF or JPEG format
- Group membership information
- Access information for Reports and Forms applications

User Profiles

When a user first logs in to the OracleAS Portal or when the portal administrator first tries to edit a user's profile, the user's profile gets created automatically. Portal administrators use the Portal User Profile portlet to manage user profiles. The Portal User Profile portlet enables the user to configure various user settings such as database schema, default group, default mobile home page, and the default page style. Note that new users are associated with the PORTAL_PUBLIC database schema by default.

Managing Groups

To implement base user privileges as well as more advanced portal-level privileges, OracleAS Portal creates the following groups.

- *AUTHENTICATED_USERS* Member of this group are able to log in to the OracleAS Portal; by default, all users have this privilege. The group includes all authenticated (logged in) users. This group is used to assign default privileges to all logged in users, and the members of this group have the CREATE GROUP privilege.

- *DBA group members* These members belong to the highest privileges level, and initially the user PORTAL is the only member of this group. The DBA group is meant for the OracleAS administrators so they can use various OracleAS components. The DBA group confers all global privileges on its members.

- *PORTAL_ADMINISTRATORS* Confers all OracleAS Portal global privileges except database-related privileges on its members and is meant for administrators of the OracleAS Portal. The user PORTAL_ADMIN is the initial member of this group. Members of the PORTAL_ADMINISTRATORS group can perform portal administrative tasks such as managing pages, styles, portlets, page groups, and providers.

- *PORTAL_DEVELOPERS* Members of this group can build and manage local database providers and their portlets.

- *PORTLET_PUBLISHERS* The members of this privileged group can add portlets to portal pages and publish those pages to other portal users.

In addition, users who plan on accessing and deploying reports through Oracle Reports should belong to one of the following reports-related portal groups:

- *RW_BASIC_USER*   Members are limited to the ability to execute deployed reports.
- *RW_POWER_USER*   These members can execute deployed reports as well as receive detailed error messages.
- *RW_DEVELOPER*   Members can execute deployed reports and develop and test reports using the OracleAS Reports Services.
- *RW_ADMINISTRATOR*   In addition to the privileges of the RW_DEVELOPER group, members of this group have several Oracle Reports–related administrative privileges.

A member of any of the preceding groups must be explicitly granted the appropriate portal privilege by the OracleAS Portal administrator, in order for them to run reports from the OracleAS Portal.

Creating Groups

You use the *Group Portlet* to create portal groups. By default, the creator of a group is the group's owner, but you may specify additional group owners. You can add not only users but other groups as members of a group. You can specify the following types of information when creating a group:

- *Basic information*   This includes, for example, the name and a description of the group.
- *Visibility of the group*   You can specify a group as private or public. A private group is visible only to its owners. By default, all groups have a public visibility.
- *Privileges*   By designating a group as *privileged,* you can assign privileges to it.

Managing Group Profiles

When the portal administrator first tries to edit a group's profile, the group's profile gets created automatically. Portal administrators use the Portal Group Profile portlet to manage group profiles. The administrator can specify the default home page for the members of a group and assign global portal privileges for a group.

OracleAS Portal User and Group Privileges

You can assign and control privileges on a per-user or a per-group basis. There are three types of user and group privileges, as explained in the following subsections.

Oracle Application Server Privileges

These privileges are stored in the OID and enable users to perform user and group administration using the Delegated Administrative Service (DAS).

OracleAS Portal Global Privileges

These privileges are assigned on the basis of a portal object type (e.g., like page groups, pages, styles, and portlets). A user or group can be assigned similar privileges on all objects belonging to one of the portal object types.

OracleAS Portal Object Privileges

These are the most limited privileges, and they are conferred only on a particular instance of a portal object.

CERTIFICATION OBJECTIVE 7.04

Administering the Portlet Repository

During the installation of the OracleAS Portal, a portlet repository is created that automatically stores information about providers and their portlets. Initially, the repository will contain information about the built-in providers and their portlets. These providers and portlets are created mainly for portal administration and portal development, although all portal users can use them.

Before further discussion of the Portlet Repository, let's quickly review portlet providers.

Providers

A provider is a *container of portlets* that helps link up the OracleAS Portal and the provider's portlets. The OracleAS Portal first contacts the provider that communicates with the portlets it contains. Providers help simplify the implementation of numerous portlets in the OracleAS Portal. Note that the OracleAS Portal never talks to a portlet *directly*, but does so through the provider that contains the portlet.

There are two main types of provider interfaces—*database* and *Web-based*—and these are described briefly next.

Database Providers

Portlets written as a PL/SQL package are known as *database providers*. You must use database providers for creating database-based PL/SQL portlets. When you're going to heavily interact with databases, use PL/SQL portlets, which are implemented as stored procedures and can be written either in PL/SQL or in Java Stored Procedures wrapped in PL/SQL.

on the
ⓘob

The Federated Portal Adapter enables database providers to be accessed as though they were Web providers.

Web Providers

A *Web provider* is a Web application, written in any Web language and hosted by a Web server separately from the OracleAS Portal. The OracleAS Portal communicates with the Web provider using the traditional HTTP protocol. You gain the following benefits by exposing portlets as Web providers:

- Use of existing application code to create new portlets
- Capability to be managed independently of the OracleAS Portal
- Use of any of several Web languages
- Capability to act as a hosted server for OracleAS Portal users

on the
ⓘob

To expose your portlets as a Web provider, you must create providers that can communicate with the OracleAS Portal using SOAP (XML) and manage your portlets. You use the Portal Developer Kit (PDK) to do this.

Figure 7-5 shows all providers registered with the OracleAS Portal, including Web and database providers.

The portal repository is part of the PORTAL product schema described previously. During the installation of the OracleAS Portal, the Portlet Repository is created as a *page group*, which includes all available portlets. In the Portlet Repository, there can be multiple providers, each with its sub-page, and the portlets are stored in the sub-pages.

The Portlet Repository page group content populates the *Add Portlets* page when a user wishes to add a portlet to a portal page. The portal administrator manages the Portlet Repository.

FIGURE 7-5

The OracleAS
Portal Providers
Page

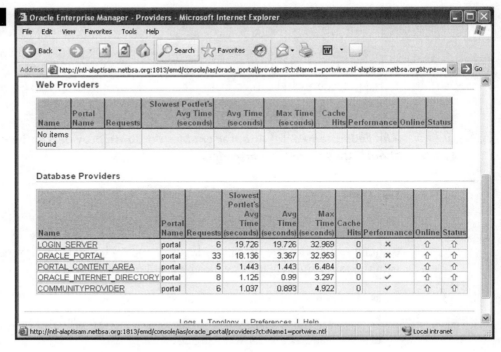

Organization of the Portlet Repository

OracleAS Portal creates a page for each provider's portlets under the New Page in the Portlet Repository whenever a new local provider or a remote provider group is registered. In addition, a page is created under New Page for a page group when any object in that page group is published to the OracleAS Portal. When you manually add pages to the Portlet Repository, the provider's portlets won't be available until you register the provider with the OracleAS Portal. You can edit the Port Repository page group to manage providers and portlets as you would any other page group. The portal administrator controls access to the providers in the Portlet repository by editing the provider page's Access tab or by directly editing the portlet itself.

Figure 7-6 shows the Portlet Repository Page Group, accessible by clicking the portal navigator link on the Portal home page. You can also access the Portlet Repository from the Portlet Repository administrative portlet.

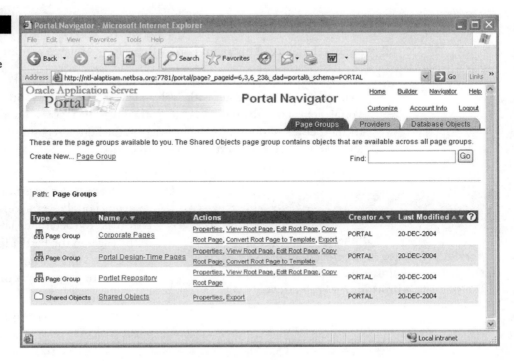

FIGURE 7-6

The Portlet Repository Page Group

Providers

The OracleAS Portal divides providers into three groups, which are discussed in the following subsections.

Locally Built Providers   *Locally built providers* are automatically registered by the OracleAS Portal instance and are created by portal tools such as the Portlet Builder.

Registered Providers   *Registered providers* are registered by the portal administrator with the OracleAS Portal instance.

Provider Groups   A *provider group* is a logical collection of Web providers. The remote Provider Groups Service handles the definition of the provider groups.

Portlet Repository Administrative Tasks

Following is a summary of the main Portlet Repository–related administrative tasks:

- Registration of new providers so their portlets are known to the Portlet Repository. You can register both Web and database providers with OracleAS Portal. For each of the providers, the portal saves the registration information in the portlet repository, creates a new page on the Portlet repository page group, and adds the necessary portlet items to that page.
- Controlling access to the Portlet Repository.
- Updating provider registration details and changing portal users' access to existing providers. You determine users' access to the pages in the Portlet Repository Page Group, by granting privileges in the Access settings section of the Access tab.
- Reorganizing Portlet repository page group content so users can easily locate various portlets.
- Refreshing either individual portlets or the entire Portlet Repository when there are changes in the provider implementation—for example, by adding new portlets to the provider.

To make user and group portlet privileges immediately effective, the portal administrator must invalidate the portal content in the Web cache.

CERTIFICATION OBJECTIVE 7.05

Exporting and Importing Portal Content

In order to *consolidate* multiple OracleAS Portal instances, or to *move and update* portal objects between development and production instances, or to *deploy the same content* across multiple OracleAS Portal instances, you can migrate portal content using the set of *export and import utilities* provided by the OracleAS Portal. The portal export and import feature migrates the OracleAS registration information but doesn't really migrate the Web or database providers themselves. The following subsections summarize the export and import methodology used to move content from one OracleAS Portal instance to the other. Figure 7-7 shows the Export Object(s) page, showing how you can select objects for the transport set.

Creating a Transport Set

The *transport set* consists of the list of all the portal objects you plan to export to another OracleAS Portal instance. In order to create the transport set, follow these steps:

1. From the Portal Navigator, select the object you wish to export and click **Export.**
2. Provide a name for the transport set you chose.
3. You can export the transport set now and also save it for later use. When you edit a saved transport set, you select the Add to an Existing Transport Set option, as shown in Figure 7-7.

FIGURE 7-7

The Export Object(s) Page

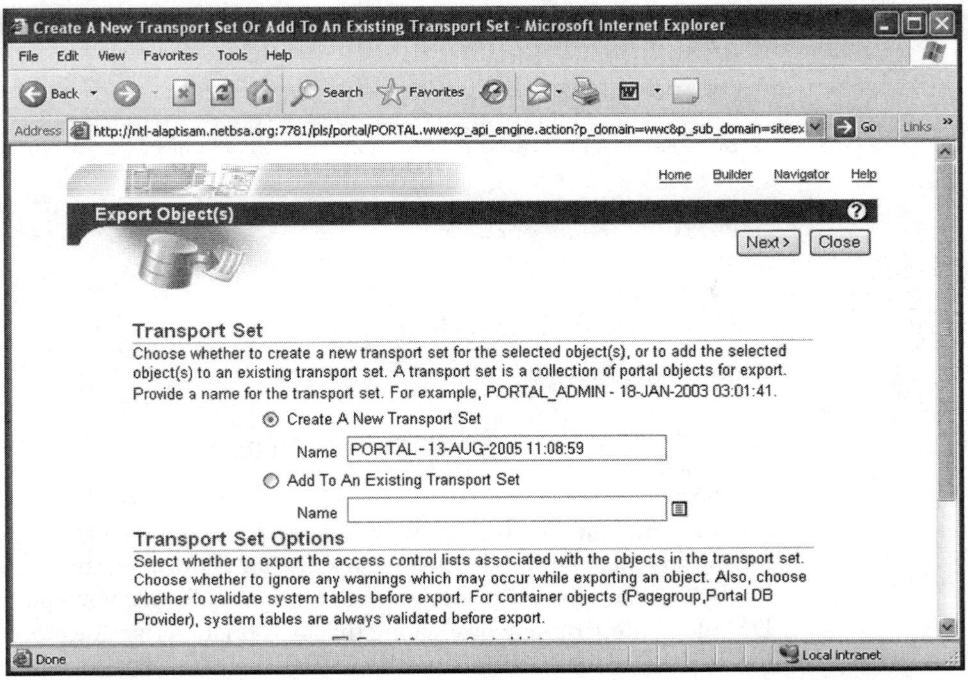

Note that you must first export an entire portal page group, before you can export its components, which are individual objects such as categories, styles, or a perspective. The OracleAS Portal will attempt a registration of the Web provider metadata by contacting the provider during the migration. If the OracleAS Portal can't contact the provider, the migration will fail and a message will be logged in the import log file.

Exporting the Transport Set

To export the select transport set of objects, you follow these steps:

1. From the available saved transport set, select a transport set you wish to export by selecting Export This Transport Set Immediately or select the Export Later, More Objects Have to Be Added option if you want to add more objects later.

2. Export the transport set. The following is an abbreviated log of the export process:

```
Validating System Tables in preparation for Export...
Beginning outer script: wwutl_schema_validation.validate_all
Validate Page Groups
Validate categories associated with page groups
Success: All categories associated with page groups are valid
Validate Pages
Validate Portlets
Validate page portlets
Extracting metadata for the export objects...
Exporting Pages...
Exporting Page Groups ...
. . .
Completed On: 13-AUG-05 13:08:28
```

3. After the export is completed, review the export log for any errors during the export.

OracleAS employs the well-known data export and import utilities for the migration and also provides two scripts, one for performing the migration from a UNIX shell and the other for performing it from a Windows command window. Download the script file by clicking the appropriate script download link. Figure 7-8 shows the Download Scripts and View Logs page. Run the downloaded export script with the *-mode export* option and make a note of the dump file that's created by the

FIGURE 7-8

The Download
Scripts and View
Logs Page

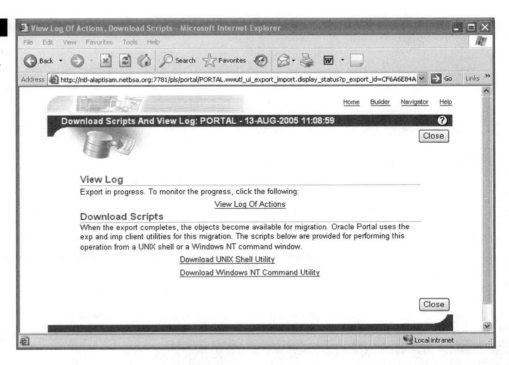

export. This dump file will contain the migration-ready export set. Here's the syntax of the export script:

```
$ -mode export <-s portal_schema>
<-p portal_password> <-pu portal_username>
<-pp portal_userpassword><-company company_name>
<-c connect_string> <-d dump_file_name(s)>
<-automatic_merge>
```

Here's an example showing how the script is run in the EXPORT mode:

```
$ -mode export -s myportal -p myportal123
        -c mydb -d myexport.dmp
```

exam
ⓦatch

You need command-line access to execute the shell or command-line utilities generated by the export-import process. These utilities access the Oracle EXP (export) and IMP (import) utilities as well as the Portal instance.

Importing the Transport Set

Before you can run the import process, you must first transfer the *export dump file* to the target server. Once you transfer the export dump file to the target server, you must import the data in the dump file into the target OracleAS Portal instance. You import the data from the export dump files by using the same script as you did for export, with one change: change the mode to import instead of export, by setting the *-mode* parameter to *import*, as shown in the following example:

```
$ -mode import -s myportal -p myportal123<<">>
        -c mydb -d myexport.dmp<<">>
```

The steps for importing the portal content follow.

1. Log into the Portal instance, and go the Administer tab of the Portal Builder Page. Click **Import,** after selecting on the transport set you wish to import into this OracleAS Portal instance.
2. Select the import mode and click **Start Import.**
3. After the import has been completed, check the log for any errors.

CERTIFICATION OBJECTIVE 7.06

OracleAS Portal Configuration Tasks

Using the OracleAS Portal administrative user interface, the Oracle Application Server Control, or configuration scripts, you can configure various OracleAS Portal tasks. The following subsections describe the major portal configuration tasks.

Configuring the Self-Registration Feature

The *self-registration feature* enables users to create their own portal accounts. Users fill a self-registration form, and if it's approved, a portal account is immediately created for the user, enabling the user to log in to the OracleAS Portal.

The portal administrator should first configure and then enable the self-registration feature. Here are the steps for doing so:

1. Click the Global Settings link in the Services portlet.
2. In the middle of the page, you'll see the following section on self-registration:

```
Self-Registration Options
```

3. Select whether to allow users to register their own user accounts. Select whether self-registered users need to be approved before they are able to log on, and click **Configure** to specify the approval process. If approval is not required, self-registered users can log on immediately after registering.

```
Enable Self registration
    Approval Required
    No Approval Required
```

4. Select either the Approval Required or the No Approval Required option.

5. You must also enter the information under the E-Mail (SMTP) Host section if you choose the Approval Required option.

6. Click **OK** to confirm your changes.

Once you configure the self-registration feature, the OracleAS Portal administrator must enable the self-registration feature by editing the Portal Login portlet settings. For production portals, the page designer usually configures the self-registration feature in the User Login portlet.

Configuring the OracleAS Portal for WebDAV

WebDAV stands for "Web-based Distributed Authoring and Versioning," which is a set of extensions to the standard HTTP protocol that enables users to collaboratively edit and manage files on remote Web servers. One of the major goals of WebDAV is to fulfill an original vision of the Web as a collaborative medium. Often, Web sites gather information from a large number of geographically separated sources.

The OracleAS Portal enables you to gather documents in a centralized place. However, there remains the problem of moving and publishing content from various sources into the OracleAS Portal. If it's a simple set of documents, you can map the PORTAL schema in the OracleAS Metadata Repository to a Web folder. Using WebDAV, the HTML pages and related information can be directly authored by their primary sources.

Because OracleAS supports WebDAV, you can use a WebDAV client such as Web Folders, Cadaver, Oracle Drive, Dreamweaver, Adobe Photoshop, or SiteCopy to manage Web content by directly moving files between file systems on your desktop and the OracleAS Portal page groups, among other things. You can use any WebDAV-compliant desktop application (e.g., Microsoft Office 2000) to edit and save portal content.

The big advantage provided by WebDAV clients is that they enable users to manage portal content right from their own file systems, while adhering to the structure and rules specified by the OracleAS Portal.

on the job

A WebDAV client lets you map the PORTAL schema in the OracleAS Metadata Repository as a drive, in order to perform authoring and publishing tasks right from your desktop. You can edit documents in place and save them back to the Metadata Repository.

Setting Up the OracleAS Portal for WebDAV

In order to set up the OracleAS Portal for WebDAV, you must configure WebDAV by setting up a WebDAV client on a user's personal computer. You must also configure it on the server side by specifying WebDAV defaults inside the OracleAS Portal.

On the server side, you can configure WebDAV by modifying the *oradav.conf* file, which contains various OraDAV parameters. When you install OracleAS, the OraDAV parameters are assigned default values, enabling you to access Oracle Databases through the WebDAV client (or a Web browser). Of course, as a portal administrator, you can modify the *oradav.conf* file.

To enable the uploading of content through WebDAV clients, you can set options within the OracleAS Portal user interface. You may configure the following items this way:

- Specify default item types for Zip and WebDAV uploads.

- Select target regions for any content a client adds through the WebDAV client.

Following are the major features of the WebDAV protocol, which facilitates the creation of interoperable, collaborative applications:

- *Locking (concurrency control)* WebDAV makes use of long-duration exclusive and shared write locks to prevent overwriting when multiple collaborators write without first merging their changes.

- *Properties* Use of XML properties enables the storing of arbitrary metadata. DASL, the DAV searching and locating protocol, provides searches based on property values to locate Web resources.

- *Namespace manipulation* WebDAV supports copy and move operations, as well as the creation and listing of collections, which are similar to file system directories.

The Apache server implements WebDAV through the *mod_dav* module, which supports read and write access to local files through a Web browser or a WebDAV client. Oracle's own *mod_oradav* module extends the functionality of the *mod_dav* module. The *mod_oradav* module enables users to read Oracle database content and write to the database.

The *oradav.conf* file, located in the $ORACLE_HOME/Apache/oradav/ directory, contains the configuration parameters for OraDAV. Note that the *oradav.conf* file is included in the *oracle_apache.conf*, which in turn is included in *httpd.conf*, the main HTTP configuration file. You can either edit the *oradav.conf* file directly or use the Application Server Control to do so. The latter is the recommended way. All the OraDAV parameters are contained within the <Location> container and start with either DAV or DAVParam in front of the parameter name.

```
<Location /dav_portal/portal>
    Options Indexes
    DAV oracle
    DAVDepthInfinity On
    DavParam ORACONTAINERNAME wwdav
    DavParam ORACookieMaxAge 28800
    DavParam ORASERVICE cn=oas10g,cn=oraclecontext
    DavParam ORAUSER portal
    DavParam ORACRYPTPASSWORD BYfJ+k80wzSBJ+h51RJc+RZ15s7ToLpT2Q==
    DavParam ORAPACKAGENAME portal.wwdav_api_driver
</Location>
```

By default, the OracleAS Portal DAV URL is

```
http://hostname:port/dav_portal/portal/
```

In the foregoing URL, *dav_portal* stands for the default name of the virtual directory used, to distinguish between a WebDAV client portal access and a regular portal access using the *pls* virtual directory. The portal item refers to the *DAD* of the portal installation. Users need to provide the same username/password combination to log in to a portal in WebDAV as they do to log in to the regular portal. Here's an example:

```
http://mysite.oracle.com:7777/dav_portal/portal
```

The Oracle Portal Configuration Assistant

You configure the OracleAS portal with the help of the Oracle Portal Configuration Assistant (OPCA), which is automatically invoked by the Oracle Universal Installer during the installation of the OracleAS instance. You can manually invoke the OPCA by using the *ptlasst* script, located in the $ORACLE_HOME/assistants/opca directory.

Using the Portal Dependency Settings Tool

The OracleAS Portal has to work with several OracleAS components such as the OracleAS Web Cache and the Oracle Internet Directory. You must therefore configure the OracleAS Portal to work effectively with these components. You use the *iasconfig.xml* file, also called the *Portal Dependency Settings File*, to configure the data about the portal-related components of the OracleAS.

If you want to make configuration changes by editing the *iasconfig.xml* file, you must use the *ptlconfig* (*ptlconfig.bat* in Windows systems) script, also known as the *Portal Dependency Settings Tool*, to update portal information in the OracleAS Metadata Repository.

Here's a typical *iasconfig.xml* file, showing configuration settings for the OracleAS Web Cache, the OID, and the OEM Application Server control (EM, standing for Enterprise Manager):

```
<IASConfig XSDVersion="1.0">
- <IASInstance Name="portwire.ntl-alaptisam.netbsa.org" Host="ntl-alaptisam.
netbsa.org">
  <OIDComponent AdminPassword="@BQGUNSNJdm1qxqpjZ/R/WVyugCfzLg36WQ=="
AdminDN="cn=orcladmin" SSLEnabled="false" LDAPPort="389" />
  <WebCacheComponent AdminPort="4006" ListenPort="7781" InvalidationPort="4007"
InvalidationUsername="invalidator" InvalidationPassword="@Bb1hmSOpcJnXggHE5AxUfQ
i05twMursi8A==" SSLEnabled="false" />
  <EMComponent ConsoleHTTPPort="1813" SSLEnabled="false" />
  </IASInstance>
- <PortalInstance DADLocation="/pls/portal" SchemaUsername="portal" SchemaPassw
ord="@Bb1hmSOpcJnXfdeRd0Q3DDygCZMyjcnIoA==" ConnectString="cn=oas10g,cn=oraclec
ontext">
  <WebCacheDependency ContainerType="IASInstance" Name="portwire.ntl-alaptisam.
netbsa.org" />
  <OIDDependency ContainerType="IASInstance" Name="portwire.ntl-alaptisam.
netbsa.org" />
  <EMDependency ContainerType="IASInstance" Name="portwire.ntl-alaptisam.netbsa.
org" />
  </PortalInstance>
  </IASConfig>
```

Using the *ptlconfig* script, you can

- Update the OracleAS Metadata Repository with the new configuration settings in a specific or in multiple Portal instances.
- Encrypt the plain text passwords in the *iasconfig.xml* file.

Configuring Language Support

The OracleAS Portal supports portal development and deployment in 29 languages. The self-service content management supports all these languages as well. During the installation of the OracleAS Middle Tier, you can configure the language that will show up in the Set Language portlet. You can then use the OracleAS Portal either in the browser's language setting or in the language that was selected using the Set Language portlet.

You can configure additional languages by using the *ptllang* tool. You must run the *ptllang* tool from the MID_TIER_ORACLE_HOME, where the OracleAS Portal is installed.

```
$ ptllang -lang lang_code [-i install_type] [ -s portal_schema]
[-sp portal_schema_password] [-c portal_db_connect_string]
```

In the preceding illustration of the *ptllang* script syntax, this is what each of the parameters stand for:

- *lang*   This is the abbreviation for the language you wish to install.
- *-i*   This refers to the installation type, with the two types being *typical* and *custom*. In the typical mode, the script connects to the OracleAS Metadata Repository, and in the custom mode, it connects to a portal schema in a customer database.
- *-s*   This is the OracleAS Portal schema name.
- *-sp*   This refers to the password for the OracleAS Portal schema.
- *-c*   This refers to the connect string for the OracleAS Metadata Repository Oracle database (*DbHostName:DbPortNumber:DbServiceName*).

on the **Job**   *Because the Set Language portlet isn't available by default, you must add it to the Portal Builder page.*

on the **Job**   *You can diagnose portal performance issues by running the OracleAS Portal Diagnostics Assistant.*

TWO-MINUTE DRILL

OracleAS Portal

- ❏ A portal is a collection of one or more page groups.
- ❏ A portal organizes and arranges diverse information in the form of portal pages.
- ❏ A portal page consists of one or more portlets, which are reusable building blocks.
- ❏ Each portal page is divided into several regions, each with a separate set of display and other options.
- ❏ Portlets and items are the two basic types of OracleAS Portal building blocks.
- ❏ You can have content items and navigational items.
- ❏ There are several portlets ready to use when you install the OracleAS Portal.
- ❏ Page definitions are stored separately from the content of the portal pages.
- ❏ The OracleAS Portal architecture consists of the client, the middle tier, and infrastructure tiers.
- ❏ The Parallel Page Engine (PPE) runs as a servlet and builds portal pages for display.
- ❏ Providers are the backbone of the portal page; they provide the content for the portlets displayed in a portal page.
- ❏ Portlets providers can be Web providers or database providers.
- ❏ The portal may dynamically assemble and format either a portal page or server-cached pages.

Managing the OracleAS Portal

- ❏ You can manage the OracleAS Portal through the Application Server control or the administrative portlets in the OracleAS Portal. You can also use various configuration scripts.
- ❏ The portlet repository contains information about the portlets and the registered providers.
- ❏ The *mod_plsql* performance logging service enables you to collect user request performance statistics.

OracleAS Portal Schema, User, and Group Management

❏ By default the PORTAL, PORTAL_PUBLIC, the PORTAL_DEMO, and the PORTAL_APP database schemas are created in the OracleAS Metadata Repository.

❏ The PORTAL schema is the product schema for the OracleAS Portal.

❏ PORTAL_PUBLIC is the default OracleAS Portal access schema.

❏ The portal administrator uses DAS to enter user and group information in the OID.

❏ The four default OracleAS Portal users are orcladmin, portal, portal_admin, and public.

❏ The *portal* user is the superuser for the OracleAS Portal.

❏ The portal_admin user account has limited administrative privileges.

❏ The *public* user account is used by unauthenticated user sessions.

❏ The portal administrator uses the User portlet to create new users.

❏ A user's profile is created automatically when the users first log in or when the administrator first tries to edit the user's profile.

❏ By default, new users are associated with the PORTAL_PUBLIC schema.

❏ You use the Groups portlet to create groups.

❏ The OracleAS Portal creates the following default groups: AUTHENTICATED_USERS, DBA, PORTAL_ADMINISTRATORS, and PORTAL_DEVELOPERS.

❏ There are also four reports-related portal groups.

❏ You can assign and control privileges on a per-user or a per-group basis.

❏ The three types of portal privileges are the OracleAS privileges, OracleAS Portal Global privileges, and OracleAS Portal Object privileges.

Administering the Portlet Repository

❏ The portlet repository stores information about the various portal providers and their portlets.

❏ A provider is a container of portlets that links up the OracleAS Portal and the provider's portlets.

❏ The OracleAS Portal always talks to portlets indirectly, through the providers that contain the portlet.

❑ You can have Web providers or database providers.

❑ Database providers are written as PL/SQL packages, whereas Web providers can be written in any Web language.

❑ A provider's portlets are visible only after the provider is registered with the OracleAS Portal.

❑ Providers are divided into three groups.

❑ Locally built providers are created by portal tools such as the Portal Builder.

❑ Registered providers are those registered by the portal administrator.

❑ Provider groups are logical collections of Web providers.

❑ To make users and groups immediately effective, the portal administrator must invalidate the portal content in the Web cache.

Exporting and Importing Portal Content

❑ You can use the export and import utilities to move portal objects between OracleAS Portal instances.

❑ The transport set consists of all the portal objects you plan to export.

❑ You must first export the entire page group before you can export its components.

OracleAS Portal Configuration Tasks

❑ The self-registration feature enables users to create their own portal accounts.

❑ After the self-registration feature has been configured, it should be enabled by editing the Portal Login portlet settings.

❑ WebDAV allows users to collaboratively edit and manage files on remote Web servers.

❑ Oracle's *mod_oradav* module extends the functionality of the *mod_dav* module.

❑ The *mod_oradav* module uses the OraDAV driver to map WebDAV activity to database activity.

❑ The *oradav.conf* file is included in the *oracle_apache.conf* file.

❏ The portal-related components are configured using the *iasconfig.xml* file, also called the *portal dependency settings file*.

❏ The *ptlconfig* file, also known as the *portal dependency settings tool,* is used to update information in the OracleAS Metadata Repository.

❏ You can configure additional languages after the installation, using the *ptllang* tool.

SELF TEST

1. The two types of portal providers are

   A. Web providers and database providers

   B. Web providers and portal providers

   C. Portal providers and database providers

   D. Reusable providers and nonreusable providers

2. Which of the following is the product schema for the OracleAS Portal?

   A. PORTAL_APP

   B. PORTAL

   C. PORTAL_DEMO

   D. PORTAL_PUBLIC

3. Which of the following users is the portal "superuser"?

   A. orcladmin

   B. portal

   C. portal_user

   D. portaladmin

4. What does the Parallel Page Engine do?

   A. Caches the portal pages.

   B. Builds portlets.

   C. Runs parallel portal sessions.

   D. Builds portal pages for display.

5. OracleAS Portal

   A. always talks to portlets indirectly, through the providers.

   B. always talks to portlets directly, through the providers.

   C. always talks to providers indirectly, through the portlets.

   D. always talks to providers indirectly, through the providers.

6. To make user and groups immediately effective,

   A. the portal administrator must invalidate the portal content in the Web cache.

   B. the portal administrator must validate the portal content in the Web cache.

C. the portal administrator must remove the portal content in the Web cache.

D. the portal administrator must add the portal content in the Web cache.

7. During an OracleAS export of the portal content,

   A. you must first export the categories.

   B. you must first export the page styles.

   C. you must first export the portlets.

   D. you must first export the entire page group.

8. The OracleAS Portal self-registration feature

   A. enables users to register providers.

   B. enables users to register portal applications.

   C. enables users to register their own portal accounts.

   D. enables applications to automatically register themselves.

9. Which of the following is true?

   A. You must execute the *ptlconfig* script after editing the *iasconfig.xml* file.

   B. You must edit the *iasconfig.xml* file after executing the *ptlconfig* script.

   C. You must edit the *ptlconfig* script after executing the *iasconfig.xml* script.

   D. You must execute the *iasconfig.xml* script and the *ptlconfig* script simultaneously.

10. What does the *ptllang* script help you do?

   A. Add additional languages to the OracleAS Portal during the installation.

   B. Add additional languages to the OracleAS Portal after the installation.

   C. Define the default language for the OracleAS Portal.

   D. Remove unwanted languages from the OracleAS Portal.

SELF TEST ANSWERS

1. ☑ **A** is correct. Web providers and database providers are the two types of portal providers.
   ☒ **B, C,** and **D** are wrong because they all contain at least one nonexistent type of provider.

2. ☑ **B** is correct. PORTAL is the product schema for the OracleAS Portal.
   ☒ **A** is wrong because PORTAL_APP contains portal applications, not the product schema. **C** is wrong because PORTAL_DEMO contains the portal demonstration code. **D** is wrong because it's the default database mapping account.

3. ☑ **B** is correct. The portal user is the superuser for the OracleAS Portal.
   ☒ **A** is incorrect because orcladmin is the user account for the OracleAS administrator. **C** and **D** are wrong because they are made up user names.

4. ☑ **D** is correct because the Portal Parallel Engine builds portal pages for display by taking data related to the page layout and converting it into a page containing portlets.
   ☒ **A** is wrong because the PPE isn't concerned with Web caching at all. **B** is wrong because the PPE doesn't build portlets—it builds portal pages. **C** is wrong because the PPE has nothing to do with parallelizing the portal operations.

5. ☑ **A** is correct. The OracleAS Portal always talks to portlets indirectly, through the providers.
   ☒ **B** is wrong because it's the opposite of what the portal does, which is to talk to the portlets indirectly through the providers. **C** and **D** are wrong because the OracleAS Portal talks directly to the providers.

6. ☑ **A** is correct. To make user and group information immediately effective, the portal administrator must *invalidate* the portal content in the Web cache.
   ☒ **B** is wrong because the information in the Web cache must be invalidated, not validated. **C** is wrong because the portal administrator doesn't remove anything from the Web cache. **D** is incorrect because the portal administrator doesn't have to add anything to the Web cache.

7. ☑ **D** is correct because you must first export the entire page group.
   ☒ **A, B,** and **C** are incorrect because all of these refer to individual portal objects. You must first export the entire page group before you can export any of these objects.

8. ☑ **C** is correct because the self-registration feature enables users to register their own portal accounts.
   ☒ **A** is wrong because the feature doesn't allow users to register providers. **B** is wrong because the feature doesn't allow users to register applications. **D** is wrong because the self-registration feature is meant for the users, not the applications.

9. ☑ **D** is correct because you must edit the *iasconfig.xml* script before executing the *ptlconfig* script.

   ☒ **A** and **B** are wrong because they contain the wrong sequence and the wrong action; you edit the *iasconfig.xml* first and execute the *ptlconfig* script after that. **D** is wrong because you can't execute the *iasconfig.xml* file. You can edit this file and finalize the changes you made only by executing the *ptlconfig* script afterwards.

10. ☑ **B** is correct because the *ptllang* script is used to add additional languages to the OracleAS Portal after OracleAS installation.

    ☒ **A** is wrong because the *ptllang* script isn't invoked during OracleAS installation. **C** is wrong because the *ptllang* script isn't used to set the default language for the OracleAS Portal. **D** is wrong because the *ptllang* script can't be used to remove any of the languages used by the OracleAS Portal instance.

8
Managing OC4J and Configuring J2EE Applications

Oracle Application Server 10g provides support for Java 2 Platform, Enterprise Edition (J2EE) applications, and support for J2EE is a crucial and integral part of Oracle Application Server 10g. This chapter is devoted to explaining how J2EE applications work and how the OracleAS component OC4J (Oracle Containers for Java) provides support for enterprise J2EE applications. This is in addition to supporting the work of several other OracleAS components, such as the OracleAS Portal and Delegated Administrative Services (DAS).

CERTIFICATION OBJECTIVE 8.01

Introduction to J2EE

The Java 2 Platform, Enterprise Edition (J2EE) offers a component-based framework for designing, developing, and deploying Web-based enterprise applications. J2EE defines the specification for EJBs. J2EE is a set of Java technologies, with each of them being designed for a specific purpose, such as providing security, enabling transactions, or sending email. Let's start our review of J2EE with a short summary of the various J2EE components.

J2EE Components

In this section, the main J2EE components are explained. In addition, I explain how Oracle Application Server 10g supports each of these essential features.

Java Authentication and Authorization Service

The Java Authentication and Authorization Service (JAAS) is Java's security package, which provides user authentication and user access control capabilities. OC4J implements JAAS order to provide developers a way to offer secure access to J2EE applications. You can also integrate Oracle's implementation of JAAS with the OracleAS Single Sign-On and the Oracle Internet Directory.

Java Transaction API

Java Transaction API (JTA) is the specification of standard Java interfaces between a central transaction monitor and all the parties in a distributed transaction system. JTA is used by applications deployed in the OracleAS to demarcate transactions. For single database-based transactions, JTA helps provide the Single-Phase Commit to demarcate transactions and for transactions involving multiple databases, JTA provides the Two-Phase Commit mechanism. As you'll see later, OracleAS lets you use non-emulated databases to provide support for the Two-Phase Commit mechanism.

Java Naming and Directory Interface

The Java Naming and Directory Interface (JNDI) is an independent directory service that enables Java applications to access various naming and directory services with a common Application Programming Interface (API). OC4J implements the JNDI service to provide necessary naming and directory functionality to applications.

Java Message Service

The Java Message Service (JMS) provides standard messaging API, which enables application components to pass data among themselves. Java programs use JMS to access enterprise message systems. JMS helps you integrate heterogeneous systems using the standard messaging API.

Remote Method Invocation

Remote Method Invocation (RMI) helps distributed applications communicate through invoking procedure calls. Using RMI, methods of Java objects can be invoked remotely from other Java Virtual Machines. OC4J provides RMI support over two protocols: the Oracle Remote Method Invocation (ORMI) protocol and the Internet Inter-ORB Protocol (IIOP). EJBs, by default, use the RMI/ORMI protocol to communicate, instead of the alternative RMI/IIOP protocol.

Data Sources

Data sources are encapsulations of database server connections that help provide database connectivity to your J2EE applications. OracleAS provides support for emulated and non-emulated data sources, which are discussed in detail later in this chapter.

Java Transaction API

EJBs use Java Transaction API (JTA) 1.0.1 for managing transactions. These transactions involve single-phase and two-phase commits.

J2EE Connector Architecture

The J2EE Connector Architecture (J2CA) provides a standard architecture for connecting the J2EE platform to non-Java-based enterprise systems such as ERPs and relational database management systems and legacy applications.

Java Object Cache

The Java Object Cache provides Java classes to improve performance by caching local copies of Java objects within a process.

Terminology

Because the main topic in this chapter, OC4J, is all about enabling J2EE-based applications, it's important for the reader to understand the common terminology used when dealing with J2EE applications. The following sections are devoted to that.

Servlets

Servlets are small programs that run on the server, and you use them to enable dynamic content in your Web pages or JSP documents. During their execution, servlets can access the Enterprise Java Beans (which are defined later).

Java Server Pages

Java Server Pages are HTML pages that contain embedded Java code.

JavaBeans

JavaBeans are reusable components that implement the functionality you need in J2EE applications. You can use various JavaBeans in your J2EE applications.

J2EE Containers

A J2EE container contains the framework for running EJBs, such as starting an EJB, and provides necessary support services for the EJB to perform its magic. OC4J is one type of J2EE container, and you'll learn a lot about it later in this chapter.

Enterprise JavaBeans

Enterprise JavaBeans (EJBs) are Java components that implement business logic. EJBs follow JavaSoft's specifications. You use Enterprise JavaBeans to implement the business logic in your J2EE applications. While you must use JavaBeans as part of an application, Enterprise JavaBeans are self-contained J2EE components that can service users' requests. EJBs live inside, and are always run inside, an EJB container, which provides the necessary support infrastructure, such as connectivity to clients and other EJBs, as well as access to server resources, connectivity, and transactional support.

Note that you must deploy an EJB inside a J2EE container, unlike regular JavaBeans. A client application can access an EJB, which contains the business logic, only through a container.

An EJB can either use JDBC connections to connect directly to a database or let the container handle the database connectivity for it. The container holding an EJB is responsible for satisfying requests made by clients by either instantiating an EJB afresh, or letting the client access an already running EJB. The container will maintain the transactions, security issues, and other EJB operational details.

There are *three basic types* of Enterprise JavaBeans, which are described briefly in the following subsections.

Session EJBs   Session EJBs support a client during the execution of its tasks and last only as long as the client's session does. You can have *stateful* or *stateless* EJBs. A stateless session EJB won't store the state between method calls, whereas a stateless session EJB maintains state. Each stateful EJB is associated with a single client only.

Entity EJBs   Entity EJBs represent an object of data, usually of a persistent nature, such as the table rows in a database. Similar to database data, Entity EJBs have a primary key to uniquely identify them. Usually, the container wherein the Entity EJBs resides will implement the database connectivity for the entity EJBs.

Entity EJBs can reflect two types of persistence: *container-managed persistence* (CMP) and *bean-managed persistence* (BMP). Persistence in this context refers to database transactions. When session beans choose container-managed persistence, the bean writer declares necessary transaction attributes in the deployment descriptor. The EJB container then manages the transactions automatically, without the bean writer having to write code for transaction management. Under bean-managed persistence, the user transaction interface is used to manage transactions. The bean writer decides when, exactly, the transactions are committed or rolled back instead of the container itself deciding it. The recommended approach is to use CMP in preference to BMP.

Message-Driven EJBs   Message-Driven EJBs represent the integration between Java Message Service (JMS) and EJBs. These EJBs perform asynchronous messaging within the server, serving as JMS Message Listeners instead of interacting directly with clients and becoming involved in client transactions. When clients publish messages to JMS destinations, the JMS provider and the EJB container coordinate their work in delivering the message to the message-driven EJBs.

With this quick review of J2EE, let's turn our attention to OC4J, which is the framework for the development and deployment of EJB applications in the Oracle Application Server.

Deploying EJBs

You deploy EJBs as well as all the other components of your J2EE application by packaging together all the necessary modules for an application. You put all relevant components into a zipped file, ending with a specific extension denoting the type of file; the Java Virtual Machine will then execute that single file. J2EE applications can have three types of application deployment files, also called archives: *JAR* files, *WAR* files, and *EAR* files.

JAR Files   JAR (*Java Archive*) files can represent an application's EJB application module as well as a client application. The EJB JAR files, which include the Enterprise JavaBeans (EJBs) along with the JSP files, images, and the like are packaged together into one file archive, named a *JAR*, that's executed by the Java Virtual Machine as one. JAR files have the extension *.jar*.

WAR Files   A WAR (*Web Application Archive*) file is used to package Web application module components such as HTML pages, servlets, and JSP pages. Typically, a WAR file contains an XML file named *web.xml*, which serves to describe the various Web components inside the WAR file.

EAR Files   You use an EAR (*Enterprise Archive*) file to package an entire enterprise Java application, including both the Java and the Web components, for deployment to OC4J. Therefore, an EAR file can contain both JAR and WAR files. The *application.xml* XML file included in an EAR file describes the contents of the EAR file.

Java provides a utility to zip the deployment files, in order to create the three types of archives. You can use the jar utility to create a JAR and a WAR file, as shown here:

```
$ jar -cvfM <application-name>.ear
$ jar -cvfM <application-name>.war
```

CERTIFICATION OBJECTIVE 8.02

Oracle Containers for Java

The Oracle Application Server 10g provides its own J2EE container, called the Oracle Containers for J2EE (OC4J). OC4J is an easy-to-use, lightweight, and highly scalable J2EE container that is written entirely in Java. OC4J is a complete Java 2 Enterprise Edition (J2EE) environment that runs on the Java Virtual Machine (JVM) of the standard Java Development Kit (JDK). OC4J runs on the standard JDK that's a part of your operating system. Oracle bases its OC4J framework on technology licensed from Ironflare Corporation, developers of a leading J2EE container called the Orion Server. Thus, you'll see several references in the OracleAS OC4J documentation to the Orion Server, and some of the OC4J executables contain their original Orion Server–based names.

OC4J is a set of containers that enable J2EE application deployment. For example, OC4J provides a Web Container to support JSP page translation as well as execution with a servlet engine. OC4J also provides an EJB container. As mentioned earlier, OC4J provides J2EE services such as JNDI, JDBC, JTA, JCA, and JAAS.

In this chapter, OC4J is discussed as part of the full OracleAS 10g product set, not its alternative pure Java standalone distribution. The pure Java standalone distribution is easy to download (one Zip file), install, and configure. However, the standalone distribution is really suited for development and testing only. For large-scale applications, you must use OC4J with the full OracleAS environment to take advantage of the full-fledged Oracle HTTP Server, Single Sign-On, and many other advanced features.

However, because the standalone and the OracleAS-based OC4J distributions are identical, you can use the standalone version to develop enterprise applications that you can later deploy on the Oracle Application Server 10g.

on the job

The mod_oc4j module routes requests from the Oracle HTTP Server to OC4J.

Default OracleAS OC4J Instances

When you create a new OracleAS instance under the Portal and Wireless middle-tier option (and also have the OracleAS Infrastructure instance installed), you automatically have the following OC4J instances:

- *Home*   This is the default OC4J instance that comes with every OracleAS installation.
- *OC4J_Portal*   This contains a servlet to support OracleAS Portal (middle tier).
- *OC4J_Security*   This supports Identity Management Services (infrastructure).
- *OC4J_Wireless*   This contains a servlet to support OracleAS Wireless (middle tier).
- *oca*   This supports the OracleAS Certificate Authority (infrastructure).

Although you can manage the OC4J process running inside OracleAS by editing the OC4J configuration files directly, that's not the recommended way to manage OC4J when you use it as part of the OracleAS, as compared with using it in a standalone mode. The purpose behind including OC4J inside the OracleAS stack is to help manage J2EE enterprise systems. You must use the Oracle Application Server to manage all components of OracleAS, including OC4J.

Using the Application Server Control, it's possible to manage and configure clustered OC4J processes across multiple OracleAS instances and hosts. Application Server Control provides clustering, high availability, load balancing, and failover capabilities to help you manage multiple OC4J instances.

on the **You must run OC4J with the JDK that is installed with Oracle Application**
ⓙ o b **Server Release 2 (JDK 1.3.x) for optimal performance.**

You can use either Application Server Control or command-line tools to start, stop, configure, and deploy applications. The two command-line tools you can use to manage OC4J instances are the familiar *opmnctl* and *dcmctl* utilities.

CERTIFICATION OBJECTIVE 8.03

Creating an OC4J Instance

Each OracleAS instance is created with a default OC4J instance named *home*, as shown here:

```
$ opmnctl status
Processes in Instance: infra_10_1_2.ntl-alaptisam.netbsa.org
ias-component       | process-type       |    pid | status
-----------------------------------------------------------------
LogLoader           | logloaderd         |    N/A | Down
DSA                 | DSA                |    N/A | Down
HTTP_Server         | HTTP_Server        |   3744 | Alive
dcm-daemon          | dcm-daemon         |   7176 | Alive
OC4J                | home               |   6268 | Alive
OC4J                | oca                |   9164 | Alive
OC4J                | OC4J_SECURITY      |   7596 | Alive
OID                 | OID                |   7172 | Alive
$
```

You can create a new OC4J instance either by using the command-line utility *dcmctl*, or by using the Application Server Control. Let's review the creation of a new OC4J instance using both methods in the following subsections.

Using the dcmctl Utility

You can use the *dcmctl* command-line utility to perform several OC4J administration tasks, including the following:

- Deploying and undeploying an application
- Creating and destroying an OC4J instance
- Listing applications
- Resynchronizing an OC4J instance
- Starting and stopping an OC4J instance
- Updating an OC4J instance configuration

You use the *dcmctl* utility with the *createComponent* option to create a new OC4J instance. The standard syntax for using the *dcmctl* command is as follows:

```
$ ORACLE_HOME/dcm/bin/dcmctl command [options]
```

You can use the *dcmctl* command with various options. You use the *createComponent* option to create a new OC4J instance, as shown here:

```
$ dcmctl createComponent -ct oc4j -co component_name
```

In the *dcmctl* command, the two options denote the following:

- *-ct* (component type) is a scope option that specifies that the *dcmctl* command be applied to the named component type, which in our case is oc4j.

- *-co* (component name) is also a *dcmctl* scope option; it designates the name of a component during the creation of that component.

Here's an example showing how to create a new OC4J instance (the *command type* is oc4j, of course, and the *component name*—that is, the name of our new OC4J instance—is OC4J_Test):

```
$ dcmctl CreateComponent -ct oc4j -co OC4J_Test
Component Name: OC4J_Test
Component Type: OC4J
Instance:       infra_10_1_2.ntl-alaptisam.netbsa.org
$
```

To check that the new OC4J instance, OC4J_Test, has been successfully created, use the *ListComponents* option of the *dcmctl* utility, as shown here:

```
C:\OraHome_2\dcm\bin> dcmctl ListComponents
1
Component Name: home
Component Type: OC4J
Instance:       infra_10_1_2.ntl-alaptisam.netbsa.org
2
Component Name: HTTP_Server
Component Type: HTTP_Server
Instance:       infra_10_1_2.ntl-alaptisam.netbsa.org
3
Component Name: oca
Component Type: OC4J
Instance:       infra_10_1_2.ntl-alaptisam.netbsa.org
4
Component Name: OC4J_SECURITY
Component Type: OC4J
Instance:       infra_10_1_2.ntl-alaptisam.netbsa.org
5
Component Name: OC4J_Test
Component Type: OC4J
Instance:       infra_10_1_2.ntl-alaptisam.netbsa.org
6
Component Name: OID
Component Type: OID
C:\OraHome_2\dcm\bin>
```

The *dcmctl listComponents* command returns a list of all OracleAS components within the scope you specify. If you don't specify the scope (i.e., use the command without any arguments), you'll get a list of all OracleAS components in that instance. If you're using *dcmctl shell,* you can limit the list of components using a pattern. In the following example, I use "4" as a pattern matcher in order to get a list of all OC4J instances within an OracleAS instance:

```
$ dcmctl listComponents *4*
```

To remove an OC4J instance with the *dcmctl* utility, use the *dcmctl* command with the *removeComponent* option (*co* again stands for the component name):

```
$ dcmctl removeComponent -co nameOfOC4JInstance
```

on the
job

When you create a new OC4J instance, the OC4J instance isn't automatically started. You must start the new instance either through Application Server Control or through the opmnctl utility.

Sometimes, you may have to remove an entire OracleAS instance using operating system commands (by removing the files and directories belonging to the OracleAS installation). When you adopt this much wider-scoped procedure to remove an OC4J instance instead of using the *removeComponent* command just shown, the DCM repository will continue to retain the removed OC4J instance's information. This information may potentially hurt you during a subsequent reinstallation of OracleAS. You can use the *destroyInstance* command to clear the repository of all information pertaining to the removed OracleAS instance, as shown here (*-i* stands for the OracleAS instance name):

When you execute the following command, the *dcm.conf* file, the *targets.xml* file, and the repository directory are all automatically purged of all the OracleAS instance–related information:

```
$ dcmctl destroyInstance -i instance1
```

Using the Application Server Control

Using the Application Server Control is the recommended way to create a new OC4J instance. You can create a new OC4J instance using the Application Server Control by following these steps:

1. Go the System Components table and click the Create OC4J Instance button, which is shown in the upper right-hand corner of Figure 8-1.
2. Provide a name for the new OC4J instance in the page that comes up.
3. Click the Create button.
4. Application Server Control will confirm that the new OC4J instance was created.

When you create a new OC4J instance, either through the *dcmctl* utility or through the Application Server Control, *a new directory* will be created with the name of the new OC4J instance under the $ORACLE_HOME/j2ee directory. In our case (refer to the OC4J creation example using the *dcmctl* utility), this directory's name would be OC4J_Test.

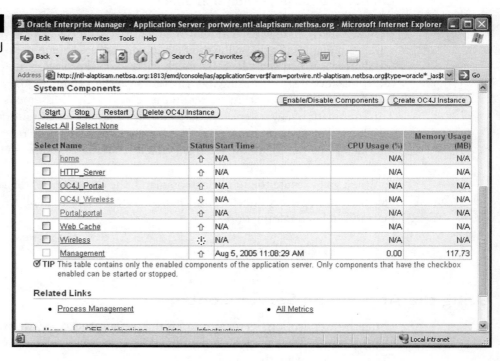

FIGURE 8-1

Creating an OC4J Instance

Managing the OC4J Instance

You can manage OC4J with the Application Server Control or OPMN, in addition to the DCMCTL utility. The recommended approach is to use the Application Server Control for performing day-to-day management of the OC4J instances. The Application Server Control makes the creation and management of OC4J instances a snap. However, you can also use the command-line utilities *opmnctl* and *dcmctl* to manage the OC4J instances noninteractively. These tools are ideal when you are using scripts to perform batch jobs, or for scheduled maintenance jobs. Let's start by reviewing OC4J instance management using the two command-line utilities *opmnctl* and *dcmctl*, and then go on to learn how to use the Application Server Control for managing an OC4J instance.

Using OPMN

You use the *opmnctl* command-line utility to stop and start OC4J instances. As you may recall from Chapter 3, when you use the *opmnctl* utility with the *ias-component* option, you start or stop all subprocesses of a component. In this case, using the *ias_component* option, you can start and stop all OC4J instances running in an OracleAS instance, as shown here:

```
$ opmnctl startproc ias_component=OC4J
$ opmnctl stopproc ias_component=OC4J
```

These two commands will start and stop all the OC4J instances in an OracleAS instance.

By using the *process-type* option, you can start and stop a *specific* OC4J instance. Here I show how you would start and stop a specific OC4J instances (named oc4J_Test) using *opmnctl*:

```
$ opmnctl startproc process_type=OC4J_Test
$ opmnctl stopproc process_type=OC4J_Test
```

Note that these two commands will start and stop the *single* OC4J instance, OC4J_Test, respectively.

Using DCMCTL

Earlier in this chapter you learned how to create and delete OC4J instances using the *dcmctl* utility. You also learned how to use the *listComponents* command to list all the applications deployed in an OC4J instance. The *dcmctl* utility contains commands you can use to deploy an OC4J application, as you'll see later in this chapter.

Using the Application Server Control

Every OC4J instance, including the new OC4J instance OC4J_Test that you created earlier, will have its own OC4J home page. You can perform the following OC4J management tasks using the Application Server Control Console:

■ Start an OC4J instance.

■ Configure an OC4J instance.

■ Manage the data sources and security.

■ Monitor the availability, usage, and performance of the OC4J instance.

■ Stop an OC4J instance.

■ Restart an OC4J instance.

■ Disable and enable an OC4J instance.

Figure 8-2 shows the OC4J home page in the Application Server Control Console.

Following are the main sections of the OC4J home page:

■ The General section shows a snapshot of the status of the OC4J server and also lets you stop and start the OC4J server.

■ The Status section shows a summary of the performance of the server, including CPU and memory usage.

■ The JDBC Usage section shows information about the open JDBC connections and active transactions, rollbacks, and commits.

■ The Response–Servlets and JSPs section shows details about the response times for processing requests, the active sessions, and the active requests.

■ The Response–EJBs section shows EJB transactional details.

FIGURE 8-2

The Application
Server Control
OC4J Home Page

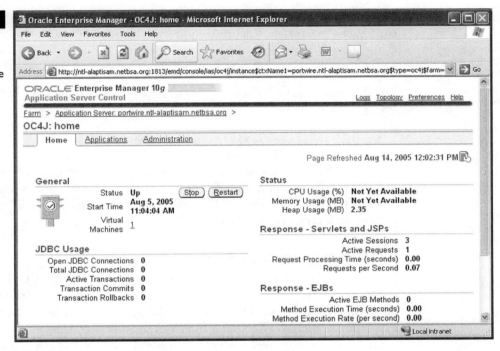

FIGURE 8-2

The Application
Server Control
OC4J Home Page

You can *start* and *stop* the OC4J instance from either the Application Server
Control Instance home page or the OC4J home page, by clicking on the Start and
Stop buttons. Note that you can also start and stop OC4J instances from the Oracle
Application Server Control Instance home page as well. If you wish to disable an
OC4J instance, you can do so by clicking the Enable/Disable Components in the
OracleAS Instance page. Similarly, you can reenable a disabled OC4J instance from
the Enable/Disable Components page by removing the selected instance from the
disabled components table. However, note that an enabled component won't start
automatically.

You perform most OC4J configuration and management tasks from the OC4J
home page. Each of the OC4J instances will have its own home page. You drill
down to any OC4J instance home page by selecting the name of the OC4J instance
in the System Components table. The OC4J home page has two tabs: *Applications*
and *Administration*. Clicking on the Applications tab will take you to the OracleAS

Console Applications page and clicking on the Administration page will take you to the OracleAS Console Administration page. Let's briefly review these two pages.

Testing the Default OC4J Instance

To test the default OC4J configuration, specify the following URL in your Web browser:

```
http://<hostname>:7777/j2ee/j2ee-index.html
```

In the URL, *hostname* stands for the name of the server on which your Oracle HTTP Server is running, and 7777 is, of course, the default *port number* for the OHS. If you type the following URL, you should see a "Hello World" greeting. The HelloWorldServlet is part of the OC4J installation.

OC4J Administration Page

Using the OC4J Administration page, you can perform various OC4J server configuration tasks. You can also access other pages so you can set the directory and file paths for the default application and the configuration file. Under the Instance Properties section, you'll see a set of links that will take you to the relevant page for configuring the OC4J server, the Web site, and the like. You can edit the key OC4J configuration file (the *server.xml* XML file) either by using the Server Properties link or by clicking on the Advanced Properties link. Under the Application Defaults section, there are links that enable the configuration of data sources, security, and JMS providers.

Let's take a brief look at three important links under the Instance Properties section: Server Properties Page, Website Properties, and Advanced Properties.

Server Properties You can view and edit the OC4J server properties from the Server Properties page, as shown in Figure 8-3. You'll find the following sections in the Server Properties page:

■ *General* Contains the name, server root, and configuration file names, which you can't change after creating the OC4J instance. The default Web module properties field contains the *global-web-applications.xml* file. The Applications Directory field is the default directory for the EAR files of deployed applications. The deployment directory field lets you specify the default directory for placing modified module deployment descriptors.

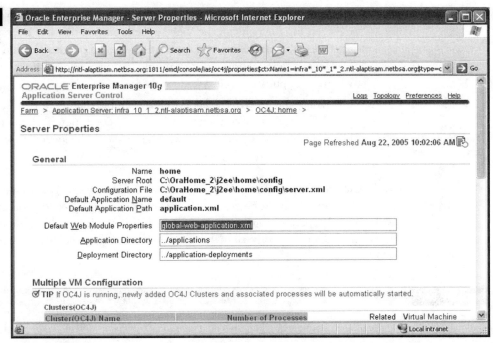

FIGURE 8-3

Server Properties
Page

- *Multiple VM Configuration*   Helps you configure multiple OC4J Java Virtual Machines.
- *Ports*   Enables the configuration of various ports. These ports include Remote Method Invocation (RMI), Java Message Services (JMS), AJP, and RMI-IIOP ports. The JMS, RMI, and RMI-IIOP were explained earlier in this chapter and AJP (Apache Java Protocol) is explained a little later in the chapter. The *mod_oc4j* module uses the AJP protocol to talk to an OC4J instance.
- *Command-line options*   Lets you configure Java executable commands.
- *Environment variables*   Helps set the environment for the OC4J instance.

Website Properties   The Website Properties home page lets you specify which Web applications are loaded when you start the OC4J instance. The parameters you specify are stored in the configuration file named *web-site.xml*. The following list gives the two major sections on this page:

■ *Default Web Module*   This section contains three nonconfigurable fields representing the name of the Web application, the name of the parent J2EE application, and whether the applications should be loaded when you start OC4J. Loading the applications at startup time improves application response time when the application is invoked for the very first time.

■ *URL Mappings for Web Modules*   This is a table that provides information about all the Web modules contained in the OC4J container. Each module's name, the URL to which it's mapped, and whether it should be loaded on OC4J instance startup is specified in this section.

Advanced Properties   You can view and edit any OC4J configuration file using the Advanced Properties page, as shown in Figure 8-4. As you can see, the Advanced Properties page contains a list of all the configurable files along with their locations. Click on *server.xml* (this configuration file is explained in detail later in

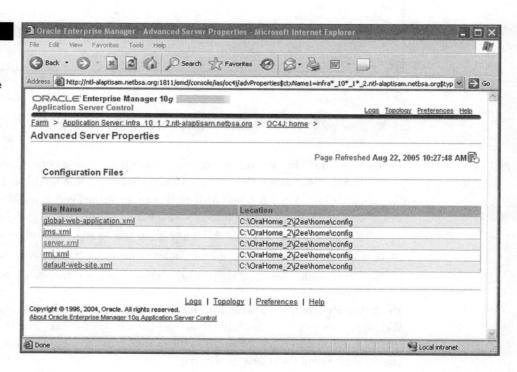

FIGURE 8-4

The OC4J
Advanced
Properties Page

this chapter), for example, if you wish to edit that file. That will take you to the Edit Server.xml page, which you can edit, thus modifying the configuration of the OC4J instance.

You can configure the following configuration files from the Advanced Properties page:

- *server.xml*
- *default-web-site.xml*
- *rmi.xml*
- *jms.xml*
- *global-web-application.xml*

In addition to the foregoing configuration files, you can edit the following files if you access the Advanced Properties page from an application:

- You can edit the *application.xml, oc4j-connectors.xml, principals.xml* and *data-sources.xml* files if you access the Advanced Server Properties page from the default application.
- You can edit the *principals.xml* and the *orion-application.xml* files if you access the Advanced Server Properties page from any deployed application.

All the files mentioned here are discussed later in this chapter.

exam watch

If you want to modify the global definitions of the data-sources. xml and principals.xml files, you must modify them under the default application. If you want to modify them only locally, you must modify them under the deployed application.

OC4J Applications Page

The OC4J Applications page lets you deploy and maintain Web applications. Using this page, you deploy WAR files or new OC4J applications. When you deploy a new WAR file, the WAR application is automatically wrapped by the Application Server Control into a J2EE application—that is, into a *.ear* file. This *.ear* file is used to deploy the Web application's WAR file. After you deploy a new WAR application,

Watch   *The default application is the parent application for all applications in an OC4J instance.*

its name will appear in the form of a *.ear* file in the Deployed Applications table on the OC4J Server Applications page. The Deployed Applications table shows the name, path, and parent application of all deployed applications as well as the application's performance metrics, such as the number of active requests and request processing time.

You can deploy a new *.ear* file to a single OracleAS instance, or it can be simultaneously deployed to several OC4J instances that are part of a cluster.

You can *undeploy* a WAR file by using the OC4J Applications page. If you wish to *redeploy* an application, you can't use the Applications page directly. In order to redeploy an application, you must first undeploy the application and deploy it again. Here are the steps for redeploying a WAR file:

- Click the Applications tab in the OC4J home page.
- Select the application you wish to deploy from the Deployed Applications table.
- Click the Undeploy button.
- Click the Deploy WAR file. You must use the name of the original application you undeployed before performing this step.

on the **job**   *You can't manage OC4J instances using the OC4J standalone tool admin.jar. However, you can manually modify the XML configuration files and then use the* **dcmctl** *tool to notify the Application Server that the files were edited by you directly. The* **dcmctl** *command to do this is* **dcmctl updateconfig -ct oc4j**.

Watch   *In order to deploy, redeploy, or undeploy a J2EE application, the application files must be archived in an EAR or WAR file archival format.*

You will learn how to deploy Web and J2EE applications using the OC4J Applications page later in this chapter.

Configuring OC4J

When I mention configuring OC4J, I mean something broader than merely configuring the OC4J server itself. Our main motivation in learning about the OC4J server is to learn how to deploy J22 applications with it. Thus, configuring OC4J involves the configuration of the OC4J server itself, as well as the configuration of the J2EE applications framework. In addition, you must configure the *mod_oc4j* module, which lets the Oracle HTTP Server communicate with the OC4J server instance.

An OC4J instance has *three* groups of configuration files: *mod_oc4j* configuration files, OC4J server configuration XML files, and the J2EE application deployment XML files. As you can tell, you use the first set of files to configure the interaction of the *mod_oc4j* module with the Oracle HTTP Server. You use the second set of files to configure the OC4J server proper, and the last set of configuration files to configure the deployment of J2EE applications via the OC4J server. These three groups of configuration files are reviewed in the following subsections.

on the
(j) o b

Port number 7777 is the default port for the Oracle Web listener. You must specify the port number if you are using a non-default port number. However, OracleAS Web Cache uses port 7777, and the HTTP server will actually be listening on port 7778.

on the
(j) o b

You can't modify J2EE XML files such as web.xml and ejb-jar.xml after deploying an application. You can, however, modify the OC4J-specific XML files of the application.

The mod_oc4j Configuration Files

The *mod_oc4j* HTTP server module facilitates communication between the Oracle HTTP Server and the OC4J instance and enables access to HTTP clients. The *mod_oc4j* module runs within the HTTP server and performs the following functions:

■ Identifying the requests it needs to serve

■ Determining the particular OC4J instance it should route the request to

■ Communicating with the selected OC4J instance backend processes

OPMN keeps *mod_oc4j* aware of the status of the instances, and thus, oc4j will route jobs only to the running processes. Because *mod_oc4j* is aware of the OracleAS Clusters and OC4J *islands* (an OC4J island is a set of OC4J processes that replicates session state among all the OC4J processes that are part of the island) the OC4J processes can run on multiple nodes, and its routing is calculated to provide transparent failover as well.

By default, the *mod_oc4j* module will direct all *j2ee/* context-bound applications to the OC4J server. You can, however, add other mount points for this context in the mod_*oc4j.conf* file, if you plan on using other contexts (for example, *test/*). Once you start your Oracle HTTP Server, the context changes will be in effect and all new requests for the *test/* context will be sent to the OC4J server. The *mod_oc4j* configuration files are located in the following directory:

```
$ORACLE_HOME/Apache/Apache/conf
```

Here's a typical *mod_oc4j* configuration file, named *oc4j.conf*:

```
##############################################
# Oracle iAS mod_oc4j configuration file: mod_oc4j.conf
##############################################
LoadModule oc4j_module modules/ApacheModuleOc4j.dll
<IfModule mod_oc4j.c>
    <Location /oc4j-service>
        SetHandler oc4j-service-handler
        Order deny,allow
        Deny from all
        Allow from localhost ntl-alapatisam.netbsa.org ntl-alapatisam
    </Location>
Oc4jMount /j2ee/*
Oc4jMount /forms90 FORMS_PROD
</IfModule>
```

Let's briefly analyze the *oc4j.conf* file, which is called as part of the Oracle HTTP Server configuration file *httpd.conf*.

- The *LoadModule* directive tells the Oracle HTTP Server that the *oc4j_module* should be loaded each time the Oracle HTTP Server starts.

- The *<IfModule>* directive tells the HTTP server what it should do when it encounters the *oc4j_module* in the *httpd.conf* file, which is the configuration file for the Oracle HTTP Server.

- The *<Location>* directive specifies the virtual path /oc4j-service, which will launch the oc4j-service handler, but only if the URL comes from the address specified within the Location directive.

- The lines starting with the *Oc4jMount* command help set the URL mapping. The *Oc4jMount* command lines specify the virtual paths for *mod_oc4j* to route to a particular OC4J instance. For example the virtual path /j2ee/* belongs to the OC4J *home* instance. Any request that contains the regular expression /j2ee/* is then routed to the home OC4HJ instance. In this example, the URL mapping for this OC4J instance makes the Oracle Application Server route all requests for /forms90 FORMS_PROD to this OC4J instance. You can look at this as the rough *mod_oc4j* equivalent of an OHS Alias. All deployed J2EE applications must be associated with a "root context" (an URL prefix), which serves to identify the requests that need to be handled by *mod_oc4j*. The *Oc4jMount* command maps the root context to the particular OC4J instance to which an application is deployed.

CERTIFICATION OBJECTIVE 8.06

The OC4J Server Configuration Files

The OC4J *server configuration files* (also known as OC4J configuration files) help configure the OC4J server and are located in the following directory:

```
$ORACLE_HOME/j2ee/<instance>/config
```

The OC4J server configuration files configure various OC4J instance–related items such as ports, security, and basic J2EE services. These XML files are purely

about configuring the OC4J instance itself and aren't directly related to the deployment of the J2EE applications.

The OC4J server configuration files consist mainly of a set of *Server XML configuration files* and a set of *Web site XML files*. The server configuration files specify various properties of the OC4J server such as the listening ports, passwords, security, and related basic J2EE services as well as the data sources and Web sites. The Web site XML files are used to configure ports, Web contexts, and protocols to facilitate the functioning of the OC4J Web site.

Let's review the important OC4J server XML files.

server.xml

The *server.xml* file is *the key OC4J server configuration file*; it contains references to most of the files used by the OC4J server. Besides configuring the OC4J server, the *server.xml* file also points to other configuration files, such as the *jms.xml* file for JMS support. This way, you can configure the various services in their own configuration files, but by referring to them in the *server.xml* file, you let it be known that these services are for the use of the OC4J instance. The server configuration files are OC4J instance specific and refer to the key J2EE configuration files. You don't usually need to modify the OC4J server configuration files when you deploy J2EE applications. Here's how the *server.xml* file references other configuration files:

```
server.xml
|----→rmi.xml
|----> jms.xml
|----→application.xml
|          |--------→principals.xml
|          ---------→data-sources.xml
|-----→global-web-application.xml
------→default-web-site.xml
            |------→default-web-app
            -------→web-app
```

Together, the *server.xml*, the *application.xml*, and the *default-web-site.xml* files define an application's configuration.

You use the *server.xml* file for the following purposes:

■ Configuring OC4J
■ Referencing other configuration files
■ Specifying J2EE applications

Let's look at each of these three categories of tasks in detail in the following subsections.

Configuring OC4J

You configure the OC4J server by modifying the following elements in the *server.xml* file:

■ Global application, global Web application, and default Web site
■ Number of HTTP connections the OC4J server will permit
■ Logging settings
■ Transaction time-input settings
■ SMTP host

Referencing Other Configuration Files

You can reference other configuration XML files and directories in the *server.xml* file. Following are the important configuration files referenced in the *server.xml* file:

■ *data-sources.xml* location
■ *jazn-data.xml* location
■ *jms.xml* and *rmi.xml* locations

on the Job

If you're using a standalone OC4J instance, port 8888 is used by default to access the OC4J listener. In the OracleAS environment, OPMN overrides this port setting. OracleAS by default allocates port 7777 for access via the Oracle HTTP Server when you enable the OracleAS Web Cache.

Specifying Other J2EE Applications

You specify the deployed J2EE applications in the *server.xml* file by using the <application> element.

Structure of the server.xml File

The *server.xml* file consists of several *elements*, each of which is responsible for a certain area of OC4J-related configuration. Here's a typical *server.xml* file:

```
<?xml version="1.0" standalone='yes'?>
<!DOCTYPE application-server PUBLIC "Orion Application Server Config"
"http://xmlns.oracle.com/ias/dtds/application-server-9_04.dtd">
<application-server
      application-directory="../applications"
      deployment-directory="../application-deployments"
  connector-directory="../connectors"
>
      <rmi-config path="./rmi.xml" />
      <!--Interoperability config link-->
      <sep-config path="./internal-settings.xml" />
      <!--JMS-server config link, uncomment to activate the JMS service-->
      <jms-config path="./jms.xml" />
      <javacache-config path="../../../javacache/admin/javacache.xml" />
      <j2ee-logging-config path="./j2ee-logging.xml" />
      <log>
            <file path="../log/server.log" />
            <!--Uncomment this if you want to use ODL logging capabilities
            <odl path="../log/server/" max-file-size="1000" max-directory-size=
"10000"/>
            -->
      </log>
      <global-application name="default" path="application.xml" />
      <global-web-app-config path="global-web-application.xml" />
      <!--<web-site path="./secure-web-site.xml" />-->
      <web-site default="true" path="./default-web-site.xml" />
        <!--Add the http-web-site in this way and uncomment this line
      <web-site path="./http-web-site.xml" />
      </application-server>
```

Note that all the directories referred to inside the *server.xml* file are relative to the $ORACLE_HOME/j2ee/config directory. In the example shown previously, there are several *elements* such as application-server and the like. I'll briefly describe the *important elements of the server.xml* file in the rest of this section. Note that the example file shown in the previous section doesn't happen to contain all of the following elements.

<application-server> You use the top-level element of the *server.xml* file, called the <application-server> element, to specify the application server configuration information. The <application-server> element has attributes such as the following:

■ The application-auto-deploy element specifies the directory the OC4J server automatically deploys applications from.

■ The application-directory element specifies the directory where the OC4J instance will store the application *.ear* files. If you don't specify any directory values for this element, the *.ear* files are, by default, stored in the $ORACLE_HOME/j2ee/home/applications directory. The application-directory element specifies that any files placed in the directory you specify for this element should be automatically deployed.

■ The deployment-directory element specifies the directory where the OC4J instance should store the files it generates for permanent storage. Each of the applications you deploy will have its own deployment-directory element.

<application>   The <application> element specifies the name of the application and the path to the application archive (EAR).

<global-application>   The <global-application> element specifies the default application for an OC4J server.

<global-web-app-config>   The <global-web-app-config> element specifies the location of the *web-application.xml* file.

<jms-config> and <rmi-config>   The <jms-config> and <rmi-config> elements specify the path to the *jms.xml* and the *rmi.xml* files, respectively.

<max-http-connections>   The <max-http-connections> element specifies the number of maximum concurrent connections that the Web site can accept.

<web-site>   The <web-site> element specifies the path to a *web-site.xml* file that's used to define a Web site, as shown in the following example:

```
Path=''. . . /my-web-site.xml''
```

Other OC4J Server XML Files

Besides the main OC4J configuration file, *server.xml*, several other OC4J server XML files help to configure the OC4J instance. Let's take a quick look at these.

jazn.xml and jazn-data.xml   The *jazn-data.xml* and the *jazn.xml* files are used for security configuration if you're using the Java Authentication and Authorization

(JAAS) Service. The file contains user and group configuration information for the default *JAZNUserManager* client-admin console.

The data-sources.xml file To make their applications portable across servers, application developers use logical representation of databases and publish these data sources in the Java Naming and Directory Interface (JNDI) tree. The applications retrieve database connections through *javax.sql.dataSource* objects and look up the objects through the JNDI. These objects are called *data sources,* and the deployer must specify the mapping between a logical dataSource object and the physical databases. The connection methods that are specified are used by the applications to connect to the specified database.

on the
()o b

The properties and methods of the data source objects are specified by the javax.sql.DataSource interface.

The *data-sources.xml* file lets you configure OC4J database sources used by the various applications hosted by the OC4J instance. In addition, the file contains information on retrieving JDBC connections. The *data-sources.xml* file contains the following types of information:

- JDBC driver
- JDBC URL
- Database schema
- Maximum number of database connections allowed
- Username and password for the data source
- JNDI name in the JNDI lookup, to retrieve the data source

Note that the *data-sources.xml* file establishes the data source object definitions at the OC4J instance level. These *global data sources* are specified by an XML tag, and the XML attributes for each data source include the JDBC connection string and sometimes the username and password information. All applications deployed in the OC4J container can share the data sources defined at the container level. Applications can also use application-specific data sources by incorporating the *<data-sources>* tag in the *application.xml* file to refer to the *data-sources.xml* file and directly use the data sources defined therein.

When the OC4J instance starts, it parses the *data-sources.xml* file, instantiates the DataSource objects, and binds them into the JNDI namespace. After you deploy an application, the application accesses the data sources by looking up the JNDI tree. Note that there's a separate JNDI namespace for each application.

The different types of data sources, such as emulated and non-emulated data sources as well as native data sources, are discussed in detail later in this chapter. Here's a typical *data-sources.xml* file showing how to use the Oracle JDBC driver to create a JDBC thin connection type data source:

```
<data-sources><data-source>
class=<<">>com.evermind.sql.DriverManagerDataSource
name="OracleDS"
location="jdbc/OracleCoreDS"
xa-location="jdbc/xa/OracleXADS"
ejb-location="jdbc/OracleDS"
connection-driver="oracle.jdbc.driver.OracleDriver"
 username="scott" password="->pwForScott"
url="jdbc:oracle:thin:@localhost:1521:oracle"
 inactivity-timeout="30"
 connection-retry-interval="1" />
<data-source>
</data-sources>
```

In the sample *data-sources.xml* file, this is what the various elements stand for:

- *Class* is the type of data resources or the DataSource class.
- *Name* is the name of the data source—in our case, OracleDS, which is the default data source.
- *Location*, *xa-location*, and *ejb-location* are the JNDI names that the data source will bind to. You must specify all three of the location attributes for emulated data sources, but you use only the value specified for the ejb-location attribute.
- *Connection-driver* is the type of connection to be returned. This attribute refers to the class that actually implements the data source connection.
- *Username* and *password* are the username and password for the database users.
- *url* is the JDBC connection URL for the database being mapped to this data source.
- *Inactivity-timeout* and *connection-retry-interval* are the default timeout and connection retry intervals, in seconds.

principals.xml The *principals.xml* file contains user and group information as well as permissions and certificates.

rmi.xml The *rmi.xml* file contains Remote Method Invocation (RMI) configuration information. The RMI listener, which provides remote access for EJBs, has its settings defined in this file as well. Here are the main components of the *rmi. xml* file:

- Host name or IP address
- Port number to which the RMI server binds
- Clustering and log settings

jms.xml The *jms.xml* file contains the OC4J Java Messaging Service (JMS) implementation configuration information. The following are the key components in this file:

- Host name or IP address
- Port number to which the JMS server binds
- Settings for queues bound to the JMDI tree
- Log settings

on the *Job*
The global application for the OC4J server acts as the parent for all applications in that OC4J instance. The applications inherit the parent application's properties, but you can override the default parent application properties with application-specific properties.

The Web Site XML Files

The Web site–related XML files configure ports, protocols, and Web contexts for the OC4J Web site, and are in the following format:

```
*-web-site.xml
```

The *web-site.xml* file contains the Web site configuration information, including the following:

- Host name, IP addresses, and listener ports
- Default Web application for the site
- SSL configuration
- Settings for user Web applications

Here's a typical *web-site.xml* file:

```xml
<?xml version="1.0" standalone='yes'?>
<!DOCTYPE web-site PUBLIC "OracleAS XML Web-site"
 "http://xmlns.oracle.com/ias/dtds/web-site-9_04.dtd">
<web-site host="localhost" port="3302" protocol="ajp13"
 display-name="My Java Web Site" cluster-island="1" >
<web-site port="3302" protocol="ajp13"
display-name="My Java Web Site">
<!--The default web-app for this site, bound to the root-->
<default-web-app application="default" name="defaultWebApp" root="/j2ee" />
<web-app application="default" name="dms" root="/dmsoc4j" access-log="false" />
<access-log path="../log/default-web-access.log" />
</web-site>
```

Here are the key elements of the
web-site-xml file:

- *web-site*   The name of your Web site.
- *host*   The name of the server hosting the Web server.
- *display-name*   A user-friendly Web site name.
- *default-web-app*   The default Web application.
- *name*   The name of the WAR file for the application, minus its *.war* extension.
- *port*   The Oracle HTTP Server forwards requests over the AJP listening port defined here. The OPMN configuration contains information about the range of AJP ports that can be used.
- *protocol*   The protocol used is AJP1.3, which is the Apache Jserver Protocol, used by *mod_oc4j* running on the Oracle HTTP Server (which is based on the Apache Web server), to communicate with the OC4J instance.
- *root*   The value for this attribute is /j2ee in our example; note that this must match the value specified for the *Oc4jMount* command in the *oc4j.conf* file. The root variable shows the *root context* for the application off your Web site. If your Web site is http://myhost:7777/j2ee, you initiate your application by going to http://myhost:7777/j2ee/testapp (testapp is the name of your J2EE application).
- *access-log*   Name of the log where access information is logged.

J2EE Application Deployment Files

Now that you have reviewed the OC4J server XML files (which include the server configuration files and the Web site configuration file), let's turn our attention to J2EE application XML files. There are two basic types of application configuration XML files: *J2EE deployment* (configuration) files and an *OC4J-specific* configuration file.

The application configuration XML files are meant for deployment of J2EE applications defined in an Enterprise Application Archive (EAR) file. The applications can include Web application components such as servlets and JSP pages, as well as EJB applications. A J2EE application can contain various types of modules, listed as follows:

- Web applications modules (WAR files), which include servlets and JSP pages
- EJB applications modules (EJB JAR files), which include Enterprise JavaBeans (EJBs)
- Client applications contained in JAR files (JSPs)
- Connectors

In order to deploy an application to OC4J, you archive the JAR and WAR files that belong to the enterprise Java application into an EAR file, whose layout follows J2EE specifications.

Applications that include only a Web application are bound to a UR, to make the application accessible to the Web clients. Applications with the EJB application component, however, aren't bound to a URL. These can be accessed either through Remote Method Invocation (RMI) or locally, through the JVM running on a server.

OracleAS lets you create clusters of OC4J processes. The Oracle Enterprise Manager provides built-in support for managing such OC4J clusters across the enterprise. You must, therefore, rely on the Oracle Enterprise Manager 10*g* (Grid Control) and not use the *admin.jar* tool to manage the OC4 instance by itself. For the same reason, you are advised not to edit a single OC4J instance configuration file directly, but rather, use the Application Server Control. Although only the EJB modules and Web modules have been described thus far, there are actually four J2EE application types: *EJB, Servlet (Web modules), JSP,* and *Client.* You've already seen that J2EE applications have *two types of deployment (or configuration) files,* namely:

- A J2EE deployment descriptor XML file (stored in the $ORACLE_HOME/ applications/<app-name> directory)
- An OC4J-specific deployment descriptor XML file (stored in the $ORACLE_HOME/application-deployments/<app-name> directory), denoted by the prefix of *orion*

You thus end up with a total of *eight* J2EE Deployment XML files for the four types of applications, four of which are the OC4J-specific Orion XML files and the other four, J2EE XML files.

In addition to the eight possible J2EE deployment XML files, you have a set of *four common global configuration files* for all types of applications. The four global application configuration files are as follows:

- *application.xml*   This is the global application configuration file, which contains the common settings for all applications in an OC4J instance.
- *orion-application.xml*   This contains OC4J-specific global application information for all applications.
- *web-application.xml*   This contains OC4J-specific global Web application configuration information that specifies common settings for all Web modules.
- *oc4j-connectors.xml*   This contains information about global connector configuration.

To summarize our discussion, you can have the following J2EE application deployment files in an OC4J environment:

- Four common Global Configuration Files: *application.xml, orion-application.xml, global-web-application.xml,* and *oc4j-connectors.xml*
- Two configuration files for *each of the four J2EE application types,* one a J2EE deployment descriptor and the other an OC4J-specific deployment descriptor. The resulting files are the following:
  - For EJBs: *ejb-jar.xml* and *orion-ejb-jar.xml*
  - For Web modules: *web.xml* and *orion-web.xml*

■ For client modules: *application-client.xml* and *orion-application-client.xml*

■ For connectors: *ra.xml* and *oc4j-ra.xml*

In the following subsections, the main application XML configuration files are discussed briefly.

w a t c h   *If you don't create the OC4J-specific deployment XML files, they will be automatically created when you deploy J2EE applications.*

Description of the Application (J2EE Deployment) XML Files

In this section, each of the eight types of application XML files, also known as the J2EE Deployment XML Files, are discussed. First, let's review the four common global application configuration files.

Following are the four common global configuration files for all J2EE application components.

o n t h e
Ó o b   *All the configuration XML files starting with Orion are also referred to as OC4J-Specific Orion files. The other set of configuration files consist of J2EE-related XML files.*

The J2EE application.xml File

The J2EE *application.xml* file is stored in the j2ee/home/config directory and is the global application configuration file *for all J2EE applications* in an OC4J instance. The *application.xml* file identifies all the Web and EJB applications that are part of a J2EE application. This file points to the location of the *jazn-data.xml* and the *data-sources.xml* file. Note that the J2EE *application.xml* file isn't the same as the local *application.xml* files. The latter describe the J2EE EAR files.

w a t c h   *The application.xml file is the main J2EE application deployment descriptor file.*

The following subsections state the important elements in the *application.xml* file. The <application> element is the top element in the *application.xml* file. Within the <application> element, you can use the following elements.

<ejb>pathToEJB.jar</ejb>   The ejb element refers to an EJB JAR.

<alt-dd>path/to/dd</alt-dd>   The alt-dd element represents an optional Uniform Resource Indicator (URI) to the deployment descriptor file for a J2EE module. The deployer will read the deployment descriptor from the default location if you don't specify the alt-dd element.

<connector>context</connector>   The connector element refers to the URI of a resource adapter archive file.

<context-root>thedir/</context-root>   The context-root descriptor shows the URI of a Web application.

<description>A description.</description>   The description element is a simple description of the application being deployed.

<icon>   The icon element is used to specify the location of application images used in GUI tools.

<java>pathToClient.jar</java>   The java element refers to a Java application client module.

<module>   There are as many module elements as there are separate J2EE modules, and each of them contains EJB, Java, and Web elements.

<web>   The Web element shows the `web-uri` and the `context-root` of a Web application module. The <web-uri> element indicates the URI of a Web application file. (A URI is an Internet protocol element consisting of a name or address you can use to refer to a resource. A URL is just an URI that additionally provides a way of accessing and obtaining a representation of the resource.) The URI is relative to the top level of the application package. Here's the syntax for the <web> element:

```
<web-uri>thePathToThe.war</web-uri>
```

Here's a simple *application.xml* file:

```
<application>
  <display-name>myapp j2ee application</display-name>
  <description>
    A sample J2EE application that uses a Container Managed
    Entity Bean and JSPs for a client.
  </description>
  <module>
    <ejb>myapp-ejb.jar</ejb>
  </module>
  <module>
    <web>
      <web-uri>myapp-web.war</web-uri>
      <context-root>/myapp</context-root>
    </web>
  </module>
</application>
```

The orion-application.xml File

The *orion-application.xml* file is the OC4J-specific global configuration file for all applications in an OC4J instance. You specify the following types of configuration information in the *orion-application.xml* file:

- *autocreate-tables* and *autodelete-tables:* You must define a data source for all container-managed persistence (CMP) beans. The *autocreate-tables* attributes determine whether to automatically create tables for CMP beans for entity bean persistence, thus ensuring that fields and database types are mapped correctly. The *autodelete-tables* attribute determines whether to automatically delete the tables. By default, *autocreate-tables* is set to true and *autodelete-tables* is set to false.
- Default data sources for CMP beans
- Default security user manager
- JNDI authorization

If you want to bind EJBs to existing database tables, set the *autocreate-tables* attribute to false. You then deploy the EJB in a *.ear* file. Finally, you reconfigure the newly generated *orion-ejb-jar.xml* file so it uses the existing database tables.

global-web-application.xml   The *global-web-application.xml* file contains common settings for all the Web modules in an OC4J instance. The file contains OC4J-specific global Web application configuration details.

oc4j-connectors.xml   The *oc4j-connectors.xml* file is a connector configuration file that contains the global OC4J-specific connector configuration information.

Now that you've reviewed the four global J2EE configuration files, let's turn our attention to the two types of configuration files (J2EE-specific files and OC4J-specific files) that each of the four application types (EJB, Web module, client, and connector) can have.

EJB

The EJB-related XML files are J2EE EJB application configuration files, used to define EJB deployment descriptors; they are part of the EJB JAR file. There are two EJB XML files: the J2EE *ejb-jar.xml* file and the OC4J-specific *orion-ejb-jar.xml* file.

J2EE ejb-jar.xml   The *ejb-jar.xml* file defines EJB deployment parameters in a JAR file. If you're using CMP, the file contains definitions for the container-managed EJBs.

OC4J-Specific orion-ejb-jar.   The *orion-ejb-jar.xml* file defines OC4J-specific deployment descriptors for EJBs and thus contains the deployment time information for EJBs. The file provides the mapping for EJBs to the OC4J server environment. You can specify the following attributes in the *orion-ejb-jar.xml* file:

- Session persistence settings
- Time-out settings
- Transaction retry settings
- CMP, ORMI, and JNDI mappings

The *orion-ejb-jar.xml* file is located in the $ORACLE_HOME/j2ee/home/ application-deployments directory. After you deploy an application, you'll find the *orion-ejb-jar.xml* file in the /deploymentName/jarname(.jar)/orion-ejb-jar.xml directory. If you bundle the EJB with the application or if you don't specify a deployment directory in the OC4J main configuration file (*server.xml*), the *orion-ejb-jar.xml* file will be stored under the META-INF/orion-ejb-jar.xml directory.

The *orion-ejb-jar.xml* file will be copied to the directory specified for the *deployment-directory* attribute, but only if there are no prior files in that directory. Note that that you use the *orion-ejb-jar.xml* file only for the initial configuring of an application deployment. After this, the OC4J instance will modify the files to add pertinent information to it.

Web Module

There are two Web-related XML files, one of which is the J2EE-specific XML file and the other, the OC4J-specific XML file.

J2EE web.xml All servlets, EJBs, and JSPs that are part of the J2EE application are described in the J2EE *web.xml* file. Here are the contents of a typical *web.xml* file:

```
<web-app>
    <display-name>myapp web application</display-name>
    <description>
        Web module that contains an HTML welcome page, and 4
JSP's.
    </description>
    <welcome-file-list>
        <welcome-file>index.html</welcome-file>
    </welcome-file-list>
    <ejb-ref>
        <ejb-ref-name>TemplateBean</ejb-ref-name>
        <ejb-ref-type>Entity</ejb-ref-type>
        <home>TemplateHome</home>
        <remote>Template</remote>
    </ejb-ref>
    <servlet>
        <servlet-name>template</servlet-name>
        <servlet-class>TemplateServlet</servlet-class>
        <init-param>
            <param-name>length</param-name>
            <param-value>1</param-value>
        </init-param>
    </servlet>
</web-app>
```

OC4J-Specific orion-web.xml The *orion-web.xml* file contains the mappings for Web settings. Here are important items that are part of this file:

- Auto-reloading
- Buffering
- Directory browsing
- Document root
- Virtual directories

- Clustering
- Session tracking
- JNDI mappings

Client

There are two XML files that contain client configuration information: *application-client.xml* and *orion-application-client.xml*.

J2EE application-client.xml   The *application-client.xml* file contains the JNDI information necessary for accessing the server application.

```
<application-client>
     <display-name>TemplateBean</display-name>
     <ejb-ref>
          <ejb-ref-name>TemplateBean</ejb-ref-name>
          <ejb-ref-type>Entity</ejb-ref-type>
          <home>mTemplateHome</home>
          <remote>Template</remote>
     </ejb-ref>
</application-client>
```

OC4J-Specific orion-application-client.xml   The *orion-application-client.xml* file contains JNDI mappings for the client. The JNDI mappings map the EJB reference logical name to the JNDI name for the EJB, as shown in this example:

```
<orion-application-client>
   <ejb-ref-mapping name="TemplateBean"
   location="myapp/myapp-ejb/TemplateBean" />
</orion-application-client>
```

Connector

There are two connector-related XML files: *ra.xml* and *oc4j-ra.xml*.

ra.xml   The *ra.xml* file contains J2EE-related configuration information.

oc4j-ra.xml   The *oc4j-ra.xml* file contains OC4J-specific configuration information.

Using the Application Server Control to Configure OC4J

In the previous subsections, you learned how to manually edit the various OC4J configuration files. However, you can change OC4J configuration easily through the Application Server Control. To edit OC4J server configuration files using the Application Server Control, follow these steps:

1. On the OC4J home page, click the Administration tab to display the Administration page.
2. On the Administration page, click the Advanced Properties button.
3. The OC4J Advanced Properties page appears listing all configuration files available for editing for the current OC4J server.
4. The OC4J Advanced Properties Page appears, listing all the OC4J configuration files you can edit. Click the configuration file you want to edit. You can then make your configuration changes in the editable text box that appears.
5. Click the Apply button to save your configuration changes.

CERTIFICATION OBJECTIVE 8.07

Deploying J2EE Applications

Oracle recommends that you use consistent and meaningful naming conventions when developing Web applications. You must create your applications as a set of modules and place them under a directory that's named for the application. All your directories under the main application directory should be consistent with the directory structure for creating the necessary JAR, WAR, and EAR archives to facilitate the archiving of the application modules. Here's the standard development application directory structure for J2EE-based Oracle applications:

```
Applications/<application_name>/
        META-INF
                application.xml
        <ejb_modules>/
                EJB classes
                META-INF/
                        ejb-jar.xml
```

```
                        orion-ejb-jar.xml
            <web-module>/
                index.html
                JSP pages
                WEB-INF/
                    |               web.xml
                    |               orion-web.xml
                    |               classes/
                    |                       ----Servlet classes
                    |--------------Lib/
    <client_module>/
                Client classes
                META-INF/
                    |
                    ---------     application-client.xml
                                  orion-application-client.xml
```

Note that the *application.xml* file, which is the main application descriptor file, defines each of the modules. When you create a directory structure such as the one shown here, the modules are easily distinguishable from each other. For example, the EJB package class "testapp.ejb.Prod" should be located in the directory *<testapp>/ <ejb_module>/testapp/ejb/Prod.class*.

Deployment Methodologies

As mentioned previously, you can deploy Web applications as well as EJB applications through OC4J. You can deploy applications through the Application Server Control, or by using the *dcmctl* utility. The recommended approach is to use the Application Server Control. You can also deploy applications by manually editing the configuration files, of course, as well as by unpacking the deployment archive files in their deployment directories.

Data Sources

A *data source* is an object that lets you retrieve a connection to a database server. Data sources are encapsulations of connections to a database server, and they are instantiations of objects implementing the *javax.sql.dataSource* interface. Data source objects are bound to the JNDI name space, and the J2EE applications use the JNDI tree to look up various DataSource objects. Data sources offer you portable methods for creating JDBC connections across servers.

Because of their vendor-independent nature, Oracle Corporation recommends that you use data sources to retrieve database server connections.

Types of Data Sources

There are three types of data sources you can use in OC4J:

- Emulated data sources
- Non-emulated data source
- Native data sources

Emulated Data Sources   *Emulated data sources* emulate the XA (Transactional) protocol for JTA (Java Transaction API) transactions and offer features such as OC4J caching and pooling and Oracle JDBC extensions (for Oracle databases). The need for emulated data sources arose because many JDBC drives didn't offer XA capabilities in earlier days.

An emulated data source doesn't provide full XA global transactional support, such as the two-phase commit, which is unsupported under emulated data sources. However, because they lack full transactional support, emulated data source connections tend to be quite fast in nature. If you're using local transactions or global transactions that don't require the two-phase commit mechanism, emulated data sources are the recommended type of data source for you to use.

The following is a *data-sources.xml* configuration entry for an emulated data source:

```
<data-source
    class="com.evermind.sql.DriverManagerDataSource"
    name=ÓOracleDSÓ
    location="jdbc/OracleCoreDS"
    xa-location="OracleDS"
    ejb-location="jdbc/OracleDS"
    connection-driver="oracle.jdbc.driver.OracleDriver"
    username="scott"
    password="tiger"
    url="jdbc:oracle:thin:@//localhost:5521/oracle.regress.
rdbms.dev.us.oracle.com"
    inactivity-timeout=Ó30Ó
/>
```

Although you specify values for the *location, ejb-location*, and *xa-location* attributes when configuring an emulated data source in your *data-source.xml* file, you must only use the value specified by the *ejb-location* attribute when looking up that emulated data source. By now, you're well aware that you use a JNDI tree to look up a data source. You must look up a data source in the following way (only the "jdbc/OracleDS" value is used in the JNDI lookup):

```
Context ic = new InitialContext();
DataSource ds = (DataSource) ic.lookup("jdbc/OracleDS");
```

Or this:

```
DataSource ds = (DataSource) ic.lookup("java:comp/env/jdbc/OracleDS");
Connection con = ds.getConnection();
```

exam

ⓦatch   *In the data-sources*
.xml file, you must specify values for the
location, xa-location, *and* **ejb-location**
attributes. The first two attributes,
however, are actually deprecated now, and
only the value you specify for **ejb-location**
is actually used as the location string. To
be used in a JNDI lookup for retrieving the
data source. Applications, EJBs, Servlets,
and JSPs should use the **ejb-location** *value*
to look up emulated data sources in the
JNDI tree.

on the   *If you want true two-phase commits in your transactions, you must use a*
ⓙob   *non-emulated data source.*

Non-Emulated Data Sources   A *non-emulated data source* provides full JTA services, meaning that the two-phase commit mechanism is provided as well. Oracle Corporation recommends you use non-emulated data sources. A non-emulated data source provides higher recovery and reliability as well as distributed database features, unlike the emulated data sources. Note that to run a non-emulated data source, you must use a Java-enabled database, such as the Oracle Database.

Here's a typical *data-sources.xml* file for a non-emulated data source:

```
<data-source
  class="com.evermind.sql.OrionCMTDataSource"
  location="jdbc/OracleDS"
  connection-driver="oracle.jdbc.driver.OracleDriver"
  username="scott"
  password="tiger"
  url="jdbc:oracle:thin:@//localhost:5521/oracle.regress.rdbms.dev.us.oracle.com"
</data-source>
```

Note that JNDI lookups are performed using the value of the *location* attribute in the *data-sources.xml* file.

In the *data-sources.xml* file,

- *Location* refers to the JNDI name bound to the data source in the JNDI name spaces.
- The *url*, *username*, and *password* attributes refer to the database and default user name and password for retrieving connections to the database.
- *Class* is the type of data source class to bind in the name space.

Native Data Sources   *Native data sources* are supplied by JDBC vendors, and are used to implement data sources. Vendors provide extensions to facilitate capabilities such as caching and pooling. OC4J supports native data sources, but because they don't provide JTA services such as commits and rollbacks, they can't be used in global transactions. Here's how a *data-sources.xml* file looks for a native data source:

```
<data-source
    class="com.my.DataSourceImplementationClass"
    name=ÓNativeDSÓ
    location="jdbc/NativeDS"
    username="user"
    password="pswd"
    url="jdbc:myDataSourceURL"
</data-source>
```

Native data sources don't support JTA transactions. Both emulated as well as non-emulated data sources support JTA transactions, but only the non-emulated data sources support true two-phase commit (an emulated data source can only emulate a two-phase commit).

You can manage data sources through the Application Server Control's Application Data Sources page. You can reach this page by clicking the Administration tab on the OC4J home page, and then clicking on Data Sources under the Application Defaults section. From the Application Data Sources page, you can perform the following functions:

- View data source information for all applications, including the data source name, the JNDI location, and class and JDBC Driver information.
- Create, delete, and modify data sources.
- View performance statistics for data sources (only for non-emulated data sources).

The Data Sources page can be used to connect top Oracle as well as non-Oracle databases. For Oracle database connections, you must either configure a non-emulated Data Source that is purely Oracle based or use an emulated Data Source, which involves a wrapper around an Oracle Data Source.

on the job

Use the com.evermind.sql.DriverManagerDataSource with the Merant JDBC drivers to connect to Oracle databases.

Creating Data Sources

I'll briefly describe how you can create data sources using the Application Server Control. Here are the steps:

1. Go to the OC4J home page, click the Administration tab, and then click Data Sources.
2. In the Application Data Sources page, click the Create button (you can also click the Create Like button if you want to pattern a new data source after an existing one).
3. There are several sections in the Data Source Properties page (actually titled *Create Data Source*), which appear next. In the General section, fill in the name and description of the data source as well as the following information:
   - Data source class
   - JDBC URL
   - JDBC driver
   - Schema

*Your default **data-sources.xml** file provides predefined data sources that may suit your needs.*

4. In the Data Source Username and Password section, specify the username and password using the schema you chose in the previous section.

5. In the JNDI Locations section, you specify the JNDI location string that is used for JNDI tree lookups when the application is retrieving the data source. Of the three attributes—Location, Transactional (XA) Location, and EJB Location—you are required to specify only the *Location* attribute. If you plan on having the EJBs use the database for Container Managed Persistence (CMP), you must specify the XA and EJB Location attributes. For a non-emulated data source, you must specify all three JNDI location attributes, although only the *ejb-location* is actually used.

6. In the Connection Attributes section, you specify various connection-related attributes, such as the following:

   ■ Connection retry interval

   ■ Maximum connection attempts

   ■ Inactivity timeout period

   ■ Maximum and minimum number of open connections

7. In the Properties section, you can specify properties for any custom or third-party data source you may be configuring.

8. Once you have made the necessary configuration, click the Create button to create your new data source.

A DataSource object is used by developers to provide a logical representation of a database. It's the job of the deployer to map this logical representation to a physical database. Using the logical DataSource object to look up the JNDI, the J2EE applications will retrieve the database names so they can connect to them. The deployer first uses the J2EE application file (EAR file), to locate the DataSource references in the deployment descriptor. The deployer will then create mappings between the database schemas matching the DataSource requirements, so the application can connect to it.

You must use an emulated data source for a single-phase commit, and you can utilize the default data source (*data-sources.xml*) for this purpose. Here's the default *data-sources.xml* file:

```
<data-source
    class="com.evermind.sql.DriverManagerDataSource"
    name="OracleDS"
    location="jdbc/OracleCoreDS"
    xa-location="jdbc/xa/OracleXADS"
    ejb-location="jdbc/OracleDS"
    connection-driver="oracle.jdbc.driver.OracleDriver"
    username="scott"
    password="tiger"
    url="jdbc:oracle:thin:@//localhost:1521/ORCL"
    inactivity-timeout="30"
/>
```

Plug in your database URL information instead of the default URL shown in the *data-sources.xml* file. You must do this for each of the databases that are part of the transaction. The data source retrieval, as mentioned earlier, is done through a JNDI lookup. The JNDI name is shown by the *ejb-location* attribute.

Retrieving the Data Source Connection   Your first task before using the database for queries is to retrieve a connection to the database. To retrieve the database connection, you can perform a lookup on the JNDI name bound to the data source definition. Note that you may also perform a JNDI lookup by looking up the logical name that you defined in the environment of the bean container. You retrieve the database connection using the *getConnection* method. Using the data source definition, for example, you retrieve a database connection as follows:

```
Context ic = new InitialContext();
DataSource ds = (DataSource) ic.lookup("jdbc/OracleDS");
Connection conn = ds.getConnection();
```

Because the data source already contains the username and password attributes, you can use the *getConnection* method without the username/password attributes.

Managing Data Sources

Here are the steps that enable you to manage data sources using the OC4J home page of the Application Server Control:

1. On the OC4J home page, click the Administration tab.
2. In the Application Defaults section, click Data Sources.

3. In the Application Data Sources page (titled Data Sources), you'll see a list of all the available global data sources, which all the deployed applications can use. Figure 8-5 shows the Data Sources page. Notice the OracleDS default data source shown in that page, which is an emulated data source. This means that applications can use only a specific database through this data source. A non-emulated data source will let the application access multiple databases.

4. You can create a new data source by clicking the Create button or edit a data source by clicking the Edit button in the Data Source Properties page. You've already seen how you can create a new data source in the previous section. Let's see how you can edit a data source's properties by using the Edit Data Source page, which you reach by clicking the Edit button.

5. In the Edit Data Source page, shown in Figure 8-6, you can configure data sources so they are mapped to Oracle and non-Oracle databases. You can configure the following data source–related attributes from this page:

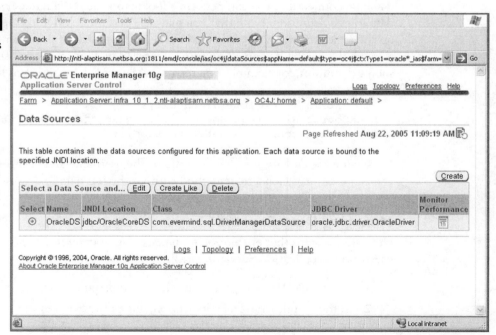

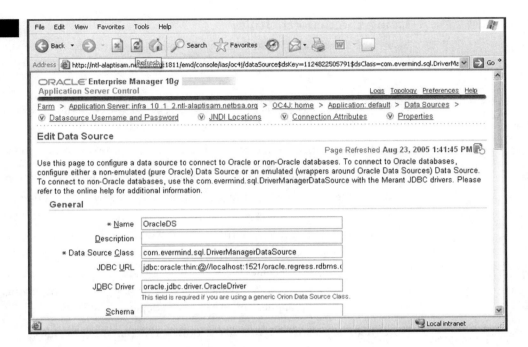

- Data source name
- Data source class
- JDBC URL
- Database username and password
- JNDI locations
- Connection attributes

Now that you have learned how to create and manage data sources, let's turn to a discussion of the deployment methodologies for Web and EJB applications in the following subsections.

Deploying Web Application Modules

You can use either the Application Server or the *dcmctl* utility to deploy Web applications. In the following subsections, examples are given of both approaches to Web application deployment.

Using the dcmctl Utility

Using the *dcmctl* utility, you can deploy, undeploy, and redeploy Web applications by using the supplied WAR files. Here's an example showing how to use *dcmctl* to deploy a WAR file:

```
dcmctl deployapplication -file /test/testapp.war -a testapp \
-co home -rc /myiAS/myWebapps
```

In the preceding *dcmctl* command, the various options stand for the following:

- *file* refers to the WAR file (it could also be an EAR file) that you want to deploy.
- *a* refers to the name of the application being deployed (testapp in our example).
- *-co* (*component name*) specifies the OC4J instance to which this WAR file will be deployed. If you leave this parameter out, the application will, by default, be deployed to the *home* OC4J instance.
- The *-rc* option specifies the base path a URL will use to access the Web module (for example, http://hostname:port/context_root) you are deploying. Note that the *-rc* option applies only when you're deploying WAR files.

Note that you mustn't use the *-rc* option when deploying EAR files.

To redeploy a Web application, use the *dcmctl* command as in the foregoing example, but with the *redeployApplication* option instead of the *deployApplication* option. To undeploy an application, use the *undeployApplication* option.

Using the Application Server Control

You deploy WAR files in order to deploy Web applications. However, when you deploy a WAR file for the first time, the Application Server Control wraps the application in an EAR file, thus making it a J2EE application. Use the following steps to deploy a Web application through the Application Server Control's Deploy Web Application page, which displays a list of all OC4J applications deployed on the OC4J server:

1. Go to the OC4J home page and click the Applications tab.
2. In the OC4J server Applications page, click the Deploy WAR file, under the Deployed Applications section.
3. In the Deploy Web Applications page, supply the path to the Web application, the Web application's name, and the URL it should be mapped to. Figure 8-7 shows the Deploy Web Application page.

FIGURE 8-7

The Deploy Web
Application Page

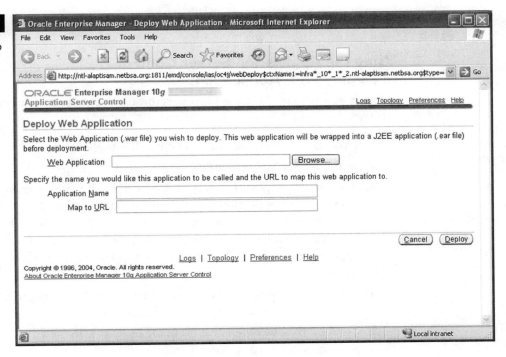

4. Click the Deploy button to deploy the Web application.

5. Note that once you deploy a Web application file through the Application Server Control, you can't redeploy it by using the EAR file created for it by the Application Server Control. You must first undeploy the application and then deploy the WAR file again.

Deploying J2EE (EJB) Applications

EJB modules depend on *deployment descriptors* to specify the runtime attributes of the enterprise beans. Deployment descriptors are saved in *ejb-jar.xml* files. EJBs are packaged and shipped along with their deployment descriptors (contained in the *ejb-jar.xml* file) in a standard format, in the form of a *.jar* (dot jar) file. When you deploy an EJB application, the deployment tool first reads the deployment descriptors specified in the *ejb-jar.xml* file. From this, the deployment tool gets information about the EJB, such as the type of beans packed in the *.jar* file, their transaction attributes, and their access permissions.

The ejb-jar.xml file specifies the run-time behavior of EJBs.

Using the Application Server Control to Deploy J2EE Applications

It is very easy to deploy J2EE applications through the Application Server Control. Here are the steps:

1. Go to the OC4J home page and click the Applications tab.

2. In the Deployed Applications section, click the Deploy EAR file.

3. The Deploy Application Wizard—Select Application page appears next. The Deploy Application Wizard will deploy the selected EAR file and apply any configuration changes you may make. Select the J2EE application you wish to deploy by providing the name and the location of the application's EAR file. You must also select the parent application here. Click Continue.

4. The URL Mapping for Web Modules page is next. You map a Web module to a URL pattern on your Web site and click Next.

5. On the Resource References Mapping page, you do the following:

   - Select the JNDI location.
   - Select the data source.
   - Select the JNDI location.
   - For each CMP entity bean, select a data source location and the tables.
   - Click Next.

6. On the User Manager page, select the User Manager you want to use for security. The JAZN XML User Manager provides complete security; to do this, you must set up a default realm and the *jazn-data.xml* file. The XML User Manager requires you to additionally configure the *principals.xml* file. Click Next.

7. In the Security Role Mappings page, assign security roles to the users and groups that are part of the OC4J container.

8. In the Publish Web Services page, click the Publish button if you want to publish and Web services has defined your application. Click Next.

9. In the Summary page, review your selections and click Deploy.

Using dcmctl to Deploy EJBs

You can use the *dcmctl deployApplication* command, explained previously to show how to deploy Web application modules (WAR files), to deploy J2EE applications as well. Here's an example:

```
$ dcmctl deployapplication -file /test/testEAR.ear -a testEAR -co OC4J_Test
```

The *dcmctl deployApplication* command is similar to the command you use to deploy Web applications, with the difference that you don't have to specify the *-rc* option in the case of J2EE application deployment. If you use the *-co* (component name) option to specify a particular OC4J instance, the operation applies to only that OC4J instance within an OracleAS instance. In our example, the EAR module will be deployed to the OC4J instance named *OC4J_Test*. If you don't specify the *-co* target option, the operation applies by default to the OC4J instance named *home*.

The following things happen when you execute the *deployApplication* command:

- The WAR or EAR file is copied to the server.
- The WAR or EAR Zip file is then expanded into runtime directories.
- If necessary, the context root in the *httpd.conf* file and the mount points in the *oc4j.conf* file and *server.xml* are modified. A new mount point is added to the *oc4j.conf* file to match the root context.
- All files are copied to the DCM repository.

Changes in Configuration Files

When you deploy applications, either by using the *dcmctl* utility or through the Application Server Control, several changes are made in the OC4J configuration. The following text gives a brief summary of the changes made in the main configuration files.

The application name is added to the *server.xml* file:

```
<application name=''testapp''
    path=''../applications/testapp.ear'' />
```

The context root for your new application (*testapp*) is added to the *default-web-site.xml* file, as shown here:

```
<web-app application=XXXX;testapp'' name=''testapp''
    root=''/testapp''/>
```

The *application.xml* file, located in the $ORACLE_HOME/applications/testapp/META-INF/ testapp directory is modified by adding the application module definitions to it:

```
<web><web-uri>webtestapp.war</web-uri></web>
```

In addition, a new *Oc4jMount* command line is added to the *oc4j.conf* file to match the root context /testapp.

Maintaining and Monitoring Applications

The OC4J home page shows all the deployed Web and EJB modules for an OC4J instance. The same page also shows a summary of application performance statistics, such as request processing time and method execution time. You can perform various management tasks by clicking the appropriate links which are grouped under the properties, resources, and security groups.

If you want to drill down into an individual application, click the link to the relevant application on the OC4J home page to get to the OC4J Application home page. Figure 8-8 shows the OC4J Application home page. From an application's

FIGURE 8-8

The OC4J
Application
Home Page

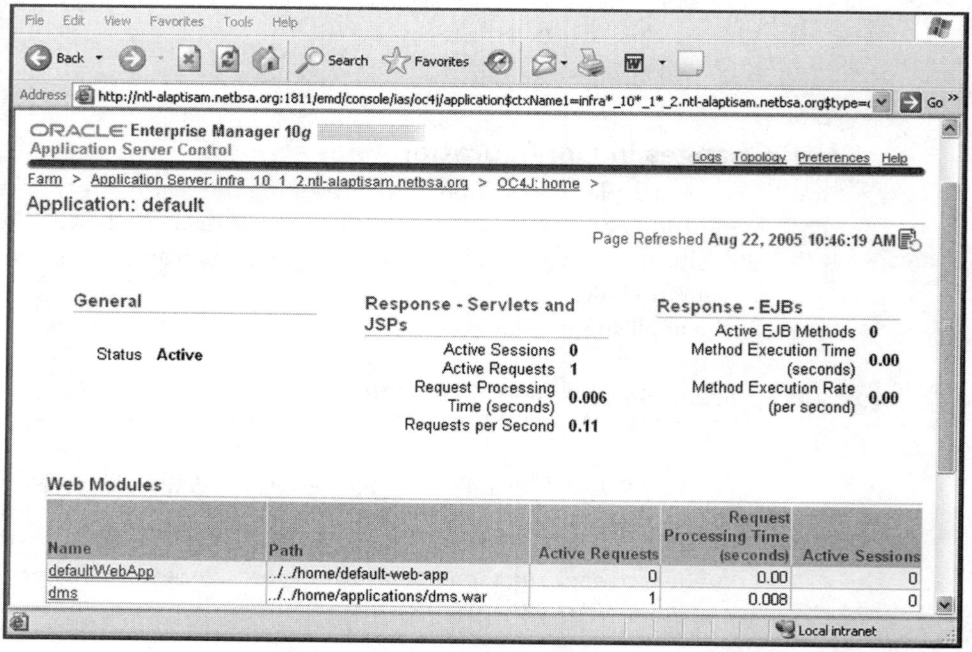

home page, you can monitor the status and performance metrics in the General section, right at the top of the page.

The two important sections in the Application home page are the Web Module and EJB Modules sections, which show the status and performance details about these two types of modules. You can drill down to the home pages of the various components of the two types of modules such as servlets, JSPs, and EJBs from the Web Module and EJB Module home pages.

Deploying and Registering Web Providers

You use Web providers to provide content to OracleAS Portal. Chapter 7 explains how Web and database providers work. Deploying Web providers is similar to deploying J2EE applications, because Web providers are regular J2EE applications. Portlet developers can use EAR files to deploy Web providers to the OracleAS Middle Tier. After you deploy a Web provider, you test the deployment using the URL of the provider adapter server, as shown here:

```
http://hostname:port/context_root/providers
```

If your deployment is successful, you'll see the test page. If you disable the test page, client browsers will get a "403 Forbidden" response.

All Web providers must be registered with the OracleAS Portal, using the OracleAS Portal Web user interface. Registering the providers lets OracleAS Portal know how to access the providers. The portlet developer must provide the portal administrator the necessary deployment and registration instructions.

TWO-MINUTE DRILL

Introduction to J2EE

❑ J2EE is used to build and deploy Web-based applications.

❑ JTI is used by applications deployed in the OracleAS to demarcate transactions.

❑ JNDI is an independent directory service that enables Java applications to access various naming and directory services.

❑ JMS provides a standard messaging API that enables application components to pass data among themselves.

❑ RMI helps distributed applications communicate by invoking procedure calls.

❑ Data sources encapsulate database connections and help provide database connectivity to J2EE applications.

❑ The J2EE Connector Architecture (J2CA) provides a standard architecture for connecting the J2EE platform to non-Java-based enterprise systems.

❑ Servlets are small programs that run on the server and are used to enable dynamic content in Web pages and JSP documents.

❑ JavaBeans are reusable components that implement the functionality needed in J2EE applications.

❑ A J2EE container contains the framework for running EJBs, such as starting an EJB, and provides necessary support services for EJBs.

❑ Enterprise JavaBeans (EJBs) are Java components that implement business logic.

❑ Session EJBs support clients during the execution of their tasks and last for the duration of a session.

❑ Entity EJBs represent an object of data, usually of a persistent nature, such as the table rows in a database.

❑ Entity EJBs can reflect two types of persistence: *container-managed persistence* (CMP) and *bean-managed persistence* (BMP).

❑ Message-driven EJBs represent the integration between the JMS (Java Message Service) and EJBs.

❑ J2EE applications can have three types of application deployment files, also called archives: *JAR* files, *WAR* files, and *EAR* files.

Oracle Containers for Java

❏ OC4J is a set of containers that enable J2EE application deployment.

❏ When you create a new OracleAS instance, you automatically install a set of default OC4J instances, to support the various OracleAS components.

❏ You must use the Oracle Application Server to manage OC4J.

❏ The two command-line tools you can use to manage OC4J instances are the familiar *opmnctl* and *dcmctl* utilities.

Creating an OC4J Instance

❏ The name of the default OC4J instance is *home*.

❏ You can create new OC4J instances with either the *dcmctl* utility or the Application Server Control.

❏ The *dcmctl createComponent* command helps you create a new OC4J instance.

❏ The *ListComponents* command helps you view all OC4J components.

❏ You must start a newly created OC4J instance using the Application Server Control or the *opmnctl* utility.

❏ You use the *destroyInstance* command to clear repository information about a removed OracleAS instance.

Managing the OC4J Instance

❏ The recommended way to manage the OC4J instance is to use the Application Server Control.

❏ To start or stop a single OC4J instance, use the *opmnctl* command with the *ias-component* option.

❏ To start or stop all the OC4J instances in an OracleAS instance, use the *opmnctl* command with the *process-type* option.

❏ Every OC4J instance has a separate OC4J home page in the Application Server Control Console.

❏ You can start and stop an OC4J instance either from the Application Server Control home page or from the OC4J home page.

❏ You can edit the *server.xml* file either by using the Server Properties link on the Administration page or by clicking the Advanced Properties link.

❏ The Website Properties home page lets you specify which Web applications are loaded when you start an OC4J instance.

❏ You can deploy a *.ear* file to a single OC4J instance or to all OC4J instances in a cluster.

❏ You can't directly redeploy an application; you must first undeploy and then deploy the application again.

❏ You use the *dcmctl updateConfig* command to let the OracleAS instance know that you have manually updated the configuration files using the standalone tool *admin.jar*.

Configuring OC4J

❏ An OC4J instance has three types of configuration files: *mod_oc4j* files, server configuration files, and application deployment files.

❏ The default port for the Oracle Web Cache on a UNIX system is 7777.

❏ The *mod_oc4j* module facilitates communication between the Oracle HTTP Server and the OC4J instance.

❏ The *mod_oc4j* module helps to provide transparent failover for clustered OracleAS instances.

❏ The *server.xml* file is the key OC4J server configuration file.

❏ The *server.xml* contains references to other configuration files, including J2EE configuration files.

❏ The *server.xml*, *application.xml*, and the *default-web-site.xml* files together define an application's configuration.

❏ The *default-web-site.xml* file contains the default Web site configuration details.

❏ The *jazn.xml* and *jazn-data.xml* files are used for security configuration, if you're using the Java Authentication and Authorization Service (JAAS).

❏ Logical data source objects are published in the JNDI tree.

❏ Applications retrieve database connections through the java.sql.DataSource objects and look up the objects through the JNDI.

❏ The java.sql.DataSource object specifies the properties and methods of the data source objects.

❏ You use the *data-sources.xml* file to configure the OC4J database sources used by various applications.

❏ An application can also specify data sources at the application level, using the <data-sources> tag in the *application.xml* file.

❏ Each application has a separate JNDI namespace.

❏ Managed data sources are directly managed by OC4J, whereas native data sources are provided by vendors and implement the java.sql.dataSource interface but aren't wrapped by OC4J.

❏ The *principals.xml* file contains user, group, and other security-related information.

❏ Web application modules are contained in WAR files and include servlets and JSP pages.

❏ EJB applications are contained in EAR files and include EJBs.

❏ Client applications (JSPs) are contained in JAR files.

❏ To deploy an application to OC4J, you archive the JAR and WAR files into an EAR file.

❏ Each J2EE application type has two types of OC4J application configuration files: an OC4J specific file (Orion files) and a J2EE deployment descriptor file.

❏ If you don't explicitly create the OC4J-specific deployment file, they'll be automatically created at deployment time.

❏ The J2EE *application.xml* file is the global configuration file for all applications.

❏ Each application has its own local *application.xml* file.

❏ The *orion-application.xml* file is the OC4J-specific global configuration file for all applications.

❏ The *autocreate-tables* and *autodelete-tables* attributes determine whether to automatically create and delete tables for CMP beans.

❏ You must set *autocreate-tables* to false if you want to bind EJBs to existing tables.

❏ The *orion-ejb-jar.xml* file contains the mapping of EJBs to the OC4J server environment.

The OC4J Server Configuration Files

❏ The OC4J *server configuration files* help configure the OC4J server.

❏ The configuration settings in the OC4J configuration files apply directly to the OC4J server and not to the deployed J2EE applications.

❏ The *server.xml* file is the *key OC4J server configuration file*; it contains references to most of the files used by the OC4J server.

❏ The *jazn-data.xml* and the *jazn.xml* files are used for security configuration if you're using the Java Authentication and Authorization (JAAS) Service.

❏ The *data-sources.xml* file lets you configure OC4J database sources used by the various applications hosted by the OC4J instance.

❏ The *principals.xml* file contains user and group information as well as permissions and certificates.

❏ The *rmi.xml* file contains Remote Method Invocation (RMI) configuration information.

❏ The *jms.xml* file contains the OC4J Java Messaging Service (JMS) implementation configuration information.

❏ The *web-site.xml* file contains Web site configuration information.

❏ There are two basic types of application configuration XML files: *J2EE deployment* (configuration) files and an *OC4J-specific* configuration file.

❏ There are four J2EE application types: *EJB, Servlet (Web Modules), JSP,* and *Client.*

❏ Each J2EE application has a J2EE deployment descriptor XML file and an OC4J-specific deployment descriptor XML file.

❏ In addition to the different J2EE deployment XML files, there is also a set of *four common global configuration files* for all types of applications.

Deploying J2EE Applications

❏ Application directory naming conventions must be consistent with the appropriate directory structure for creating necessary JAR, WAR, and EAR files.

❏ You can deploy applications through *dcmctl* or the Application Server Control.

❏ You can also deploy applications by manually editing the configuration files and if you do so, you must run the *dcmctl updateconfig* command to record, in the Metadata Repository, the changes you made.

❏ When you are specifying JNDI locations as part of a data source creation, you must specify the XA and EJB locations only if you plan on having the EJBs use the database for CMP. Otherwise, specify only the Location attribute.

❏ The default data source (OracleDS) is emulated, which means you can connect only to a specific database.

❏ You must use a *non-emulated* data source if the application must access multiple databases.

❏ When you deploy a WAR file for the first time, it's wrapped inside an EAR file.

❏ EJB deployment descriptors are saved in the *ejb-jar.xml* files.

❏ Web providers are regular J2EE applications.

❏ All Web providers must be registered with the OracleAS Portal, using the OracleAS Portal Web user interface.

SELF TEST

1. What is the name of the default OC4J instance?

    A. Home
    B. Default OC4J
    C. OC4J Home
    D. OC4J

2. Which two of the following statements are true, regarding a data source for a J2EE application?

    A. For an emulated data source, you must specify only the ejb-location attribute to look up the data source in the JNDI space.
    B. For a non-emulated data source, you must specify only the value for the location attribute to look up the data source in the JNDI space.
    C. For an emulated data source, you must specify the location, the xa-location, and the ejb-location attributes to look up the data source in the JNDI space.
    D. For a non-emulated data source, you must specify the location, the xa-location, and the ejb-location attributes to look up the data source in the JNDI space.

3. Which of the following *opmnctl* commands would you use to start all the OC4J instances?

    A. `$ opmnctl startproc ias-component=OC4J_HOME`
    B. `$ opmnctl startproc process-type=OC4J_HOME`
    C. `$ opmnctl startproc process-type=OC4J`
    D. `$ opmnctl startproc ias-component=OC4J`

4. Which of the following is the main OC4J configuration file?

    A. *server.xml*
    B. *web.xml*
    C. *oc4j_module*
    D. *application.xml*

5. Which of the following would you use to deploy J2EE applications?

    A. A WAR file
    B. An EAR file
    C. A JAR file
    D. An APP file

6. What is the *mod_oc4j*?

   A. A key configuration file that facilitates communication between the Oracle HTTP Server and the OC4J instance.

   B. A key configuration file that helps configure the Web server.

   C. A module that's a part of the HTTP server and facilitates communication between the HTTP server and the OC4J instance.

   D. A module that's a part of the HTTP server that determines the OC4J configuration settings.

7. Where are data sources published?

   A. Java Naming and Directory Interface

   B. Java.sql.dataSource object

   C. *httpd.conf* file

   D. *server.xml* file

8. Which of the following is the OC4J-specific global configuration file?

   A. *orion-application.xml*

   B. *server.xml*

   C. *application.xml*

   D. *global-application.xml*

9. What happens when you deploy a Web application for the first time?

   A. Its EAR file is wrapped into a JAR file.

   B. Its JAR file is wrapped into a WAR file.

   C. Its WAR file is wrapped into a JAR file.

   D. Its WAR file is wrapped into an EAR file.

10. Which of the following must you do to connect an application to multiple databases?

   A. You must use an emulated data source.

   B. You must use a non-emulated data source.

   C. You must use the default data source.

   D. You must not use the data-sources file at all.

SELF TEST ANSWERS

1. ☑ **A** is correct. The default OC4J instance is named *home*.
    ☒ **B, C,** and **D** are wrong because there are no such default OC4J instances.

2. ☑ **B** and **C** are correct. **B** is correct because you must only specify the location attribute when looking up a non-emulated data source in the JNDI tree. **C** is correct because you must specify all three attributes for emulated data sources, although only the ejb-location attribute is used by the applications, servlets, JSPs, and EJBs.
    ☒ **A** is wrong because you must specify all three attributes for emulated data sources, and **D** is wrong because you must specify only the location attribute for a non-emulated data source.

3. ☑ **C** is correct. The *opmnctl* startproc process-type=OC4J command will start all OC4J instances in an OracleAS instance.
    ☒ **A** is wrong because the *ias-component* option starts only the specified OC4J instance, not all OC4J instances. **B** is wrong because the process-type option can't be used to start a single instance of OC4J. **C** is wrong because the command is missing the process-type option.

4. ☑ **A** is correct. The *server.xml* file is the main OC4J configuration file.
    ☒ **B** is wrong because the *web.xml* file contains the Web configuration information. **C** is wrong because the *oc4j_module* is part of the Oracle HTTP Server configuration, not the OC4J configuration. **D** is wrong because the *application.xml* is the key configuration file for an application, not the OC4J instance.

5. ☑ **B** is correct. You use EAR files to deploy J2EE applications.
    ☒ **A** is wrong because WAR files are used to deploy Web applications, not J2EE applications. **C** is wrong because JAR files are used to deploy client applications only. **D** is wrong because it refers to a nonexistent type of file.

6. ☑ **C** is correct. The *mod_oc4j* module is part of the Oracle HTTP Server, and it is instrumental in facilitating communications between the Web server and the OC4J instance.
    ☒ **A** and **B** are wrong because the *oc4j_module* isn't a configuration file but an HTTP module. **D** is wrong because the *oc4j_module* has nothing to do with the OC4J configuration.

7. ☑ **A** is correct. Data sources are published in the Java Naming and Directory Interface (JNDI).
    ☒ **B, C,** and **D** are the wrong locations for publishing the data sources.

8. ☑ **A** is correct. The OC4J-specific global configuration file is named *orion-application.xml* (all OC4J-specific files have the *orion* prefix in the XML files).

    ☒ **B** is wrong because the *server.xml* file is the main configuration file for the OC4J instance. **C** is wrong because the *application.xml* file is the main J2EE-specific application configuration file. **D** is wrong because it refers to a nonexistent configuration file.

9. ☑ **D** is correct. When you deploy a Web application for the first time, its WAR file is wrapped into an EAR file.

    ☒ **A, B,** and **C** are wrong because they provide the wrong filenames.

10. ☑ **B** is correct. You must use a non-emulated data source to access multiple databases.

    ☒ **A** is wrong because an emulated data source will let you connect only to a single database instance. **C** is wrong because the default data source (OracleDS) is an emulated data source that allows you to connect to just a single Oracle database. **D** is wrong because you must use a datasource file when you're using data sources.

9

OracleAS
Web Cache

CERTIFICATION OBJECTIVE 9.01

Introduction to the OracleAS Web Cache

Application Servers manage a Web site and control access to Web site data. Application Servers respond to requests from client browsers and request the applications on the Web server interface to interact with the database and perform jobs requested by the clients. Peak loads on Web sites could potentially slow down the Web site and led to diminished productivity and lower revenues for the business. One way out of an overloaded application server situation is, of course, to add more servers to the mix, which may or may not help. First of all, you'll spend additional money to set up the Web servers, and second, even the additional servers may be overloaded during peak times. Creating custom Web caching solutions is another way out of this problem, but it's costly and takes time to develop.

Before you delve deeper into the capabilities of the OracleAS Web Cache, it's important to get familiar with a few key definitions. An *origin server* is another term for a regular Web application server. A *proxy server* substitutes for the real server. A proxy server doesn't actually serve the client directly—it channels the client requests to the origin server, or to another proxy server. Proxy servers are useful for setting up a security framework and for caching content. A *reverse proxy server* looks like a regular origin server to the user: actually, however, it serves content by first retrieving the content from a real origin server, thus acting as a kind of a gateway to the origin server. The OracleAS Web Cache acts as a reverse proxy server by intercepting client requests and responding to those requests by retrieving the content from the backend origin servers.

The OracleAS Web Cache is also called a "content-aware" server accelerator. With the Web cache, the origin servers are spared the job of processing a huge number of requests of URLs that are cached in the OracleAS Web Cache. The OracleAS Web Cache also has a much higher cache capacity than legacy proxies and performs much faster than object caches running as part of the application tier.

You can deploy the OracleAS Web Cache on the same machine as the application Web server or on a dedicated server.

The OracleAS Web Cache works as a *server accelerator*, and acts as a virtual server on behalf of the OracleAS instance. The Web cache caches specified Web application server content and passes it to the clients. The Web cache sits in front of the application servers and intercepts HTTP and HTTPS requests from client browsers. The Web cache then provides the cached content of the application servers to the client browsers, if the page contents are already in the cache. If the client browser requests pages that aren't in the cache (a new page) or pages that refer to stale or invalid content, the Web cache sends the requests along to the origin Web server. Once the origin Web server sends the new page content, it's sent to the user through the Web cache again, where the page content is cached. The Web cache thus performs as a virtual server or a reverse proxy server, enhancing the availability, scalability, and performance of Web sites. In addition to the caching features, the Web cache provides load balancing and failover capabilities.

Here are the main features of the OracleAS Web Cache:

e x a m

⍟ a t c h *When a Web page stored in the cache becomes invalid or outdated, the OracleAS Web Cache marks the page for removal.*

e x a m

⍟ a t c h *A Web cache cluster lets the caches read documents from each other, similar to the way the Oracle Real Application Clusters (ORAC) functions, where each database instance is aware of the contents of the other instances' buffer cache.*

- Can run on the same or different host as the application server.
- Caches both static and dynamically generated Web content.
- Supports partial page caching with the help of Edge Side Includes (ESI) technology.
- Provides Web server load-balancing and failover capabilities.
- Includes clustering capabilities.
- Provides compression features to enable faster delivery of large Web files.
- Removes invalid or outdated Web pages automatically.
- Provides HTTP header information (along with cookies), which is used to provide content-aware caching and routing.

- Handles thousands of concurrent connections, unlike the Oracle HTTP server, thus providing scalability and protecting against "denial of service" attacks.

Figure 9-1 shows the OracleAS Web Cache Administration welcome page.

FIGURE 9-1

The OracleAS
Web Cache
Welcome Page

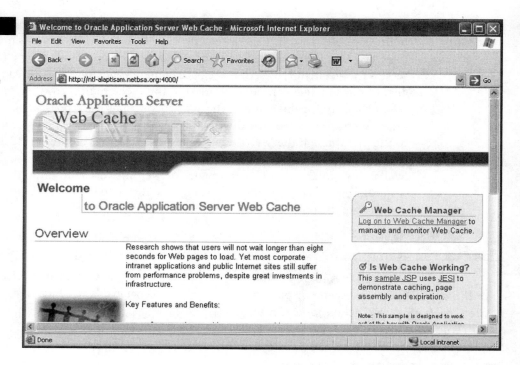

The Reverse Proxy Web Caching Mechanism

When a client browser requests information from a Web site, the OracleAS Web
Cache works as a reverse proxy server and serves the client request. Let's say you
have an OracleAS Web Cache running on the IP address 176.17.15.12 and the
Oracle Application Server's IP address is 176.17.15.14. The sequence of events that
occurs when the client browser contacts the Web site is as follows:

1. The client browser sends a request to www.anycompany.com. The Domain
   Name System accepts the request for the IP address of the Web site.
2. The Domain Name System will return the IP address of the load balancer for
   the Web site, which is assumed to be 176.17.15.10 in our example.
3. The browser will send the request for this page to the load balancer, which
   sends the request on to the OracleAS Web Cache running on 176.17.15.12.
4. If the OracleAS Web Cache has the requested page cached, it will send the
   page content to the client browser.

5. If the OracleAS Web Cache doesn't have the requested page, it has to send the request to the Oracle Application Server at 176.17.15.14. This will also happen if the requested content is stale or invalid.

6. The Oracle Application Server will send the requested content back to the OracleAS Web Cache.

7. The OracleAS Web Cache will send the Web page along to the client browser after first copying and storing the page contents.

Maintaining Consistency and Reliability

In order to maintain consistency between the origin Web server and the Web cache content and thereby increase reliability of the cached content, the OracleAS Web Cache relies on the following four features:

- Invalidation
- Expiration
- HTTP cache validation
- Performance assurance heuristics

Invalidation

When it encounters frequently changing content, the OracleAS Web Cache marks them as *invalid,* to prevent stale data and outdated data from being sent out to the browsers. When a client requests an object marked invalid, the OracleAS Web Cache will refresh the object with fresh content from the origin Web server. You can also remove and refresh invalid objects immediately or base the refresh and removal timing based on the workload of the origin Web server.

Expiration

Expiration policies enable the OracleAS Web Cache to mark an object invalid after it spends a certain predetermined amount of time in the cache. Oracle Corporation recommends that you put in place expiration policies for all cached objects.

HTTP Cache Validation

The OracleAS Web Cache compares validators in the request header and the cached object's response header to check if they are the same, so it can determine if the content is valid.

Performance Assurance Heuristics

If the Web cache indiscriminately invalidates or expires content, you could very well see a deterioration in the performance of your origin Web servers, with users constantly encountering the dreaded "HTTP 503 Server Unavailable" errors. Thus, the Oracle Web Cache will sometimes serve information that's outdated (stale), when the workload is heavy and the origin server doesn't have sufficient time to get the refreshed versions of requested Web pages. The key idea is not that the Web cache will sometimes serve a stale document—but rather, the fact that it will make a smart decision as to whether it can serve a document stale if it has to. The Oracle Web Cache won't serve just any page stale; it uses performance assurance heuristics to decide which objects it can safely serve stale. Following are some of the factors it uses to determine whether it can serve a stale Web document:

- *Validity*   This is based on the expiration and invalidation times.
- *Popularity*   This is based on the total number as well as the number of recent requests for a Web page.
- *Total available capacity of origin servers*   This is based on the difference between the total capacity and the total current load of the origin Web servers.

Of course, if you've configured a Web document to be immediately refreshed upon a change, you don't need to apply any performance heuristics to determine whether you can serve stale versions of that page.

Request and Response Headers

The OracleAS Web Cache uses four types of HTTP request- and response-header fields. The four types are described briefly in the following subsections.

Surrogate-Capability Request-Header Field

The OracleAS Web Cache will attach a Surrogate-Capability request-header field to each object's request message, thus making the applications aware that the content is coming from the Web cache. This applies to all the objects that are requested from the Web cache.

Server Response-Header Field

The OracleAS Web Cache attaches *diagnostic information* to the Server response-header field of the HTTP response messages for all objects sent to a browser.

Surrogate-Control Response-Header Field

This is a key response-header field, because it lets application developers *override the caching rules* that they have set (say, through the Application Server Control or the OracleAS Web Cache Manager), with their own custom caching rules.

Surrogate-Key Response-Header Field

Application developers can use the Surrogate-Key response-header field to specify search-key strings, which can be used as additional criteria for invalidation of content. The Web Cache administrator can use these search-key strings along with the URL of the objects as invalidation criteria.

Compression

The OracleAS Web Cache can compress various types of Web content. You can enable compression either through the OracleAS Web Cache Manager or by incorporating a *compress* control directive in the Surrogate-Control response-header field. Certain types of files (e.g., GIF files) are not compressed, to ensure that they appear correctly in the browser. Compression decreases latency, which is the time taken to make network round trips. Because compressed objects are small, they need less time to make network round trips. The average compression ratio is a factor of 4, meaning a 400Kb file will be compressed to just 100Kb.

on the job

Compressing Web content leads to a reduction in network latency.

OracleAS Web Cache Ports

The default HTTP protocol port for OracleAS Web Cache is port 7777 on UNIX and port 80 on Windows systems. If port 7777 is already taken, the installer will allocate an alternative port in the range 7777–7877. Port 7777 is the default port for client requests, whether they are HTTP or HTTPS. The OracleAS Web Cache uses other listening ports for administration, invalidation, and statistics monitoring requests. The port numbers for these HTTP protocol–based listening ports have to be within the range 9400–9499. The following are the defaults for the management-related port numbers:

Whenever you change the
OracleAS Web Cache configuration, you
must restart the OracleAS Web Cache
processes (the admin server process and
the cache server process). Remember that
all cached content will be wiped out when
you shut down the OracleAS Web Cache.

■ Administration requests use port 9400.

■ Invalidation requests use port 9401.

■ Statistics monitoring requests use
port 9402.

Caching Principles

The OracleAS Web Cache sits in front of the
application server and services client requests
for Web pages by storing the pages in its cache.
However, this doesn't mean that the Web cache
indiscriminately stores all of a Web site's content and continues to serve those same
pages forever. The OracleAS Web Cache determines how long to cache documents,
based on *caching rules* and *expiration policies*. After you configure the OracleAS
Web Cache with a set of cacheability rules or a document, that document isn't
automatically placed in the cache. The document goes into the cache only after the
first request for it from a user's browser. Upon the first request, because the document
isn't in the cache, the OracleAS Web Cache sends the request on to the Application
Web server. Subsequent requests for the document will be served from the OracleAS
Web Cache itself.

Static Web content is typically an HTML file that doesn't change—the same
Web page is served repeatedly to all requestors. Thus, the Web server can safely
cache static Web pages without problems. The content of a dynamic Web page, on
the other hand, can change, whether due to user-initiated changes sent through a
Web form for example, or to database-generated changes (say, additions or deletions
to an online store's catalog). Thus dynamic content means that the same URL
(from the same user or from different users) might require different results, because
of different parameters or perhaps because the data has changed. So, while you can
cache dynamic pages (as far as the Web cache is concerned, they are just pages
identified by a URL), due to their very nature, you'll most likely not want to cache
them for long periods of time, unlike static Web pages.

Let's discuss some of the important principles relating to how Web content is
cached by the OracleAS Web Cache.

Cacheability Rules

Only content that's specified for caching using *cacheability rules* is cached for
subsequent requests.

Invalidation and Expiration of Content

Cached content becomes irrelevant over time as a result of changes in the origin server's content. By using an invalidation mechanism, you mark cached documents as invalid when you decide they should be refreshed. When browsers request documents marked invalid, the Web cache will try to refresh them immediately. If the Web server is very busy, in order to prevent performance degradation due to a heavy cache invalidation or expiration, the Web cache continues to serve the stale documents until they can be refreshed by the Application server. Using an expiration mechanism, you can automate the document-invalidation mechanism after the stale documents stay for a specified length of time in the Web cache.

Dynamically Generated Content

As mentioned previously in this chapter, caching static documents is a trivial task compared to the caching of dynamic Web content. Dynamically generated Web content includes pages representing product catalogs and search results, both of which can be dynamically modified as a result of changes made by the user. You use technologies such as Java Server Pages (JSP), Active Server Pages (ASP), PERL, servlets, PHP, and Common Gateway Interface (CGI), to design dynamic Web applications.

Invalidation of cached content is especially critical in the context of dynamically generated Web pages. For dynamically generated Web content, it's important the Web server and the client have some means of sharing session information so that the cached content can be invalidated or refreshed as necessary. The OracleAS Web Cache recognizes several methods of sharing information and caches dynamically generated Web pages on the basis of information passed through these methods which are as follows:

- Using session cookies
- Embedding parameters in the URLs
- Embedding parameters in the POST body

The client browser and the origin server exchange session and category information with the help of cookies or embedded parameters in the URLs or the POST body.

A *cookie* is a string of text that the Web server stores on the client machine to help identify the client visiting a Web site. A session cookie is a cookie that enables Web sites to track user sessions, thus maintaining state in the essentially stateless

HTTP environment. Cookies enable the Web server to correlate a particular client with the Web page requested, thus letting the Web server serve appropriate content to the user. Session tracking devices such as cookies are extremely useful in the context of applications that make use of shopping carts and other such online devices. When the client first requests a page from the Web server, a cookie is sent by the server and stored in the client's file system. A cookie is of this general format:

```
Cookie:cookie=value
```

For example, this cookie identifies a username:

```
username=salapati
```

When clients send subsequent requests to the Web server, the request will contain the cookie name/value pair in the Cookie request-header field of the request.

Instead of using cookies stored on the user's machine, the Web server can use embedded parameter information in the URLs to identify the user. The OracleAS Web Cache can use either cookies or the parameters in the URLs to identify and cache multiple versions of documents and personalized attributes, in addition to session information.

As mentioned previously, efficient invalidation mechanisms are critical to the serving of dynamically changing Web content. The OracleAS Web Cache uses different *mechanisms* to ascertain the validity of dynamically generated Web pages by checking the content of the source origin server that generated the pages. The three important mechanisms that enable the serving of dynamic pages are as follows:

- Personalized attributes
- Multiple document versions
- Session information

Note that any one of the three session-tracing devices mentioned earlier — session cookies, embedded URL parameters, or embedded parameters in the POST body — can be used with the three mechanisms that enable dynamic content. These three important mechanisms are reviewed in the following subsections.

Personalized Attributes Using personalized attributes enables the OracleAS Web Cache to use common pages for multiple users, by employing categorization. Essentially the same Web page is served to multiple users, with values of personalized attributes being substituted for different clients. When the initial request comes in, it sets the personalized attribute cookie or URL or POST body parameters, which are then used to serve cached content for all subsequent requests for the page with identical cookie attributes or parameters. It's common for Web pages to use personalized greetings or icons on Web pages. The OracleAS Web Cache HTML tags <!--WEBCACHETAG--> and <!--WEBCACHEEND--> help mark the personalized attribute information on Web pages. The OracleAS Web Cache processes these tags by using cookies, embedded URL parameters, or POST body parameters to substitute the values for personalized attributes.

When the first request for the page comes in, the OracleAS Web Cache gets it from the origin server and caches it. The Web cache also processes the WEBCACHETAG tags and gets ready to substitute the values for various personalized attributes, based on the cookie values or parameters sent through URL (GET) or POST requests. Later requests for that page will receive personalized versions of the same page from the OracleAS Web Cache, based on their session cookie or parameter values.

Multiple Document Versions   The OracleAS Web Cache follows caching rules for pages with multiple versions of the same Web page. The OracleAS Web Cache can create multiple versions of a document by using either of the two methods discussed in the following paragraphs.

Different cookie-value combinations   When a browser makes the initial request, the OracleAS Web Cache sends the request to the origin server, which includes a Set-Cookie response header as part of its response to the browser, as shown here:

The OracleAS Web Cache doesn't cache the Set-Cookie response-header field.

```
Set-Cookie:cookie=value
```

The browser stores this cookie/value combination and issues it the next time it makes a request:

```
Cookie:cookie=value
```

If the cookie/value pair in the browser's request header matches the cookie/value pair in the response header that was last received, the OracleAS Web Cache will cache the response. The OracleAS Web Cache will then use the cookie's value to serve the correct version of the multi-version document to the browser.

For example, an online store can show an identical page displaying various products to its regular customers and the customers who receive preferential treatment based on some criteria. You can do this using values of the cookies for a page, or the HTTP request headers for that page. For example, you serve multiple versions of a welcome page for a company (http://www.mycompany.com/welcome.htm) to different categories of users, such as employees, general customers, and suppliers. You simply configure the OracleAS Web Cache to recognize a cookie with the name user_type, which will have three possible values: employees, general_customers, and suppliers. This will enable the OracleAS Web Cache to cache three different versions (you must create the three versions beforehand) of the welcome page.

Here's an example showing multiple versions of the same URL. Once you configure the OracleAS Web Cache to recognize the cookie user_type, it can cache all three versions of the URL http://www.testhost.com/page1.htm.

```
http://www.testhost.com/page1.htm. user_type=Customer
http://www.testhost.com/page1.htm. user_type=Employer
http://www.testhost.com/page1.htm. user_type=Management
```

Different HTTP request headers for the pages   You can also configure caching rules using HTTP request headers instead of cookies. HTTP request headers enable browsers to specify more information about their request as well as about themselves, enabling the OracleAS Web Cache to select the correct version of the URL to serve to that browser.

A client can use an HTTP request-header field to pass information about itself. You can configure the OracleAS Web Cache to serve the appropriate version of a URL, such as a welcome page, based on the value of the information in the request header. As an example, the User-Agent request header contains information about the Web browser making a request, as shown here:

```
User-Agent: Mozilla/4.61 [en] (WinNT; U)
```

As another example, the Accept header specifies acceptable media types, as shown here:.

```
Accept: image/gif, image/x-xbitmap, image/jpeg, image/pjpeg, image/png, */*
```

Session Information   A Web site can track user sessions by using unique *session IDs*, by including a Set-Cookie response header when it responds to a browser's initial request to establish a session. Origin servers can also track sessions by including the session value in an embedded URL parameter (using the GET method) or using the POST method, wherein the session values are embedded in the POST body. Using one of these parameters, the origin server can then track the browser's session. If the Web server isn't tracking the sessions with cookies, it will compare the client's request headers with the Web server's response header to determine the session.

Whether the origin servers use cookies, embedded URL parameters, or POST body parameters, the OracleAS Web Cache can be configured to perform the following functions:

Exclude embedded URL or POST body parameters   When a request contains embedded URLs or POST body parameters, each URL appears to be distinct, thus forcing the OracleAS Web Cache to cache all these "distinct" URLs. By excluding the value of these embedded URL or POST parameters, the OracleAS Web Cache can serve identical pages to multiple sessions. Here's an example that shows the POST body for the same Web page for two users:

```
User 1:
section=999
&session_ID=1234
User 2:
section=999
&session_ID=5678
```

As you can see, only the value of SESSION_ID parameter is different in the POST body. You can then configure the OracleAS Web Cache to ignore the value of the SESSION_ID parameter, thus ensuring that the same object can be cached for both the users, instead of caching separate pages for each of them.

Substitute session information in session-encoded URLs   Session-encoded URLs are specified by using tags such as <A HREF = . . . > to embed session information inside HTML pages. The session-encoded URLs help distinguish between users and result in varying responses from the origin server for different sessions. The OracleAS Web Cache can use session values from cookies, embedded URL parameters, or POST body parameters to substitute the session value contained within the session-encoded URLs. By configuring the OracleAS Web Cache to substitute session information in this way, combined with the ability to exclude embedded parameters as discussed in the preceding paragraph, the OracleAS Web Cache succeeds in caching the same object for multiple sessions, even when the session-encoded URL session parameters are different for each session.

Edge Side Includes and Partial Page Caching

The OracleAS Web Cache uses both cacheable and noncacheable Web page fragments to dynamically assemble Web pages. The OracleAS Web Cache uses Edge Side Includes (ESI), which employs a markup language similar to XML, to dynamically assemble Web page fragments. A Web page is divided into several fragments, each with a possibly different caching profile. The Web cache will then independently cache each of the fragments as a separate element in the page, instead of caching the entire Web page as a single element. When the end user requests the Web page, the OracleAS Web Cache will assemble the fragments into HTML pages. Using the new ESI standard, the edge server caches the common elements of a Web page and asks the database only for personalized information related to a page request. This ability to cache fragments of a Web page is called *partial page caching*. Thus, several users can use the same common elements that are cached, thus eliminating the need to store individual pages for each of them, covering virtually identical content. Based on the information provided through the request headers or through cookies, the Web pages are assembled on a customized basis. The end result is that the OracleAS Web Cache has fewer copies of Web pages to cache and invalidate, thus enabling it to cache and serve a much larger amount of HTML content with the same or fewer resources.

Page Assembly

Developers use a template page (configured with ESI tags) containing fragments, to create content for partial-page caching. Fragments are simply HTML files containing text and other elements. The templates consists of common elements such as logos and navigation bars ("look and feel" page elements), and the fragments represent the dynamic sections of the Web page. Template pages are associated with URLs requested by the users. ESI markup tags in the template page configuration tell the OracleAS Web Cache which HTML fragments to include in the Web page.

Note that each page fragment may have its own caching policy, and the fragments are stored as distinct elements inside the OracleAS Web Cache. You may also have some types of fragments that can never be cached—for example, a user's bank account information.

The following is a simple example of how ESI markup tags are used to include HTML page fragments inside a page:

```
<H3>Today's News</h3>
<esi:comment text='' Shows the HTML Source with ESI tags.'' /><esi:choose>
    <esi:when test="$(Profile{PersonalInterests}) == 'Sports'">
      <H4>Sport News</H4>
      <esi:include src="/SportNews.jsp?sessionID=$(QUERY_STRING{sessionID})" />
    </esi:when>
    <esi:when test="$(Profile{PersonalInterests}) == 'Career'">
      <H4>Financial News</H4>
      <esi:include src="/FinancialNews.jsp?sessionID=$(QUERY_STRING{sessionID})"
/>
    </esi:when>
    <esi:otherwise>
      <H4>General News</H4>
      <esi:include src="/DefaultNews.jsp?sessionID=$(QUERY_STRING{sessionID})" />
    </esi:otherwise>
</esi:choose>
```

The ESI example shown here illustrates the use of some common ESI tags. You'll notice that this particular ESI markup opens with the <esi:choose> tag and ends with the </esi:choose) tag. The <esi:choose> tag lets you perform conditional processing, as shown by the use of the <esi:when> and <esi:otherwise> tags inside our example text. Similarly, the <esi:include> tag lets you include an HTML fragment (a file). The <esi:comment> tag lets you specify comments for informational purposes. You can also use the <esi:inline> tag (not shown in our example) to specify fragments as separately cacheable, embedded in the HTTP response of other objects. By the way, the example shown belongs to an online newspaper; it specifies that the Sports News section be shown to those viewers of the newspaper whose profile indicates they're interested in sports. It specifies that the Financial News page be shown to users who have indicated "career" in their profiles, and finally, it specifies that the General News sections be shown to all other viewers.

CERTIFICATION OBJECTIVE 9.02

OracleAS Web Cache Management

You use several tools to manage the OracleAS Web Cache, among which are the Oracle Application Server Control and the *opmnctl* utility. The Oracle Application Server enables you to monitor and configure several aspects of the Web cache. Here are some of the important tasks you can perform using the Application Server Control:

- Configuring the OracleAS Web Cache
- Monitoring the Web cache status
- Monitoring the origin server status
- Starting and stopping the OracleAS Web Cache
- Configuring sites and origin servers and mapping the sites to hosts
- Invalidating content
- Configuring cache expiration policies

watch *You can use the opmnctl command-line utility or the Oracle Application Server Control to start and stop (and restart) the OracleAS Web Cache processes.*

The OracleAS Web Cache Manager is another GUI tool that lets you manage virtually all aspects of the OracleAS Web Cache.

Default Oracle Web Cache Users

There are two default OracleAS Web Cache users: *administrator* and *invalidator*. The administrator account represents the main administrative user and it is used to configure, start, and stop the Web cache. In addition, you use the administrator account to send invalidation requests and monitor statistics. The invalidator user account is used exclusively to send invalidation requests.

Using opmnctl

You use the command-line tool *opmnctl*, which as explained in Chapter 3, starts and stops the OracleAS Web Cache processes.

You use the *opmnctl* command with the status option to check whether the Web cache processes are running, as shown here (the status column will show *alive* for a running Web cache process):

```
$ opmnctl status
Processes in Instance: portwire.ntl-alaptisam.netbsa.org
------------------+--------------------+---------+---------
ias-component     | process-type       |     pid | status
------------------+--------------------+---------+---------
LogLoader         | logloaderd         |     N/A | Down
DSA               | DSA                |     N/A | Down
HTTP_Server       | HTTP_Server        |    5352 | Alive
dcm-daemon        | dcm-daemon         |    5424 | Alive
WebCache          | WebCache           |    2840 | Alive
WebCache          | WebCacheAdmin      |    2924 | Alive
OC4J              | home               |    5248 | Alive
OC4J              | OC4J_Portal        |    9252 | Alive
wireless          | performance_server |    5784 | Alive
wireless          | messaging_server   |    8120 | Alive
wireless          | OC4J_Wireless      |    7064 | Alive
$
```

Note that under the ias-component Web cache, there are two components—*webcache* and *webcacheadmin*—that are different processes. The *webcacheadmin* component is in charge of managing the administrative interface and provides configuration and monitoring capabilities. The *webcache* component is for the cache server process, and it manages the Web cache itself through request processing and connection pooling. The two processes, WebCache and WebCacheAdmin, are independent. Although the WebCacheAdmin process may be running, you can't submit invalidation requests without starting the WebCache process.

When you modify the OracleAS Web Cache configuration, you must restart both OracleAS Web Cache processes. For example, you can change the OracleAS Web Cache administrator password using the Security page in the Application Server Control. Once you change the password, you must restart the cache server and the admin server processes using *opmnctl*, as shown here (you may also use the *webcachectl* restart command for standalone Web cache installations):

```
$ opmnctl restartproc ias-component=WebCache
```

on the **job**

The WebCacheAdmin (administration server process) manages the administrative interface, and the WebCache (cache server process) actually manages the cache.

Note that the command shown here uses the *ias-component* and not the process-type attribute. Thus, both the OracleAS admin server and the cache server processes are restarted together.

To start and stop the two OracleAS Web Cache processes together, use the following two commands:

```
$ opmnctl startproc ias-component=WebCache
$ opmnctl stopproc ias-component=WebCache
```

To start and stop a single component, you use the *process-type* attribute, in addition to the *ias-component* attribute, as shown here:

```
$ opmnctl startproc ias-component=WebCache process-type=WebCache
$ opmnctl startproc ias-component=WebCache process-type=WebCacheAdmin
$ opmnctl stopproc ias-component=WebCache process-type=WebCache
$ opmnctl stopproc ias-component=WebCache process-type=WebCacheAdmin
```

e x a m

ⓦ a t c h

You can't use the Restart option in the Application Server Control (cache operations page) to restart the WebCacheAdmin component after you make a configuration change. You must use the opmnctl tool to restart the process. If you have a standalone OracleAS Web Cache installation, you must use the webcachectl command-line utility to start and stop the Web cache.

Using the Application Server Control

You can also use the Application Server Control to start and stop the OracleAS Web Cache, although the preferred way to perform those tasks is to use the *opmnctl* utility. In order to start and stop the OracleAS Web Cache through the Application Server Control, go to the System Components table and click the Start, Stop, or Restart buttons. In addition, you can start and stop the OracleAS Web Cache from the home page of the OracleAS Web Cache.

Once you start the OracleAS Web Cache (either both processes or at least the WebCacheAdmin process), you can use Application Server Control to access the Web cache; you can also use it as the primary tool to manage the OracleAS Web Cache. Figure 9-2 shows the OracleAS Web Cache home page, which you can

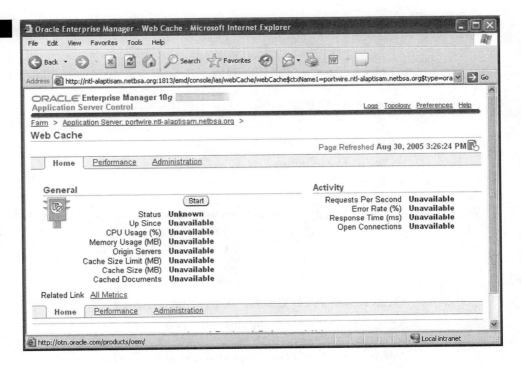

FIGURE 9-2

The OracleAS
Web Cache
Home Page

access from the System Components table in the Application Server Control
home page.

OracleAS Web Cache Home Page

Note that in addition to using the *opmnctl* utility, you can also start and stop the
OracleAS Web Cache from its home page (you may also start and stop the Web
cache by clicking the OracleAS Web Cache link in the System Components table
on the Application Server home page and using the Start/Stop buttons). Besides
starting and stopping the Web cache, the Web cache home page lets you monitor
OracleAS Web Cache performance as well as the caching activity level. The Web
cache home page contains two sections: General and Activity. The General section
shows the following types of information:

- OracleAS Web Cache status
- Web cache size and limit
- Number of cached documents

- Memory usage
- CPU usage

The Activity section of the home page shows the following types of data:

- Requests per second
- Data served
- Open connections
- Active sessions
- Errors per second

The OracleAS Web Cache home page contains two tabs—Administration and Performance—which take you to the OracleAS Web Cache Administration page and the OracleAS Web Cache Performance page, respectively. Let's look at these key pages in detail.

OracleAS Web Cache Administration Page

Using the Web Cache Administration page, you can perform tasks such as configuring the initial cache setup properties, invalidating cached content, and establishing rollover times for event and access log files. There are four links on this page:

- You can invalidate cache content or rollover log files using the Operations link.
- To configure cache clusters, use the Cluster Properties link.
- To modify OracleAS Web Cache configuration, use the Web Cache Properties link.
- To modify the application environment, use the Application Properties link.

There are two key OracleAS Web Cache configuration files—*webcache.xml* and *internal.xml*—both located in the $ORACLE_HOME/webcache directory. The *webcache.xml* file is for configuring the OracleAS Web Cache (all configuration changes made through the OracleAS Web Cache Manager become a part of the *webcache.xml* file), and the *internal.xml* file is for internal settings of the Web cache. The *webcache.xml* file contains configuration information such as passwords, listener addresses, site-server mappings, and rules. When you use either the Application Server Control or the Web Cache Manager to configure the OracleAS Web Cache, the *webcache.xml* file is automatically modified. You mustn't edit either of these files directly, unless you're asked to do so by the Oracle Support Services personnel.

OracleAS Web Cache Performance Page

The OracleAS Web Cache Performance page lets you evaluate the efficiency of OracleAS Web Cache and provides the following key performance metrics:

- Documents currently being served by the OracleAS Web Cache per second (current)
- Percentage of objects currently being served by the OracleAS Web Cache per second (current requests)
- Average number of objects served per second since the OracleAS Web Cache was started (average)

From the Performance page, you can navigate to the following areas:

- Web site statistics
- Requests for Web cache content
- Origin server performance
- Popular requests
- Error information, including network errors and "site busy" errors
- Metrics related to cache hits and cache misses
- Compression metrics

Standalone Configuration Management Tools

If you install the OracleAS Web Cache not as part of the OracleAS instance, but separately as a standalone installation, you can't use the Application Server Control or *opmnctl* to manage it. You must use either the OracleAS Web Cache Manager or the *webcachectl* utility to manage the standalone OracleAS Web Cache instance.

The OracleAS Web Cache Manager

You can use the OracleAS Web Cache Manager to configure and monitor the OracleAS Web Cache, as well as the Web sites that are being cached by the Web cache. Using the OracleAS Web Cache Manager, which is a GUI tool, you can do the following:

- Start and stop the OracleAS Web Cache.
- Configure the Web cache.
- Configure caching rules.

■ Monitor Web cache performance.

■ Configure origin servers and sites.

■ Invalidate cached content.

■ Rollover log files.

You log into the OracleAS Web Cache Manager using the following link:

```
http://your_SiteName:port/webcacheadmin
```

The port number will be listed in the $ORACLE_HOME/install/portlist.ini file in the following format:

```
Web Cache Administration port = 4006
```

On the OracleAS Web Cache Manager home page, you'll see a navigation bar on the left with various links. When you click any of the links, the content will be displayed on the right. Following are the groups in which the links are organized:

■ *Operations* includes cache operations and content invalidation.

■ *Monitoring* includes Web cache and origin server statistics, health monitor, popular requests, and end-user performance analysis.

■ *Properties* include security, auto-restart, network timeouts, resource limits, and clustering.

■ *Logging and diagnostics* includes links to event and access logs and diagnostic logs.

■ *Ports* include listening ports and operations ports.

■ *Origin servers, sites, and load balancing* include links to origin servers, site definitions, and site-to-site mapping.

■ *Rules for caching, personalization, and compression* include caching and compression rules, expiration policy definitions, session definitions, and cookie definitions.

■ *Rule association* includes links such as compression and expression policy association and cookie and header association.

Using the webcachectl Utility

You must use the *opmnctl* utility to manage an OracleAS Web Cache that's installed as part of OracleAS. If you're running the OracleAS Web Cache as a standalone instance, use the *webcachectl* utility to start and stop the OracleAS Web Cache processes.

CERTIFICATION OBJECTIVE 9.03

OracleAS Web Cache Administration Tasks

The OracleAS Web Cache administrator performs configuration and administration tasks relating to the OracleAS Web Cache.

Modifying Security Settings

As explained earlier, two default users come with the OracleAS Web Cache installation: *administrator* and *invalidator*. Both of these have passwords that you specify during the installation. You can change the administrator password in the following way:

- Click the Administration page in the OracleAS Web Cache home page.
- On the Administration page, click the Security link under the Properties => Web cache section.
- You can change either or both the administrator and invalidator user' passwords by entering a new password for them. Click **OK** after entering the new password. You must restart the Web cache using *opmnctl* commands for the new passwords to take effect. Figure 9-3 shows that the password was successfully changed.

When you modify the configuration of any of the following items, you must restart both the *cache* server and the *admin* server:

- Administration port properties
- Administrator password
- Trusted subnets
- User and group ID information

Configuring Listening Ports

By default, the OracleAS Web Cache will use port 7777 to listen for HTTP requests. Of course, if this port is already in use, the installer will assign a different port number. You can also assign ports by using the Application Server Control's Administration page. On this page, click the Ports link to go to the Ports page.

FIGURE 9-3

Changing the
Administrator
Password

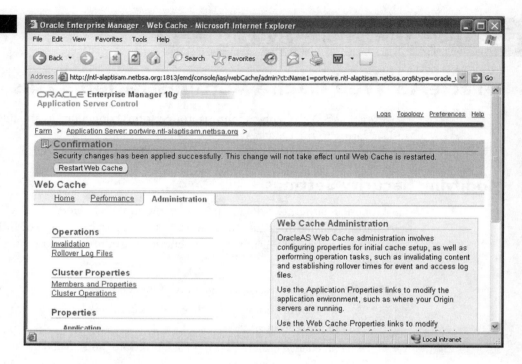

In the Ports page, you can modify two types of port settings:

■ *Listen ports*   Listen Ports are the ports that the OracleAS Web Cache uses for
incoming browser requests. As mentioned previously, the default listen port
for the OracleAS Web Cache is 7777. You can modify the port settings or add
additional ports for listening.

■ *Operation ports*   Operation ports are used for receiving non-browser requests and
are mainly used for administrative, invalidation, and monitoring-related requests.
Unless there's a port conflict, you don't have to change the operation ports.
Following are the default HTTP port numbers for these request types:

  ■ Port 4000 is used for requests made to the administrative listener and from
  the Application Server Control.

  ■ Port 4001 is used for invalidation requests.

  ■ Port 4002 is used for statistics monitoring requests.

Configuring Site Definitions

A *site* in the OracleAS Web Cache context is composed of a server and a port number. Each site has its own caching rules, error pages, and aliases. By defining a site in a particular way, you affect how the OracleAS Web Cache forwards requests to an origin server. You can have the following *two types of sites* when you're using the OracleAS Web Cache:

- *Virtual host site*   The OracleAS Web Cache hosts all virtual host sites and supplies the cached content from these sites in response to user requests. In addition, the OracleAS Web Cache is capable of assembling ESI fragments from the virtual host sites.

- *ESI provider site*   An ESI provider site is meant exclusively for assembling ESI fragments by the OracleAS Web Cache. Users can't connect these sites to request Web content.

You can create a new site or edit an existing one, using the Create or Edit Named Sites page, shown in Figure 9-4.

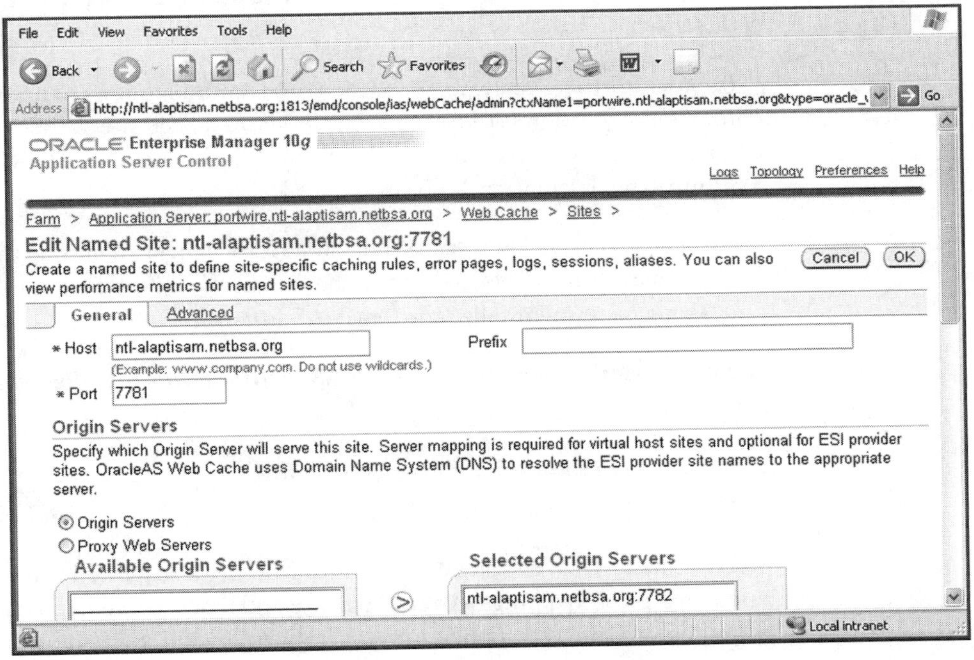

FIGURE 9-4 The Create or Edit Named Sites Page

You must specify the origin server that will serve the new site you're creating if you're using a virtual host site. For an ESI provider site, server mapping is optional.

Specifying Origin Server Settings

The Oracle AS Web Cache tries to serve a browser request first from its own cache. If it fails to find the necessary document in its cache—that is, if there's a cache miss—the request is routed to the Web server from which the OracleAS Web Cache gets the original content, also known as the *origin server*. One of the major OracleAS Web Cache administrative tasks is to configure the location of the origin servers. The OracleAS Web Cache uses the origin server to send all requests for internal sites. For external sites that are protected by firewalls, the OracleAS Web Cache uses *proxy servers*. You must configure origin servers to serve such objectives as load balancing, failover, and site-to-site mappings.

You can configure the origin servers from the Origin Servers home page, which you access by clicking the Origin Servers link in the OracleAS Web Cache Administration page.

on the **j o b**   ***An origin server could be either an application Web server or a proxy Web server.***

In order for the OracleAS Web Cache to forward requests to an origin server (or a proxy server), you must first map that server to a Web site. When a user sends in a request for a document, the OracleAS Web Cache uses the following attributes to determine the destination Web site:

- The request's *Host request-header field* (If the request is missing the Host request-header field, it's sent to the default Web site, which is the computer on which you installed the OracleAS instance.)

on the **j o b**   ***The computer on which the OracleAS instance was installed serves as the default site.***

- The *Host* specified in the requested URL
- The *arc* attribute of the ESI tag

The OracleAS Web Cache determines whether a requested site is supported, based on a prior mapping between that site and a host server. You can create an origin server using the application server, by following these steps:

1. Go the OracleAS Web Cache home page and click Administration.
2. Under the Properties => Application section, click the Origin Servers link.
3. In the Origin Servers page, you can view and modify the origin server settings. Click the Create button to create a new origin server.
4. The Create or Edit Origin Server page will appear next. Figure 9-5 shows the Create or Edit Origin Servers page.
5. At the top of the Create or Edit Origin Server page, you specify *general settings* for the new origin server:

   - Host
   - Port
   - Protocol
   - Capacity (maximum number of connections)
   - Routing Enabled (determines whether the OracleAS Web Cache routes requests to this server)

FIGURE 9-5

The Create or Edit Origin Server Page

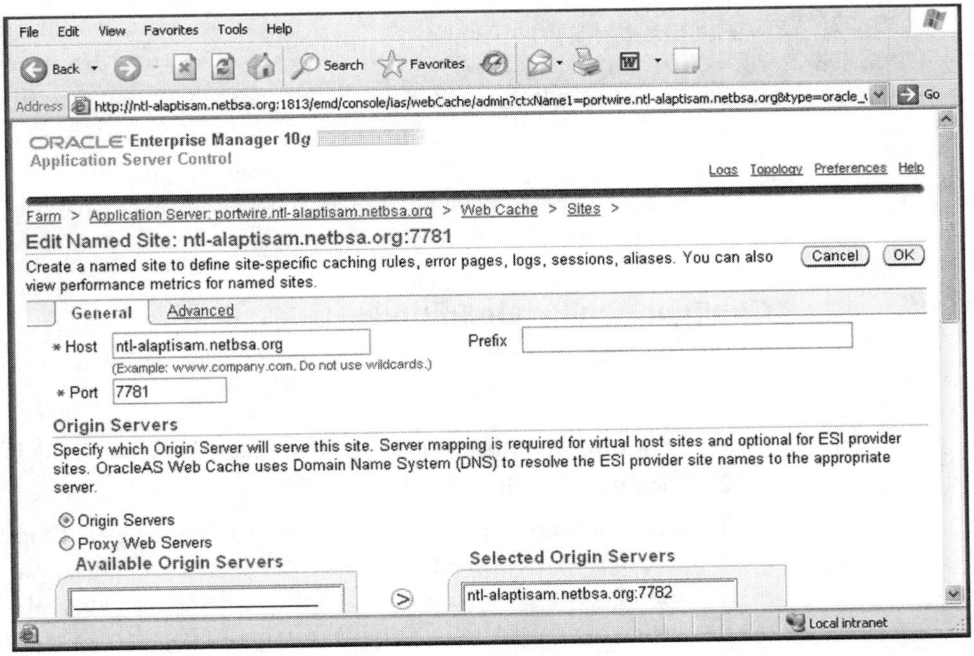

6. Next, you specify the *Failover* configuration, so the OracleAS Web Cache knows how often to ping a failed origin server.. Here are the failover parameters:

■ *Failover threshold* This specifies the number of failed contact attempts before declaring the server "down."

■ *Ping URL* The URL the OracleAS Web Cache must periodically ping until the server is up.

■ *Ping frequency* This determines how often the OracleAS Web Cache should ping the failed Web server.

If there are any external sites behind a firewall, you must also provide the username and password for the proxy server.

Types of Site Definitions

Broadly speaking, you have two types of site definitions:

■ *Named Site Definitions* These are known sites supported by the OracleAS Web Cache; and they define sites and their mappings to origin servers.

■ *Server Mappings for Unnamed Site* These are mappings to origin servers for sites that don't match any named virtual host

The OracleAS Web Cache will forward requests to an origin server only if you map the server to a Web site.

sites. The Server Mappings for Unnamed Site is an ordered list of hosts and ports. The first match is selected as the candidate site from this ordered list.

Configuring Site Definitions

You can use the Oracle Application Server to configure site definitions. Here are the steps you must follow to configure a new site:

1. Click the Administration tab in the OracleAS Web Cache home page.

2. Click the Sites link under the Properties => Application section.

3. In the Sites home page, you can configure Named Sites Definitions, Server mappings for Unnamed Site, as well as default and global settings for session binding, error pages, among other things. Because your goal is to create a named site, click the Create button under the Named Sites Definitions section.

4. You have to configure various things for the new site under the following tabs:

   ■ *General*   Here you specify the host name and port number.

   ■ *Origin servers*   You must specify the origin server or proxy server that will serve this site. As mentioned previously, when configuring a virtual host site, this is mandatory, whereas it's optional for ESI provider sites.

   ■ *Aliases*   You need to specify all the aliases for the site so that the OracleAS Web Cache can cache content for requests made to the named site and all its aliases as well.

   ■ *Error pages*   When the OracleAS Web Cache can't provide the requested content, it must return an error page instead. You must specify the following error pages, depending on what caused the error:

      ■ Network Error page

      ■ Site Busy Error page

      ■ ESI Default Fragment Server Error page

If you don't specify site-specific error pages for each error type, the default error pages are served instead.

If you don't specify your own error pages in the OracleAS Web Cache, the user is served the default error page. It's a good idea to set up your own error pages, so your Web site problems don't have to be exposed to the users. For example, it's common to return a 4004 error (indicating a user error) rather than the 500 error that's caused when the HTTP Server is too busy.

Using OracleAS Diagnostic Tools

You can use either the Application Server Control or the Web Cache Manager to view the contents of the Web cache—for example, to determine which are the most popular page requests. You can generate a list of all URLs currently in the Web cache. You can also generate a list of the most popular URL requests depending on their recentness and frequency. You can further classify the list according to whether the objects were cached or not cached by the Web cache. You can list the popular requests by following these steps:

   ■ Go to the OracleAS Web Cache home page and click the Performance tab.

   ■ In the Performance page, click the Popular Requests link.

Figure 9-6 shows the Popular Requests table, showing the most popular requests since the OracleAS Web Cache was started. The page ranks various URLs by the

FIGURE 9-6

The Popular
Requests Table

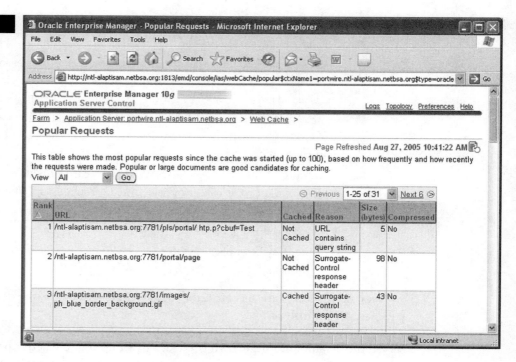

FIGURE 9-6

The Popular
Requests Table

number of times they were requested, along with information as to whether they
are cached and/or compressed. Of course, a popular or a large document is a good
candidate for caching.

Configuring Access and Event Logs

There are two important types of OracleAS Web Cache logs: event logs and access
logs. Figure 9-7 shows the two types of logging files in the Application Server
Control Console. Let's briefly review these two types of logs and their confirmation.

Event Logs

Event logs contain event information as well as logging all error messages. You can
check the event log to see which objects are being cached and monitor port conflicts
and any issues relating to starting and stopping the Web cache. By default, the access
log is named *access_log*, and is located in the $ORACLE_HOME/webcache/access
directory. The access log contains alert, notification, warning, and informational
messages. Here's a small segment of an access log:

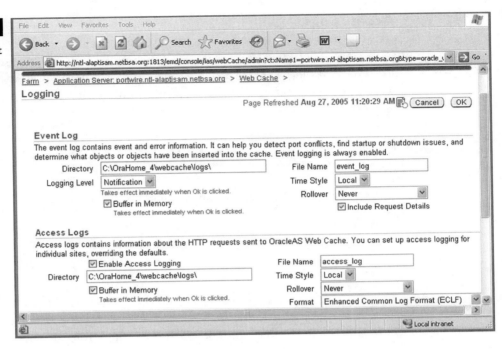

FIGURE 9-7

Configuring Event and Access Logs

```
24/Aug/2005:10:18:25 -0500] [notification 9608] [ecid: -] The cache server
process started successfully.
 [24/Aug/2005:10:43:09 -0500] [notification 13002] [ecid: -] Maximum allowed
incoming connections are 700
[24/Aug/2005:10:43:09 -0500] [warning 11917] [ecid: -] SSL wallet Origin Server
Wallet file SYSTEM DEFAULT LOCATION (See Documentation)\ewallet.p12 does not
exist.
 [24/Aug/2005:10:43:09 -0500] [notification 12209] [ecid: -] A 1 node cluster
successfully initialized
```

You can configure the access log settings using the Application Server Control or the Web Cache Manager. As Figure 9-7 shows, you can configure the following settings relating to the event logs, using the Application Server Control:

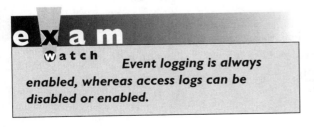

Event logging is always enabled, whereas access logs can be disabled or enabled.

- Directory
- Logging level
- File name
- Time style
- Rollover

Access Logs

All HTTP requests sent to the OracleAS Web Cache are logged in the access log, just as the all HTTP requests to the HTTP server are logged in that server's access log. The access log is named *access_log,* and is located in the $ORACLE_HOME/ webcache/logs directory. Here's a short snippet from the *access_log* file:

```
127.0.0.1--- [21/Jun/2005:16:02:52 -0500] "GET /_oracle_http_server_webcache
_static_.html HTTP/1.1" 200 99 "3044628623536,0"
127.0.0.1--- [21/Jun/2005:16:03:12 -0500] "GET /_oracle_http_server_webcache
_static_.html HTTP/1.1" 200 99 "3061808513674,0"
```

As shown in Figure 9-7, you can configure the following access log settings:

- Directory
- File name
- Time style
- Rollover
- Format

In addition to the foregoing configuration settings, you can perform the following tasks in the Application Server Control access log section:

- Enabling and disabling access logging
- Including or excluding ESI fragment requests

Manual Rollover of the Access and Event Logs

Previously, you saw how you can set the *log rollover frequency* settings for both the access and the event logs. You can also manually rollover these two logs by using the OracleAS Web Cache Manager, which will automatically save the current log file. Here are the steps to manually rollover the two log files:

1. In the OracleAS Web Cache navigator pane, select Operations => On-Demand Log File Rollover.
2. In the On-Demand Log File Rollover page that appears, go to either the Event Logs table or the Access Logs table and select an individual cache or click the Select All button.
3. Click Submit.

Creating and Configuring Caching Rules

You create caching rules in order to specify which objects the OracleAS Web Cache should cache. The Web cache will actually cache a specified object only after a client requests that object. Thus, upon the first request for an object, the OracleAS Web Cache will have to direct the client request to the origin server (*a cache miss*). If the request URL has a caching rule associated with it, the object is cached and for subsequent requests, the OracleAS Web Cache will serve the object directly from its cache (*a cache hit*).

When you stop and start the OracleAS Web Cache, all objects in the cache are cleared.

As mentioned earlier, the OracleAS Web Cache doesn't automatically cache all Web site content, but rather does so, based on explicit *caching rules*. Caching rules dictate whether or not the OracleAS Web Cache should cache content as well as the type of content it should cache. You can configure caching rules in the following two ways:

- Specify URL-based caching attributes through the OracleAS Application Server Control or the OracleAS Web Cache Manager.
- Specify caching rules for specified objects within their Surrogate-Control response-header field.

The OracleAS Web Cache caches objects using the following priority:

1. Surrogate-Control response header
2. Caching rules based on the URL using the page

If the following response headers are present, the OracleAS Web Cache *doesn't perform any caching* of objects:

- Authorization request header
- Proxy-Authorization request header
- Pragma: no-cache response header

■ Warning response header

■ The two cookie-related headers: Cookie request header and the Set-Cookie response header

Finally, the OracleAS Web Cache will look for the Cache-Control and the Expires response headers, if none of the headers in the preceding list are present. Any directives and settings in the Surrogate-Control response header will override all other caching rules. The OracleAS Web Cache always merges the caching rules for an object with the Surrogate-Control response header, but in cases where there's a conflict, it's the Surrogate-Control response-header settings that will prevail.

How Caching Rules Work

Caching rules specify how the OracleAS Web Cache should respond to requests from Web browsers. All caching rules are ordered according to priority and only the first matching rule is used. Each caching rule has two components: a *selector* and *instructions*. When a new request comes in, it's compared with the selector and provided there's a match, the Web cache will follow the corresponding instructions. If there's no match, of course, the Web cache won't cache any content.

The OracleAS Web Cache supports the POSIX standard for regular expressions. Here's a simple summary of the main POSIX-type regular expression syntax rules:

■ A carat (^) denotes the beginning of a URL, and a dollar sign ($) denotes the end of a URL.

■ A period (.) will match any single character.

■ A question mark (?) matches zero or one occurrence of the character that it follows, thus making that character optional.

■ An asterisk (*) matches zero or more occurrences of the pattern that it follows.

■ Use a slash (/) to escape special characters such as periods and asterisks, as shown here:

```
/.  /*
```

Here's a typical caching rule named *cache compress html,* with a selector and instructions:

```
Name: cache compress html
Selector: Reg: \.html?$
Instructions: Compress
Expires: Max Time in Cache, 5 Minutes,
Refresh: Immediately
```

This caching rule will immediately cache all Web documents whose URL ends in ".htm" or ".html," for a maximum period of five minutes.

Figure 9-8 shows the Rules Overview page of the Application Server Control. The important components of the Caching Rules table—Select, Order, Name, Selector Summary, Enabled, Cache, and Instructions—are described in the following subsections.

Select

The select column lets you select the rule you want to configure.

FIGURE 9-8

The Rules Overview Page

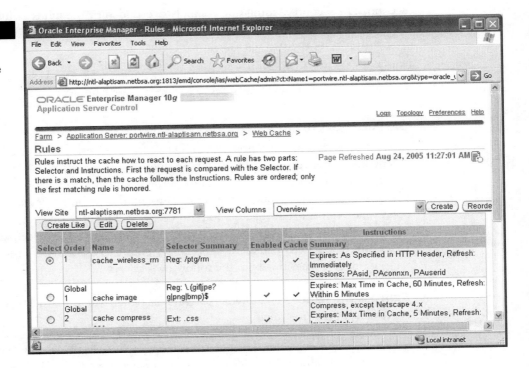

Name

The name column simply shows the name assigned to each of the caching rules.

Order

The order column shows the priority of the caching rule. Note that the caching rules with the wildcard * are given lower priority, because of their broader scope. You can use the Reorder button to rearrange the priorities of the caching rules. A caching rule with a higher priority matches first and is thus processed, and the other caching rules are ignored. Let's say you specify the following two caching rules:

```
^/abc/.*index\.htm$  // cache all index.htm[l] files in the "/abc/" virtual path.
^/abc/bc/index\.htm$ // don't cache the /abc/bc/index.htm[l] file(s)
```

Although the second rule specifies that you don't want the */abc/bc/index.htm[l]* file(s) to be cached, that directive will be ignored, because the more general directive of the first caching rule (cache *all index.htm[l]* files) takes priority over the second. The second caching rule is simply overridden by the more inclusive first caching rule. If you want to ensure that the */abc/bc/index.htm[l]* file(s) aren't cached, you must reverse the two rules as shown here:

```
^/abc/bc/index\.html?$ // don't cache the /abc/bc/index.htm[l] file(s)
^/abc/.*index\.html?$  // cache all index.htm[l] files
```

Selector Summary

In order to select the appropriate caching rule for a request, the OracleAS Web Cache must filter through all the caching rules that are available. Using a selector simplifies this task by limiting the range of the search. When the OracleAS Web Cache receives a user request, it searches through the caching rules and finds the appropriate rule for that request. You can use several types of selectors during the creation of caching rules: expression type, URL expression, HTTP request method, URL, and POST body parameters and POST body expressions. Let's review the various selector types briefly in the following sections.

Expression Type The OracleAS Web Cache lets you use three types of expression in caching rules:

- *Ext* (file extension expression type) You specify a file extension type such as *.gif* or *.html*. The caching rule is applied to all objects ending with that file extension.

Note that you don't have to specify the dot (.) in front of extensions such as .gif or .html, because the OracleAS Web Cache starts all file extensions with a dot (.) anyway.

- *Dir* (path prefix)   The caching rule is applied to all objects with a matching path prefix. The path prefix specifies the directory to be traversed in order to locate objects. The OracleAS Web Cache starts all paths with either http://hostname: port/ or slash (/), thus making it unnecessary to specify them explicitly. You can use regular expression characters such as periods (.), question marks (?), asterisks (*), brackets ([]), curly braces ({}), carets (^), dollar signs ($), and backslashes (\) inside the path prefix.
- *Reg* (regular expression)   The caching rule is applied to all objects matching regular expression syntax.

The Selector Summary column lists the expression type and the URL of the objects based on that expression type.

URL Expression   You specify the URL based on the expression type you chose.

HTTP Request Method   All HTTP client requests include a method, which tells you the purpose of the request. Here's a brief summary of the main HTTP request methods:

- *The GET method*   The GET method uses a URL to submit information and is normally used to make simple Web page requests.
- *GET method with query string*   The GET method with query string consists of a URL with a query string attached to it, containing parameters. Here's an example:

```
http://www.testserver.com/test/config/navframe?frame=default
```

The request shown here executes the *navframe* script located in the /*test*/.*config* directory. The request passes the value/pair *frame = default*.

- *The POST method*   You use the POST method for user requests that add or change data on the Web server, such as submitting a form with values for variables.

The most commonly used are the GET and POST methods. As you've seen, you can have two types of GET methods: GET and GET with query string. You must specify one of these three methods as the HTTP request method for an object.

URL and POST Body Parameters   You can enter any parameters embedded either in the URLs or in the POST body. You may use these characters as delimiters: question mark (?), ampersand (&), dollar sign ($), or semi-colon (;).

POST Body Expression   If you chose the POST method as the HTTP request method, you can then specify the HTTP POST body in regular expression syntax.

Enabled

This column lets you know whether a caching rule is enabled or not.

Instructions

The instructions column, as you can see in Figure 9-8, consists of two subcolumns. The *cache* column indicates whether the OracleAS Web Cache should cache an object. The summary column consists of two items—compression and expiration. The compression item specifies whether cacheable and noncacheable objects are compressed before being sent to a browser. The expiration item specifies how long an expired object can stay in the Web cache. Here's an example:

```
Compress, except Netscape 4.x
Expires: Max Time in Cache, 5 Minutes, Refresh: Immediately
```

Predefined Caching Rules

The OracleAS Web Cache provides several predefined caching rules, designed to accelerate Web sites and to reduce the risk of serving stale data. The predefined caching rules are summarized as follows:

- \.*html?*$ All files whose URL ends with html or htm
- \.*(gif | jpe?g)*$ All files ending with gif, jpeg, or jpg
- \.*(bmp | png)*$ All files ending with bmp or png
- \.*js*$ All files ending with .js (JavaScript files)
- \.*pdf*$ Documents ending with .pdf

From the foregoing list, you can determine that all pdf, html, jpeg/bmp, and JavaScript files are cached automatically by the OracleAS Web Cache.

Creating Your Own Caching Rules

You can create caching rules using the OracleAS Web Cache Manager or the Application Server Control. Here's a brief description of how you create caching rules using the Application Server Control:

1. In the Rules Overview page, shown in Figure 9-8, click the Create button.
2. In the Create Rule page, shown in Figure 9-9, first enter general information in the General section at the top of the page. This includes the name and description of the caching rule you're going to create and the site name. Select Enabled if you want to enable the rule upon its creation.

FIGURE 9-9

Creating a Caching Rule Using Application Server Control

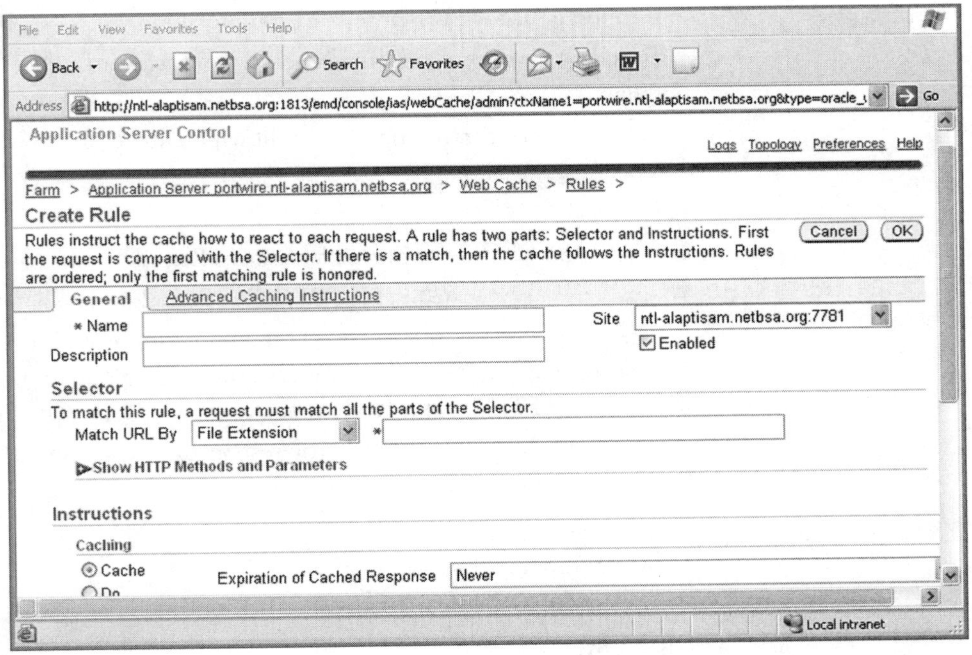

3. Specify the type of selector you wish to use, in the Selector section. As explained previously, you can choose among a file extension, a path prefix, or a regular expression. In the box next to the Selector box, specify the URL you want to match to the selector you chose. Note that a request must match all parts of the selector in order to match a certain rule.

Click the Show HTTP Methods and Parameters link to specify the request methods. You have to configure three things on this page:

- *HTTP methods*   Your new rule will apply only to requests using one of the selected HTTP request methods. You must choose among the following: GET, GET with query string, or POST.

- *POST body*   You can restrict the POST body by specifying a POST body expression.

- *URL parameters*   You may specify URL parameters if the HTTP request method is GET with a query string, or if the request method is POST and the Match URL by Type is either File Extension or Path Prefix.

Under the Instructions section, you must configure three things: caching, expiration of cached response, and compression.

Specify your caching choice by selecting *Cache* or *Do Not Cache* for the documents.

You must select from one of the following choices for the Expiration of Cached response box:

- Never

- Expires: Max time in Cache, 5 Minutes, Refresh: Immediately

- Expires: As Specified in HTTP Header, Refresh: Immediately

- Expires: Max time in Cache, 60 Minutes, Refresh: Within 6 Minutes (This means that the Web cache can serve stale content up to six minutes if the Oracle HTTP server is too busy to deliver a fresh copy.)

Configure the compression of the responses by the OracleAS Web Cache. Select from one of the following choices:

- Do not compress.

- Compress for all browsers.

- Compress for all browsers except Netscape 4.x.

4. Click **OK.**

CERTIFICATION OBJECTIVE 9.05

Expiration Policies

A document's life in the Web cache is determined by the *expiration policy* relating to that document. Any document that displays periodically updated information, say, stock market quotes, is a good candidate for invalidation according to a preset *expiration policy*. Using expiration policies, the OracleAS Web Cache can mark an object as invalid after it spends a prespecified time in the cache. Objects that are marked invalid can be either refreshed immediately, or they can be made available when the origin server becomes available, if the origin server load is heavy. Invalidated objects aren't automatically removed immediately from the cache. You can specify when to expire an object and how long the object can be retained in the cache after its expiration (thus letting the OracleAS Web Cache serve "stale" content).

Oracle recommends creating an expiration policy for every object, to keep objects from staying indefinitely in the cache.

Configuring Expiration Policies

To set an expiration policy, you must first define a rule to match the request and then, associate an expiration policy with it. You can configure expiration policies using the OracleAS Web Cache Manager, or the Application Server Control Console. Let's learn how to configure expiration policies, using the Application Server Control:

1. Click on the Administration tab in the OracleAS Web Cache home page.
2. Go to Properties => Application => Rules => Expiration Policies.
3. In the Expiration Page, click the Create button to create a new expiration policy. To modify an existing policy, click Edit; to remove an expiration policy, click Delete.

In the Expiration Page, you can do the following things:

- View expiration policies of cached objects.
- Create new expiration policies.
- Specify the length of time objects can stay in the cache after their expiration.

FIGURE 9-10

The Expiration
Policies Table

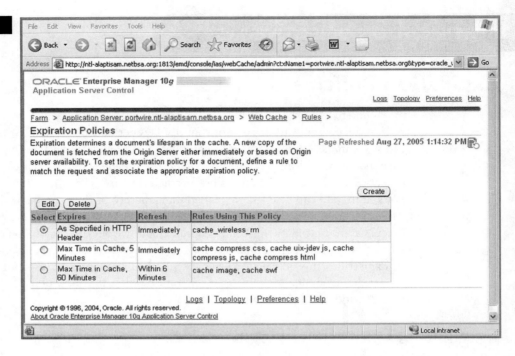

The Expiration Policies table, shown in Figure 9-10, shows all current expiration policies in the OracleAS Web Cache. The table has three important columns, as described subsequently:

- *Refresh* The Refresh column states when the page should be refreshed—for example, immediately, or "within 10 minutes."
- *Expires* The Expires column specifies the expiration rules; the following types of rules are used:
    - *Max Time in Cache* Base expiration on when a document enters the cache
    - *Max Time Since Document Created* Base expiration on when a document was created
    - *As Specified in the HTTP Expires Header* Base expiration on the HTTP Cache Control or Expires response-header fields

The default expiration rules use the As Specified in the HTTP Expires header criterion.

■ *Rules Using This Policy*   Lists the associated caching rules

Creating Expiration Policies

You use the Application Server Control of the OracleAS Web Cache Manager to create a new expiration policy. To create a new expiration policy, follow these steps:

1. Go the OracleAS Web Cache home page and click the Administration button.
2. Click the Rules link.
3. Click Expiration Policies at the bottom of the Rules page.
4. Click the Create button to navigate to the Create Expiration Policy page.
5. Figure 9-11 shows the Create Expiration Policy page. In the Objects Expire section, select one of the following criteria to expire an object:

FIGURE 9-11
The Create Expiration Policy Page

File   Edit   View   Favorites   Tools   Help

Back ·   Search   Favorites

Address http://ntl-alaptisam.netbsa.org:1813/emd/console/ias/webCache/admin?ctxName1=portwire.ntl-alaptisam.netbsa.org&type=oracle_   Go

ORACLE Enterprise Manager 10*g*
Application Server Control

Logs Topology Preferences Help

Farm > Application Server: portwire.ntl-alaptisam.netbsa.org > Web Cache > Rules > Expiration Policies >
Create Expiration Policy

Expiration determines a document's lifespan in the cache. A new copy of the document is fetched from the   Cancel   OK
Origin Server either immediately or based on Origin server availability. To set the expiration policy for a
document, define a rule to match the request and associate the desired expiration policy.

Objects Expire   Expired objects Are Refreshed
◉ As Specified in the HTTP Expires Header   ◉ Immediately
○ Max Time in Cache   ○ Within a Time Limit, Based on Origin Server Availability
○ Max Time since Document Created   Removal Time Limit [   ] Seconds ▾
    Max Time Limit [   ] Seconds ▾

                                                                                              Cancel   OK

Logs | Topology | Preferences | Help

Copyright © 1996, 2004, Oracle. All rights reserved.
About Oracle Enterprise Manager 10g Application Server Control

Local intranet

- As specified in the HTTP Expires header
- Max time in Cache
- Max Time since Document Created

In the Expired Objects Are Refreshed section, specify the disposition of the expired objects.

- *Immediately* The OracleAS Web Cache will mark objects as invalid and refresh them immediately with new content from the application Web servers.
- *Within a time limit, based on HTTP availability* The OracleAS Web Cache will mark objects as invalid and refresh them according to the ability of the application Web server. You must enter the maximum time for which an object can be kept in the cache.

6. Click **OK.**

CERTIFICATION OBJECTIVE 9.06

Sending Invalidation Requests

The OracleAS Web Cache uses invalidation for content that changes frequently—stock quotes, for example. Invalidating documents stored in the Web cache is one of the key administrative tasks relating to the OracleAS Web Cache. When you aren't sure of the length of time for which an object in the cache remains useful, you use OracleAS's *invalidation mechanisms*. When it can't predict the frequency of change of cached objects, OracleAS interactively marks the objects invalid. For example, when a user empties a shopping cart, the cached content must, of course, be invalidated. OracleAS provides the default user INVALIDATOR for marking the cached Web pages invalid. Besides the INVALIDATOR account, you can also use the *ias_admin* or the *administrator* account to invalidate cached objects. Any of these three accounts can be used to send invalidation messages, which are HTTP post requests. A brief summary follows of when the OracleAS Web Cache uses each of the three accounts for invalidation of Web cache contents.

The *central* or *provider* cache in an OracleAS Web Cache hierarchy uses the subscriber Web cache's invalidator credentials to specify the objects to be invalidated. In addition to the list of objects, the site host name is also needed. The site host will invalidate objects only if the site host name matches the IP address of the cache making the invalidation request.

When the invalidation requests are sent using the ias_admin or administrator account, there's no need for specifying the site host name.

Structure of the Invalidation Requests

HTTP POST requests in the XML format contain the invalidation messages that identify the documents the OracleAS Web Cache must invalidate. These messages are sent to the OracleAS Web Cache through an invalidation listening port. In a Web cache hierarchy or a Web cache cluster, the invalidation messages are propagated from one OracleAS Web Cache server to another. When an invalidation message is sent to a central cache, it's automatically propagated to the remote cache.

Invalidation Request Methods

You can send cache invalidation requests *manually*, using the Application Server Control, the Oracle Web Cache Manager, or telnet. You can also send the requests *automatically*, using applications, database triggers, or scripts. These two types of invalidation mechanisms are reviewed in the following subsections.

Manual Invalidation Methods

You can manually send invalidation messages to the OracleAS Web Cache using *telnet*, the Application Server Control, or the OracleAS Web Cache Manager.

Using Telnet   You can send invalidation messages using telnet by specifying the OracleAS Web Cache host server name, the port number for the invalidation listening, and, finally, the invalidation message itself. You connect to the OracleAS Web Cache at the listening port and use the telnet command to specify a POST message header. You first authenticate the invalidator account before sending out the XML-formatted invalidation message. The OracleAS Web Cache can make invalidation requests in both a BASICSELECTOR and an ADVANCEDSELECTOR format. Because the OracleAS Web Cache has to traverse the content of its entire cache to locate the objects to invalidate, it could take considerable time when the OracleAS Web Cache receives an advanced invalidation request. Therefore, when you need only to invalidate a single object in the cache, just send a basic invalidation request instead of an advanced invalidation request. Here's an example, showing an invalidation request in the BASICSELECTOR mode, which invalidates a file named *images/logo.gif*:

```
<?xml version="1.0"?>
<!DOCTYPE INVALIDATION SYSTEM "internal:///WCSinvalidation.dtd">
<INVALIDATION VERSION="WCS-1.1">
    <OBJECT>
      <BASICSELECTOR URI="http://www.company.com:80/images/logo.gif"/>
      <ACTION/>
    </OBJECT>
</INVALIDATION>
```

The invalidation response for the invalidation request shown here would look like this:

```
<?xml version="1.0"?>
<!DOCTYPE INVALIDATIONRESULT SYSTEM "internal:///WCSinvalidation.dtd">
<INVALIDATIONRESULT VERSION="WCS-1.1">
    <OBJECTRESULT>
      <BASICSELECTOR URI="http://www.company.com:80/images/logo.gif"/>
      <RESULT ID="1" STATUS="SUCCESS" NUMINV="1"/>
    </OBJECTRESULT>
</INVALIDATIONRESULT> ??//
```

Using the Application Server Control for Invalidation
The Application Server Control offers you a quick and efficient way to invalidate cached objects without having to understand any complicated HTML or XML formats. To invalidate an object, follow these steps:

1. Go to the Web cache home page and click the Administration tab.

2. Select Operations.

3. Select Invalidation and use the wizard-driven process to invalidate objects.

Using the OracleAS Web Cache Manager
You can also use the OracleAS Web Cache Manager to manually invalidate Web cache objects. Here are the steps for submitting a basic invalidation request:

1. Select Operations => Basic Content Invalidation, from the navigator frame.

2. In the Basic Content Invalidation page that appears, select a cache from the For Cache list.

3. In the Search Criteria section, select the search criteria, which lets you invalidate a single object or a set of objects:

   ■ Remove all cached objects.

   ■ Enter exact URL for removal.

4. You can preview the objects that will be invalidated, by choosing Preview list of objects that match the invalidation criteria, in the Action section.

5. Click Submit.

6. In the Action section, select from the following choices regarding the processing of invalid objects:

   ■ Remove immediately.

   ■ Remove objects no later than <number><time> after submission.

7. Click Submit.

Automated Invalidation Requests

You can automate invalidation requests using database triggers, scripts, or applications.

Using Database Triggers   Database triggers are pieces of Oracle code that are executed or "fired" when a DML operation occurs. You can use the UTL_TCP package to send invalidation requests through triggers. Triggers come in very handy when handling DML changes. For example, several users could be querying a catalog, and the Web cache will be populated with the catalog pages. If you then update the catalog (using a DML operation), all these cached pages can be invalidated by using a database trigger that's executed automatically by the Oracle database following a DML operation.

Using Scripts   You can use a script to send an invalidation message to the OracleAS Web Cache—for example, following a data reload every night.

Using Applications   The OracleAS Web Cache ships with several APIs you can use to send invalidation requests. These APIs are located in the $ORACLE_HOME/webcache/toolkit directory. In addition, you can find sample code for Java, C, PERL, and PL/SQL programs in the $ORACLE_HOME/webcache/examples directory.

Performance Assurance with Expiration and Invalidation

To avoid frequent generation of "Server Unavailable" errors to Web browsers due to frequent invalidation or expiration, the OracleAS Web Cache will serve stale documents until the origin servers have a chance to refresh them. This is done on the premise that serving a stale document is better than producing an error message in response to a browser request.

Because there's a trade off between performance and fresh content, the OracleAS Web Cache uses performance assurance heuristics to decide which objects it can serve stale. The performance heuristics act as rules of thumb in assigning a priority order to the various Web pages. Documents with a higher priority are retrieved immediately, without serving stale versions of those pages. Objects with a lower priority might be served stale and retrieved later on. The priority of a Web document is based on how popular that document is. The most popular and the most recent documents are refreshed first, subject to the load and capacity limits of the origin server. Here's a summary of the factors the OracleAS Web Cache bases its performance assurance heuristics on:

- *Validity*   This is based on the expiration, invalidation, and removal times of a Web document.

- *Popularity*   This is based on the number of total requests as well as the number of recent requests for an object.

- *Total available capacity of origin servers*   This is based on the difference between the total capacity (maximum number of concurrent connections of all origin servers) and the total load (total number of connections currently used by the origin servers combined) being carried by the OracleAS Web Cache.

The OracleAS Web Cache uses the heuristics listed here, to build its queues of objects it should update with fresh content from the origin servers.

✓ TWO-MINUTE DRILL

Introduction to the OracleAS Web Cache

- ❑ The OracleAS Web Cache works a server accelerator.
- ❑ The OracleAS Web Cache also performs as a virtual server or a reverse proxy server.
- ❑ The OracleAS Web Cache also provides failover and load balancing capabilities.
- ❑ If the requested content is found in the cache, it's considered a cache hit.
- ❑ If the requested content isn't in the cache, or if it's stale or invalid, it's considered a cache miss.
- ❑ Cacheable content goes in the cache only after the first request is made by a browser.
- ❑ When the origin server is busy, the OracleAS Web Cache may continue serving stale documents.
- ❑ For dynamically generated content, cookies and embedded HTML parameters are used to exchange information between the browser and the Web server.
- ❑ The OracleAS Web Cache can use personalized attributes to serve common pages to different users.
- ❑ The OracleAS Web Cache can create multiple document versions using different cookie/value pairs or by using different HTTP request headers for pages.
- ❑ By using session values in embedded URL parameters or the POST body parameters, origin servers can tract browser sessions.
- ❑ By excluding embedded URLs or POST body parameters, the same cached pages are served to multiple sessions.
- ❑ Session-encoded URLs are used to serve varying responses for different sessions.
- ❑ Edge Side Includes (ESI) involves the use of special markup tags to dynamically assemble Web page fragments.
- ❑ Page fragments represent the dynamic component of a Web page.
- ❑ Page fragments can have different caching profiles and are treated as separate elements in a page.

❏ Partial page caching involves the caching of Web page fragments, which are actually HTML files.

OracleAS Web Cache Management

❏ You manage the OracleAS Web Cache with the Application Server Control and the *opmnctl* utility.

❏ You use the *webcachectl* utility to manage standalone OracleAS Web Cache instances.

❏ The user *administrator* is the main administrative user of OracleAS Web Cache.

❏ The *invalidator* account is used to send invalidation requests only.

❏ There are two OracleAS Web Cache processes: *cache* and *webcacheadmin*.

❏ When you configure the OracleAS Web Cache, the *webcache.xml* file is automatically modified.

OracleAS Web Cache Administration Tasks

❏ By default, the OracleAS Web Cache uses port 7777 to listen for HTTP requests.

❏ There are two types of ports: listening ports and operation ports.

❏ A site consists of a server and a port number.

❏ There are two types of sites: virtual host sites and ESI provider sites.

❏ Users can connect only to the virtual host sites.

❏ ESI provider sites are for assembling ESI fragments only.

❏ If you're configuring a virtual host site, you must map it to an origin server.

❏ The OracleAS Web Cache uses origin servers for internal requests and proxy servers for external sites that are protected by firewalls.

❏ You must map origin servers to a Web site before you can forward requests to it from the OracleAS Web Cache.

❏ There are two types of site definitions: named and unnamed site definitions.

❏ Named site definitions are known sites supported by the OracleAS Web Cache.

❏ Server mappings for unnamed sites are mappings to origin servers for sites that don't match any named virtual host sites.

❑ Event logs contain event and error information.
❑ The access log records all HTTP requests sent to the OracleAS Web Cache.
❑ You can manually rollover the event and access logs, using the OracleAS Web Cache Manager.

Creating and Configuring Caching Rules
❑ Caching rules determine whether the OracleAS Web Cache should cache Web site content.
❑ You can configure caching rules by using URL-based caching attributes, through Surrogate-Control response-header fields.
❑ The Surrogate-Control response-header settings will prevail in case there's a conflict.
❑ Caching rules are ordered according to priority, and the first matching rule is always the one that's used.
❑ A caching rule has two components: a selector and instructions.
❑ The selector in a caching rule limits the range of search for caching rules.
❑ You can use three types of selector formats: file extension (Ext), path prefix (Dir), or a regular expression (Reg).
❑ The OracleAS Web Cache provides several predefined caching rules.

Expiration Policies
❑ Periodically updated information can use preset expiration policies to invalidate content.
❑ Invalid objects can be refreshed immediately or when the origin server is available.
❑ Oracle recommends creating expiration policies for every Web page so that no page can stay indefinitely in the cache.
❑ To set an expiration policy, you must define a rule to match the request and associate an expiration policy with it.
❑ The OracleAS Web Cache uses invalidation techniques to invalidate content that changes frequently.
❑ Invalidation messages are HTML POST requests to invalidate content.

❏ You can send manual invalidation messages through telnet, through the Application Server Control Console, or through the OracleAS Web Cache Manager.

❏ When invalidating a single object, use a basic invalidation request instead of an advanced invalidation request.

❏ You can send automatic invalidation messages using database triggers, scripts, or applications.

❏ The OracleAS Web Cache uses performance heuristics to determine which objects it can serve stale.

❏ Performance heuristics don't apply to objects that will be refreshed immediately.

❏ The priority of a page depends upon how popular the page is.

Sending Invalidation Requests

❏ The OracleAS Web Cache uses invalidation for content that changes frequently.

❏ When it can't predict the frequency of change of cached objects, OracleAS interactively marks the objects invalid.

❏ You can send cache invalidation requests manually or automatically.

❏ You can manually send invalidation messages to the OracleAS Web Cache using *telnet*, the Application Server Control, or the OracleAS Web Cache Manager.

❏ You can automate invalidation requests using database triggers, scripts, or applications.

❏ The OracleAS Web Cache will serve stale documents until the origin servers get a chance to refresh them.

❏ The OracleAS Web Cache uses performance assurance heuristics to decide which objects it can serve stale.

❏ The main factors the OracleAS Web Cache bases its performance assurance heuristics on are validity, popularity, and the total available capacity of origin servers.

SELF TEST

1. Which of the following does the OracleAS Web Cache act as? (Choose two)

   A. Server accelerator

   B. Secure server

   C. Proxy server

   D. Origin server

2. Which of the following does the OracleAS Web Cache use to substitute values for personalized attributes?

   A. Cookies, user IDs, and embedded URL parameters

   B. Cookies, embedded URL parameters, and POST body parameters

   C. Cookies, embedded URL parameters, and GET body parameters

   D. Cookies and SSO and POST body parameters

3. Which of the following is a task of different HTTP request headers for Web pages?

   A. Serving identical content to all users

   B. Serving different content to different users

   C. Serving static content only

   D. Serving invalidated and stale content

4. Which of the following files is updated when you configure the OracleAS Web Cache?

   A. *update.xml*

   B. *internal.xml*

   C. *server.xml*

   D. *webcache.xml*

5. Which of the following types of port settings must you configure for the OracleAS Web Cache?

   A. Listen ports and response ports

   B. Request ports and response ports

   C. Listen ports and operation ports

   D. Operation ports and response ports

6. Which of the following sites do server mappings for unnamed sites refer to?

   A. Sites that don't match any proxy server host sites

   B. Sites that don't match any named virtual host sites

   C. Sites that don't have any ports

   D. Sites without a name

7. Which of the following can you use to specify caching rules?

   A. Surrogate-Control response-header field

   B. Server mappings for unnamed sites

   C. Host request-header field

   D. Cache request-header field

8. Which of the following components does each caching rule have?

   A. Selector and rule

   B. Selector and port

   C. Selector and instructions

   D. Selector and site

9. Which of the following selector formats does the OracleAS Web Cache use?

   A. ext, dir, web

   B. ejb, ext, file

   C. ext, file, dir

   D. ext, dir, reg

10. Which of the following expiration rules does the Default OracleAS Web Cache use?

    A. HTTP Expires Header criterion

    B. Max time in cache principle

    C. Min time in cache principle

    D. Max time since document created principle

SELF TEST ANSWERS

1. ☑ **A** and **C** are correct. **A** is correct because the OracleAS Web Cache sits between the browser and the origin server and helps accelerate the serving of Web content using cached Web pages. **C** is correct because the OracleAS Web Cache also acts as a proxy server.
   ☒ **B** is incorrect because the OracleAS Web Cache isn't concerned with security. **D** is incorrect because the origin server actually creates the Web pages that the OracleAS Web Cache ends up caching.

2. ☑ **B** is correct. The OracleAS Web Cache uses cookies, embedded URL parameters, and POST body parameters to substitute values for personalized attributes.
   ☒ **A** is incorrect because user IDs aren't used directly for setting personalized attributes. **C** is incorrect because it's the POST body parameters that are used, not GET parameters. **D** is incorrect because the SSO server doesn't play any part in this process.

3. ☑ **B** is correct. Different HTTP request headers for Web pages help serve different content for different users.
   ☒ **A** is wrong because different HTTP request headers are used to serve customized content to users. **C** is wrong because the different HTTP request headers help serve dynamic, not static Web content. **D** is wrong because different HTTP request headers aren't used for the explicit purpose of serving invalidated and stale content.

4. ☑ **D** is correct. When you reconfigure the OracleAS Web Cache with the help of the Application Server Control or the OracleAS Web Cache Manager, the *webcache.xml* file is automatically modified.
   ☒ **A** is wrong because it's a made-up name. **B** is wrong because the *internal.xml* is for internal OracleAS Web Cache purposes. **C** is wrong because the *server.xml* isn't used in the context of the OracleAS Web Cache.

5. ☑ **C** is correct. You must configure listen ports for listening to browser requests and operation ports for operational reasons.
   ☒ **A, B,** and **D** are wrong because there are no such things as response ports.

6. ☑ **B** is correct. Server mapping for unnamed sites is for sites that don't match any named virtual host sites.
   ☒ **A** is wrong because it's the virtual host sites, not the proxy host sites, that are being mapped here. **C** and **D** are wrong because the sites must have a port number and a name.

7. ☑ **A** is correct. One of the two ways of specifying caching rules is to specify them in the Surrogate-Control response-header field.
   ☒ **B, C,** and **D** are wrong because you can't specify caching rules with any of these.

8. ☑ **C** is correct. Each caching rule has two components: *selector* (ext, dir, or reg) and *instructions*.

   ☒ **A, B** and **D** are wrong because they're all missing one of the components.

9. ☑ **D** is correct. The OracleAS Web Cache uses the following three selector formats:

   - *Ext* (file extension)   The caching rule is applied to all objects ending with a file extension, such as *.html*.
   - *Dir* (path prefix)   The caching rule is applied to all objects with a matching path prefix.
   - *Reg* (regular expression)   The caching rule is applied to all objects matching regular expression syntax.

   ☒ **A, B,** and **C** are wrong because they don't specify the three correct selector formats.

10. ☑ **A** is correct. By default, the OracleAS Web Cache uses the HTTP Expires header criterion.

    ☒ **B** and **D** are incorrect because they are alternative criteria for setting expiration rules, but not the default criteria. **C** is wrong because there is no "min time in cache" principle.

A

About the CD

T he CD-ROM included with this book comes complete with MasterExam and the electronic version of the book. The software is easy to install on any Windows 98/ NT/2000 computer and must be installed to access the MasterExam feature. You may, however, browse the electronic book directly from the CD without installation. To register for a second bonus MasterExam, simply click the Online Training link on the Main Page and follow the directions to the free online registration.

System Requirements

Software requires Windows 98 or higher and Internet Explorer 5.0 or above and 20 MB of hard disk space for full installation. The electronic book requires Adobe Acrobat Reader.

Installing and Running MasterExam

If your computer CD-ROM drive is configured to auto run, the CD-ROM will automatically start up upon inserting the disk. From the opening screen you may install MasterExam by pressing the *MasterExam* button. This will begin the installation process and create a program group named "LearnKey." To run MasterExam use START | PROGRAMS | LEARNKEY. If the auto run feature did not launch your CD, browse to the CD and click the "LaunchTraining.exe" icon.

MasterExam

MasterExam provides you with a simulation of the actual exam. The number of questions, the types of questions, and the time allowed are intended to be an accurate representation of the exam environment. You have the option to take an open-book exam, including hints, references, and answers; a closed-book exam; or the timed MasterExam simulation.

When you launch MasterExam, a digital clock display will appear in the upper left-hand corner of your screen. The clock will continue to count down to zero unless you choose to end the exam before the time expires.

Electronic Book

The entire contents of the Study Guide are provided in PDF. Adobe's Acrobat Reader has been included on the CD.

Help

A help file is provided through the help button on the main page in the lower left-hand corner. An individual help feature is also available through MasterExam.

Removing Installation(s)

MasterExam is installed to your hard drive. For *best* results for removal of programs, use the START | PROGRAMS | LEARNKEY | UNINSTALL options to remove MasterExam.

Technical Support

For questions regarding the technical content of the electronic book or MasterExam, please visit www.osborne.com or email customer.service@mcgraw-hill.com. For customers outside the 50 United States, email international_cs@mcgraw-hill.com.

LearnKey Technical Support

For technical problems with the software (installation, operation, removing installations), please visit www.learnkey.com or email techsupport@learnkey.com.

Glossary

access control lists (ACLs)   ACLs are lists of resources and the usernames of those who are permitted access to these resources within a system. The OID access control list shows the permissions users have regarding various OID directory objects.

access control policy point (ACP)   An ACP is an OID entry that contains the access control policies applying to all entities below that entry within a Directory Information Tree. You use ACPs to apply access control policies in an OID subtree.

access log   The access log logs all HTTP requests sent to the OracleAS Web Cache for an origin Web server. The default location is $ORACLE_HOME/ webcache/logs (ORACLE_HOME\webcache\logs in Windows).

admin server process   The admin server process is one of two OracleAS Web Cache components, the other being the cache server process. The admin server process supports administrative and monitoring tasks.

Advanced Encryption Standard   Advanced Encryption Standard (AES) is a cryptographic algorithm that has been approved for replacing DES.

anonymous authentication   Anonymous authentication is the process by which the OID authenticates users without asking for their credentials and authorizes users to exercise privileges granted to anonymous users.

Application Server Control   The Application Server Control is a GUI tool that lets you administer, configure, and monitor the Oracle Application Server and its components.

application Web server   The application Web server is also called the *origin server* and is responsible for responding to client requests for a Web site.

attribute   An attribute in an LDAP directory such as the OID is used to specify various data elements (e.g., the name and phone number of a directory entry). Each of the attributes belongs to an object class. Attributes are type/value pairs. For example, you might have the attribute value salapati@netbsa.org, for the attribute type email.

authentication   Under authentication, the server checks to see whether clients are authorized to access certain objects by verifying the identification credentials supplied by the client. You can authenticate messages using public key cryptography, which verifies whether a message was indeed originated by a certain entity.

authentication method   An authentication method helps verify an entity's credentials. Oracle uses various authentication methods, including Kerberos and Secure Sockets Layer (SSL).

authorization   Authorization is the granting (or denial) of access to a service or resource. Authorization is based on the organization's authorization policies and follows the initial step of authentication.

auto login wallet   The auto login feature in the Oracle Wallet Manager allows PKI or password-based access without having to provide credentials. Because the auto login features provide single sign-on capabilities, they are also referred to sometimes as *SSO wallets*.

base   In the OID, the base refers to the root of a subtree search.

basic authentication   Basic authentication, also known as plain text authentication, is a simple authentication protocol used by Web servers to authenticate entities. It involves the use of encoded user credentials, but not encryption.

bean-managed persistence (BMP) bean   A bean-managed persistence (BMP) bean stores state information within the bean itself.

binding   In the context of the OID, binding refers to the process of authenticating users to the directory.

CA certificate   The CA certificate, also known as the root certificate, contains the public key of a Certificate Authority (CA). Your browser needs to have the CA certificate as part of its trusted root certificates if it has to trust messages signed by the CA. Note that the CA signs all certificates with its private key.

cache hit   A cache hit occurs when the OracleAS Web Cache can serve an HTTP request from its cache without having to go the origin server.

cache miss   A cache miss occurs when the OracleAS Web Cache can't serve HTTP requests from its cache, forwarding requests to the origin server instead.

cache server process   The cache server process belongs to the OracleAS Web Cache; it helps manage the cache by managing connections and processing requests.

category cookie   A category cookie is a type of cookie that lets the Web server serve multiple versions of a page to various user categories.

certificate   A certificate provides a way to confirm that an entity's public key does indeed belong to that entity. A Certificate Authority, which is a trusted entity, creates a certificate by signing an entity's public key. A certificate usually contains the entity name and other identifying information including its public key, along with information about the Certificate Authority that issued the certificate. Public key certificates use the CA's signature to attest that the public key that's a part of the certificate indeed belongs to the entity that claims to have signed it.

certificate authentication   Certificate authentication is the process whereby clients authenticate themselves through the use of X.509 v3 certificates.

Certificate Authority   A Certificate Authority is a trusted party that certifies the identity of various entities such as users and servers. After it first verifies a user's identity, the CA issues a certificate and signs it with the CA's private key. Servers and clients use the CA's own certificate along with its published public key to verify its signatures on the certificates the CA issued.

certificate chain   A certificate chain is a list of certificates containing an end-user certificate and its Certificate Authority certificates.

certificate request   A certificate request consists of a request for a certificate, a signature algorithm identifier, and a digital signature.

certificate revocation list (CRL)   A CA maintains a list of all digital certificates it revokes in a CRL.

cipher suite   A cipher suite is a set of authentication, encryption, and data integrity algorithms used for exchanging messages between connections in a session.

ciphertext   Ciphertext is encrypted message text.

cluster   An OracleAS cluster is a set of application server instances that are identically configured, with the same application deployment on all the instances. A cluster simplifies application deployment across multiple instances, besides providing fault tolerance.

common log format (CLF)   The common log format is a standard format for Web transaction log files.

connect descriptor   A connect descriptor describes a network connection's destination by providing the destination service and network route details.

connect identifier   A connect identifier is a name that maps to a connect descriptor.

connected directory   A connected directory concept is relevant to the Oracle Directory Integration and Provisioning environment and refers to directories that require full synchronization between the Application Server Certificate Authority and themselves. For example, a company's human resources database falls under the category of a connected directory.

container   Containers contain components such as servlets and help to manage the runtime execution of the servlets. Web servers pass HTTP servlet requests to containers, which translate those requests into Java method invocations and pass the requests along to the servlets.

container-managed persistence (CMP) bean   CMP beans are EJBs that store their information in the container itself.

cookie   A cookie is a text string of information sent by a Web server to the user's browser and saved there to maintain state between multiple HTTP calls. The browser will pass the cookie back to the server during subsequent requests, thus letting the Web server track the state of the transactions.

credentials   Credentials refer to the username and password used to access a database, an application server, or an identity-management infrastructure.

cryptography   Cryptography refers to the techniques used to encode and decode data.

DAD   A database access descriptor (DAD) specifies how applications connect to an Oracle database in response to HTTP requests. A DAD includes the username, password, connect-string, and other related information needed to make the database connection.

Data Encryption Standard (DES)   Data Encryption Standard (DES) is a widely used symmetric cryptography algorithm.

data integrity   Data integrity guarantees that the contents of a message you receive are unaltered versions of the original message.

decryption   Decryption is the process whereby you convert an encrypted message into a readable, plain text format.

default DAD   When an application doesn't specify a DAD, PL/SQL applications use the default DAD (database access descriptor) to access a database.

default identity management realm   A default identity management realm is the enterprise that acts as a host for other enterprises, by making various Oracle components available to the enterprises. The hosted enterprises have their own identity management realm in the DIT.

default realm location   The default realm location is an attribute in the root Oracle Context that identifies the root of the default identity management realm.

delegated administrator   A delegated administrator performs roles in a specific identity-management realm or for specified applications, as opposed to a global administrator, whose domain is the entire OID.

deployment descriptor   A deployment descriptor is an XML file that contains a description of the deployment settings for an application component. The J2EE Server reads the deployment descriptor at runtime and implements the deployment settings.

digital signature   You use digital signatures by applying special algorithms (e.g., DSA, RSA, and ECDSA) to data to provide the objectives of integrity, authentication, and non-repudiation of data. Note that the digital signature is created by using the special public key algorithm to sign the sender's message with the sender's private key. First, a hash function is applied to the block of data, and then the result is encrypted using the signer's private key. The signature vouches for the authenticity of the document, and the sender can't repudiate it. A digital signature identifies the author or sender of an electronic document and verifies that the document hasn't been tampered with.

directory information base (DIB)   A DIB refers to the entirety of information in a directory, and consists of all entities in a directory information tree (DIT).

directory information tree (DIT)   A directory information tree (DIT) is a hierarchical tree-like structure consisting of the DNs of the entries.

directory integration and provisioning server   The directory integration and provisioning server synchronizes data between the OID and a connected directory, such as a human resources database of an organization.

directory manager   *See* Oracle Directory Manager.

directory naming context   A directory naming context is a subtree within the DIT that is usually the top of some organizational subtree.

directory server instance   A directory server instance is an invocation of the directory server, and you may have multiple directory server instances.

directory-specific entry (DSE)   A DSE is a directory entry whose contents are specific to the directory server holding it.

distinguished name (DN)   A distinguished name is a unique name for an OID directory entry that helps to uniquely identify any directory entry. A DN for a directory entry is the concatenation of the RDNs of each of the nodes in the DIT, from the root node to that entity's node. For example, an entity named Sam Alapati working for MyCompany's India office would have this DN: "cn=Sam Alapati", ou=People, o=MyCompany, c=India."

domain   A domain is any tree or subtree under the Domain Name System (DNS) namespace.

domain component attribute   The domain component (DC) attribute is used in constructing a distinguished name (DN) from a domain name.

EAR file   An Enterprise Archive (EAR) file is used to deploy an entire J2EE application; it contains both the JAR and WAR files relating to that application.

Edge Side Includes (ESI)   ESI is a markup language that enables the OracleAS Web Cache to perform *partial page caching* of HTML fragments.

EJB   *See* Enterprise JavaBean (EJB).

EJB containers   EJB containers coordinate the components in an EJB application and provide the runtime support for them.

EJB deployment descriptor   An EJB deployment descriptor provides information such as transaction and security policies regarding EJB deployment.

embedded URL parameter   Embedded URL parameters provide information that's embedded in the URLs.

encryption   Encryption is the conversion of plain text data to ciphertext using cryptographic algorithms. Only authorized recipients can read encrypted data, by first decrypting the data.

encryption certificate   An encryption certificate contains the public key that's used for encrypting messages. You can also use this public key to establish or exchange session keys when transmitting messages, documents, and data.

enterprise beans   Enterprise beans encapsulate the business logic of applications.

Enterprise JavaBean (EJB)   Enterprise JavaBeans (EJBs) define a platform-independent, object-oriented component architecture for multi-tier client/server systems.

entity bean   Entity beans model a business entity and are used to facilitate business services involving the computation of data, such as a purchase order.

entry   In the OID, an entry stands for a basic entity in the directory and contains a set of information about an object. Entries contain attributes, which help describe the object that the entry represents. You uniquely identify an entity using the distinguished name (DN) of that entry.

expiration   Expiration is the marking of objects as invalid after they spend a specified amount of time inside the OracleAS Web Cache. Objects marked invalid can be refreshed either immediately or when the origin server is able to do it.

external application   An external application authenticates itself by displaying HTML login forms instead of delegating the authentication function to the OracleAS Single Sign-On Server. During the initial login, users may choose to have their credentials retrieved by the OracleAS Single Sign-On Server, in which case they will log in to the application transparently during subsequent logins.

external verification   External verification is the practice of using a third-party service such as Kerberos to verify a user's identity.

farm   An OracleAS Farm is a collection of OracleAS instances that share the same OracleAS Infrastructure. You can have a database-based or a file-based OracleAS Farm.

GET method   The GET method is one type of an HTTP request method that uses URLs to send information to the Web server. You usually use the GET method for making simple Web page requests.

GET method with query string   The GET method with query string is a type of HTTP request method that is composed of a URL and a query string that contains parameters. Here's an example, where the request executes the navframe script and passes it to the frame variable with a value of *default*:

```
http://www.myserver.com/setup/config/navframe?frame=default
```

global administrator   A global administrator performs directory-wide functions in a hosted environment where the host makes various Oracle components available to multiple enterprises.

globalization support   Globalization support is the capability for multiple language support. OracleAS provides globalization support by supporting 29 languages.

group search base   The group search base is an OID term that refers to the node in the identity-management realm under which all groups are located.

HTTP   Hypertext Transfer Protocol (HTTP) is the predominant communication protocol used by the Web browsers and Web servers to communicate and transmit messages.

HTTP header   The HTTP headers are part of both a browser request message and the response message that's sent back by the Web server. Headers include information such as the user, server, MIME types, content type, and content length.

HTTP request header   The HTTP request header is a header that lets a Web browser pass information to the Web server about both the browser and the request.

HTTP request method   An HTTP request method is part of the HTTP request that tells the Web server what the client request's purpose is. The three main HTTP request methods are GET, GET with query string, and the POST method.

HTTP Server   The Oracle HTTP Server serves client requests by providing requested files to the client, based on the information provided in the requested URL.

httpd.conf   The *httpd.conf* file is the configuration file for the Oracle HTTP Server.

HTTPS   HTTPS stands for the Secure Hypertext Transfer Protocol and uses the Secure Sockets Layer (SSL) under the normal HTTP application layer to provide secure encryption and decryption of Web pages.

HTTPS protocol   HTTPS stands for the Secure Hypertext Transfer Protocol, which uses the Secure Sockets Layer (SSL) to encrypt page requests and responses.

iASAdmins   The iASAdmins group (administrative group) takes care of user and group management in OracleAS. Note that the OracleAS Single Sign-On administrator belongs to this group.

identity management   Identity management is the management of an organization's security life cycle for entities such as users, customers, trading partners, and Web services. Management includes the management of users and groups as well as the administration of user privileges.

identity-management infrastructure database   The identity-management infrastructure database is the Oracle database that stores data for the OID as well as for OracleAS Single Sign-On.

identity-management realm   An identity-management realm is a collection of all enterprise identities that are subject to the same administrative policies; it is represented in the OID as a specific entry.

identity-management realm–specific Oracle Context   In each identity-management realm in the OID, there's an Oracle Context containing information such as the user-naming policies, location of groups, assignment of privileges, and application-specified data for the realm, including authorization information.

IIOP   Internet Inter-ORB protocol (IIOP) is the protocol used by CORBA objects to communicate. EJB objects use RMI.

infrastructure tier   The infrastructure tier contains the Oracle Metadata Repository and the identity-management-related components, which include OracleAS Single Sign-On, Oracle Delegated Administration Services, and the Oracle Internet Directory.

instance   In the context of OracleAS, an instance refers to the set of processes that are associated with the running of the various OracleAS components that you have installed during the OracleAS installation. You can have a single OracleASD instance for each OracleAS installation.

integrity   Integrity refers to the assurance that a message's content was received without any alterations being made to the content after it was sent.

invalidation   Invalidation is the marking of OracleAS Web Cache objects as invalid, thus keeping the OracleAS Web Cache content consistent with the origin server's content. Invalid objects are refreshed when users request them.

J2EE   Java 2 Platform, Enterprise Edition (J2EE) is a platform that helps you develop and deploy enterprise applications.

J2EE Server   The J2EE Server provides EJB containers, Web containers, or both, and provides the runtime services for J2EE applications.

JAAS   Java Authentication and Authorization Service (JAAS) provides authentication and access control services for J2EE applications.

JAR files   JAR files stands for Java Archive (JAR) files, which are packaged together with WAR files into EAR files.

Java 2 Platform, Enterprise Edition (J2EE)   The Java 2 Platform, Enterprise Edition (J2EE) consists of a set of services, application programming interfaces (APIs), and protocols that enable you to develop Web-based enterprise applications.

Java beans   Java beans are portable components that let developers write reusable program components.

Java Database Connectivity (JDBC)   JDBC is a standard Java interface for connection to a database from within a Java program.

Java Server Page (JSP)   Java Server Pages or JSPs enable you to provide dynamic Web content; they can be embedded within an HTML page.

JCA   The Java Connector Architecture (JCA) is the standard architecture for integrating heterogeneous enterprise information systems.

JDBC   Java DataBase Connectivity (JDBC) provides connectivity to databases from within a Java program.

JMS   The Java Message Service (JMS) API facilitates the asynchronous exchange of enterprise-wide business data and events.

JNDI   Java Naming and Directory Interface (JNDI) is a set of standard APIs that provide directory and naming services.

JSP   Java Server Pages (JSPs) help provide dynamic functionality to Web pages through special tags and embedded Java code executed on the Web server. The JSPs are first compiled into servlets and are run in the servlet container.

JTA   Java Transaction API (JTA) lets applications take part in distributed transactions and access transaction services provided by other components.

JTS   Java Transaction Service (JTS) is the set of services that help applications and databases become part of a transaction.

key   A key is a secretly held string of characters used to encrypt or decrypt data. Of course, larger keys are more hacker proof. Thus, a 128-bit key provides less security than a 256-bit key.

key pair   A key pair is a pair of related public key and private key associated with a user. Key pairs are used in public key encryption.

latency   Latency is the network round-trip time.

LDAP   Lightweight Directory Access Protocol (LDAP) is a well-known protocol used for accessing information from directory servers that use a hierarchical structure to store corporate directory entries. The LDAP protocol is a standard language used by LDAP clients and servers. Oracle Internet Directory uses the LDAP protocol.

LDAP Data Interchange Format (LDIF)   LDIF is a common set of standards for data exchange, and the LDAP command-line utilities accept input files only in the LDIF format.

load balancing   Load balancing is the distribution of HTTP requests among several Web servers to avoid the overloading of a single server.

message authentication   Message authentication is the process by which you verify that a message did indeed come from the entity that is supposed to have sent it.

message digest   A message digest is an encrypted text converted into a string of digits, using a one-way hash function. The message digest can be compared with the message digest that's decrypted using a public key, to make sure they are the same and haven't been tampered with during the message-transmission process.

mod_osso   The mod_osso module is run as part of the Oracle HTTP Server and enables OracleAS Single Sign-On. The mod_osso cookie stores the values for the user's HTTP headers once a user logs into the OracleAS Single Sign-On Server. These headers are later used for the Single Sign-On feature instead of requesting the user's credentials each time the user goes into an application.

mod_osso cookie   The mod_osso cookie is created on a user's initial authentication and is stored on the Oracle HTTP Server, which uses the cookie for subsequent authentication to other applications.

naming context   A naming context is a contiguous subtree of a directory information tree (DIT) that resides on one server. It can be as small as just one entry or as large as the entire DIT.

nickname attribute   The OID uses the nickname attribute to uniquely identify a user in the OID, and the default value for this attribute is *uid*. Applications use the nickname attribute to resolve simple usernames to distinguished names.

nonrepudiation   Nonrepudiation is a non contestable proof about the authenticity of the origin, delivery, submission, or transmission of messages.

object class   An object class is a named group of attributes that you can then assign to entries in a directory.

OPMN   *See* Oracle Process Manager and Notification (OPMN) Server.

Oracle Application Server Containers for J2EE (OC4J)   Oracle Application Server Containers for J2EE (OC4J) is a set of J2EE containers that execute on the Java Virtual Machine (JVM) of the standard Java Development Kit (JDK).

Oracle Application Server Infrastructure   Oracle Application Server Infrastructure provides support for the OracleAS Middle Tier and consists of the Oracle Application Server Metadata Repository, a directory server, a management server, and the Single Sign-On Server.

Oracle Application Server Metadata Repository   Oracle Application Server Metadata Repository is an Oracle database containing metadata required by Oracle Application Server instances.

Oracle Application Server Web Cache   Oracle Application Server Web Cache caches static as well as dynamic content from one or more origin servers. It serves as a server accelerator, helping to improve the performance and availability of frequently used Web content.

Oracle Context   An Oracle Context is usually located in an identity-management realm in the OID. Oracle Context is simply an entry in the OID that's named oracleContext, under which all Oracle software information is kept. You can have multiple Oracle Contexts in the OID.

Oracle Delegated Administration Service   Oracle Delegated Administration Service units perform directory operations on behalf of a user.

Oracle Directory Integration Platform   The Oracle Directory Integration Platform helps integrate multiple applications around the Oracle Internet Directory.

Oracle Directory Manager   The Oracle Directory Manager is a GUI tool that enables you to administer the Oracle Internet Directory.

Oracle HTTP Server   Oracle HTTP Server is a Web server that's built using the Apache Web Server technology. OracleAS uses the Oracle HTTP Server to serve Web applications.

Oracle Internet Directory (OID)   Oracle Internet Directory (OID) is a directory service that facilitates easy retrieval of enterprise-wide information about users and resources. OID runs as an application that's part of an Oracle database.

Oracle Internet Directory Monitor   The Oracle Internet Directory Monitor monitors and controls the Oracle Internet Directory Server processes, as well as the optional replication server and the Oracle Directory Integration and Provisioning Server.

Oracle Process Manager and Notification (OPMN) Server   The Oracle Process Manager and Notification (OPMN) Server manages the various Oracle Application Server processes and channels notifications among the components.

Oracle Wallet Manager   You use the Oracle Wallet Manager application to manage public key credentials such as a public/private key pair and certificates.

OracleAS Web Cache Manager   The OracleAS Web Cache Manager is a tool that helps you configure and manage the OracleAS Web Cache.

ORACLE_HOME   ORACLE_HOME is the directory in which you installed the Oracle software binaries.

origin server   An origin server is a regular Web server that serves content directly to the browsers. For sites outside a firewall, it could act as a proxy server.

partial page caching   The partial page caching feature enables the OracleAS Web Cache to cache fragments of HTML objects that are actually HTML files. OracleAS Web Cache uses template pages with ESI markup tags to determine which HTML fragments to fetch and include.

partner application   A partner application could be an OracleAS or non-Oracle application that delegates authentication chores to the OracleAS Single Sign-On Server. Partner applications accept *mod_osso* headers, thereby doing away with the need to sign on multiple times to different applications.

performance assurance heuristics   Oracle Web Cache uses performance heuristics to assign priorities to various objects, using the heuristics to determine which objects can be served stale and which have to be immediately removed from the cache. The queue order or priority of the objects is determined by the popularity, as well as the validity, of the objects. The priority rules dictate that the most popular and the least valid objects be refreshed before the others.

PKCS   PKCS stands for Public Key Cryptography Standards, which are specifications to be used in public key cryptography.

popularity   Popularity in the context of the OracleAS Web Cache refers to the number of requests for a page from the time it was cached as well as the number of recent requests for the page.

portal   A portal site provides a personalized and central view of applications and data.

portlet   Portlets are the basic building blocks of an OracleAS Portal page; they are reusable components that summarize information or provide access to an information source.

POST body parameter   POST body parameters are those parameters that are embedded in the POST body.

POST method   The POST method is a popular HTTP request method that involves modifying the content on the Web server (e.g., by posting messages or submitting information through a form).

private key   In a public/private key pair, the public key of an entity is used for the encryption of data, and entities use their secret private key to decrypt the messages. A private key is used to decrypt data encrypted with a public key and is not distributed to everyone.

provisioned applications   A provisioned application is one that runs under an Oracle Internet Directory–based centralized user and group information management.

proxy server   A proxy server intercepts requests to the origin server by forwarding those requests to the origin server, as well as sending the server responses back to the browser that made the original request.

public key   A public key is a key known to everyone; it is used to encrypt data so that only specific users can decrypt it. Entities use a public key to encrypt data that can be decrypted only by the public key owner using the corresponding private key. You also use public keys to verify digital signatures that an entity creates with the associated private key.

public key cryptography   Public key cryptography or asymmetric cryptography uses a private and a public key pair to exchange messages, whereby the private key is secret and the public key is known. An entity uses its private key to decrypt messages encrypted by the associated public key. The entity can also use the public key to verify signatures made with its associated private key.

public key encryption   Public key encryption uses a public key and a private key pair to encrypt as well as decrypt data.

public key infrastructure (PKI)   A public key infrastructure (PKI) typically consists of a Certificate Authority and a Registration Authority to help manage public and private keys, in order to verify digital signatures and encrypt data.

query string   You can use a query string as an optional addition to a URL to pass parameters to applications.

realm   OracleAS uses realms to store the security policies and roles that relate to a group of users, in order to make them easier to administer.

Registration Authority (RA)   The Registration Authority (RA) verifies and enrolls users before a certificate is issued by a Certificate Authority (CA).

reverse proxy server   A reverse proxy server retrieves content from backend origin servers but appears to be a normal server to client browsers.

RMI   Remote Method Invocation (RMI) lets Java programs running on one server access the methods of Java programs running on other servers.

root key certificate   *See* trusted certificate.

Secure Sockets Layer (SSL)   SSL is a standard protocol for secure network transport. SSL provides security-related services such as authentication, encryption, and data integrity.

selectors   The OracleAS Web Cache uses various selectors, such as URL expressions and the HTTP request method, to filter through various caching rules and find the ones suitable to a particular request.

servlet   A servlet is a small Java program that runs on the Web server. Servlets are used to generate dynamic content, usually by interacting with databases, and provide the response to the browser request.

servlet container   Servlet containers provide the runtime environment for Java servlets. The container calls the servlet's methods and provides runtime services to the servlet.

session bean   You use a session bean to implement business tasks—for example, for querying and retrieving data from a database.

session-encoded URLs   Session-encoded URLs are HTML hyperlink tags containing embedded session information. The OracleAS Web Cache can substitute the embedded session parameters with the session information obtained from cookies.

session key   SSL uses a secret key called the session key to encrypt data. Clients generate the session key after OracleAS authenticates itself and sends the session key to the OracleAS using public key encryption.

SSL   You use the Secure Sockets Layer (SSL) for the secure transmission of data over the internet. You use the HTTPS instead of the usual HTTP protocol, when using SSL.

SSL handshake   An SSL handshake is the procedure two entities use to initiate their session.

stateful session bean   A stateful session bean is a type of EJB bean that retains the state of a user session.

stateless session bean   A stateless session bean is a type of EJB that doesn't maintain state for clients.

superclass   Superclass is the object class from which you can derive another object class, known as the subclass of the superclass. For example, the object class organizationalPerson is a subclass of the object class person.

symmetric cryptography   Symmetric cryptography, also known as shared secret cryptography, uses identical keys to encrypt and decrypt data. The DES, RC2, and RC4 algorithms are symmetric cryptography algorithms.

trusted certificate   Trusted certificates are usually issued by a Certificate Authority (CA) that you trust; they help to qualify the identity of a third party.

Uniform Resource Locator (URL)   A URL is used by a browser to specify the location and the route to a document on the Internet. A URL consists of a protocol (http), a domain name (www.oracle.com), a directory path, and the document or file name.

user search base   In the OID directory information tree, the user search base is the node in the identity-management realm under which all the users are located.

virtual host   A virtual host is a Web server that hosts multiple Web sites or domain, or a Web server that acts as a proxy to other servers.

wallet   You use a wallet to manage security credentials of entities. A wallet is an abstraction that acts as a database to store and manage security credentials for entries. These credentials include authentication data such as private keys, certificates, and trusted certificates necessary for SSL.

WAR files   You use Web Application Archive (WAR) files to deploy the Web component modules (JSPs and servlets) of J2EE applications.

Web component   Java Server Pages (JSPs) and servlets are considered Web components under the J2EE specification.

Web services   Web services are Web applications that use open standards such as XML, SOAP, WSDL, and UDDI for transmission over the Internet.

webcachectl utility   You use the webcachectl utility to manage the OracleAS Web Cache admin server and cache server processes. Note that if you've installed the OracleAS Web Cache as part of the OracleAS installation, you must use OPMN instead of the webcachectl utility to manage the Web cache processes.

X.509   X.509 is a commonly used standard for defining digital certificates.

INDEX

Italic page numbers indicate material in tables or figures.

P

R

S

T

U

V

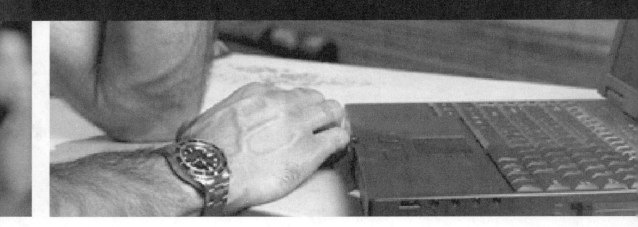

GET YOUR FREE SUBSCRIPTION
TO ORACLE MAGAZINE

Oracle Magazine is essential gear for today's information technology professionals. Stay informed and increase your productivity with every issue of *Oracle Magazine.* Inside each free bimonthly issue you'll get:

- Up-to-date information on Oracle Database, Oracle Application Server, Web development, enterprise grid computing, database technology, and business trends
- Third-party vendor news and announcements
- Technical articles on Oracle and partner products, technologies, and operating environments
- Development and administration tips
- Real-world customer stories

IF THERE ARE OTHER ORACLE USERS AT YOUR LOCATION WHO WOULD LIKE TO RECEIVE THEIR OWN SUBSCRIPTION TO ORACLE MAGAZINE, PLEASE PHOTOCOPY THIS FORM AND PASS IT ALONG.

Three easy ways to subscribe:

① Web
Visit our Web site at otn.oracle.com/oraclemagazine. You'll find a subscription form there, plus much more!

② Fax
Complete the questionnaire on the back of this card and fax the questionnaire side only to +1.847.763.9638.

③ Mail
Complete the questionnaire on the back of this card and mail it to P.O. Box 1263, Skokie, IL 60076-8263

ORACLE
MAGAZINE

ORACLE

FREE SUBSCRIPTION

O **Yes, please send me a FREE subscription to *Oracle Magazine*.**
To receive a free subscription to *Oracle Magazine*, you must fill out the entire card, sign it, and date it (incomplete cards cannot be processed or acknowledged). You can also fax your application to +1.847.763.9638
Or subscribe at our Web site at otn.oracle.com/oraclemagazine

O N●

O From time to time, Oracle Publishing allows our partners exclusive access to our e-mail addresses for special promotions and announcements. To be included in this program, please check this circle.

O Oracle Publishing allows sharing of our mailing list with selected third parties. If you prefer your mailing address not to be included in this program, please check here. If at any time you would like to be removed from this mailing list, please contact Customer Service at +1.847.647.9630 or send an e-mail to oracle@halldata.com.

signature (required)

X

date

name   title

company   e-mail address

street/p.o. box

city/state/zip or postal code   telephone

country   fax

---

① WHAT IS THE PRIMARY BUSINESS ACTIVITY OF YOUR FIRM AT THIS LOCATION? (check one only)
- ☐ 01 Aerospace and Defense Manufacturing
- ☐ 02 Application Service Provider
- ☐ 03 Automotive Manufacturing
- ☐ 04 Chemicals, Oil and Gas
- ☐ 05 Communications and Media
- ☐ 06 Construction/Engineering
- ☐ 07 Consumer Sector/Consumer Packaged Goods
- ☐ 08 Education
- ☐ 09 Financial Services/Insurance
- ☐ 10 Government (civil)
- ☐ 11 Government (military)
- ☐ 12 Healthcare
- ☐ 13 High Technology Manufacturing, OEM
- ☐ 14 Integrated Software Vendor
- ☐ 15 Life Sciences (Biotech, Pharmaceuticals)
- ☐ 16 Mining
- ☐ 17 Retail/Wholesale/Distribution
- ☐ 18 Systems Integrator, VAR/VAD
- ☐ 19 Telecommunications
- ☐ 20 Travel and Transportation
- ☐ 21 Utilities (electric, gas, sanitation, water)
- ☐ 98 Other Business and Services

② WHICH OF THE FOLLOWING BEST DESCRIBES YOUR PRIMARY JOB FUNCTION? (check one only)
Corporate Management/Staff
- ☐ 01 Executive Management (President, Chair, CEO, CFO, Owner, Partner, Principal)
- ☐ 02 Finance/Administrative Management (VP/Director/ Manager/Controller, Purchasing, Administration)
- ☐ 03 Sales/Marketing Management (VP/Director/Manager)
- ☐ 04 Computer Systems/Operations Management (CIO/VP/Director/ Manager MIS, Operations)
IS/IT Staff
- ☐ 05 Systems Development/ Programming Management
- ☐ 06 Systems Development/ Programming Staff
- ☐ 07 Consulting
- ☐ 08 DBA/Systems Administrator
- ☐ 09 Education/Training
- ☐ 10 Technical Support Director/Manager
- ☐ 11 Other Technical Management/Staff
- ☐ 98 Other

③ WHAT IS YOUR CURRENT PRIMARY OPERATING PLATFORM? (select all that apply)
- ☐ 01 Digital Equipment UNIX
- ☐ 02 Digital Equipment VAX VMS
- ☐ 03 HP UNIX
- ☐ 04 IBM AIX
- ☐ 05 IBM UNIX
- ☐ 06 Java
- ☐ 07 Linux
- ☐ 08 Macintosh
- ☐ 09 MS-DOS
- ☐ 10 MVS
- ☐ 11 NetWare
- ☐ 12 Network Computing
- ☐ 13 OpenVMS
- ☐ 14 SCO UNIX
- ☐ 15 Sequent DYNIX/ptx
- ☐ 16 Sun Solaris/SunOS
- ☐ 17 SVR4
- ☐ 18 UnixWare
- ☐ 19 Windows
- ☐ 20 Windows NT
- ☐ 21 Other UNIX
- ☐ 98 Other
- 99 ☐ None of the above

④ DO YOU EVALUATE, SPECIFY, RECOMMEND, OR AUTHORIZE THE PURCHASE OF ANY OF THE FOLLOWING? (check all that apply)
- ☐ 01 Hardware
- ☐ 02 Software
- ☐ 03 Application Development Tools
- ☐ 04 Database Products
- ☐ 05 Internet or Intranet Products
- 99 ☐ None of the above

⑤ IN YOUR JOB, DO YOU USE OR PLAN TO PURCHASE ANY OF THE FOLLOWING PRODUCTS? (check all that apply)
Software
- ☐ 01 Business Graphics
- ☐ 02 CAD/CAE/CAM
- ☐ 03 CASE
- ☐ 04 Communications
- ☐ 05 Database Management
- ☐ 06 File Management
- ☐ 07 Finance
- ☐ 08 Java
- ☐ 09 Materials Resource Planning
- ☐ 10 Multimedia Authoring
- ☐ 11 Networking
- ☐ 12 Office Automation
- ☐ 13 Order Entry/Inventory Control
- ☐ 14 Programming
- ☐ 15 Project Management
- ☐ 16 Scientific and Engineering
- ☐ 17 Spreadsheets
- ☐ 18 Systems Management
- ☐ 19 Workflow

Hardware
- ☐ 20 Macintosh
- ☐ 21 Mainframe
- ☐ 22 Massively Parallel Processing
- ☐ 23 Minicomputer
- ☐ 24 PC
- ☐ 25 Network Computer
- ☐ 26 Symmetric Multiprocessing
- ☐ 27 Workstation
Peripherals
- ☐ 28 Bridges/Routers/Hubs/Gateways
- ☐ 29 CD-ROM Drives
- ☐ 30 Disk Drives/Subsystems
- ☐ 31 Modems
- ☐ 32 Tape Drives/Subsystems
- ☐ 33 Video Boards/Multimedia
Services
- ☐ 34 Application Service Provider
- ☐ 35 Consulting
- ☐ 36 Education/Training
- ☐ 37 Maintenance
- ☐ 38 Online Database Services
- ☐ 39 Support
- ☐ 40 Technology-Based Training
- ☐ 98 Other
- 99 ☐ None of the above

⑥ WHAT ORACLE PRODUCTS ARE IN USE AT YOUR SITE? (check all that apply)
Oracle E-Business Suite
- ☐ 01 Oracle Marketing
- ☐ 02 Oracle Sales
- ☐ 03 Oracle Order Fulfillment
- ☐ 04 Oracle Supply Chain Management
- ☐ 05 Oracle Procurement
- ☐ 06 Oracle Manufacturing
- ☐ 07 Oracle Maintenance Management
- ☐ 08 Oracle Service
- ☐ 09 Oracle Contracts
- ☐ 10 Oracle Projects
- ☐ 11 Oracle Financials
- ☐ 12 Oracle Human Resources
- ☐ 13 Oracle Interaction Center
- ☐ 14 Oracle Communications/Utilities (modules)
- ☐ 15 Oracle Public Sector/University (modules)
- ☐ 16 Oracle Financial Services (modules)
Server/Software
- ☐ 17 Oracle9i
- ☐ 18 Oracle9i Lite
- ☐ 19 Oracle8i
- ☐ 20 Other Oracle database
- ☐ 21 Oracle9i Application Server
- ☐ 22 Oracle9i Application Server Wireless
- ☐ 23 Oracle Small Business Suite

Tools
- ☐ 24 Oracle Developer Suite
- ☐ 25 Oracle Discoverer
- ☐ 26 Oracle JDeveloper
- ☐ 27 Oracle Migration Workbench
- ☐ 28 Oracle9i AS Portal
- ☐ 29 Oracle Warehouse Builder
Oracle Services
- ☐ 30 Oracle Outsourcing
- ☐ 31 Oracle Consulting
- ☐ 32 Oracle Education
- ☐ 33 Oracle Support
- ☐ 98 Other
- 99 ☐ None of the above

⑦ WHAT OTHER DATABASE PRODUCTS AR IN USE AT YOUR SITE? (check all that apply)
- ☐ 01 Access
- ☐ 02 Baan
- ☐ 03 dbase
- ☐ 04 Gupta
- ☐ 05 IBM DB2
- ☐ 06 Informix
- ☐ 07 Ingres
- ☐ 08 Microsoft Access
- ☐ 09 Microsoft SQL Serv
- ☐ 10 PeopleSoft
- ☐ 11 Progress
- ☐ 12 SAP
- ☐ 13 Sybase
- ☐ 14 VSAM
- ☐ 98 Other
- 99 ☐ None of the above

⑧ WHAT OTHER APPLICATION SERVER PRODUCTS ARE IN USE AT YOUR SITE? (check all that apply)
- ☐ 01 BEA
- ☐ 02 IBM
- ☐ 03 Sybase
- ☐ 04 Sun
- ☐ 05 Other

⑨ DURING THE NEXT 12 MONTHS, HOW MUCH DO YOU ANTICIPATE YOUR ORGANIZATION WILL SPEND ON COMPUTER HARDWARE, SOFTWARE, PERIPHERALS, AND SERVICES FOR YOUR LOCATION? (check only one)
- ☐ 01 Less than $10,000
- ☐ 02 $10,000 to $49,999
- ☐ 03 $50,000 to $99,999
- ☐ 04 $100,000 to $499,999
- ☐ 05 $500,000 to $999,999
- ☐ 06 $1,000,000 and over

⑩ WHAT IS YOUR COMPANY'S YEARLY SALES REVENUE? (please choose one)
- ☐ 01 $500,000,000 and above
- ☐ 02 $100,000,000 to $500,000,000
- ☐ 03 $50,000,000 to $100,000,000
- ☐ 04 $5,000,000 to $50,000,000
- ☐ 05 $1,000,000 to $5,000,000

1001

LICENSE AGREEMENT

THIS PRODUCT (THE "PRODUCT") CONTAINS PROPRIETARY SOFTWARE, DATA AND INFORMATION (INCLUDING DOCUMENTATION) OWNED BY THE McGRAW-HILL COMPANIES, INC. ("McGRAW-HILL") AND ITS LICENSORS. YOUR RIGHT TO USE THE PRODUCT IS GOVERNED BY THE TERMS AND CONDITIONS OF THIS AGREEMENT.

LICENSE: Throughout this License Agreement, "you" shall mean either the individual or the entity whose agent opens this package. You are granted a non-exclusive and non-transferable license to use the Product subject to the following terms:

(i) If you have licensed a single user version of the Product, the Product may only be used on a single computer (i.e., a single CPU). If you licensed and paid the fee applicable to a local area network or wide area network version of the Product, you are subject to the terms of the following subparagraph (ii).

(ii) If you have licensed a local area network version, you may use the Product on unlimited workstations located in one single building selected by you that is served by such local area network. If you have licensed a wide area network version, you may use the Product on unlimited workstations located in multiple buildings on the same site selected by you that is served by such wide area network; provided however, that any building will not be considered located in the same site if it is more than five (5) miles away from any building included such site. In addition, you may only use a local area or wide area network version of the Product on one single server. If you wish to use Product on more than one server, you must obtain written authorization from McGraw-Hill and pay additional fees.

(iii) You may make one copy of the Product for back-up purposes only and you must maintain an accurate record as to the location of the back-up at all times.

COPYRIGHT; RESTRICTIONS ON USE AND TRANSFER: All rights (including copyright) in and to the Product are owned by McGraw-Hill and its licensors. You are the owner of the enclosed disc on which the Product is recorded. You may not use, copy, decomp disassemble, reverse engineer, modify, reproduce, create derivative works, transmit, distribute, sublicense, store in a database or retrieval system of any kind, rent or transfer the Product, or any portion thereof, in any form or by any means (including electronically or otherwise except as expressly provided for in this License Agreement. You must reproduce the copyright notices, trademark notices, legends and lo of McGraw-Hill and its licensors that appear on the Product on the back-up copy of the Product which you are permitted to make hereund All rights in the Product not expressly granted herein are reserved by McGraw-Hill and its licensors.

TERM: This License Agreement is effective until terminated. It will terminate if you fail to comply with any term or condition of this License Agreement. Upon termination, you are obligated to return to McGraw-Hill the Product together with all copies thereof and to pu all copies of the Product included in any and all servers and computer facilities.

DISCLAIMER OF WARRANTY: THE PRODUCT AND THE BACK-UP COPY ARE LICENSED "AS IS." McGRAW-HILL, ITS LICENSORS AND THE AUTHORS MAKE NO WARRANTIES, EXPRESS OR IMPLIED, AS TO THE RESULTS TO BE OBTAIN BY ANY PERSON OR ENTITY FROM USE OF THE PRODUCT, ANY INFORMATION OR DATA INCLUDED THEREIN AND/C ANY TECHNICAL SUPPORT SERVICES PROVIDED HEREUNDER, IF ANY ("TECHNICAL SUPPORT SERVICES"). McGRAW-HILL, ITS LICENSORS AND THE AUTHORS MAKE NO EXPRESS OR IMPLIED WARRANTIES OF MERCHANTABILITY OR FITNESS FOR A PARTICULAR PURPOSE OR USE WITH RESPECT TO THE PRODUCT. McGRAW-HILL, ITS LICENSORS, AND THE AUTHORS MAKE NO GUARANTEE THAT YOU WILL PASS ANY CERTIFICATION EXAM WHATSOEVER BY USING THIS PRODUCT. NEITHER McGRAW-HILL, ANY OF ITS LICENSORS N THE AUTHORS WARRANT THAT THE FUNCTIONS CONTAINED IN THE PRODUCT WILL MEET YOUR REQUIREMENTS (THAT THE OPERATION OF THE PRODUCT WILL BE UNINTERRUPTED OR ERROR FREE. YOU ASSUME THE ENTIRE RIS WITH RESPECT TO THE QUALITY AND PERFORMANCE OF THE PRODUCT.

LIMITED WARRANTY FOR DISC: To the original licensee only, McGraw-Hill warrants that the enclosed disc on which the Product recorded is free from defects in materials and workmanship under normal use and service for a period of ninety (90) days from the date o purchase. In the event of a defect in the disc covered by the foregoing warranty, McGraw-Hill will replace the disc.

LIMITATION OF LIABILITY: NEITHER McGRAW-HILL, ITS LICENSORS NOR THE AUTHORS SHALL BE LIABLE FOR A INDIRECT, SPECIAL OR CONSEQUENTIAL DAMAGES, SUCH AS BUT NOT LIMITED TO, LOSS OF ANTICIPATED PROFIT. OR BENEFITS, RESULTING FROM THE USE OR INABILITY TO USE THE PRODUCT EVEN IF ANY OF THEM HAS BEEN ADVISED OF THE POSSIBILITY OF SUCH DAMAGES. THIS LIMITATION OF LIABILITY SHALL APPLY TO ANY CLAIM O CAUSE WHATSOEVER WHETHER SUCH CLAIM OR CAUSE ARISES IN CONTRACT, TORT, OR OTHERWISE. Some states de not allow the exclusion or limitation of indirect, special or consequential damages, so the above limitation may not apply to you.

U.S. GOVERNMENT RESTRICTED RIGHTS: Any software included in the Product is provided with restricted rights subject to subparagraphs (c), (1) and (2) of the Commercial Computer Software-Restricted Rights clause at 48 C.F.R. 52.227-19. The terms of this Agreement applicable to the use of the data in the Product are those under which the data are generally made available to the general publ by McGraw-Hill. Except as provided herein, no reproduction, use, or disclosure rights are granted with respect to the data included in the Product and no right to modify or create derivative works from any such data is hereby granted.

GENERAL: This License Agreement constitutes the entire agreement between the parties relating to the Product. The terms of any Purch Order shall have no effect on the terms of this License Agreement. Failure of McGraw-Hill to insist at any time on strict compliance with this License Agreement shall not constitute a waiver of any rights under this License Agreement. This License Agreement shall be constr and governed in accordance with the laws of the State of New York. If any provision of this License Agreement is held to be contrary to l that provision will be enforced to the maximum extent permissible and the remaining provisions will remain in full force and effect.